MLS
$37.05
PO 73810
5-18-01

D1590960

Politicians,

the Press,

&

Propaganda

POLITICIANS,

Lord Northcliffe &

THE PRESS, &

the Great War, 1914–1919

PROPAGANDA

J. Lee Thompson

The Kent State University Press

KENT, OHIO, & LONDON

© 1999 by The Kent State University Press,

Kent, Ohio 44242

All rights reserved

Library of Congress Catalog Card Number 99-24205

ISBN 0-87338-637-x

Manufactured in the United States of America

06 05 04 03 02 01 00 99   5 4 3 2 1

Frontispiece: Lord Northcliffe, 1916

Library of Congress Cataloging-in-Publication Data

Thompson, J. Lee, 1951–

Politicians, the press, and propaganda : Lord Northcliffe and
the Great War, 1914–1919 / J. Lee Thompson.

p.   cm.

Includes bibliographical references and index.

ISBN 0-87338-637-x (cloth : alk. paper) ∞

1. Northcliffe, Alfred Harmsworth, Viscount, 1865–1922.
2. World War, 1914–1918—Great Britain.   3. Press and
politics—Great Britain—History—20th century.   4. Press
and propaganda—Great Britain—History—20th century.
I. Title.

D544.T49   1999

940.4'88941—dc21   99-24205

British Library Cataloging-in-Publication data are available.

CONTENTS

            Preface and Acknowledgments   vii
ONE   Introduction
            Background, and Prelude to War   1
TWO   "A Boomerang Policy"
            Censorship and Recruiting Battles, August to December 1914   23
THREE   "A Very Big and Difficult Thing"
            Munitions and Coalition, January to June 1915   42
FOUR   "A Very Hard Nut to Crack"
            The Conscription Question, July to December 1915   66
FIVE   "No More Shilly-Shallying"
            Air Power and Conscription, January to June 1916   88
SIX   "Asquith's Head on a Plate"
            The Fall of Asquith and the Rise of Lloyd George,
            July to December 1916   103
SEVEN   "To Tell the People of America the Truth"
            The United States Enters the War, January to May 1917   123
EIGHT   Deeds and Words
            Chairman of the British War Mission to the United States,
            June to November 1917   148
NINE   "Pegasus in Harness"
            Politics and Propaganda, November 1917 to April 1918   170
TEN   "Great Propaganda"
            From War to Peace, May to November 1918   195
ELEVEN   "The Huns Must Pay"
            Politics and Peacemaking, November 1918 to June 1919   219
TWELVE   Conclusion
            Politicians, the Press, and Propaganda   238
            Notes   245
            Selected Bibliography   302
            Index   311

Preface & Acknowledgments

THIS BOOK REPRESENTS THE FIRST DETAILED EXAMINATION OF LORD Northcliffe during the Great War, at the pinnacle of his power and influence. There was little middle ground for the Titan of Fleet Street, over which, as his contemporary Lord Beaverbrook noted, he towered as has no other personality. Northcliffe was capable of astounding triumphs and equally colossal blunders that make his career fascinating, particularly in the atmosphere of careful correctness and decision by focus group that marks the end of the twentieth century. Driven to succeed in order to please his mother and to achieve for the Harmsworth family what his father could not, Alfred Harmsworth, through hard work, luck, and driving ambition, succeeded beyond the wildest dreams of avarice. Wealth and accomplishment garnered for him a place in the ruling class of Edwardian England, and his stature was only increased by the stresses the Great War placed on Britain's society and political system. Northcliffe's prewar political and imperialist enthusiasms carried over into the 1914–18 period. The war for him became a crusade to protect the empire and to ensure that Britain would emerge from the conflict not only victorious but preeminent. The initial wartime policy battles between the press lord and his government concerned censorship and recruiting. In the following four years, he became embroiled in controversies over almost every issue of national interest, from munitions to propaganda and the peace settlement.

This study focuses on the political and propaganda aspects of Northcliffe's wartime career. Within the realm of politics several areas are of particular interest: his newspaper activities, especially his use of the *Daily Mail* as his most direct mass press instrument to bring public pressure to bear on the politicians; his support and criticism of the government policies of two prime ministers, Herbert Henry Asquith and David Lloyd George; the fall of Asquith and the rise of Lloyd George; and his duel with the generals for control of war strategy. Northcliffe's propaganda efforts encompassed the entire period. In this sphere falls the press lord's preoccupation with America, an understanding of which aids the explanation of many actions widely considered to be the result of megalomania or the beginnings of his final illness. Both his unofficial and official publicity activities are considered, as well as his attempt to project this work into the peace process, which led to his final breach with Lloyd George.

From the outbreak of hostilities in August 1914, Northcliffe became actively involved in the war effort not only through his newspapers but also, as the manuscript record clearly shows, through intimate interaction with the leading characters in British political and social life. He corresponded and met personally with an impressive number of the most influential political figures of the period, including both wartime prime ministers. The most powerful individuals in British political life sought his views on a bewildering variety of subjects.

There is voluminous manuscript evidence available of the courtship of Northcliffe by the British political and military elite. The majority of the press lord's public papers and diaries are in 245 volumes designated as the Northcliffe Additional Manuscripts in the British Library Manuscript Collection. Significant material also can be found at the Archive of *The Times* (London), which also holds the most recently discovered Northcliffe material available to scholars and allows this book to be based partly on evidence not previously published. A final repository examined for this work, the private Harmsworth Archive, includes much political and family correspondence that has been unavailable for several decades. More than fifty other sets of papers consulted for this study, encompassing many of the principal political, military, and press figures of the period, leave no doubt as to the influence of Northcliffe in the calculations and policy decisions of the nation's leadership.

There exists no separate study of Northcliffe in World War I, but numerous other published works have dealt with aspects of his life and career since the 1918 American publication of William Carson's *Northcliffe: England's Man of Power*. Many biographies of greatly varying merit have followed. Reginald Pound and Geoffrey Harmsworth's massive and detailed 1959 study continues to be recognized as the benchmark and also contains the most wartime material. This collaborative work is a thorough examination by a press historian and the nephew of Northcliffe that makes extensive use of family papers as source material. The press studies concerned with Northcliffe published since 1959, such as Tom Ferris's *House of Northcliffe* (1972), Richard

Bourne's *Lords of Fleet Street: The Harmsworth Dynasty* (1990), and S. J. Taylor's *The Great Outsiders: Northcliffe, Rothermere and the Daily Mail* (1996), have made no attempt to consider Northcliffe in regard to recent historical scholarship or debates on the Great War, such as the battle over strategy between the political "frocks" and the military "Brass Hats." One aim of the present work is to address the latest historical research.

A study of Northcliffe in these years involves many of the questions that scholars continue to debate, beginning with how real or illusory the power of the press was during the war. Other pertinent historical issues considered to one extent or another include the growth of state control during the war and the decline in the power of Parliament. An area of recent historical interest concerns the importance of what came to be called the home front in the new total war fought between nations-in-arms. Many of the latest works on the war have also emphasized that Britain was fighting alongside allies whose opinions had to be taken into consideration at all times. Northcliffe was very cognizant of this fact and worked for cooperation between Britain, its allies, and its associate, the United States. He told Lloyd George in 1914, after the stalemate in France and Flanders began, that the United States would win the war. American opinion, while a neutral and then as an associate, was a constant concern of the press lord.

Scholars have heretofore considered Northcliffe almost exclusively in light of his press achievements, with a nod to his 1918 propaganda work. A. J. P. Taylor summed up the press lord as "a newsman first, last and all the time." Northcliffe holds a prominent place in accounts of the rise of the New Journalism, the press barons and the political press in the late nineteenth and early twentieth centuries. He also has been widely criticized as a prime example of the dangers of press "power without responsibility." E. T. Raymond warned in 1919 that his "present indirect power was one of the chief dangers of the State." Winston Churchill's 1927 very personal account of events, *The World Crisis,* criticized Northcliffe's wartime role, stating that he "wielded power without official responsibility, enjoyed secret knowledge without the general view, and disturbed the fortunes of national leaders without being willing to bear their burdens." Many more recent authors have been equally hostile. In *The Prerogative of the Harlot: Press Barons and Power,* Hugh Cudlipp described Northcliffe as a man corrupted by power and wealth who desecrated journalistic standards and became dominated by "the pursuit of political power, unguided by political prescience."

Recent political and general studies of the 1914–18 period for the most part have overlooked the place of Northcliffe and the press. Cameron Hazlehurst's important political history of the first ten months of the war, *Politicians at War July 1914 to May 1915: A Prologue to the Triumph of Lloyd George* (1971), does give some limited consideration to the impact of the press in the fall of the last Liberal government in England. The political work that considers the rest of the war, John Turner's *British Politics and the Great War: Coalition and Conflict 1915–1918* (1992), gives little notice to the role of the press in the end of the Asquith government in December 1916. The book does not consider Northcliffe's 1917 appointment as head of the British War Mission to the United States, which caused a political furor. Only brief mention is made of his controversial public refusal of the Air Ministry on his return and his running duel with Lloyd George for the rest of the war. Recent general histories of the war that are mute on or give scant notice to Northcliffe include Martin Gilbert's *The First World War: A Complete History* (1994) and J. M. Bourne's *Britain and the Great War 1914–1918* (1989). Authorities on World War I who acknowledge the press lord's efforts have concentrated on his official propaganda work after he returned to England from America in late 1917. These revisionist studies reflect, in part, a reaction against the immediate postwar praise Northcliffe received for his work as head of Propaganda in Enemy Countries, as in, for example, Sir Campbell Stuart's *The Secrets of Crewe House* (1922). The historians concerned specifically with propaganda during the war largely have overlooked the publicity effort in America.

Northcliffe's concern with America (which made him an ideal choice to head the 1917 British War Mission to the United States) constitutes a continuing theme of this work and almost a case study in Anglo-American relations before and during the war. He came to believe early in the war that only American power could break the terrible stalemate in the trenches of Flanders and France. In late May 1917, despite years of proclaiming he would never join the government and give up his independence, the press lord became an important and official part of the state war machine when he agreed to head the British War Mission to the United States. The unofficial propaganda role Northcliffe assumed in the States is of particular significance to this study.

The final aspect considered in this essay is official propaganda. After Northcliffe's return to England from America in November 1917, Lloyd George again requested his services, and in February 1918 he became head of Propaganda in Enemy Countries. Northcliffe occupied this position until the end of the war, and his department was widely credited at the time with substantially weakening enemy morale and hastening the collapse of the Central Powers. In the last months of the war, Northcliffe attempted to turn his department into a propaganda arm for the coming Peace Conference but was thwarted both by the Foreign Office and by Lloyd George, who reasserted their traditional powers as the war came to an end.

Besides the press lord's ultimate failure and untimely death, perhaps a further reason for the historical neglect is that his activities transcended easy categorization and were not kept within neat boundaries. Consequently, this study also crosses historical lines by intertwining the political, social, and military with the press and propaganda areas. Northcliffe's success and his mercurial temperament have spawned countless colorful stories. Separating fact from the many recorded fictions has been often difficult, but always interesting. The following is an attempt to throw light on the press lord's role in the war, heretofore obscured.

I must express my thanks to the following individuals and institutions who made materials available to me without which this study could not have been completed: Mr. Vyvyan Harmsworth, Associated Newspaper Holdings Limited; the British Library, Great Russell Street, Oriental and India Office Collections and Colindale Newspaper Library; Mr. Eamon Dyas, archivist of *The Times*, News International; the Imperial War Museum; Ms. Katharine Bligh, the House of Lords Record Office; the Bodleian Library, Oxford; the Cambridge University Library; the Churchill Archives Centre, Churchill College, Cambridge; the National Library of Scotland; the Public Record Office; the British Library of Political and Economic Science; Liddell Hart Centre for Military Archives, King's College, London; the Library of Congress; and Ms. Judith Ann Schiff, the Yale University Library.

For permission to quote materials for which they hold copyright, I wish to thank Ms. Alison Kagamaster Bullock, granddaughter of Walter Frederick Bullock; Lord Burnham; Mr. Rupert Murdoch; Mr. Vyvyan Harmsworth; Lord Rothermere; Mr. A. J. Maxse; the British Library Board; the Science Museum Library; the Clerk of the Records of the House of Lords Record Office, on behalf of the Beaverbrook Foundation; Lord Fisher; Mr. and Mrs. William Bell; Lord Derby; Lord Scarsdale; Thomas Arthur and Caroline Kenny; the Mariam Coffin Canaday Library, Bryn Mawr College; Milton Gendel; Edward Rory Carson; Professor A. K. S. Lambton; Lord Coleraine; the Wardens and Fellows, New College, Oxford; *The Spectator;* David McKenna; Leo Amery; Lady Patricia Kingsbury; News International; Lt. Col. J. A. Charteris; the National Library of Scotland; the Syndics of Cambridge University Library; the Controller of HM Stationery Office; and the Yale University Library.

Many people helped this project to completion. Special thanks are due to Professor R. J. Q. Adams, my teacher and friend, who suggested this topic, and to Mr. John Grigg, who read the manuscript, offered kind criticism, and stands as an inspiration to us all of what a historian should be. Two other readers, Professor James Startt and Professor Thomas Kennedy, also improved this work with their insightful comments.

My most heartfelt thanks, however, is reserved for my wife, Diane, to whom I dedicate this work, and without whose unwavering support this project would never have been completed.

Politicians,

the Press,

&

Propaganda

ONE

Introduction
Background, & Prelude to War

ON 28 JUNE 1919 THE GREAT WAR BETWEEN BRITAIN AND GERMANY finally came to an official end with the signing of the Versailles treaty. That same day Sir William Robertson Nicoll, editor of the *British Weekly* (the voice of nonconformity during the Great War), addressed a letter to Lord Northcliffe, who was convalescing from throat surgery. After expressing his pleasure at the news that the press lord was well on the road to recovery, Nicoll went on, "I do not think the country adequately appreciates the tremendous services you have rendered during the war. I am sure no one did more if anyone did as much.... The future holds great things for you and we look to you."[1] The letter closed with the hope that "a great and worthy record of your war work will be written without exorbitant delay."

To cheer his press compatriot and in the general euphoria which followed the end of the war, Nicoll undoubtedly somewhat exaggerated Northcliffe's place in the conflict; however, his considerable role has been neglected by historians in the years since 1919. No study of Northcliffe in the Great War was ever published, and in 1922 the press lord was dead at age fifty-seven. His premature end ensured that the history of the terrible struggle would be written by a long list of other notable figures, including David Lloyd George, Winston Churchill, and Lord Beaverbrook, most of whom were, to varying degrees, the targets of the press lord's criticisms during the conflict. It became convenient for his many opponents to forget just how influential and feared Northcliffe was from 1914 to 1918. Subsequent histories have followed this lead. His substantial role and his service to the nation have either gone unnoticed or else been relegated to narrow studies of the press and propaganda.[2]

The completely novel circumstances of a stalemated total war that dragged on for long and bitter years without significant victories to sustain the national will or to bolster its leaders brought many well-documented changes to Britain. One significant shift that has gone largely unexamined was the major rise in the power of the press, particularly in regard to its relationship with the political leaders, who feared defeat and groped for any path to victory. Northcliffe, already a force to be reckoned with before 1914, became the chief beneficiary of the wartime intensification of press influence. During the conflict he intruded himself into British decision making concerning the most urgent issues that faced the nation, from recruiting and press censorship in 1914 to propaganda and the approaching peace settlement in 1918. He particularly objected to what he considered the muddle that plagued Britain's wartime governments and saw it as his duty as a British patriot to prod the wobbling politicians to new efforts and at all costs to ensure that the war would be won. To this end, the press lord supported a succession of military leaders against political interference in their realms. The prime minister from August 1914 to December 1916, Herbert Henry Asquith, failed to come to an arrangement with his chief newspaper critic, but his successor, David Lloyd George, was much more canny in his relations with the press. This was in part by necessity, as the Welshman was a premier without a party and the press formed one of the pillars that kept him in office. Lloyd George brought several newspaper lords into his government, including Beaverbrook, Rothermere, and Northcliffe.

As the preeminent journalistic force in Britain, by 1914 Northcliffe controlled roughly 40 percent of the morning, 45 percent of the evening, and 15 percent of the Sunday total newspaper circulations.[3] By far the two most important weapons in his press arsenal were *The Times* and the *Daily Mail*. Historical accounts of the war have tended to overlook the statements of the mass circulation *Daily Mail* in favor of the pronouncements of *The Times*. Though in doddering financial condition when Northcliffe acquired controlling interest in 1908, *The Times* remained the most politically influential newspaper among the elite classes of Britain.[4] His intervention saved the paper from ruin. Although he interfered from time to time, the press lord allowed a measure of wartime independence under the strong-willed editor Geoffrey Robinson (later Dawson).

In contrast, the *Daily Mail*'s editor from 1899, Thomas Marlowe, was more deferential to his owner and the newspaper represented the views of the press lord with less editorial filter than seen in *The Times*. Created by Northcliffe in 1896, within a few years the *Daily Mail* reached a million, mainly lower- and middle-class, readers, and its circulation remained near this level through the war.[5] Until Northcliffe's death it remained closer to his heart than any of his other publications. The *Daily Mail* aimed its appeals at the mass audience, to the people who, as the press lord predicted during the war, would return from the trenches and the munitions factories to claim their proper share of political power. Northcliffe was perhaps more in touch with and concerned by the "home front" during the war than any other figure, and the *Daily Mail* targeted this reservoir of future political power.

In addition to the *Daily Mail* and *The Times,* the other mass-circulation journals controlled by Northcliffe included the *Evening News* and the Sunday *Weekly Dispatch.* This unmatched collection of morning, evening, and Sunday newspapers gave the Northcliffe press a strong daily presence in almost all news markets, from the elite political audience of *The Times* to the national readership of the *Daily Mail.* With this supremacy already in place, the addition of wartime circumstances gained the press lord an influence more powerful than that of any British press figure before or afterward.

Well aware of his unique position, Northcliffe made his press support available to the British government, but at a price—a place in deciding the life-and-death issues involved in winning the war. The politicians paid this levy only grudgingly, and in the end withdrew as quickly as possible from what they considered something of a partnership with the devil. During the conflict a few notable figures, including Austen Chamberlain, openly attacked what they considered the undue and corrupting influence on the Lloyd George government of Northcliffe and his brethren. The majority, fearful of the power of the press in the novel circumstances of the war, kept silent. In the end, it took Britain's final victory and the following 1918 election to confirm the transitory nature of Northcliffe's influence in comparison to the formidable power Lloyd George was able to exert as the "Man Who Won the War." Even then, the prime minister found himself harried by his former press ally well into the 1919 peace making.

Before a consideration of his place in the First World War, some explanation of how Northcliffe came to his influential position in prewar Britain is necessary. This involves two broad areas. The first of these concerns two intertwined late nineteenth- and early twentieth-century newspaper developments: the rise of the popular New Journalism and the general growth in the political power of the press. The second is his personal background and involvement in the major domestic political and social controversies in the period before August 1914.

With the presence of no significant competition from other sources, the press was the most important single medium for the communication of ideas in nineteenth-century Britain and by midcentury was becoming part of the "normal furniture of life" for all the classes.[6] This growth was facilitated by the repeal of the so-called taxes on knowledge, which made printed material more generally affordable. Press innovations, coupled with the rise in literacy brought about, in part, by the 1870 Education Act, also fueled its expansion.[7] Between 1880 and 1895, all these developments gave rise to what has come to be called the New Journalism.[8] The appellation originated in an 1887 Matthew Arnold article on the problems in Ireland in which the essayist labeled the new style, like the democracy to which he compared it, "featherbrained."[9] In an attempt to entertain the public, the New Journalism used interviews, photographs, and typographical features, such as bold headlines, to break up the page. It had a more personal tone, more of a thrust toward social concerns, and became synonymous with lower standards and cheap effects. Attention shifted away from parliamentary politics. The papers published abridgments of speeches rather than the traditional unbroken verbatim columns, which were relegated to the pages of *Hansard*. The vacated space was filled, in part, by revenue-producing advertisements. The 1890s were marked by robust growth in both the advertising and consumer goods industries. The two went hand in hand. Without advertising in mass circulation newspapers, the high volume production of "branded goods" would have been impossible and without the enormous advertising revenue, cheap daily newspapers would also have been impossible.[10] The *Daily Mail* and its owner Alfred Harmsworth, later Lord Northcliffe, the most successful practitioners of this new commercial style, came to symbolize the New Journalism.

From the mid-Victorian period, British political factions recognized the need for newspaper publicity. The press became a tool of party management, used to communicate with the public, foreign powers, and other politicians. In the new age of mass politics, party funds often paid for expensive modern equipment which printed an unparalleled volume of attractive and affordable news. These papers supported the party programs, as well as the strategies and personal aims of the politicians and their press allies. The influence of the press on the public has been questioned, but its strong effect on the parties and their leaders was clear. By the decade preceding 1914, a handful of newspaper proprietors, editors, and reporters reached positions of unprecedented influence in the political decision-making process. Men such as C. P. Scott at the *Manchester Guardian*, W. T. Stead at the *Pall Mall Gazette* and the *Review of Reviews*, J. L. Garvin at the *Outlook* and the *Observer*, and Lord Northcliffe were consulted for their advice and counsel by the most powerful political leaders of the day.[11]

Northcliffe, the man who perhaps most embodied both the New Journalism and the political influence of the press, had a humble beginning. He was born Alfred Charles William Harmsworth on 15 July 1865 at Chapelizod, near Dublin. His mother Geraldine, née Maffett, to whom Northcliffe was "almost fanatically devoted" for his whole life, dominated his father, also named Alfred.[12] She pushed her husband to become a barrister and the family moved to London in 1867 in an attempt to further his new career and to escape anti-English Fenian threats.[13] The second of Northcliffe's numerous and useful siblings, Harold (later Lord Rothermere), was born in London on 26 April 1868. Despite his wife's prodding, Alfred senior had only limited success as a member of the legal profession after being called to the bar in 1869. A lack of ambition and a fondness for drink combined to the detriment of his career. Consequently, the Harmsworths moved into successively less comfortable dwellings more distant from central London, arriving by 1870 in the Vale of Health at Hampstead where the family continued to increase in numbers.[14]

At Hampstead, young Alfred made the acquaintance of George Samuel Jealous, editor of the *Hampstead & Highgate Express*. As an influential and important member of the boy's neighborhood, Jealous represented an example of the prestige the press could afford. The editor gave the lad an old set of print and, perhaps, set in motion the greatest career Fleet Street has known.[15] The used print helped young Alfred, who was not sent to school until he was eight, to learn the alphabet. His early education came mainly from observation, the uncanny use of which, whether developed as a child or inherent, proved invaluable to his later endeavors. Once at the local school he was not a good student, particularly in arithmetic, and was easily distracted. Brother Harold, on the other hand, displayed a real acumen for figures. Alfred distinguished himself more by his blond good looks, which were remarked upon from an early age, being described by one admirer as "a young Apollo." Another dubbed him the "Adonis of Hampstead."[16] Both Alfred's personality and the straitened financial circumstances of his family stimulated an entrepreneurial spirit. For example, among his early failures was a patent medicine scheme with the slogan, "Tonk's Pills—Guaranteed to Cure All Ills."[17] He was to have more luck in journalism.

Alfred Harmsworth's first practical experience of the press came at private school, where he edited the *Henley House School Magazine* and showed glimpses of his ambition and talent, and the future direction his life would take. The proprietor of the school, John Vine Milne, considered him one of the brighter pupils and noted his natural leadership of the other boys, but viewed him, as many others would in future, as "something of a puzzle."[18] At the same time, Alfred met fellow cycling enthusiast Max Pemberton, who became a longtime friend and future employee. At the age of sixteen, Alfred left home and school to pursue a career as a freelance journalist, sharing rooms for a time with the equally impecunious Pemberton.[19] The rest of his education would come from Fleet Street, not Oxford or Cambridge.[20]

Despite advice to avoid Fleet Street and a disreputable career in journalism from his father and George Augustus Sala of the *Daily Telegraph*, Alfred persevered through several lean years, which included a brief stint as editor of the periodical *Youth*. Pemberton and others have credited his meeting with George Newnes, editor of the very successful London periodical, *Tit-Bits,* as pivotal in the development of his future career.[21] The brief, interesting articles and more open format of *Tit-Bits* had caught the attention of the newly literate British public. In *Tit-Bits,* information became entertainment. It was also, the young Harmsworth did not fail to notice, a great commercial success.

While seeking financial support for a venture of his own, Harmsworth edited *Bicycling News,* and his efforts revived the failing periodical. In 1888 he found sufficient backing to produce *Answers to Correspondents,* soon shortened simply to *Answers.* The weekly, which appropriated a feature of *Tit-Bits* and also was heavily influenced by American periodicals, proposed that its readers send in their own questions, which the journal would attempt to address. In reality most of the questions at first were made up in the offices. The sales of *Answers* did not really boom, however, until the paper began to offer contest prizes and puzzles, most notably one that offered a pound a week for life to the person who could guess the amount of gold in the Bank of England.[22] The journal's huge success provided the financial foundation for subsequent Harmsworth publishing triumphs. One other development of note in the year *Answers* debuted was Alfred's marriage to Mary Elizabeth Milner, daughter of a merchant in the West India trade. Though childless, the union lasted until Northcliffe's death.

Harold Harmsworth was persuaded to leave a secure position at the Mercantile Marine Office and joined the publishing business in June of 1889. His invaluable financial skills balanced Alfred's more flamboyant entrepreneurial talents, and he played a central role in the startling growth of the Harmsworth publishing empire.[23] As they came of age several other brothers, including Cecil, Hildebrand, and Leicester also joined the burgeoning concern. Another important addition to the staff in this period was George Sutton, who joined as Alfred's secretary and soon gained more and more responsibility within the organization. Building on the success of *Answers,* the Harmsworths added to the business other periodicals that emphasized disparate topics including humor, patriotism, fitness, foreign adventure, and domestic enterprise. All these newer ventures, as did *Answers,* purposefully took a higher moral tone than the usual inexpensive popular fare which had aimed at the lowest tastes and was often, in Alfred's view at least, vulgar and obscene. Some of the titles included *Comedy Cuts, Pluck Library*, and the *Boy's Home Journal,* making a total of thirteen by 1894.[24] By this time the various

Harmsworth journals enjoyed a total circulation of two million, then the world's largest. The Harmsworths strove to price their products below the competition. They produced inexpensive "reading matter for the masses" by using new mass production techniques.[25] A. A. Milne wrote that "Harmsworth killed the penny dreadful by the simple process of producing a ha'penny dreadfuller."[26] Their sensational publications may have confused news with opinion; however, it was impossible to say they did not sell.

The great success of the Harmsworth publications drew the notice of the British political world. In 1892 *Answers* surpassed the million-copy circulation mark. Leaders in both parties made favorable remarks concerning the popular weekly with the improving tone. William Ewart Gladstone, the living embodiment of Victorian Liberalism, granted the publication an interview in which he stated that the "gigantic circulation" of *Answers* was "undeniable proof of the growth of sound public taste for healthy and instructive reading. The journal must have vast influence."[27] From the Conservative camp, Lord Randolph Churchill appraised the weekly as an "instructive and valuable" instrument that would aid the masses toward an appreciation of English literature and predicted that the "Harmsworth sort of journalism" would "become a permanent feature of our time."[28]

When the opportunity presented itself to purchase the foundering London *Evening News* at a bargain price in 1894, the Harmsworths decided to broaden their businesses to include daily newspapers. The *Evening News* was a voice of the Conservative party, and the Liberal Harold had been hesitant to become associated with it, warning his brother that it would not suit their purposes to do so. Alfred, not as inclined to Liberalism as the rest of the family, forged ahead. After he helped with the purchase negotiations, William Kennedy Jones, who had been a subeditor under Louis Tracy at the *Sun*, became editor and Tracy manager. Using the methods that had made *Answers* a success, the Harmsworth team transformed the *Evening News* into a prototype for their future newspaper endeavors, substituting new type, a more open format, and simplified news reporting, and adding a woman's column.[29] New advertisers soon flocked to the publication.

Early the same year, Alfred Harmsworth made his first trip to the United States and closely studied American newspaper methods.[30] An avid fisherman, he took numerous excursions over the following years to Florida's waters. During one of these sporting outings he fell prey to what was described as a malarial fever, which returned intermittently thereafter. Additionally, by the mid-1890s, the strains associated with supervising the many businesses had taken a physical and mental toll. For the rest of his life, Harmsworth was subject to a long list of ailments, some real, some hypochondriacal, to the great benefit of numerous Harley Street specialists.

The rehabilitation of the *Evening News* brought Alfred Harmsworth even more into the political spotlight. He was able to report this success for the Conservative party to its leader, Lord Salisbury, a few months before he replaced the Liberal Lord Rosebery as prime minister. Harmsworth's political philosophy combined Tory populism, Disraelian imperialism, and a firm belief in the "Anglo-Saxon future." Consequently, some aspects of the Liberal Unionist and Liberal Imperialist programs also appealed to the future press magnate. The *Evening News* promoted Joseph Chamberlain's idea of a bigger and better Britain, and Harmsworth, for a time, was captivated by Rosebery's Liberal Imperialism.

His rising position allowed the proprietor of the *Evening News* to meet with other "upbuilders" of the Empire, including Dr. Leander Starr Jameson and Cecil Rhodes, under whose imperial vision he fell. Another such promoter, Sir Charles Dilke, was impressed by Harmsworth after hearing him speak at the Anglo-Saxon Club in London in May 1896. Dilke wrote to the *Pall Mall Gazette* correspondent G.W. Steevens that, even though Harmsworth rated Rhodes "too high," he was "the most remarkable man I have ever seen."[31] Later that year, Alfred inspected the eastern empire in person, traveling to India on doctor's orders for a rest. The next year he made a similar pilgrimage to Egypt. One other apostle of empire, the South African proconsul Alfred Milner, would also play an important role in Harmsworth's future.

Since the early 1890s Alfred Harmsworth had considered a career in politics. In 1894 he declined nomination for Folkstone; however, the next year, at age thirty, he took the plunge as Conservative candidate for one of the Portsmouth seats in the Commons. To combat the local Liberal newspaper, the Harmsworth publications acquired the Portsmouth *Evening Mail* (later renamed the *Southern Daily Mail*). The newspaper campaign included a serial story, "The Siege of Portsmouth," that sensationalized Britain's lack of naval preparedness. Though the stories sold papers, they did not induce a war mood or enough sentiment to elect Harmsworth, even though he threw himself wholeheartedly into electioneering. This sortie into politics proved disheartening and expensive. Alfred concluded from the experience that "my place is in the House of Lords where they don't fight elections."[32] He did continue, however, to support the Conservative party with his newspapers and his growing personal fortune, investing a large sum in the faltering *Manchester Courier* in what would prove to be an expensive and futile challenge to the Liberal *Manchester Guardian*.[33] At this point Harmsworth may have lacked the "political nostril," but he could certainly sniff out profits to be made elsewhere.

Before the first edition of a completely new creation, the *Daily Mail*, was published 4 May 1896, its owner told Kennedy Jones that the enterprise would lead to either "Bankruptcy or Berkeley Square."[34] The paper used the latest technology, including new folding and linotype machines. Though priced at only a half-penny, the *Daily Mail* distinguished itself from the competition by being printed on more expensive white newsprint, its front page devoted to advertisements, in the style of the penny journals. The paper deliberately courted the aspirations of a new readership who envisioned themselves "tomorrow's £1000 a year men."[35] Once again, better value was a key to Harmsworth success, and the new venture was an immediate hit. The first day circulation of 397,215 almost equaled the total sales figure for all of the one-penny papers combined. The purchasers of the *Daily Mail* have been described as "not so much the newly educated as the newly better-off...clerks...willing to spend a halfpenny, where they might balk at a penny."[36] The half-pennies added up handsomely. After the first day Harmsworth told Kennedy Jones, "we have struck a gold mine."[37] A year later, in May 1897, Mary and Alfred Harmsworth, as he had predicted, moved to 36 Berkeley Square.

The *Daily Mail*'s abridged leaders on parliamentary affairs appealed to the new voters created by the Third Reform Act of 1884. For this mass audience, the subeditors were instructed to construct their stories of many brief paragraphs to "explain, simplify and clarify."[38] The historian A. J. P. Taylor gave Northcliffe credit for being the first to truly exploit the paragraph, which Taylor called "the greatest advance in communications since the abandonment of Latin for English," as well as the gift for providing "accurate information of every kind."[39] The Harmsworths also exploited the expanding British rail system to distribute the *Daily Mail* throughout the relatively compact British market so that readers all over England could peruse the paper over their breakfasts.[40] Thus it can be argued that it became the first truly national newspaper.[41]

Though Gladstone's letter of "heartiest good wishes" on the launching of the *Daily Mail* was "played up" by the paper, it, like its owner, attempted to steer clear of open affiliation with any party. On the first anniversary of publication, George Bernard Shaw sent a letter of congratulations that urged the proprietor to put "your political criticism on the same footing as your dramatic and literary criticism. Then it would be influential and interesting."[42] Though his sympathies were Unionist, Harmsworth refused to follow any party line.[43] He described the *Daily Mail* to the Liberal Lord Rosebery, his neighbor in Berkeley Square, as "independent and Imperial."[44] For a brief time it appeared Rosebery might be "the man" of imperial vision for the nation (and Harmsworth) to follow, but his indecision disillusioned the many prospective adherents.

In 1897 the colonial premiers visited London for Queen Victoria's Diamond Jubilee. Alfred Harmsworth entertained them at Berkeley Square. He told a shareholders meeting soon after that he had no use for "old-fashioned Conservatism, which was as dead as old-fashioned Radicalism." He described his press as "Unionist and Imperialist," continuing that his papers supported "the unwritten alliance of the English speaking peoples" and the "advocacy of a big navy" to protect Britain's interests against outside threats, particularly from Germany.[45] During the Diamond Jubilee procession in London, Victoria's grandson, Kaiser Wilhelm, found himself being booed at places on the route because of his January 1896 cable of congratulations to Paul Kruger, leader of the Transvaal, on repelling the Jameson raid.

In this period Harmsworth first met many of the future leaders of Britain, including Herbert Henry Asquith, George Curzon, and Winston Churchill. In July 1899 he drove his new automobile to Oldham to aid Churchill in his election campaign, suffering several punctures en route. Churchill sent his regrets that "neither of our enterprises were successful in connection with Oldham. But I don't expect my career or your car will be seriously damaged."[46] The following year three Harmsworth brothers, Cecil, Hildebrand, and Leicester, stood as Liberal candidates for Parliament. Only the last was returned that year, for Caithness by twenty-eight votes. The two defeated brothers established a periodical, the *New Liberal Review*, which was supportive of an imperial course.

The reputation and success of the Harmsworth press began to be known worldwide by 1900, and in the following years the stature of the owner of the *Daily Mail* continued to rise, particularly in Canada and America. During his twenty prewar trips across the Atlantic, he cultivated relationships with many influential figures in business, politics, and his own profession. One such acquaintance, Joseph Pulitzer, proprietor of the New York *World*, helped ensure Harmsworth's rank in American publishing circles. For the 1 January 1901 first edition of the twentieth century, Pulitzer challenged the owner of the *Daily Mail* to produce an edition of the *World* representing the future of newspapers.[47] Though roundly criticized, the tabloid-styled creation quickly sold out. In these many trips Harmsworth acted as an unofficial spokesman for Britain and began to be considered something of an authority on the United States.[48]

At home, Alfred Harmsworth's success brought him into contact with the political and social elite. He was presented to the Prince of Wales and made the acquaintance of dukes. However, though he had attained a ducal income by 1900, as a nouveau riche, soiled by his self-made money, he was never accepted by the ruling class of his time. He in turn failed to be ensnared by the allure of "smart society." Though he was elected to memberships in clubs such as the Carlton and Beefsteak, he had little patience for or skill at drawing room repartee. The historian Alfred Gollin noted perceptively that because of

> his power, his influence, his ability, and most of all his refusal to conform to their standards . . . the established classes were hostile to Northcliffe because he came from a different background, because he had clawed his way to the top, because he was required, as an outsider, to have recourse to different methods when he sought to clutch at authority and grasp for power. The ordinary rulers of Britain were ruthless enough but a man of Northcliffe's type had to be harder, tougher, more openly brutal, or he would perish. He had no traditional base to stand upon. The essence of his success lay in the fact that he always avoided the ordinary course; he had beaten his way to a prominent position by novel means, and he was not prepared to abandon them.[49]

The most aristocratic among the ruling class especially viewed the young press magnate as hungry for power. Lord Esher, a confidant of kings and an influential figure in these years, described him as "a clever vain man — not very intelligent about anything except organization and money-making; but full of aspirations for power."[50]

Nevertheless, the Harmsworth press was recognized by all but the most hidebound reactionaries among the Conservative elite as too valuable a party asset to alienate completely. The Conservative prime minister, Lord Salisbury, has been attributed with the disdainful remark that the *Daily Mail* was "run by office boys for other office boys"; however, the marquess was one of the many who sent a telegram of good wishes to its owner after the first edition was published.[51] The problem lay in how to control a man like Alfred Harmsworth, who by 1900 had grown too wealthy to need party funding and who began to steer his own independent course.

Northcliffe's real concern with the security of Britain and her empire allowed him to combine the patriotic with the profitable. Invasion and war scare stories sold papers, whether the enemy was France, Russia, or Germany. In 1894 France and Russia signed a naval agreement that raised fears in Britain of a hostile combination. To promote a larger British navy, that year *Answers* published William Le Queux's "The Poisoned Bullet," the first serial story with a war theme.[52] The weekly installments traced the carnage of the invading Russian and French forces in their march across the country from Beachy Head to Birmingham.[53] Lord Roberts of Kandahar, the living embodiment of the British army, agreed with Harmsworth that Britain underrated her possible opponents. He wrote to the proprietor of *Answers* that "I entirely concur with you in thinking that it is most desirable to bring home to the British public in every possible way the dangers to which the nation is exposed unless it maintains a Navy and Army sufficiently strong and well organized to meet the defensive requirements of the Empire."[54] From its inception the *Daily Mail* also warned against German "militarism," in the articles of such noted correspondents as G. W. Steevens, who also led the newspaper charge to report the 1899–1902 Boer War.[55]

Interest in the South African conflict stimulated newspaper sales to new heights. The Harmsworth organization responded on a scale never seen before, both in the number of reporters dispatched and in the rail distribution of newspapers at home. "*Daily Mail* War Specials" swiftly transported the newspaper to the Midlands and the North of England, sending circulation above one million copies, then the world's largest.[56] The journal also sent the first woman war correspondent to the Boer War, Lady Sarah Wilson, the daughter of the Seventh Duke of Marlborough.[57] The Harmsworth press reflected the jingo patriotism of the day, but could act responsibly. Though the owner of the *Daily Mail* had little faith in General Buller, he restrained his press opposition to Buller's appointment to army command. The paper's comparatively measured coverage in the face of military reverses increased the prestige of the *Daily Mail* and its owner in the country.[58]

The position Harmsworth had attained allowed him to consult with the leaders of the nation, to the annoyance of his pro-Boer detractors. Discussions with Salisbury concerning the potential problems Germany posed led to fears for British paper supplies, should the normal Scandinavian sources of newsprint be cut off.[59] Over the next few years the Harmsworth enterprises secured an enormous tract of timberland in Newfoundland and built mills on site to process the wood. The owner of the *Daily Mail* was not alone in his anxiety concerning international events. The difficulties faced in South Africa fueled national worries for the future of Britain and the empire. Against such anxieties, the fourth anniversary *Daily Mail* declared itself "the embodiment and the mouthpiece of the Imperial idea. We know that the advance of the Union Jack means protection for weaker races, justice for the oppressed, liberty for the down-trodden. Our Empire has not yet exhausted itself. Great tasks lie before it, great responsibilities have to be borne. It is for the power, the greatness, the supremacy of this Empire that we have stood. In the heart of every Englishman has dawned the consciousness that a greater destiny awaits us."[60]

In 1902 Salisbury's nephew, Arthur Balfour, succeeded to the prime ministership. Balfour liked to pretend that he did not pay attention to the press, but he realized full well the value of its publicity. After the first edition of the *Daily Mail* was published he had sent a private note to its owner praising the "new undertaking."[61] The careers of these two very different men continued to intersect through the following years. In June 1904 Balfour rewarded Alfred Harmsworth's impressive achievements, and his monetary and newspaper support of the party, with a baronetcy. A year and a half later Sir Alfred was further rewarded with a peerage, becoming Baron Northcliffe.[62] After the January 1906 election debacle, Balfour led the opposition until being supplanted by Andrew Bonar Law in 1911.[63]

One of the issues that divided the Conservatives and contributed to their defeat in 1906 was tariff reform. Northcliffe's initial support of imperial preference and tariff protection, which he believed had helped build the American economic juggernaut, brought a break with his neighbor Rosebery.[64] Before long, however, Northcliffe's passion for Joseph Chamberlain's plan for imperial unity cooled in the face of the widespread unpopularity of the "stomach taxes" on food, which were part of the scheme. A lack of enthusiasm in Canada, which the press lord considered the key to any plan of imperial cooperation, also limited his support. The best efforts of perhaps the most influential Conservative journalist of the period, J. L. Garvin, failed to persuade the press lord to pledge his newspapers wholeheartedly to the tariff reform cause.[65]

With the Liberals in power after 1906, Northcliffe and the Conservatives feared military preparations would be neglected. The pressing need for readiness against the Teutonic menace became a constant theme in the press lord's publications and correspondence.[66] Northcliffe's Liberal press critics accused him of exaggerating the German threat and spreading fear to sell newspapers. They labeled the *Daily Mail* efforts as merely "scaremongering." In 1905 Lord Roberts took the presidency of the National Service League, which agitated for compulsory service to build a British counter to the German "nation in arms."[67] Northcliffe and his publications supported the efforts of the League in its unsuccessful campaign. One of the most notable episodes was the 1906 *Daily Mail* serialization of William Le Queux's *The Invasion of 1910*, which revisited the *Answers* campaign of twelve years before. In the daily installments, the routes of the invading Uhlan hordes proved more determined by possible circulation gains than worth as military objectives. Le Queux's work gained tremendous sales when published in book form later that year with a foreword by Roberts that called for preparedness to prevent such a catastrophe from occurring in reality.[68]

The Northcliffe press alternatively attacked and supported the proposed army modernization plans of the reforming Liberal war secretary, R. B. Haldane.[69] The issue that would lead to a complete break between the press lord and Haldane was Britain's course in developing the next weapon of war—the airplane. Northcliffe shared the public fascination with the technological developments of the day. His journals reflected this interest, with early articles on the automobile, the phonograph, the telephone, electricity, and air travel.[70] He was a particular visionary in regard to the future role of the airplane. In 1906, after a visit to France to witness an early powered flight, Northcliffe angrily telephoned an editor who had neglected to give enough attention to the development, demanding, "Don't you realize, man, that England is no longer an island?"[71] To spur the development of aviation in Britain, the same year the *Daily Mail* offered £10,000 for the first flight between London and Manchester. This offer was followed by a smaller prize for a successful flight across the English Channel. Both prizes were later won by Frenchmen, which only incited Northcliffe to increase his pressure on the British government. However, he was unsuccessful in his attempts to persuade Haldane to purchase planes from the American Wright brothers. Despite this failure, the press lord tirelessly campaigned for British development of the airplane and warned of the vulnerability of England through the air, especially in light of what he considered the superior French and German air arms.[72]

In the years before the beginning of World War I, Northcliffe continued to add to his newspaper empire, buying the ailing *Weekly Dispatch* and starting an *Overseas Daily Mail,* under the editorship of John Evelyn Wrench, meant to further the "bond of Empire." Northcliffe also began a Paris *Continental Daily Mail,* and bought the *Observer,* a respected Sunday journal that had fallen on hard times. In 1903 the tabloid *Daily Mirror,* a paper for women, was launched.[73] The new venture faltered at first, but later grew to have the world's largest circulation partly through its dramatic use of photographs. However, its proprietor was never quite comfortable with the *Daily Mirror* and in March 1914 sold the journal to his brother, Harold, who had only shortly before become Baron Rothermere.[74]

The most notable addition came in 1908 when Northcliffe acquired control of *The Times.*[75] Though its circulation had dwindled, the paper remained the most prestigious British journal and was still viewed by foreign powers as a voice of official government opinion. By adding *The Times* to his newspaper regiments, the press lord gained control of what was considered to be a key organ of the British establishment, much to the fury of his Liberal critics.[76] Many feared Northcliffe would destroy the paper that he had coveted for years. Instead, his reorganization brought *The Times* up to date and, in March 1914, tripled sales from 50,000 to 150,000 copies by dropping the price from threepence to a penny.[77] The paper was also left a large degree of editorial independence, in part because of the respect the new chief proprietor held both for *The Times* as a British institution and for its editor from 1912, Geoffrey Robinson (later Dawson).[78] After the acquisition of *The Times*, Northcliffe continued to use the *Daily Mail* as his personal voice, supporting conscription, army modernization, and a stronger navy.

In 1908 and 1909 the *Daily Mail*, aided by J. L. Garvin at the *Observer* and Robert Blatchford of the *Clarion*, attacked the chancellor of the exchequer, David Lloyd George, and his radical budget plans which, it was felt, did not include enough funding for the navy.[79] The *Daily Mail* demanded in February 1908 to be told whether Britain was going to "surrender her maritime supremacy to provide old age pensions?"[80] The newspaper's owner visited Germany the next year, ostensibly to see a specialist about his worrisome eyesight, but also personally to appraise the situation. He reported to H. W. Wilson, on the *Daily Mail* staff, that "every one of the new factory chimneys here is a gun pointed at England."[81] Aided by inside information provided by Sir John Fisher, the controversial first sea lord, that year's newspaper campaign culminated in the "Naval Scare" of 1909, considered the high-water mark of prewar scaremongering.[82] The June 1909 Imperial Press Conference held in London gave Northcliffe a chance personally to share his concerns with the imperial delegates, who visited Sutton Place, his historic country house.[83]

During the 1909 controversy the press lord was first introduced to Lloyd George, who was to prove both an ally and a foe in the following years. This noteworthy encounter came in the House of Commons on 3 August 1909, with the intermediary being Northcliffe's brother, the Liberal M. P. Cecil Harmsworth.[84] On this occasion, which one historian described as the beginning of "an important but uneasy association between the two men," Lloyd George gave the keen motorist Northcliffe a preview of the Development of Roads Bill before it was submitted to Parliament.[85] This application of his famous charm helped to temper the press attacks on Lloyd George. Besides the Welshman's powers of persuasion, another factor at work was Northcliffe's sensitivity to swings in public opinion. His own intuition, as it had over the tariff reform issue, brought him to dampen his attacks on the People's Budget and also brought a break with Garvin.[86]

The naval issue was carried forward into the elections of 1910 by the Northcliffe press. During the December campaign the press lord wrote to Balfour, considered an authority on military affairs, about his continuing fears. Congratulating him on the "magnificent" party leadership he had given, Northcliffe went on that "from a careful study of the German Press— of what it is printing and what it is not printing—that our friends across the North Sea are in no wise slackening their preparations, while we are amusing ourselves with an unnecessary General Election."[87] The Conservative leader replied that he trusted "that the Government will give us good naval estimates. It all turns, I suppose, on whether they are more afraid of the Germans or of their own tail—an unhappy position for the rulers of a great country."[88] Balfour also complained about the line taken by Harold Harmsworth's Glasgow *Herald*. Northcliffe replied that he never saw his brother's "beastly paper" and that Harold, as well as brothers Cecil and Leicester, "have radical bees in their bonnets. Harold is a particularly obstinate and determined man."[89] From this point Northcliffe and his siblings increasingly diverged in their political opinions. The *Daily Mail*, however, carried on with its navalist articles intermittently until the outbreak of war.

Other prewar developments carried over into the war years. Northcliffe became convinced that, in addition to France and Russia, the United States would be needed as an ally against Germany. During a trip to North America, the press lord was alarmed by what he perceived as the undue influence of German press sympathizers in Canada and the United States.[90] He thereafter kept close track of the U.S. press scene through his overseas newspaper contacts and by sending his own writers for firsthand reports. At home, the British "naval hysteria" of 1909 was accompanied by a spy mania which led to fantastic revelations including secret plans for the thousands of German waiters in London and elsewhere to rise and wreak havoc at a signal from Berlin.[91] This "enemy in our midst" paranoia later colored Northcliffe's views concerning the wartime treatment of enemy aliens in Britain, even before war fever and mounting casualty lists had their effect on public opinion.

Despite the differences between the press lord and the chancellor of the exchequer, particularly over issues of national defense, during the Agadir crisis of 1911, *The Times* and the *Daily Mail* supported Lloyd George's Mansion House warning to Germany. Otherwise, in this crisis, the Northcliffe press was subdued in tone, most probably because the fleet was not believed to be properly prepared for war. Two years later Northcliffe and his press also supported Lloyd George and others against the charges of official impropriety stemming from the Marconi shares scandal.[92] The Welshman sent thanks to the press lord for "the chivalrous manner in which you have treated the Advocate-General and myself over the case.... I feel grateful for a great kindness done to me for I know the power you wield."[93] Northcliffe replied that "I adopted my line about this Marconi business because five minutes lucid explanation showed me that it was the fairest one.... I am not personally hostile to you....You gave me some shrewd blows and I replied to them.... A weekend glance at the French and German newspapers, convinces me that this country has more urgent business before it than personal or party issues."[94]

While Northcliffe and others campaigned in Britain, mass opinion was also being cultivated in Germany. On the Continent similar written appeals found a ready audience, and conservative pressure groups also flourished in the decade before the war.[95] These played to frustrated German expansionist desires for empire and equality with the British.[96] Groups such as the Pan German League and the German Army and Navy Leagues fostered fears of "encirclement" by the Triple Entente. Influential men such as General Friedrich Von Bernhardi wrote of the inevitability and desirability of war as an agent to prove the German mettle.[97] Sentiment on both sides of the English Channel was being prepared for war.

With the possibilities of conflict with Germany in mind, in 1913 Northcliffe attempted to link a network of foreign newspapers to cover any possible occurrence. The *Daily Mail* also began to give more attention to explaining world events to its readers, and a Berlin edition was considered to give "straight English talk" to the German people as an antidote to the government-controlled press.[98] Though mock editions of this newspaper were prepared, conflicts and difficulties with the Paris *Continental Daily Mail* eventually killed the Berlin project. Had it been published, the practicality of such a journal in the German climate of 1913 must be considered very doubtful.

For Britain the immediate prewar years were filled with turmoil. In 1912 and 1913 the attention of the public and the newspapers stayed close to home with continual crises arising from striking workers, marching suffragettes, or the unrest over Irish Home Rule, both in Ireland and Parliament. Though sympathetic to working men and to women, the press lord decried violent methods and strikes. He flatly opposed the extremes of the suffragettes.[99] Northcliffe did not wish to see bloodshed in his native Ireland, but leaned toward Sir Edward Carson and the Ulster cause against a forced settlement.[100] His high regard for the M.P. for Trinity, Dublin carried on into the war years. In the spring and summer of 1914, the United Kingdom seemed literally on the verge of disintegration as the impending passage of Irish Home Rule threatened civil war in Ulster and sympathetic political revolt at home.[101] The *Daily Mail* headlines, editorials, and articles concentrated on the Irish question, but also found space for the occasional sensational photograph either of suffragettes being dragged off to prison or street scenes of worker unrest.[102] For example, the 18 May leading article, titled "Provoking Ulster," was followed a few days later by coverage of the "Scene in the House" over Ireland, which shared the page with pictures of Mrs. Emmeline Pankhurst and other women being arrested at Buckingham Palace.[103]

Other news intruded briefly in June 1914. The battle over Lloyd George's budget took center stage in the 23 June leading article, "Mr. Lloyd George's Surrender." That month as well the British admiralty allowed eight of its most modern ships to sail into the Baltic. Four battle cruisers visited the Russian port of Kronstadt, while four battleships attended the reopening of the Kiel canal in Germany. This has been called "one of the most irresponsible decisions ever made by a British Government."[104] For several days the vessels remained anchored at Kiel at the mercy of the kaiser's capricious good faith. On 25 June a *Daily Mail* news item on the visit of the four dreadnoughts reported the cheers of the British sailors for the kaiser. Ironically, these ships included the *Audacious,* which would later be sunk by the Germans. A day later, a related story indignantly noted the arrest of the seventy-seven-year-old naval authority, Lord Brassey, at Kiel on suspicion of spying when his yacht strayed too close to an off-limits German naval dock.[105] The article put down his arrest to a spy mania in Germany.

On Sunday, 28 June 1914 the Austrian archduke Franz Ferdinand was murdered by a Slav nationalist at Sarajevo in Bosnia. The next morning's *Daily Mail* recounted the events in Sarajevo, and sympathetically traced other Hapsburg family tragedies in an article by the foreign correspondent, Valentine Williams.[106] Though newsworthy, the event was not seen to involve the direct interests of England. The same issue devoted almost as much space to a sports-page account of the American Jack Johnson's latest boxing victory. The *Daily Mail* did send one of its leading correspondents, George Ward Price, to Austria to cover the funeral of the archduke, and his account was published on 3 July.[107] Events on the Continent seemed almost normal. The automobile correspondent, John Prioleau, continued a series of articles on his driving tour of Germany.[108]

The July 1914 European crisis caught all of Britain, including the foreign office, Northcliffe, and his newspapers, by surprise. The 1 July *Daily Mail* editorial, "Drifting to Disaster," referred to the Irish question, not the Balkans. Northcliffe made a personal visit to Ulster, ostensibly to ensure the quality of the press coverage of the emergency, in which he met with Irish leaders.[109] Amidst mounting tensions, the 7 July *Daily Mail* supported "No Surrender" in Ulster. Three days later the newspaper traced Sir Edward Carson's trip to Belfast and his speech the night before. On the 11th the *Daily Mail* announced that a special contingent of journalists has been sent to Ireland to ensure proper coverage of events. Twelve representatives spread out from the *Daily Mail* office in Belfast to cover the story, "Ireland Under Arms: The War Preparations."[110] One of the correspondents, J. M. N. Jeffries, later wrote that "several of us had gone from the Reporters' Room over the wrong channel."[111]

Meanwhile, the British prime minister, Herbert Henry Asquith, attempted to find a peaceful solution for the Irish unrest that would also keep his Liberal government in office. Since the end of March, when his war secretary had resigned over the Curragh incident, Asquith had also taken this office.[112] It was his dual responsibility, then, to find a solution for the two to three hundred thousand armed men on the opposing Nationalist and Ulster sides in Ireland who daily drilled in the glare of newspaper publicity. Asquith's "wait and see," compromising style maddened his opponents, including Northcliffe, who wanted decisive action. The Conservative journalist L. S. Amery wrote anonymously of Asquith that "for twenty years he had held a season ticket on the line of least resistance and has gone wherever the train of events has taken him, lucidly justifying his position at whatever point he has happened to find himself.... And if Civil War breaks out...next month, or the month after, he will still be found letting things take their course, and justifying himself with dignity, conciseness and lucidity."[113]

The prime minister was not an admirer of newspapers, even those of sympathetic persuasion.[114] Unquestionably, Asquith reserved a special antipathy for the parvenu Northcliffe, whose newspapers had condemned the Liberals throughout their eight years of power. The premier wrote on 10 July to his confidant Venetia Stanley that "Northcliffe, who has been spending a week in Ulster, and has been well fed up by the Orangemen with every species of lurid lie, has returned in a panic. The Master [Lord Murray of Elibank]...is anxious that I should see him. I hate & distrust the fellow & all his works...so I merely said that if he chose to ask me directly to see him, & he had anything really new to communicate, I would not refuse. I know of few men in this world who are responsible for more mischief, and deserve a longer punishment in the next."[115]

However contemptuous Asquith was of Northcliffe, he did meet with him about the Irish situation. Another letter to Miss Stanley on 13 July revealed this clandestine conference at Lord Murray's London flat, reporting that the press lord had "been 'doing' Ulster, & is much struck with the Covenanters, whom he regards...as a very formidable tho' most unattractive crew. I talked over the question...with him, & tried to impress upon him the importance of making *The Times* a responsible newspaper."[116] Even had Asquith been sympathetic, Northcliffe's voice would likely have been lost amid the Liberal and army opinion which surrounded the prime minister. Rothermere reported to Murray that the interview with Asquith made a "profound impression" on his brother; nevertheless, *The Times* leader of 14 July remained critical of government efforts.[117] This was not pleasing to Murray, who voiced his rancor to the prime minister. Two days later, however, the *Daily Mail* editorial, "Time to Make Peace," reflected a change in course brought on by Asquith's plea and Northcliffe's own reading of the situation. Still, much to the premier's annoyance, *The Times* and the *Daily Mail* of 20 July revealed his secret plan to bring the king into the Irish settlement.[118]

While Britain watched Ireland, events in Austria and Germany proceeded relentlessly toward war. The assassination of Franz Ferdinand gave Austria the excuse it had long awaited to take action against the South Slav rebels within its territories. Spurred on by Germany, Austria prepared to move. A note was drafted to hand to the Serbians, "framed in terms which no self-respecting state could accept."[119] Almost lost among the reports of the king's efforts to find a peaceful settlement for Ireland, the 22 July *Daily Mail* carried a small article, "Austria Angry," which revealed the firm note to Serbia demanding the right to follow up the investigations of the assassination on Serbian soil. It also recommended that readers not take too seriously the panics caused on the Vienna bourse by the situation. The following day another small notice, headed "Austro-Servian Crisis," reported: "It is possible that the Austrian Government may have seen fit to moderate the tone of the note in view of the urgent representations of its German ally. Germany is known to be 'putting the brake on' the Austrians, who are anxious to have an immediate settlement of long-standing differences with Servia. It is generally recognized that Russia will not allow Servia to be humiliated, and Rumania is known to have left the Vienna Cabinet in no doubt that she will instantly move in the event of any attempt to crush the Servians."[120]

On 24 July 1914, while the King's exertions toward an Irish settlement failed, the crisis in Europe for the first time merited extensive space in the *Daily Mail*. Its report on the "Austrian Note" told of the demands on Serbia of "no more plots" and a reply by the following day concerning the other Austrian conditions, including the suppression of societies in Bosnia that had preached revolt. In the writer's opinion, Serbia was not likely to comply, even in the face of seven Austrian army corps marshaled for battle on the frontier. A section giving the text of the note and background on the crisis again predicted that Russia would support Serbia and pointed out that President Poincaré and Premier Viviani of France happened to be in St. Petersburg at present for consultations.

By the last week of July 1914, the European crisis had taken the headlines from Ireland. The 25 July *Daily Mail* for the first time called the situation "A Danger to European Peace":

Never has the continent had to face a situation of such extreme gravity as that precipitated by the Austrian note to Servia. Both in tenor and tone the note goes far beyond the demands which by international usage one power is entitled to make upon another… the note is virtually a declaration of war.... Austria-Hungary...has decided to grapple now and at once with the vast Pan-Servian problem in which as a state with nine million Southern slav subjects she is so vitally interested. She has cast down the gauntlet.... If Austria refuses Russia's request [for a forty-eight hour extension of the deadline] it means that the conflict cannot be localized and that the Great Powers will find themselves confronted with a European question of the first magnitude...the Triple Entente will find itself face to face with the Triple Alliance.

Expressing grave doubts as to whether Austria would listen to Russia's "admirable proposal," the newspaper reiterated that Russia would likely intervene, and called for an extension of the deadline in the "arrogant" Austrian note. The *Daily Mail* Berlin correspondent added that Germany was ready to move if Austria was attacked from anywhere other than Serbia, meaning, of course, from Russia.

Britain's "drift to commitment" in the days leading up to the declaration of hostilities with Germany has been well documented.[121] In the last days of July, Asquith and Sir Edward Grey skillfully maneuvered the "wavering" Liberal party toward support for action against Germany if necessary, predominantly because it was in Britain's best interest to do so. The war coincidentally saved the Liberal party from what appeared to be a gloomy electoral future by dwarfing the many problems of 1914 in comparison.[122]

The *Daily Mail* reflected the dwindling chances for peace. On 27 July an editorial page article by Valentine Williams, "The Crisis in Europe," outlined the questions involved and the alliances, and included a European map clearly illustrating the projected military consequences. In Williams's words, "the appalling conflagration which would then inevitably result could not leave Great Britain indifferent." That day's political news page included pieces that asserted there was still time for peace in Europe since Austria had not yet declared war, but also recounted the panics on European stock exchanges, the return of the kaiser from his Norwegian trip and the "war excitement" in Berlin. The Irish news was relegated to a distant second place. The 28 July editorial, "Sir Edward Grey's Effort for Peace," supported a conference of Great Britain, France, Germany, and Italy to offer mediation to Austria-Hungary, Russia, and Serbia and warned of the grave consequences of failure. The appeal ended with a hope that reports of an Austrian attack were false. Once confirmed the next day, the newspaper condemned Austria's decision for war, but nonetheless prayed the spread of hostilities could be avoided, for "if not Europe is face to face with the greatest catastrophe in human history."[123] Since there was still no certain news of an invasion or of fighting, at least a faint hope for peace survived. The news page reflected this view and wondered aloud if the conflict perhaps could be confined. The 30 July editorial, "All Europe Arming," spoke of the "bare possibility" that Russian mobilization might bring Austria to accept mediation, but noted that "active preparations...continue in France, Germany, Holland, Belgium and this country."

On the last day of July 1914 the *Daily Mail* proclaimed that the British people were united behind the king and the government and that the opposition leaders Bonar Law and Carson had announced they would support the nation.[124] However, in a first discordant note even before the entrance of Britain into the conflict, the paper also made it clear that, in its opinion, it was the government's previous neglect of defense that had brought England to this perilous position. Calling the threat in Europe one "not seen since the time of Napoleon," it commented that there were

> signs in every direction that the conflagration that Austria has so precipatantly and wantonly kindled is about to spread...it grows clear that whatever Servia's attitude, she was to be crushed in the pursuit of a deliberate plan. The Austrian onslaught...will, it is to be feared, draw Russia into the field....in its turn will be followed by German action. Germany's entrance will compel France....When France is in peril, and fighting for her very existence, Great Britain cannot stand by and see her friend stricken down....The hope is now only of the faintest that the war can be localized, because it is developing into a deliberate assault upon the Triple Entente. We must stand by our friends, if for no other and heroic reason, because without their aid we cannot be safe. The failure to organize and arm the British nation so as to meet the new conditions of Europe has left us dependent on Foreign allies. We have forfeited our old independent position, and as the direct consequence we may be drawn into a quarrel with which we have no immediate concern. But at least we can be true to our duty today if we have neglected it in the past.

The paper's tone was no longer hopeful, with the diplomats "almost exhausted" amid "vast preparations for war." Now the *Daily Mail* justified why Great Britain should be involved in maintaining the European balance of power. Most portentously, a "*Daily Mail* Eyewitness" reported the "Shelling of Belgrade" in the first of countless news stories from the war fronts that would follow in the next four years.

TWO

"A Boomerang Policy"
Censorship & Recruiting Battles,
August to December 1914

IN THE FIRST DAYS OF AUGUST 1914, NORTHCLIFFE RECEIVED INFORMATION from his sources close to French president Poincaré that there would be a German invasion of Belgium, but the press lord feared that an air attack on Britain would be Germany's first stroke of the war.[1] His entreaties for a stronger British air defense had fallen largely on deaf ears and he believed that the country lay literally at the mercy of the enemy. On the ground things seemed little better. The British, he felt, could not spare any divisions for France's defense; Britain's meager ground forces were needed at home to repel a likely German invasion and, further, he doubted how well prepared the army was for any campaign after eight years of Liberal government.[2]

On the press front, Northcliffe redeployed his own forces from Ireland to the continent. John Evelyn Wrench was dispatched to Paris to manage the *Continental Daily Mail*.[3] The London editors of *The Times* and the *Daily Mail* rushed their correspondents to Europe. Each man carried two hundred pounds in gold to cover his initial expenses.[4] Valentine Williams, *Daily Mail* foreign correspondent, set up a corps of couriers to ferry news back and forth.[5] The leading writers, Henry Hamilton Fyfe and George Ward Price, hurried to Paris for transport to the Franco-German frontier where the brunt of the action was expected. To support them, a supplemental body of young correspondents rode out from Paris by bicycle and car to observe the French Army.[6] The Belgian post was assigned to J. M. N. Jeffries, the youngest of the group. The *Daily Mail* news editor, W. G. Fish, informed Jeffries that "Belgium should prove an excellent news centre."[7] Thomas Marlowe, the managing editor, who perhaps knew more about Belgian conditions than he let on to Jeffries, calmly instructed him to make sure of the facts in his stories.

Marlowe's parting words were hardly reassuring, "remember... a deceased correspondent is of no use to his newspaper."[8]

The proprietor of the *Daily Mail* remained in London, either at his offices or telephoning them continually.[9] In the crisis, Northcliffe reportedly had calls waiting on ten of the thirty *Daily Mail* phone lines at all times, and he was called upon personally by many French journalists, alarmed that Britain had not yet officially committed to support France and Russia.[10] At a 1 August conference at Printing House Square, the press lord revealed that he had information that the government was going to "rat" on her Entente partners.[11] The question was how should his newspapers respond? Should they openly attack the government in this hour of national distress? In the view of its foreign editor, Henry Wickham Steed, *The Times* had to speak out to preserve its dignity as a "national institution."[12] On the other hand, the editor of the *Daily Mail*, Thomas Marlowe, feared "the country would never forgive us" for an attack on the government.[13]

Events on the Continent ensured that Northcliffe would not have to run the risk of public censure. British participation in the war appeared inevitable. Lord Milner reflected the predominant feeling when he wrote in his diary on Sunday, 2 August 1914, "everything overshadowed by the great European crisis. It seems increasingly difficult to see how England can escape being involved in a general war."[14] The Russian mobilization of 30 July triggered the timetables of the German Schlieffen plan. According to this decade-old master strategy, France must be knocked out quickly to avoid Germany having to fight a war on two fronts.[15] The bald aggression of Germany's thrust into Belgium to carry out the plan's first objective, and the plea for help of the Belgian king on 3 August, healed the remaining division in the British cabinet and swayed public opinion away from the position of neutrality that was widely called for at the time.[16] These developments cleared the way for the foreign secretary, Sir Edward Grey, head of the pro-intervention faction, to deliver an ultimatum to Germany that called for Germany to withdraw from Belgian soil by 11:00 P.M. on 4 August or face war with Britain.[17]

The 3 August *Daily Mail* headlines proclaimed "GREAT WAR BEGUN BY GERMANY—FRANCE ATTACKED WITHOUT A DECLARATION—WAR DECLARED AGAINST RUSSIA—INVASION OF LUXEMBOURG—VIOLATION OF TREATY—BRITISH WARNING TO GERMANY." The editorial was equally somber: "The shadow of an immense catastrophe broods over Europe today. All hope of peace has disappeared with a crash.... Europe might have been spared all this turmoil and anguish if Great Britain had only been armed and organized for war as the needs of our age demand. The precaution has not been taken, but in this solemn hour we shall utter no reproaches on that account. Our duty is to go forward into the valley of the shadow of death with courage and faith—with courage to suffer, with faith in God and our country." When Grey's warning was ignored by the Germans, in what has been called a "tragedy of miscalculation," Britain joined the combatants in the most horrifying war the world had yet seen.[18]

In the first few days after 4 August the threat of German invasion remained Northcliffe's paramount concern. He agreed with the majority that believed the British navy would win the war and that the few divisions of the British Expeditionary Force (BEF) would be insignificant among the grand armies of France and Germany. On 5 August, at the Admiralty, he protested to Winston Churchill, the First Lord, against any plan to dispatch the BEF.[19] During a Carmelite House conference the same night, Northcliffe declared "not a single soldier shall leave this country. We have a superb Fleet, which shall give all the assistance in its power, but I will not support the sending out of this country of a single British soldier. What about invasion? What about our own country? Put that in the leader.... Say so in the paper tomorrow."[20] In one of the rare cases in which he stood up to his chief successfully, Thomas Marlowe had Northcliffe's *Daily Mail* editorial along these lines replaced.[21] Once the final decision was made to send the BEF to the continent, the press lord put aside his misgivings and committed his considerable energies to its support. Winning the war became his mission. Steed later wrote that Northcliffe soon developed a "war mind" that "divided men into two classes—those who felt that there could be no way out except through victory, and those who bewailed the loss of peace, or sought compromises, or failed to bend all their energies to the hitting of the enemy, constantly and hard by arms and by policy."[22]

To lead the nation into battle, on 5 August Lord Kitchener was appointed secretary of state for war, a choice viewed in some quarters as a triumph for the Northcliffe press.[23] One biographer credited "the persistence of Lord Northcliffe and the insistence of the public" with ensuring the choice.[24] The military correspondent of *The Times,* Charles à Court Repington, had been clamoring for Kitchener as imperial commander since 1902 and called for his installation at the War Office on 3 August.[25] The *Daily Mail* joined *The Times* and vigorously attacked a rumored plan to bring back Haldane. The 5 August edition noted that for the past two days Haldane had been presiding over the War Office and asked what he was doing there and whether he was delaying war preparations.

No other military figure so commanded the respect of the nation as Kitchener. He had been lionized by the press for successfully fighting the country's little wars for decades and now was looked to for salvation in this larger emergency.[26] Whatever Asquith privately might have wished to do at the War Office, political and public opinion forced him to the "hazardous experiment" of bringing a soldier into the cabinet to sit at his right hand and direct the war.[27] As Cameron Hazlehurst has pointed out, it never seems to have occurred to anyone to question whether Kitchener could actually do the job.[28] It would not be many months before events changed this attitude.

Despite Sir Edward Grey's often-repeated declaration that the "lamps are going out all over Europe; we shall not see them lit again in our lifetime," the consensus in Britain held that the war would be brief.[29] It was widely regarded that the intertwined national economies of 1914 could not stand more than a few months of conflict. The industrialist Sir Alfred Mond warned in August that 300,000 British workers would be dislocated because of the loss of trade with Germany. The 12 August *Daily Mail* replied, "the British workman is not going to cry or whine, and does not want Sir Alfred Mond to cry for him." Military experts predicted that the war would involve battles of movement, fought by professional armies which would be home by Christmas. The British navy would make the crucial difference by defeating the enemy fleet and blockading Germany. Kitchener disagreed with all these assumptions and looked down upon the regular army because he thought it too small for the part he believed it would have to play.[30] In the war secretary's original scheme, his New Armies would not be ready until 1917, by which time the Russian and French forces would have worn down both the enemy and their own power to determine the settlement.[31] Both Kitchener and Northcliffe feared invasion and disagreed with the great majority that forecast a brief war.[32]

The Liberal government Kitchener joined was committed by its pre-1914 planning to a "business as usual" course in which the navy and economic support, rather than a Continental-sized army, would be Britain's contributions.[33] Sacrificing any more to the war effort, it was felt, would be disastrous. All this changed in the following months as Kitchener's plans for a "nation in arms" held sway. Parliament was asked to increase the size of the army by 500,000 men, and this was granted on 7 August 1914.[34] The same day, Kitchener issued his first appeal for one hundred thousand volunteers, and Britain was soon papered over with his image, a pointing finger emphasizing the message "Your Country Needs You!"[35] The response overwhelmed the nation's recruitment centers. Meanwhile, the BEF, under the command of Field-Marshal Sir John French, embarked for the Continent and concentrated near Amiens.[36]

After the outbreak of hostilities, conditions on the Continent were understandably chaotic. Although the French ministry of war announced that correspondents were not to be allowed at the front, many nevertheless used the general disorder to mask trips out to the fighting.[37] When detected, they were detained and then ejected from the area, often after being forced to sign statements that they would not attempt to return.[38] In Berlin, the *Daily Mail* correspondent Frederic William Wile, an American who had spent thirteen years in Germany, was forced to flee for his own safety after he was arrested and released 4 August 1914 on charges of spying.[39]

Northcliffe tried to ensure both that his press coverage in France would not break down and that his papers would provide the best reports from the field. He saw Paris as the obvious news center and insisted that its office be properly manned at all times.[40] The press lord instructed *Daily Mail* correspondent G. W. Price not to leave Paris because "from all we hear, the correspondents are going to be kept in cages like wild animals, and Paris provides a far better opportunity for you and the paper than the front."[41] This message represents one of his first remarks about government efforts to control war news.

In the decade before 1914, the British planned for censoring press coverage when the nation again became a combatant, and Northcliffe had shown sympathy for early government suggestions for some sort of press regulation. However, when it was proposed in 1908 that the newspaper proprietors be held responsible for what was published, he and other members of the recently formed Newspaper Proprietor's Association (NPA) withdrew their support.[42] The British had seen the dangers of wartime press disclosures demonstrated in the reports of the 1904–05 Russo-Japanese conflict.[43] In 1909 Northcliffe suggested to War Secretary Haldane the testing of a mock military press censorship as it would be in case of a European war.[44] Two years later an Official Secrets Act was put in place to control government information leaks. In 1912, as a result of press problems during the Agadir crisis, Sir Reginald Brade, permanent secretary at the War Office, negotiated an agreement with the NPA for a voluntary system of withholding sensitive information.[45] The joint committee set up under the agreement (and the looming threat of the 1911 Official Secrets Act) worked well before the war to prevent press mention of such activities as the BEF embarkation exercises and increased munitions production.

On 5 August 1914 another and most telling factor came into play concerning the censorship in the person of Lord Kitchener, who had only contempt for the press. Despite the fact that he had been idolized in many quarters, Kitchener felt his reputation had been sullied by past reports, in both the aftermath of Omdurman and the Boer War. To make matters worse, confidences he shared with Repington appeared in *The Times* on 15 August. In response to angry charges of favoritism to the Northcliffe press, Kitchener proclaimed a total ban on correspondents with the BEF.[46] The arbitrary manner in which the press was cut off from the consultation they had enjoyed before 1914 contributed to their wartime antagonism.[47] To guide the press and properly funnel war news, a Press Bureau was set up under Kitchener's choice, F. E. Smith (later Lord Birkenhead), a Conservative M.P.[48] It served, in the main, as a lightning rod for criticism, for the real power stayed at the Admiralty and the War Office.[49] Anxious to stay on good terms with the most powerful press lord, Smith sent a message to Northcliffe two days after he assumed his duties that "we are bound to make mistakes at the start. Give me the advantage throughout of any advice which your experience suggests."[50]

In the first few weeks of August, the British and the French strictly censored news from the front. British newspapers were supposed to voluntarily submit their articles for clearance and the Press Bureau's task was to prevent the publication of anything that would depress the public, assist the enemy, disclose movements of the army or navy or otherwise imperil the national safety.[51] To accomplish this mission the Bureau took control of the Central Telegraph Office and examined every message to and from the newspapers.[52] The ban on information concerning the BEF and serious cable delays led to a poverty of real news, which increasingly frustrated the journalists and stimulated the spread of wild rumors and fantastic reports such as *The Times* and *Daily Mail* stories of Russian soldiers passing through England.[53] Sir George Riddell, the deputy-chairman of the NPA and a confidant of David Lloyd George, recorded in his diary that there had been a "great row" in the cabinet about the suppressions and delays of news and that the press was furious over the censorship arrangements, blaming chiefly the cable censor's department.[54] Smith remarked that "Kitchener cannot understand that he is working in a democratic country. He rather thinks he is in Egypt where the press is represented by a dozen mangy newspaper correspondents whom he can throw in the Nile if they object to the way they are treated."[55]

Whether for reasons of patriotism or fear of government action, the British press was, in the main, self-censoring during the course of the war. Nevertheless, there were powerful written and unwritten strictures in place. Though the system was called "voluntary," in addition to the statutory powers of the 1911 Official Secrets Act already mentioned, the press was also made subject to several of the regulations of the first Defence of the Realm Act (DORA) passed by Parliament in August 1914.[56] Northcliffe was certainly well aware of possible penalties and, as we shall see, his publications faced government action more than once during the war.

While the British and French forbade correspondents, the Germans, on the other hand, gave the press access to their initial victorious march across Belgium and France. Those allowed with the German Army included neutral journalists, many of them Americans. The German general staff even had the temerity to offer their communiqués to *The Times*, which immediately turned them down.[57] To British newspaper men such as Northcliffe, the Germans appeared to be controlling the world's press, as well as winning it over to their side.[58] In addition to world opinion, there was in Northcliffe's view the more important question of home morale to consider. The *Daily Mail* challenged the government to "have the great courage to tell the British people the truth."[59] Noting French press revelations in August, the newspaper questioned whether the "public enthusiasm for our army is not being chilled by the insufficiency of news concerning the British troops at the front. The newspapers do not wish to publish … anything that might be injurious to the military interests of the nation … while all will agree that a careful censorship is necessary for success, it might seem that the reticence in Great Britain has been carried to an unnecessary extreme."[60]

While censorship was being put in place in England, the BEF had secretly disembarked in France between 9 and 14 August.[61] The 18 August *Daily Mail* congratulated the army on the successful transportation of the BEF to France "without a casualty." At the same time the British prepared for battle, Northcliffe's correspondents ran headlong into military intransigence. Hamilton Fyfe, who had just returned to Paris from a visit to British army headquarters, wrote to Northcliffe that "It was a difficult business…. I should very much like to be nearer the front. At Headquarters we were placed virtually under arrest, and only released on condition that we took ourselves off and did not try to get back! However I hope the French Headquarters Staff will soon let me join them."[62] Unfortunately for Fyfe the French at this point were equally hostile to press access.

Three days later Sir John French and the 90,000-man British contingent were advancing on the enemy. Though small by Continental standards, the BEF was well trained and its morale was high. The secrecy and misinformation concerning its transport was effective; the Germans had no idea the British were even in France on the 23rd at the beginning of the Battle of Mons.[63] However, because of the retreat of the French army, the BEF was soon engaged in a hazardous tactical withdrawal to escape being outflanked by the Germans.[64]

At home, the political truce that had been in place since the war crisis began was formalized by an agreement between the three parties not to contest by-elections.[65] To encourage recruiting, a nonpartisan Parliamentary Recruiting Committee was set up with Asquith, Bonar Law, and the Labour M.P. Arthur Henderson as presidents. Britain's major prewar problems— Ireland, the suffragettes, and labor unrest—all gave way to the greater national crisis. John Redmond, the Nationalist Irish leader, added his pledge of support in the House of Commons on 3 August to the one made by Sir Edward Carson on the part of Ulster.[66] Many suffragettes became fanatic supporters of the war effort, their members becoming active in "white feather" campaigns to shame men into enlisting. Labor remained restive, but as the conflict continued the jobs and higher wages it generated soothed some prewar problems. The government later proved ready, as well, to take necessary measures to keep up production in the face of strikes.[67]

The Allied news blackout during the month of August had left British newspapers to take a hopeful tone in an attempt to bolster the morale of the nation. The *Daily Mail* filled its pages with general articles about the probable course of events illustrated with maps carefully labeled as only estimates of the positions of the opposing forces. Although disturbing rumors made their way to Britain, little was printed at first about the peril faced by the BEF in its retreat from Mons. Even undoubted defeats such as France suffered in Lorraine or the Russians faced at Tannenburg were either ignored or downplayed.[68] This all changed on 30 August when *The Times* (in a special Sunday edition) and the *Weekly Dispatch* published reports of the British retreat from Mons.[69] These detailed and graphic "Amiens dispatches," written by Arthur Moore for *The Times* and Hamilton Fyfe for the *Weekly Dispatch*, shattered weeks of press optimism.[70]

On Monday 31 August the *Daily Mail* continued the story of the BEF's "heroic retreat" and in the following days assumed the defense of its Sunday associate from the widespread attacks that the articles stimulated. Not only were the reports passed by F. E. Smith at the Press Bureau; in fact, he made significant changes and additions, to the stunned surprise of the editors who fully expected the accounts would be suppressed.[71] *The Times* article, in part, read:

> Since Sunday morning last the German advance has been one of almost incredible rapidity....The Germans, fulfilling one of the best of all precepts in war, never gave the retreating army one single moment's rest. The pursuit was immediate, relentless, unresting. Aeroplanes, Zeppelins, armoured motors, were loosed like an arrow from the bow....Regiments were grievously injured, and the broken army fought its way desperately with many stands, forced backwards and ever backwards by the sheer unconquerable mass of numbers....Our losses are very great. I have seen the broken bits of many regiments....The German commanders in the north advance their men as if they had an inexhaustible supply.

The Amiens dispatches created a storm of criticism directed at Northcliffe. The reports were called exaggerated, defeatist, and a malicious attack on the Army. Asquith himself rebuked *The Times* in the House of Commons. In an effort to justify the actions of the Northcliffe press, the 1 September

Daily Mail printed Smith's addition to the dispatch: "England should realize, and should realize at once, that she must send reinforcements, and still send them. Is an army of exhaustless valour to be borne down by the sheer weight of numbers, while young Englishmen at home play golf and cricket? We want men and we want them now."[72] Smith was furious and vowed vengeance on the editors of *The Times*, who, he felt, had betrayed him, and he called Northcliffe a "dirty dog" who could not be trusted.[73] Forced to resign over the affair, Smith was replaced at the Press Bureau by Sir Stanley (later Lord) Buckmaster, the solicitor-general.[74]

To reassure the public, Asquith had Churchill compose an official press communiqué (published anonymously 5 September) on the retreat.[75] Churchill wrote to Northcliffe, "I think you ought to realize the [damage] that has been done by Sunday's publication in the 'Times.' I do not think you can possibly shelter yourself behind the Press Bureau, although their mistake was obvious. I never saw such panic-stricken stuff written by any war correspondent before; and this served up on the authority of the 'Times' can be made, and has been made, a weapon against us in every doubtful state."[76] The press lord replied,

> This is not a time for Englishmen to quarrel, so I will not say all that I might about the publication of the Amiens message in The Times. Nor will I discuss the facts and tone of the message, beyond saying that it came from one of the most experienced correspondents in the service of the paper. I understand that not a single member of the staff on duty last Saturday night expected to see it passed by the Press Bureau. *But when it was not merely passed, but carefully edited, and accompanied by a definite appeal to publish it,* there was no other possible conclusion except that this was the government's definite wish.[77]

The Amiens dispatches incident affected the relationship between the press and the government in several ways. First, it confirmed Churchill in his extreme view of naval censorship. Even though, or perhaps because, Churchill had served as a correspondent himself in the Boer War, the Admiralty was even more closed to newsmen than the army. No warship in action was able to find room for a correspondent. Naval information had to be gleaned from the occasional official communiqués the Admiralty saw fit to issue.[78] The affair also moved the War Office to take action.[79] Though the dispatches confirmed Kitchener's worst suspicions about the press, it had become apparent some news must be allowed. However, instead of authorizing press correspondents, the War Office announced that its reports would be supplied by an official "Eyewitness," Major Ernest Swinton.[80] Swinton went to France on 14 September 1914 and continued his reports until the middle of July 1915.[81] Almost the only other British Army source of war news in 1914 came in the periodic dispatches of Sir John French.

Finally, the Amiens affair put Northcliffe firmly in opposition to the government and its censorship policy, whatever his prewar sympathies might have been. He wrote on this subject to Lord Murray of Elibank that "Some things are far more than flesh and blood can stand. So far as I am concerned, I propose to keep aloof from members of this Government until the war is over."[82] Though the press lord pretended to be unruffled by the affair, he told one of his writers, R. Macnair Wilson, that the attacks that labeled him an enemy of the army "hurt me more than anything else in my life."[83] The criticism was all the more painful, said Northcliffe, because "it was true what we said about the retreat from Mons. If only we had turned that glorious truth to our advantage."[84]

In early September the advance of the German army to the outskirts of Paris became the most important story. The 3 September *Daily Mail* showcased a map of the fighting near the city.[85] That same issue carried an article by J. M. N. Jeffries reporting the "charge of the 9th Lancers," which he called "another Balaclava."[86] Hamilton Fyfe reported the German advance to within twenty-nine miles of the capital and his thrilling capture and release by Uhlan cavalry on the outskirts of Paris.[87] *The Times* and the *Daily Mail* prepared to transfer their Paris offices to Bordeaux, along with the French government. In the days before the move, the Northcliffe press arranged with the Paris *Le Temps* to exchange news, including the official communiqués of the French government, whatever its location.[88] *Daily Mail* articles described the "Flight From Paris" by the government and the populace. By Monday 7 September the *Continental Daily Mail* was being published at Bordeaux. Soon after this, the early battlefield misfortunes of the Allies were reversed when their armies successfully counterattacked at the battle of the Marne. This stroke halted the German advance, saved Paris, and spelled the end of any remaining German illusions of swift victory in the West. By 15 September the *Daily Mail* staff had returned to their Paris office. The Marne victory also convinced Northcliffe that Germany would be defeated provided Britain could be convinced to exert her full strength.[89] To this end, he spent the remainder of the war attempting to mobilize public and political opinion.

Despite Northcliffe's best efforts at circumvention, the censorship continued to plague his campaign to awaken the country to the peril it faced. Repington wrote to Lord Roberts that "the censorship is being used as a cloak to cover all political, naval and military mistakes."[90] The letters of the soldiers to their loved ones allowed at least fragmentary news to get home. The *Daily*

Mail began to feature these openhearted communications of British enlisted men and officers (forwarded at first to the paper by their families), which gave an otherwise unavailable glimpse into conditions at the front. Northcliffe used them to back up his contention that the newspaper was "THE SOLIDER'S FRIEND" and he also sent them to politicians as evidence for his arguments.[91]

In early October 1914 the press lord made his first of many trips to the front. By this time the *Daily Mail* was supplying 10,000 free copies of each edition for the troops. Major Swinton, the official "Eyewitness," had responsibility for the dispersal of the papers and met with Northcliffe in Paris. Swinton fully expected an attack on his amateur journalistic efforts and arrived for the meeting wary of divulging secrets, but he was soon charmed by Northcliffe, who offered to put the considerable intelligence resources of his newspapers at the disposal of general headquarters (GHQ).[92] The press lord asked Swinton to pass along a request to visit army headquarters to Sir John French.[93] Northcliffe later recorded that at this time he also sent a scheme for airborne propaganda against the Germans to French, but nothing came of it. When he then presented the notion to General Sir Henry Wilson, the Director of Military Operations replied that it was a only a minor matter, that the thing was "to kill Germans."[94]

Though Northcliffe apparently did not meet personally with the British commander on this first trip, he visited the Belgian and French armies and was able to make some contact with British troops. He thoroughly enjoyed the adventure. His companion, Hamilton Fyfe, recorded that during the trip their car, driving at night without lights, had several near misses with disaster and that the two men experienced a shell bombardment at Pervyse. After watching an air raid, Northcliffe commented, "We shall have those fellows dropping bombs on London before long."[95] Back in England, he wrote to Leo Maxse, editor of the *National Review*, "I have just returned from a most interesting journey to the front.... I am afraid many of our boys will be frozen to death. Lots of them foolishly sold or gave away their overcoats when they first went across."[96]

The press lord's battlefront experience left him even more convinced that the British spirit would be given a boost if correspondents could share the inspiring things he had seen with the public. The visit to the front was questioned in a House of Commons debate on censorship. A Liberal M.P., James Hogge, wondered why "a certain well-known gentleman... has actually been in the fighting at the front, a privilege which is usually reserved for Ministers and Members of the opposition of the front bench."[97] In the same debate the chief censor, Sir Stanley Buckmaster, unapologetically defended the Press Bureau from attacks on its severity and accusations that it harmed recruiting.

In fact, he professed that a more stringent censorship was needed, as an alternative to martial law. The Press Bureau and Northcliffe were "heading for a row," Buckmaster told Riddell.[98]

In October and November *Daily Mail* maps followed the so-called "race to the sea" in which the opposing armies tried to outflank each other. The triumph of modern defense over attack was demonstrated in the defeat of the German attempt to break through at the First Battle of Ypres.[99] The stalemated front soon extended from the Swiss border to the Channel, marking the end of the war of movement and the beginning of the long years of trench warfare.[100] Winston Churchill's actions at the Admiralty also came under increasing press attack in October.[101] The nation expected great things of the navy and had been disappointed by the escape of the German battle cruiser *Goeben* to Turkey, the sinking of three (admittedly antiquated) British cruisers in one day, and losses at Antwerp by the Royal Navy Division. The failed defense of Antwerp personally involved Churchill.[102] Asking "Who is Responsible?" the *Daily Mail* rebuked the First Lord for interfering "in fields which do not properly concern him" and called for his colleagues to see that he did no more "mischief."[103] In a harbinger of future developments, the piece ended with a warning that though "this last incident was not vital... some future commitment might be."

At the end of October, in response to widespread public and press demands (led by Northcliffe), Lord Fisher was recalled from retirement to right the Admiralty's course. The chief proprietor of *The Times* took Geoffrey Robinson and Lovat Fraser to visit the First Sea Lord so that they could see "what manner of man it is in whom our destiny lies."[104] He assured Fisher that he was "at one with" him and wanted to ensure that his papers would be as well. Nevertheless, Admiralty censorship continued unabated under the new regime.[105] Churchill called on Buckmaster to suppress newspaper criticism or to return the censorship to the Admiralty and the War Office.[106] Even though he remained dissatisfied with naval censorship, Northcliffe cabled Arthur Brisbane, at the *New York Evening Journal,* that the one big change in the first few months of the war had come with the return of Fisher, adding that he did not think naval arrangements could be in better hands than those of Fisher, who was "a most daring and original man—the youngest thing of seventy-four in the world, I should think."[107]

American newspapers were able to carry accounts of events that the Admiralty and War Office censors denied to the press in Britain. W. F. Bullock, the *Daily Mail* correspondent in New York, sent clippings on the 27 October sinking of the British battleship *Audacious* and the rescue of its crew by the liner *Olympic* off Ireland.[108] Northcliffe wrote to Murray about the news blackout on the sinking that "the English people do not mind bad news. In as much as the Germans know of the disaster there can be no possible reason for suppressing it. It is a boomerang policy that will hit this Government very hard in the course of the long war that we are now commencing."[109]

To circumvent the censorship, the Northcliffe newspapers often quoted the American and other presses. For example, the 4 December 1914 *Daily Mail* carried excerpts from the *Saturday Evening Post* of "the only interview Lord Kitchener has given since the outbreak of war," by the American journalist Irvin Cobb. The article revealed Kitchener's prediction that the war effort would need at least three more years and that Germany would be defeated, because "there is no other possible contingency." This policy infuriated Buckmaster, who claimed he had proof that the chief proprietor of *The Times* had American papers attack the British censorship so that his newspaper could print their comments. Although Asquith (at the chief censor's request) asked the government departments not to show preference to *The Times*, Buckmaster complained that he was not supported by the cabinet in his calls for sterner measures and that Churchill and Kitchener were afraid to use DORA to court-martial the press lord.[110] In cabinet discussions Lloyd George often defended the press and Northcliffe. Riddell noted that "L. G. not very keen about attacking the Harmsworth crowd" and felt that there was "no doubt some sort of understanding between him and Northcliffe."[111]

To the owner of the *Daily Mail*, the censorship and recruiting questions were inextricably linked, and by November 1914 the projected shortfall in men had become the war's most important issue.[112] He complained to General Sir Henry Wilson, that "the present censorship has nothing to do with the conveyance of news to the enemy, the primary object being to keep the public in a state of optimistic foolishness, and is, in effect, a general suggestion not to enlist."[113] The press lord also corresponded with General Campbell, the director of recruiting, who offered to meet and discuss press aid. Northcliffe replied that this would be useless at present because the ignorance of the public about the military situation had "rendered powerless" his newspapers. His letter went on that "unless Lord Kitchener speedily takes the public into his confidence as to the nature of the conflict in which we are engaged, recruiting will continue at its relatively par pace. My agents in Germany, on the other hand, report of the immense enthusiasm and volunteering. The German man in the street is aware that this is a life and death struggle. Unfortunately our people are not aware of that. The censorship precludes the truth being told."[114]

Frustrated with War Office intransigence, Northcliffe took the matter up directly with the prime minister. A letter to Asquith linked recruiting failures to the censorship and raised the specter of conscription and a "split in the national ranks" unless recruiting methods were improved.[115] Before the war,

Northcliffe had been in favor of compulsion, but believed in late 1914 that the political consequences would be too damaging to the nation to justify a call for its immediate inaction. He spoke of recruiting and his communication with the prime minister in a letter to Geoffrey Robinson, editor of *The Times:*

> I wish you would have a good energetic leader on the failure of the recruiting plan.... I had an urgent message for the Government last night as to the attitude of my newspapers to this recruiting question. I stated positively that a muzzled newspaper is no more effective for recruiting than a muzzled gun would be for shooting, and that under no circumstance would I support any recruiting scheme (of which they have several) until the Press was placed in a position where it could really help....
>
> I am in favour of conscription, as you know; but to institute it at this moment would be bad, and would start the beginning of a peace-at-any-price Party.[116]

In the following weeks the *Daily Mail* also harried the government over its recruiting failures, but had little apparent effect.

The end of November saw the first *Daily Mail* correspondents officially allowed at the front, but not with the British army. The French allowed George Curnock and G. W. Price a view from their lines near Ypres. Curnock described the scene as "an abomination of desolation."[117] Two days later, the *Daily Mail* expressed the hope that "from this beginning the British Government will learn that, with a press as patriotic as we believe the British press to be, the presence of war correspondents under due control with the armies is a necessary link between the forces in the field and the public at home."[118] The improved situation soon brought much more news, both in quantity and quality, for the British press. However, largely because of Kitchener's intransigence, it would still be many months before correspondents were allowed with the British army.

Besides the dominant questions of censorship and recruiting, other issues occupied Northcliffe in the first five months of the war. The most important among these were the fear of German spy activity in England, concern for American opinion, and continuing battles with the Liberal press. The national alarm over the multitude of German spies believed to be roaming England was a direct carryover from the prewar invasion and spy manias. Conservative and Liberal newspapers waged campaigns against "anything and anyone" with German associations.[119] Products with German-sounding names, such as Schweppes Mineral Water, were forced to publish denials of enemy connections.[120] Even figures in the government were not immune, as the treatment of Lord Haldane and Prince Louis of Battenburg, both eventually forced from office, demonstrated.[121] Though the actual number of German espionage operatives in Britain was relatively small, this issue struck a public nerve and anti-German spy paranoia, fed by the press, continued throughout and became linked to the question of alien internment.[122] The 23 October *Daily Mail* editorial, "Proper Precautions at Last," lauded the announced government decision to intern all resident aliens between the ages of eighteen and forty-five.[123]

The Northcliffe press also joined the rest of the British newspapers in howls of righteous indignation over German "atrocities" in Belgium and France. These stories began in the first weeks of the war. On 12 and 17 August the *Daily Mail* carried accounts of "German Brutality," including the murder of five civilians corroborated by sworn statements. A 21 August article by Hamilton Fyfe chronicled the "sins against civilization" and "barbarity" of the Germans. A week later in a story based on accounts by wounded British troops, Fyfe continued to list atrocities with examples of Germans cutting off the hands of Red Cross workers and using women and children as shields in battle.[124] At the end of August the Belgian legation in London began releasing official reports of German "excesses."[125] The 26 August *Daily Mail* declared, "The measured, detailed, and we fear unanswerable indictment of Germany's conduct of the war issued yesterday by the Belgian minister is a catalogue of horrors that will indelibly brand the German name in the eyes of all mankind . . . this is no ordinary arraignment . . . concerned not with hearsay evidence, but with incidents that in each case have been carefully investigated. . . . After making every deduction for national bias and the possibility of error, there remains a record of sheer brutality that will neither be forgiven or forgotten." In September the *Daily Mail* reported the "Horror of Louvain" and continued with subsequent revelations of outrages at Maline, Rheims, and elsewhere. The 18 September issue carried a full page of atrocity photographs including, according to the caption, a Belgian civilian holding up the charred remains of his daughter's foot. An investigative commission convened under the former British ambassador to the United States, Lord Bryce, published a condemnation of German brutalities including reports of the impaling of babies and amputations of women's breasts. Besides the domestic audience, these broadsides were also aimed at world, and most importantly, American, opinion.[126]

Carrying on Northcliffe's prewar campaign, the *Daily Mail* almost immediately began to warn of enemy publicity in the United States.[127] While his newspapers publicly proclaimed the failure of the German "campaigns of falsehoods," privately Northcliffe believed otherwise.[128] He wrote about the matter in September to *The Times* correspondent in Washington,

Arthur Willert, who reported that educated opinion was on the side of Britain and passed along many positive comments from Americans.[129] However, he sent his chief a letter, identified only as from a British sympathizer in California, which confirmed the press lord's worst suspicions of German propaganda gains.[130] At the same time, fearing the use German propagandists would make of any negative comments, the press lord gave instructions that, "no criticism of the US was to appear in my newspapers until the American Fleet bombarded Liverpool."[131]

Northcliffe hoped to use newspaper interviews with prominent British figures to influence American opinion. He asked Sir George Riddell, who acted as an intermediary between the NPA and the government, for his cooperation in obtaining interviews from the king, Asquith, Fisher, Kitchener, and Lloyd George for the United Press Syndicate, which supplied 650 American newspapers.[132] Since his "Fight to the Finish" Queen's Hall speech in September 1914, the Northcliffe press had particularly praised the Welshman among the politicians.[133] "There is no man now in public life who is better qualified to stimulate the country to put forth its last ounce of strength than Mr. Lloyd George," declared the 26 September *Daily Mail*. Northcliffe called on the chancellor of the exchequer to grant an interview to the *Chicago Tribune*, one of the most powerful American papers and considered to be pro-German in its sentiments, telling him that the "Germans are very assiduous in the United States and we want all the help we can get."[134] Unfortunately, Lloyd George had made a prior commitment and felt unable to comply.[135] Although thwarted in this instance, Northcliffe continued to push other figures to grant interviews for dissemination in America.

When others would not speak out, the owner of the *Daily Mail* gave personal interviews that played on the notoriety he had gained in many trips across the Atlantic. In the 30 December 1914 *New York Sun* he asserted that, although it might take years, Germany would be defeated as long as the Allies marshaled all their resources, including manpower: "You ask me if I believe the necessary army can be raised by voluntary service. Personally I don't. You'll remember you could not do so in 1861. My personal belief is that we shall be obliged to adopt conscription as you...did. We shall fight with all the resources of our manhood, our shipyards, our wealth...[we] will go under rather than give in. It is no doubt disappointing to English and American business men to learn that there are people like myself who regard this gigantic struggle as a matter of years rather than months."[136]

Northcliffe relied heavily on his employees for information about the United States (whether he accepted their opinions or not), but he also corresponded directly with many Americans about the war. These letters represent propaganda pieces themselves, full of bluff bravado, but often brutally honest about the many shortcomings he saw in the Allied effort. In one such missive, the press lord invited Arthur Brisbane, of the *New York Evening Journal,* to "come over and see the very interesting state of affairs in Europe. It would be quite easy for you to get among the Germans, and I daresay it could be arranged for you to spend some time with the Allied forces too."[137] Even though Northcliffe claimed the Germans were already "beaten," nevertheless, the British were preparing for "a three years' war" with many ups and downs. While he denigrated Germany's achievements so far, noting "they have lost immensely—and they lose badly," the press lord also admitted that the British had lost heavily as well. The same letter revealed his concern that "we may not be preparing sufficiently for invasion. I am inclined myself to think that we are not—perhaps because I should be one of the first people to be hanged if the Germans got here."

Although the British nation had come together in the face of war, differences between the Conservatives and Liberals remained. In late November 1914, the Northcliffe press published Twells Brex's *"Scaremongerings" of the Daily Mail,* a compilation of the newspaper's articles on the German peril from the prewar period. This work, an unabashed advertisement of Northcliffe's correct predictions, included, as well, examples of the pacific or pro-German utterances of Liberals such as Lord Haldane and A. G. Gardiner, editor of the *Daily News.* The Liberal newspaper response was immediate. *The Star* proclaimed that "next to the Kaiser, Lord Northcliffe has done more than any other living man to bring about the war."[138] Gardiner considered Northcliffe the greatest corrupting influence in Fleet Street and a real danger to national life even before the war.[139] A *Daily News* "Letter to Lord Northcliffe" pointed out some of the press lord's own published pro-German sentiments. Gardiner conceded that Northcliffe's "claim to be the true prophet of war does not call for dispute" and continued,

It has always been your part to prophesy war and cultivate hate. There is nothing more tempting to the journalist than to be an incendiary. It is the shortcut to success, for it is always easier to appeal to the lower passions of men than to their better instincts. There is a larger crowd to address and you have never deserted the larger crowd. The student of your career... will have no difficulty in pointing to the wars you have fomented, the hatreds you have cultivated, the causes you have deserted, the sensations, from the Pekin falsehood to the Mons falsehood about the defeat of the British army, that you have spread broadcast. You have done these things because...they were the shortcut to success—that success which is the only thing you reverence amidst all the mysteries and sanctities of life.... This war will change much.... It will make an end of many things, and among them may we not hope that it will make an end of the most sinister influence that has ever corrupted the soul of English journalism?[140]

In response to these attacks Robert Blatchford championed Northcliffe in the following week's *Daily Mail*, but the press lord did not rise to the bait himself.[141] He explained to Lovat Fraser, "My object in showing up the 'Daily News' is to spike their guns when the settlement comes, and I think I have done that. I do not in the least mind personal attacks nor do I care what the public think about me. The fact that my newspapers are almost the only ones that are not shrinking rapidly at the present moment shows that my readers have faith in them. If the readers attacked me, I should then begin to think that I am the wicked man the little tradesmen of Fleet Street believe me to be."[142] Despite his words to Fraser, the attacks of the Liberal papers apparently troubled the press lord. Lloyd George commented to Riddell about the affair that Northcliffe "thought he was picking up a rabbit and found it was a hedgehog."[143]

The zeppelin raids and naval bombardments on civilian targets that began in the last month of 1914 brought directly home to the English population for the first time the bitter reality of twentieth-century warfare. The *Daily Mail* howled over the "inhuman and malignant action," of the German shelling of Scarborough and other coastal towns, which killed many women and children.[144] Two months before, the newspaper had appealed for better air defense preparations "instantly" against the fifty to one hundred airships being prepared in Germany for an assault.[145] Despite their sensational coverage in the press, Northcliffe remained confident that the attacks would not cause the terror and panic which the Germans hoped. At year's end the *Daily Mail* pledged in 1915 "never to sheath the sword" until the whole of France was cleared of the enemy and Belgium was regained.[146] The fundamental job ahead, continued the paper, was to destroy Prussian militarism even though this "can only be carried out by the invasion of Germany."

Though firmly resolved to see the thing through, the first five months of war had been a frustrating nightmare for Northcliffe. While the greatest news story in history unfolded just across the channel, his correspondents could neither visit nor report it from the British army. The government proved largely deaf to his warnings about the negative effects of censorship on morale and recruiting. December 1914 saw direct German attacks on England from the air and the sea, which he considered preludes to invasion.

The press lord's battles over the censorship and recruiting continued into 1915, as did his concerns with the German "enemy within" and American opinion. In the new year they would be joined with other, even more urgent, issues such as the shortage of munitions and the need for a truly national government to replace the tired Liberal "muddlers" who after five months still failed to take the war for the life-and-death struggle Northcliffe recognized it to be.

THREE

"A Very Big and Difficult Thing"
Munitions & Coalition, January to June 1915

BY THE BEGINNING OF 1915, FIVE MONTHS OF WAR HAD CHANGED THE balance of political power in Britain between the prime minister, the House of Commons, and outside influences including the press. The role of the Commons was diminished after August 1914 by the increased need for secrecy, the numerous recesses, and the fact that many Members were abroad with the Army.[1] As the ultimate parliamentarian, Asquith's power waned in parallel. Lord Kitchener's stranglehold on the War Office also diminished the role of Parliament. Further shifts came as a result of the party truce. The efficient local Liberal agents no longer served only party ends, and the Conservatives temporarily discontinued partisan attacks.[2]

Into this power vacuum came the press—Northcliffe in the lead. The decades before the war had seen the political influence of the press increase dramatically, and once the war began, with the debates in Parliament and party speeches diminished as counterattractions, this power grew even greater. The politicians, already intimately familiar with the newspaper offices of Fleet Street, nimbly adjusted to its heightened wartime prestige. Even before Britain joined the hostilities, Northcliffe found himself courted for the information he could give allied politicians. As the war lengthened, so did the list of those who sought his aid.

During the first six months of 1915, the home population became more personally acquainted with the realities of total war. The zeppelin and naval bombardments that began at the end of 1914 continued. The mounting battlefield casualties directly affected more and more families, including the Harmsworths. Atrocity propaganda continued to fuel public hatred of Germany, producing a conviction that only total victory would be acceptable.[3] The war effort and the German submarine campaign brought the home front real shortages for the first time. By March 1915 revelations of a critical lack of high explosive shells for the British army overshadowed the two continuing problems of censorship and recruiting for Northcliffe. The munitions muddle exemplified for him the shortcomings of the wait-and-see Liberal administration. The "Shells Scandal" that followed in May 1915 was not an isolated incident, but the culmination of a months-long newspaper campaign that materially contributed to the demise of Britain's last Liberal government.

Intertwined with the munitions problem was the added issue of the Dardanelles campaign.[4] This operation against Turkey, to run the Straits and capture Constantinople, brought to light a serious division in British strategic planning. Opinion was divided into two camps. "Westerners," led by army figures like Sir John French, believed the war must be won in Flanders and France. "Easterners," led by politicians like Winston Churchill and Lloyd George, thought a breakthrough could be made in Turkey or the Balkans, ending the stalemate.[5] Churchill promoted the Dardanelles campaign as a method both to take Turkey out of the war and to open a warm-water supply line that would bolster Russia.[6] Northcliffe considered the Dardanelles a waste of men and munitions needed for the Western Front; however, he joined forces with the easterner Lloyd George over the shells question.

Before the shortfall in munitions took center stage, other concerns intruded in the first months of the year. Northcliffe's press came under heavy fire from French and British authorities and he continued to worry about Anglo-American relations, strained by the British blockade of Germany. The press lord feared that not only might American support be lost, but, because of heavy-handed British actions against her shipping, it was possible the United States could become actively hostile. He showed a deep concern, as well, over the state of relations with Britain's partners in the war— France and Russia. In 1915 it became apparent that England would have to contribute more than monetary and naval aid to her Allies while Kitchener's New Armies prepared for battle in 1917. A toll of British blood more substantial than that which had already been shed would be necessary to ensure that France and Russia stayed the course and did not fall prey to German peace maneuvers. The debate shifted from whether a large British army would be dispatched to where a morale-boosting victory might be best obtained for the Allies.[7]

The new year began inauspiciously for Northcliffe. He was notified that the Paris *Daily Mail* had been shut down for twenty-four hours by the French censor as punishment for a 30 December 1914 dispatch that the paper failed to suppress.[8] The error was blamed on a miscommunication at 3:30 A.M., after most of the staff had left for the night.[9] Appeals to the Foreign and War Offices concerning the "high-handed manner" in which the paper was suppressed (rather than only reprimanded) fell on deaf ears. The Paris staff explained to Northcliffe that the French censor had not been well disposed toward the paper and had often made harsh accusations that the *Daily Mail* was too optimistic in its news. Not in a mood for excuses, the press lord warned the Paris editor that he had had two serious complaints and added that he did "not like to be severe, but...please understand that such a thing will not happen twice under your Editorship. The London staff are particularly indignant, as the matter is causing much comment in Government circles here, and has evidently been communicated to the British Government."[10] A visit from the public prosecutor prompted a letter to the London staff as well.[11] However, Northcliffe did take the opportunity to inform Sir Edward Cook at the Press Bureau that "it may interest you to know that the French authorities have lately lectured the Paris edition of the 'Daily Mail'—a replica of the English edition—on its optimism. Here we receive daily abuse because of its pessimism."[12]

After dealing with these newspaper worries, Northcliffe departed in the first week of January 1915 for a second visit to the front. As before, his journey added fuel to his frustration with the lethargic attitude of the Asquith ministry. The government, he feared, was bungling relations with France and also with the most important neutral—America. He wrote about these matters to Samuel Storey soon after leaving the fighting line:

> It has again been brought home to me, as it was during a previous visit...
> that this country is in for the greatest struggle of its history.
>
> I fear that we are muddling and dallying. You will probably realize that
> the Government that did not see the war coming, apparently does not see
> that America is coming, and that the trouble with the French is develop-
> ing rapidly. Our American friends write me that they will not have their
> commerce directed by us. Our French friends say that England does not
> understand that we are fighting Germany on French territory or that one-
> eighth of the richest part of France is held by the Germans...starv-
> ing to death two millions of French people behind the German lines....
> You know, of course, that Germany has approached France twice about
> a separate peace.
>
> We are dealing very gently with the Government now, because the
> public, who know nothing about the war, will not tolerate criticism of our
> public men; but, believe me, we shall not be patient much longer.[13]

A 6 January Lovat Fraser article in the *Daily Mail*, "What *We* Are Doing in the War," noted the "restlessness" in France and Russia regarding Great Britain's share in the war and blamed the misunderstandings on the "business as usual" attitude of the government and the British failure to introduce conscription as had her Allies.[14]

Fearful for the health of the alliance, in 1915 Northcliffe strove to keep in touch with battlefield and political developments in Russia and, later, in Italy after that country joined the Allied cause in May. Hamilton Fyfe was dispatched to Petrograd to report on the Russian scene for the *Daily Mail*. This arrangement was never quite satisfactory. Delays caused by the long distances involved, conditions in Russia, and the censorship handicapped communications from the start. Fyfe's conciliatory attitude toward the German people also caused problems.[15] Robert Wilton, the Russian correspondent for *The Times*, reassured his worried chief in April that "the Russians will go on fighting another year if necessary. I believe they are, on the whole, playing a straight game."[16] When the Italians joined the Allied cause, Northcliffe immediately moved to secure news coverage on this new front and met the same obstacles as elsewhere. The British ambassador in Rome, Sir Rennel Rodd, replied to a query from the press lord that "as far as I understand there is no intention here at present to allow correspondents, though something probably will be arranged later."[17]

To remedy French doubts about the seriousness of Britain's commitment, Northcliffe suggested to the authorities that their reporters be allowed to tour England and view British war preparations. He began his entreaties at the top, with letters to Asquith and Sir Edward Grey, the foreign secretary.[18] The two replied that they would discuss his suggestion with Lord Kitchener, who vetoed the idea.[19] A letter from Reginald Brade at the War Office to Sir Eric Drummond, Asquith's personal secretary, summarized the arguments against Northcliffe's plan. Brade confided that, according to Kitchener's sources, the French were by no means displeased with the share the British were taking. Further, the war secretary felt that if the Frenchmen were allowed to visit, they would almost certainly be struck by the contrast between life in France and Britain. They would not see the fleet; they would not see the troops in Egypt or India. It was feared that the result would likely be "quite the contrary from what we should like." Also the British were presently prohibiting their own journalists from writing about military preparations. It would not be possible to maintain this attitude if the French were invited. Brade's letter ended, "On the whole, therefore, Lord Kitchener thinks that Lord Northcliffe should be told that in the present circumstances the scheme is not one which the Government could welcome."[20]

After the press lord learned his proposal had been rejected, he discounted the arguments against it in further correspondence with Asquith and Grey. He told Asquith that he was "not much impressed by them. They do not dispose of the fact that, among our nearest ally, the man in the street is in the mental condition which the Germans want him to be." Northcliffe then quoted Von Falkenhayn, head of the German general staff, who had said, in reply to the question "When are you going to strike?" that it was not necessary, for "We will weary out the French."[21] In his letter to Grey, Northcliffe added that he was concerned that "we are now only beginning to embark on a struggle in which we may be left almost single-handed, with the additional hostility of the United States. It seems to me as imperative that the French discontent should be allayed as that we should have a friendly America. Both these, I believe, could be helped by the aid of the Press."[22]

Frustrated in his efforts to promote a British tour of French journalists, Northcliffe turned his attention to publicizing Britain's recent battlefield accomplishments as an alternative method of appeasing French and Russian discontent. He wrote in early February to Bonar Law, who was soon to visit British headquarters in France, asking his assistance to bring the matter before Sir John French. "I do think it important for the nation," Northcliffe asserted, "as well as to assure a proper realization of our efforts by the French and Russians that some account should be published."[23] He corresponded with Colonel Brinsley Fitzgerald, Field-Marshal French's secretary, concerning plans to have John Fortescue, a leading historian, write an account of the Battle of Ypres for general newspaper release. The press lord was not in favor of this course, commenting that "Fortescue is our best military historian. He is not a correspondent."[24] The press lord also approached Fitzgerald on behalf of Mary Roberts Rinehart, a writer for the American *Saturday Evening Post*, who sought to become the war's first female correspondent. Northcliffe gave her letters of introduction to the Belgian premier and army commander, as well as Sir John French.[25] Despite the press lord's skepticism as to her chances of actually reaching the front, Rinehart used her nursing training to cross the channel on a supposed mission to report on war hospitals. Once across, she managed a wider tour of the Allied armies, which included a visit to British GHQ.[26]

Throughout the war Northcliffe maintained his own intelligence service at home and abroad. He employed observers in the Allied countries, as well as America, Sweden, Spain, and Holland, and received regular reports on conditions in Germany and the occupied countries.[27] The thousands of letters to his newspapers and the activities of his *Continental Daily Mail* staff gave Northcliffe a better view of the war than that of many members of the cabinet. Widespread business interests and cousins in Germany provided another base to which he added as needed. For example, in 1915 one agent traveled to Germany for a month to gather impressions, particularly of manufacturing centers, then reported personally to the press lord in London.[28]

The information obtained by such methods often was offered to the government and occasionally accepted. In March 1915, the War Office used Northcliffe's network to complete a set of German casualty lists. He told Edward Ingram, "I will do my utmost to procure the casualty lists, but we find that they are more and more difficult to obtain. It is necessary to send someone into Germany to get them, and already one of my agents has been caught and sent to a fortress."[29] The press lord also passed along to the War Office many ideas he received for new (and often improbable-sounding) weapons. One such letter proposed a "vortex" antiaircraft gun meant literally to knock airplanes out of the sky with a burst of air. For the trenches, Arthur Brisbane sent plans from America for a hydraulic water cannon.[30]

Northcliffe was particularly concerned with the effects of German propaganda in the United States and American reaction to the British blockade. At the beginning of the war it was assumed that the British fleet would soon defeat its enemy counterpart and blockade the German coast.[31] When the German navy stayed at anchor and refused to engage, the British erected a blockade to intercept trade and waited for the foe to emerge. A British Order in Council of 20 August 1914 unilaterally added food to the absolute contraband list drawn up before the war and made other revisions.[32] British interference with the shipping of neutrals under these modified guidelines drew protests from the United States. In the official British view, neutral hardships were unfortunate but unavoidable when balanced against the vital interests of the empire. However, when the Germans bent the rules in retaliation with their submarine campaign, their interests were not recognized.[33] Northcliffe agreed that Germany must be blockaded, but not at the cost of completely alienating American official and public opinion, which he felt the Foreign Office slighted.[34] Willert reinforced this belief with a report that the main difficulty in relations between the two countries was that "Washington is ignored to a most surprising extent."[35] In an attempt to remedy this shortcoming, Northcliffe forwarded press clippings from the United States to Sir Edward Grey, which illustrated both American hostility and the success of German efforts.[36]

On the propaganda front, the 22 January *Daily Mail* warned of "Dernburg's Lie-Campaign Succeeding in the U. S."[37] From New York, W. F. Bullock contributed a continuing series on the German campaign. That month Frederic Wile (the former Berlin *Daily Mail* correspondent) crossed the Atlantic on a fact-finding mission for his chief. He reported back that the German efforts were "acute, tremendous and insidious."[38] Wile recounted his tour of the country in the series, "The German Campaign in America," which began in the 9 March *Daily Mail*. The press lord also complained to the

First Sea Lord, Admiral Fisher, about the slighting of America due to the censorship. The same letter ascribed his newspaper criticism of the Dardanelles operation to "fear of the appalling optimism of your colleagues, who rarely see an inch before them."[39] "If they underestimate the colossal job before the country," asked Northcliffe, "do they not underestimate the Dardanelles scheme?" "Theirs," he continued, "is not the rashness of courage, but the valour of ignorance."[40]

The announcement of Germany's February submarine blockade of Britain was labeled a "bluff" by the *Daily Mail*, which called for a "real blockade" in response.[41] Northcliffe, whose press operations had already been hampered by the loss of many men to the armed forces, for the first time felt his paper supply threatened and planned for the worst. In a letter of complaint to Geoffrey Robinson at *The Times* about the downward trend in circulation and measures that might have to be taken, the press lord added that "our difficulties are going to be increased because it is said that owing to the blockade the price of paper is about to rise, and we must issue small papers I fear."[42] The British responded to Germany's submarine campaign by tightening their own surface blockade. The Order in Council of 11 March 1915 enlarged the campaign to include all German trade.[43] These actions were the subject of a letter to Northcliffe from J. C. O'Laughlin of the *Chicago Herald:*

> I assume your Government was forced by public opinion to make the reprisal which was announced.... the British declaration is as violative of recognized principles of international law as is the German decree though... your government... has announced a purpose of observing the laws of humanity.... this Government will protest emphatically.... There it will stop, for the present at least. The American people ... do not want war, especially with the Allies.... I beg you, in the interest of good relations of the two countries, to see that a measure of caution is employed that the seizures shall be limited to the zone of war.[44]

In May 1915 the German submarine campaign came to a climax with the sinking of the *Lusitania* and the resulting loss of 128 American lives. The 8 May *Daily Mail* labeled the action "Premeditated Murder." The 10 May issue included photographs of dead women and children lined up at the Queenstown "charnel house." Some expected the Americans to join the war in the spirit of Wilson's stated rule of "strict accountability," but his "Too Proud to Fight" speech soon disabused them of the idea.[45] After the disaster, Willert wrote to Northcliffe from America that "the row with Germany by no means precludes a further unpleasant controversy over our blockade. As things stand today only actual war can prevent that."[46]

On the home front, Northcliffe fully realized how unpopular he was making himself in some quarters by his constant newspaper criticisms and reminders of the long and difficult task ahead for the country.[47] By March 1915, however, increased numbers of politicians from both parties also questioned the methods of the Asquith government and the Kitchener mystique. Conservatives, particularly Walter Long and the Unionist Business Committee, muzzled by the ongoing "party truce" and unhappy with the progress of the war were increasingly impatient. Some Liberals were also restive. At Bangor, Lloyd George began a series of public pronouncements. The 1 March *Daily Mail* printed his remark that "we are conducting a war as if there was no war. I have never been doubtful about the result of the war. Nor have I been doubtful, I am sorry to say, about the length of the war and its seriousness.... we need men, but we need arms more than men and every day that produces delay is full of peril to this country." Northcliffe joined forces with Lloyd George over the issue that would dominate the next few months — the shortage of shells.

No one on either side had foreseen the unprecedented scale of western front artillery bombardments, but by October 1914 the need for an increased supply of munitions had become apparent. A Shells Committee, including Lloyd George, was created to examine and propose solutions to the problem.[48] This civilian invasion of the army sphere was resented and blocked by Kitchener and the War Office; however, the committee was able to manage some improvements.[49] The war secretary's military career outside England had not prepared him to share information in cabinet discussions, and his aloof persona intimidated the other members.[50] Stringent control of War Office matters brought him into almost immediate conflict with Lloyd George, who complained that Kitchener treated his colleagues with "the usual mixture of military contempt and apprehension."[51] In addition to the War Secretary's duties, Kitchener took it onto himself to raise, train, and equip the huge New Armies, to mobilize Britain's industries for war, and to oversee Britain's global strategy. At the same time, he acted as his own chief of staff, personally oversaw every detail, and sought to economize whenever possible. This course, so successful in smaller conflicts, proved disastrously inadequate by 1915.[52] The old methods failed to equip the multitude of soldiers Kitchener proved so adept at recruiting. His clashes with Sir John French, who feared the war secretary would take personal command in France, further complicated the situation.[53]

Because he had to take into consideration the empire and Britain's Allies, in the westerner/easterner split over strategy, Kitchener was one of the few British military figures amenable to diversions of men and material away from the western front.[54] Russian pleas for assistance in early 1915 made him open to Churchill's naval plan to open the Dardanelles, especially if, as Churchill insisted, few troops would be required.[55] After the naval bombardment failed, Kitchener was forced to divert troops from the western front to the Dardanelles, rather than face a humiliating withdrawal. This further infuriated Sir John French, who continued to plead for more resources. The lack of ammunition, particularly high-explosive shells, came to a head after the battle of Neuve Chappelle (10–13 March) once again demonstrated the futility of using shrapnel shells against heavily entrenched German positions.

Since the first months of the war, Sir John French had complained about munition shortages, which often forced miserly rationing of shells.[56] Kitchener's frugal habits led him to call French's use of shells during the Battle of Neuve Chappelle "recklessly extravagant."[57] Rather than try new channels of ordering and procurement, Kitchener continued to support the unimaginative methods of his master-general of ordnance, Sir Stanley Von Donop.[58] Faced with this War Office intransigence, French appealed for help outside of army channels, including politicians and the press.

Northcliffe's natural inclination to allow professionals to do their jobs without interference and his inspections of the front put him squarely on the side of Sir John French in this dispute. Kitchener's hostility and lack of co-operation extinguished any lingering hope Northcliffe held for success under his leadership. One biographer of Kitchener recounted a personal confrontation between the two men at the War Office over censorship, in which the war secretary threatened prosecution if the press lord published information helpful to the enemy, and showed him the door.[59] Consequently, Northcliffe transferred his confidence to Sir John French. Lloyd George became the third party in a formidable triumvirate ranged against Kitchener. Had the war secretary been more attuned to conditions in England, he might have worked with the campaign led by Lloyd George and Northcliffe. As a result of his uncooperative attitude, the agitation culminated in a bitter public attack.[60]

Even before the battle of Neuve Chappelle, Northcliffe was in contact with French about munitions and their production, including the problem of motivating worker support for the war. A 3 March letter expressed the hope that the field-marshal would "shortly receive the munitions" for his "great enterprise."[61] French also sent Colonel Brinsley Fitzgerald, his secretary, to England for discussions with his press ally about newspaper publicity.[62] The field-marshal and the press lord both considered "lamentable" the division of British forces created by the Dardanelles expedition, and Northcliffe assured French that his newspapers would not "cease to urge the sending of men to your army."[63] He also reported that Repington and Valentine Williams were coming to Flanders to "concentrate British attention on the real battle-line."[64] French replied that he "rejoiced to hear the view which you take in regard to the division of our forces. I entirely agree ... and I earnestly hope you will do your utmost in your powerful control of the Press to insist upon concentration of all available forces in this theatre."[65]

The costly British failures on both the western and eastern fronts in March brought a new urgency to the shells problem. News of Neuve Chapelle got out in letters to the papers, from Members of Parliament, and from accounts of wounded soldiers in England. Northcliffe visited the hospital established by his wife at their country house, Sutton Place.[66] Kitchener broke the silence and admitted his worries over munitions in the House of Lords on 15 March 1915, yet he told Asquith two weeks later he would resign if another Shells Committee was appointed.[67] The failure of the naval bombardment to breach the Dardanelles on 18 March added to the criticism of the government. In a 29 March *Daily Mail* interview, Sir John French stated that "the protraction of the war depends entirely on the supply of men and munitions."

The military setbacks strengthened rumors that the Conservatives, their press allies, and others were scheming to discredit the prime minister and force a coalition. Churchill and Lloyd George were accused of working to undermine the government from within. The Welshman, in particular, was brought under suspicion because he had been lauded recently in the Northcliffe press. The home secretary, Reginald McKenna, passed along the whisperings to the prime minister.[68] Asquith told Miss Stanley on 29 March,

There is, in the Tory press a dead set being made against me personally. Witness the articles in *The Times* & the *Morning Post*.

As you know, I am fairly indifferent to press criticism. I honestly don't care one damn about that. McKenna came to see me ... with a tragic history of intrigue. The idea is that Northcliffe (for some unknown reason) has been engineering a campaign to supplant me by Ll. G! McK is ... quite certain that Ll. G. & perhaps Winston are "in it." Which I don't believe. However, he (McK) ... has a certain amount of evidence as to Ll. G. to go upon.[69]

Asquith appears to have been correct in his belief that Lloyd George remained loyal in this period. No evidence to support McKenna's charges has surfaced.

In April 1915 Northcliffe made his third visit to the front. While on the Continent he saw Field-Marshal French and also met with General Joffre, the French army commander, and André Tardieu (former foreign editor of *Le Temps*), who was acting as liaison between Joffre and the French government.[70] The press lord wrote to his mother that he had a "long talk with Sir John French" and a "pleasant dinner at which was the prince of Wales."[71] At British GHQ, Northcliffe composed a rare handwritten note to his old friend Alexander Kenealy, former editor of the *Daily Mirror:* "All here most confident that by prolonged massed artillery fire on a tremendous scale they can break the German line & the next few weeks will be momentous in history I feel sure. General French [i]s calm, able & certain, & by necessity a terrific worker. I sat with him till late last night. We need shells. Today I go to stay with Joffre whose headquarters are at Chantilly a long motor ride from here right along the war front, at many places. I propose writ[ing] my impressions of the two men in the Times shortly."[72]

Kitchener used Joffre's objection to correspondents as a rationale for excluding them from the British army. Consequently, Northcliffe (probably with the aid of Sir John French) arranged a meeting with Joffre at Chantilly, the French GHQ, to dispel this argument.[73] Northcliffe sent a long memorandum detailing this conference (by Valentine Williams, who had accompanied him) to Brinsley Fitzgerald for Sir John. It revealed, among other things, Joffre's demands for more English soldiers and the fact that the French commander felt Kitchener "had not behaved quite straight...over the question of troops."[74] The press lord's efforts were rewarded when Joffre agreed to Northcliffe's suggestion that a Reuters correspondent should report news from the French army.[75] At the same time, Sir George Riddell and other press figures at home urged Kitchener to allow correspondents with the British forces. Northcliffe reported to Riddell that:

General French has come to the same opinion, as the Germans, that war correspondents are necessary to armies...in order that the troops may read about the war in which they are engaged, and, secondly, so that the public may know about their relations and friends and the war itself.

...if the Government wishes to avoid strikes and to enlist in this war the services of the whole of the people, they should strain every nerve to get really distinguished writers to make the war what it is—a matter of life or death to the nation.[76]

In May Kitchener finally allowed press representatives at general headquarters in France, where, although their movements were limited, they remained for the rest of the war.[77] Valentine Williams credited Northcliffe's visit with Joffre and his own 19 April Neuve Chapelle story with forcing Kitchener to remove his ban.[78]

The conference with Joffre increased Northcliffe's dissatisfaction with the British government's prosecution of the war. He listed several grievances in a letter to Lovat Fraser over an article in *The Times* which Northcliffe felt whitewashed government blunders:

> Anyone who has studied this war knows that our army in France is unable to move. Its position is growing harassing to the French who are anxious to move. It cannot move for three reasons: Firstly, because many of the shells that should have been sent to it have been dispatched to the Dardenelles; Secondly, because the 29th Division, which was promised to the French, has been sent to the Dardanelles; and, Thirdly, because the Government has not availed itself of the small contractors who have offered to supply shells.
>
> ...I have reason to believe, privately, that General French is on his way over to England to make urgent representations...to the Cabinet.[79]

The same letter particularly condemned the government over the shortage of shells:

> The whole question of the supply of munitions of war is one on which the Cabinet cannot be arraigned too sharply....
>
> When recently, I saw those splendid boys of ours toiling along the roads to the front, weary, but keen and bright-eyed...I could not help feeling very, very bitter at the thought that many of them were on the way to certain mutilation and death by reason of the abominable neglect of the people here.
>
> ..."The Times"...has a tremendous duty and responsibility—more especially as I feel my duty greater because I have now made three visits to this war, have talked with hundreds of people—both English and French—concerned with it, and know that, while we are talking about the alleged drunken habits of the working man (in which I do not believe), the guns at the front are starved for want of the only means of putting an end to this frightful slaughter of the best which any nation has to give.

Although he disagreed with Northcliffe concerning the Dardanelles, about the shells shortage Fraser replied, "I believe the time will come when we shall have to say that we cannot run this war with a Cabinet of tired lawyers; but we must first be very sure of our ground, and not move unless we are convinced the country will be with us. Remember that if that time comes we shall probably have to arraign Lord Kitchener also, and that will be a very big and difficult thing."[80]

The Drink Question mentioned above became another national issue of debate at this time. Lloyd George blamed alcohol for many of the country's production and labor problems and considered nationalization of the liquor industry.[81] The 1 March *Daily Mail* reported his speech at Bangor, which accused alcohol of doing more damage than German submarines. A month later the Welshman told the Shipbuilder's Employer's Federation that "Excessive drinking in the works connected with these operations is interfering seriously with that output."[82] A plan for voluntary abstinence, however, found few supporters beyond the king and Kitchener.

Northcliffe disagreed with Lloyd George on this issue and had his newspapers say so. He had made inquiries among his workers and warned Charles Beattie, night editor at the *Daily Mail,* to "go slow with the prohibition business.... I think there is going to be trouble over this matter. The suggestion that we shall have drinking to excess is untrue."[83] The 3 April *Daily Mail* suggested a reduction in legal alcohol levels, warning that "the proposal of total prohibition is fraught with danger and injustice." On 14 April the paper struck even harder, combining drink, the Dardanelles, recruiting and munitions:

> A week ago the country was told the Members of the Cabinet were about to become teetotalers. A few weeks ago the public was led to believe that Constantinople was about to become ours.
>
> The enforced temperance of the whole Cabinet seems to be about as doubtful an immediate proposition as the capture of the Sultan's capital. Both matters are, as usual, shrouded in official secrecy....
>
> At the outset of the struggle, instead of seizing the factories and making shells, as did the French and Germans, they seized the newspapers in order to shut the public mouth....
>
> At present we are in the midst of a recruiting muddle, by which hundreds of thousands of married men have been enlisted while the country is notoriously full of single slackers....
>
> But the greatest muddle of all is the combined beer and shell muddle. Our gallant commander in Flanders, Field Marshal Sir John French, has repeatedly emphasized the increasing need of shells.... the War Office which might have foreseen this, joins with Mr. Lloyd George and rends our working men, throwing all the blame on their drunken habits. Were it not so tragic, there would be something grotesque in all this.

Lloyd George unsuccessfully attempted to enlist Northcliffe's aid for his antidrink program. "I am anxious to have a talk with you on the government proposals about Drink," the Welshman wrote to the press lord, "we have overwhelming evidence of the grave mischief in the munitions and transport areas caused by excessive drinking and we must take strong action otherwise the war will go on forever.... your influence is essential."[84] Despite this flattery, Northcliffe was not persuaded and remained hostile to further proposals.

The *Daily Mail* continued to pressure the government. On 13 April the newspaper called for the publication of Sir John French's Neuve Chappelle dispatches to coincide with the week's recruiting drive, charging that "the constant suppression of news with regard to the operations in Flanders and the mysterious Dardanelles Expedition is, indeed, a matter which requires the attention of Parliament."[85] A chart (reproduced from *Le Matin*) showed the relative miles of trench line occupied by each army—with France holding 543½, the British 31¾, and the Belgians 17½. French's released dispatch was quoted two days later: "In war as it is today between civilized nations, armed to the teeth with the present deadly rifle and machine gun, heavy casualties are absolutely unavoidable.... loss and waste of life can, however, be shortened and lessened if the attacks are supported by the most efficient and powerful force of artillery available; but an almost limitless supply of ammunition is necessary and a most liberal discretionary power as to its use must be given to the artillery commanders."[86]

The 16 April *Daily Mail* blamed the government that "did not see the war coming" for the mounting casualties. It continued that even when the "war came they did not see that shells would be wanted in such quantities." Because the government also did not see the need for more men, Britain was presently in "the ignoble position of holding only 31 miles in the firing line." About the harmful charges that excessive drinking had been responsible for an inadequate supply of ammunition, it declared, "This is no hour for side-tracking the interests and energy of the nation and diverting them to tee-totaler fads and crazy plans of 'nationalizing the drinking trade.' Let Ministers get back to their own real business—the supply of shells and men." Three days later the campaign resumed, this time including the opposition and Kitchener as well:

There is a growing discontent with a Government that started last August with great popularity and a brave show of bellicose speeches. There is also considerable discontent with an opposition which does not help the Government by means of criticism and advice.... unless the Government is kept up to the mark and supplied with new ideas and energy from the opposition it will continue to hide itself behind Lord Kitchener....

We assert that Lord Kitchener has done as much as mortal man could do in the nine months he has been engaged in an entirely novel task. Where he has failed is in not ruthlessly ejecting the "old gang" with the consequent delay in making the 200,000 shells we want every day...most serious of all in failing to see that all the factories in the country capable of producing munitions of war were set to the task.[87]

Based on information from Sir John French, Kitchener assured Asquith that the supply of shells was adequate. Eager to demonstrate the wickedness of Northcliffe, the prime minister declared at Newcastle on 20 April 1915 that "I saw a statement the other day that the operations...of our army... were being crippled, or at any rate, hampered, by our failure to provide the necessary ammunition. I say there is not a word of truth in that statement, which is the more mischievous, because, if it were believed, it is calculated to dishearten our troops, to discourage our Allies, and to stimulate the hopes and activities of our enemies."[88] This speech drew immediate and widespread press criticism. *The Times* and *Daily Mail* asked how Asquith's remarks could be reconciled with statements by Lloyd George and Kitchener on the shortage of shells.[89] Asquith wrote again to Venetia Stanley, "I am so glad that you liked my speech; if you think it good, I don't care a twopenny damn what anyone else thinks about it—let alone Northcliffe & his obscene crew. I don't think we shall hear much more now on this particular line of attack, as after a very curious rapprochement between K & Ll. G.... the latter was allowed—for the first time—to give a number of most convincing figures to the House yesterday."[90]

Rather than smoothing the waters, Lloyd George's revelations in the House of Commons caused Northcliffe further concern. On 1 May he warned French that he would soon be held responsible for the military failures:

The evil effects of the secrecy with regard to your army are assuming new form. On April 21st, Mr. Lloyd George, in the House of Commons said that there were 36 divisions at the front. That statement has been interpreted by the British and French publics as meaning that you are in command of 750,000 men. People are asking...If Sir John French has three quarters of a million men, why is he only occupying thirty miles of line?... Early this week Lord Kitchener expressly forbade the newspapers analyzing Mr. Lloyd George's statement, and you are therefore believed to have this vast army at your disposal....

In the absence of some strong statement from you the Government have your friends at their mercy, because they are able to get their newspapers to say that any agitation for less secrecy is unpatriotic and playing the enemy's game.

As a further result of secrecy, Mr. Asquith is able to assure the nation that your operations have never been hampered for want of ammunition.

A short and very vigorous statement from you to a private correspondent (the usual way of making things public in England) would, I believe, render the government's position impossible, and enable you to secure the publication of that which would tell the people here the truth and thus bring public pressure on the Government to stop men and munitions pouring away to the Dardanelles, as they are at present.[91]

This advice to French plainly revealed Northcliffe's role behind the scenes in the Shells Scandal. His remarks were made two weeks before Repington's 14 May article in *The Times*, which is usually marked as its beginning. It also places the episode into the larger westerner versus easterner controversy in which the press lord supported the generals against the politicians.

Northcliffe's activities since March 1915 had not gone unnoticed among the Liberals, for many of whom he had become the "supreme bogy."[92] On 1 May, the same day the press lord advised French to look to his own defense, A. G. Gardiner struck in a *Daily News* editorial, "Mr. Asquith or Lord Northcliffe?" Gardiner commented that the campaign against the government had been "worked with characteristic astuteness as well as characteristic ruthlessness," and continued that, whether in the *Daily Mail* or *The Times*, "it is always Lord Northcliffe that is calling the tune."[93] A week later the *Daily News* charged that while most were calling for Churchill's head, Northcliffe's aim was higher—at Asquith, a new government, and conscription.[94] In Gardiner's view, only an election could show true public opinion and save the country. This was the last thing Asquith wished to hazard.[95]

Soon after the battle of Festubert began on 9 May, Kitchener notified French that 20,000 rounds (20 percent of his reserve) were to be earmarked for the Dardanelles.[96] A few days later, frustrated by failure on the battlefield, French decided to act. He shared the War Office correspondence over the shells with Repington and sent Fitzgerald and his aide-de-camp (ADC), Captain Frederick Guest, to London to show the same material to Lloyd George, Bonar Law, and Arthur Balfour.[97] Repington's account, published in *The Times* of 14 May, of the failed attack on the Aubers Ridge five days before, charged that "the want of an unlimited supply of high explosives was a fatal bar to our success."[98]

The Shells Scandal that followed the publication of Repington's disclosure was the end product of months of newspaper demands for more shells and a reorganization of the country's munitions production.[99] The article has also been viewed as the final straw that prompted Lloyd George to inform Asquith he could not go on in the government.[100] The same day Northcliffe was notified that a favorite nephew, Lucas King, had been killed in action.[101] On 15 May Lord Fisher, unable to contain his bitter disagreement with

Churchill over the Dardanelles, tendered his resignation from the admiralty. Northcliffe met with Lloyd George on 17 May to discuss the growing crisis.[102] Over the next week a coalition government was formed.[103]

The *Daily Mail* followed up Repington in *The Times* with more pointed criticisms. The 20 May editorial called for business methods to be applied to the new government and warned that its formation could not

> Follow the lines of ordinary political jobbery. Every man put in it must be put there because he has some special qualification, and not because of "claims" on either party. He must be strong and active, for whatever the shallow pates called optimists may think, we have almost certainly embarked on an undertaking of great length. The old week-end country-house Governments will not do in times like these.... If the result is a patchwork Government, the muddle and the consequent grumblings and apprehensions of the last few months will speedily recur.... If it is a real National Government ... it will receive the enthusiastic support of the nation, and especially of those upon whom has fallen the ungrateful task of criticism.

In a separate article, the same edition listed the causes for the cabinet crisis as the controversy between Churchill and Fisher at the Admiralty, the shells situation, and conscription.

When it became apparent Kitchener would remain in charge of the War Office in the reformed government, Northcliffe felt he had to take drastic action. "I don't care what they do to me, the circulation of the *Daily Mail* may go down to two and the *Times* to one—I don't care," he told W. G. Wilson. "The thing has to be done! Better to lose circulation than to lose the war."[104] Driven by his fear for the nation and his personal grief, Northcliffe composed the 21 May *Daily Mail* editorial, "Tragedy of the Shells—Lord Kitchener's Grave Error," which called for the army and navy to be "placed in the best available hands." At the Admiralty, it advised that Fisher should remain "untrammeled." For Lord Kitchener and the War Office, the piece was nothing short of an open indictment:

> In the dark days when Lord Haldane ... showed signs of renewed tinkering with the Army, the *Daily Mail* suggested that Lord Kitchener should take charge of raising the new troops ... that part of the work was done as well as anyone could do it ... the soldiers are there. How many, nobody knows.... *What we do know is that Lord Kitchener has starved the army in France of high explosive shells....*

It has never been pretended that Lord Kitchener is a soldier in the sense that Sir John French is a soldier. Lord Kitchener is a gatherer of men—and a very fine gatherer too. But his record in the South African war as a fighting general...was not brilliant....

The admitted fact is that Lord Kitchener *ordered the wrong kind of shells*—the same kind of shell which he used against the Boers in 1900. He persisted in sending shrapnel—a useless weapon in trench warfare. He was warned repeatedly that the kind of shell required was a violently explosive bomb which would dynamite its way through the German trenches and entanglements and enable our brave men to advance safely. The kind of shell our poor soldiers have has caused the death of thousands of them. Incidentally it has brought about a Cabinet crisis and the formation of what we hope is going to be a National Government.[105]

This editorial had exactly the opposite effect from that which Northcliffe wished. An affronted nation condemned the press lord and all his works and rose in fervent defense of Kitchener. *Daily Mail* circulation and advertising plummeted and papers were burned in the street and at the stock exchange, which sent messages of confidence to Asquith and Kitchener, and gave three cheers for Kitchener and three groans for Northcliffe.[106] A placard inscribed "The Allies of the Huns" was hung outside the city office of the *Daily Mail.*[107] London clubs banned the *Daily Mail, The Times, Evening News,* and *Weekly Dispatch* from their premises. Outside the metropolis, grass-roots opinion against Northcliffe's "abominable pretensions" caused the *Evening News* circulation to fall behind its competitors.[108]

The leaders of the army also rallied to the defense of the war secretary. General Haig informed Kitchener's secretary, Colonel Oswald Fitzgerald, how "thoroughly disgusted we all are here at the attacks which the Harmsworth reptile press have made on Lord Kitchener."[109] Haig went on that past indiscretions by Repington had cost lives and that in any other country those responsible would have been shot. General Rawlinson wrote that the press attack was "perfectly monstrous and has raised us out here to a pitch of fury that is quite insatiable."[110] In his opinion the failures at Aubers Ridge had been tactical, not due to a lack of high explosive shells. General Hamilton informed Kitchener that "the infamous attack upon you of the Harmsworth Press...is bitterly resented throughout the forces....They say a nation gets the Press it deserves, but surely the British Empire has never done anything bad enough to earn itself a Harmsworth!"[111]

The day after the *Daily Mail* salvo, A.G. Gardiner returned fire in the *Daily News.* "Northcliffe and Kitchener, The Meaning of the Vendetta," blamed the press lord, not Churchill, Fisher, or Kitchener, for the crisis.[112] To Gardiner, the biggest problem the country now faced was not who would form the new Government, but what it would do with Northcliffe. Two days later the *Daily News* chronicled spreading national protests against the *Daily Mail* and its owner.[113] The Liverpool Provision Exchange, it was reported, had followed London's example of cheers, groans, and telegrams of confidence to Kitchener. Northcliffe also had been attacked by the *Birmingham Post,* "one of the most influential Unionist organs in the provinces," and by the Unionist *Liverpool Courier.*

The *Daily News* continued the story of the "growing chorus of protests" in the following week. On 28 May it reported "resolutions from all quarters" including protests from the Bristol Liberal and Constitutional Club and *Daily Mail* burnings at the Liverpool University Reading Room. On 31 May the paper disclosed the hostile responses of several weekly reviews: the *Spectator* called Northcliffe's methods "outrageous," the *Nation* accused the press lord of instilling the "poison of uncertainty in our national mind," and a *New Witness* article, "The Harmsworth Plot," alleged that Northcliffe only clamored for the appointment of Kitchener so that he could then tear him down to show his power, but that Lord Kitchener "refused to conduct the War Office under orders from Carmelite Street."

In the face of this deluge of criticism, the owner of the *Daily Mail* remained defiant. John Evelyn Wrench later recalled walking with him on "the very day when the *Daily Mail* was burnt in the City of London and advertisers were canceling their contracts by thousands.... Never did Northcliffe appear to me of more heroic mould. Northcliffe knew his facts were right, he was intensely patriotic and nothing could deflect him from his purpose of telling the people the truth."[114] As a countermeasure, the *Daily Mail* began a "Truth Will Out" campaign. The 24 May editorial described the people angry at the newspaper as "the dupes of official secrecy and unthinking optimism." However, the paper was certain that "the truth cannot be hidden for long and it will be found that those who are now so active in criticising the *Daily Mail* will...turn their criticism in the right direction." In its own defense, the *Daily Mail* quoted other journals, including J. L. Garvin's comment in the *Observer,* that "we must hold it to be true that the failure and the casualties...on Sunday week were largely due to want of sufficient ammunition of the right kind.... we need far more high explosive...in vast and...almost unimaginable quantities."[115]

Within weeks the Northcliffe press was joined by many others who questioned War Office actions. The Liberal *Manchester Guardian* had already called the explosives supply "deplorable" and stated that "it is impossible Lord

Kitchener should escape...the chief responsibility for this failure."[116] The "Eyewitness" report from the front published 24 May confirmed that "the enemy's breastworks were well armed with machine guns behind steel shields which could only be destroyed by high explosives."[117] On 1 June Maj. Gen. W. L. Dalrymple "spoke of the urgent need for more men in munitions factories and said that although they learnt that the *Daily Mail* had been burnt in some places, the contentions of that newspaper regarding munitions seems to be right in many respects."[118]

Though it appears Northcliffe acted on his own in attacking Kitchener, Lloyd George was also furious with the secretary for war, and he met with Northcliffe two days after the *Daily Mail* attack began.[119] Riddell recorded in his diary that he had "a shrewd suspicion that LG has been a party to the attack on Kitchener in the 'Times' and the 'Daily Mail' and the 'Manchester Guardian.' He did not appreciate how powerful Kitchener is in the country or how much Northcliffe is hated by the Press generally and distrusted by the public. LG is very deep and subtle in all his proceedings. He rarely tells *all* the story."[120] At Manchester on 3 June Lloyd George vowed to "reveal the truth" and asserted that if the British had had the same "infinite number of guns firing an infinite number of shells" as did the Germans on the Russian front in Galicia they could have achieved the same effect in Flanders.[121] Other voices joined the Welshman. Debate in the House of Commons over the shells revealed that offers by outside suppliers had been turned down by the War Office in April.[122] In the House of Lords, Earl Stanhope charged that "the French, broadly speaking, hold their trenches by few rifles and the support of their wonderful 75 MM gun. We hold our trenches principally by rifle fire. The first system is expensive in ammunition. The second is expensive in lives."[123]

Numerous letters arrived from England, America, and France which supported Northcliffe's course. Valentine Williams sent some words of encouragement from France where he was one of the newly appointed correspondents:

> The attitude of the *Mail* has been courageous beyond words as people will find out sooner or later when they know the whole truth.... As it is Lloyd George's speech is a striking confirmation of the truth of what we have been saying for months and I am sure his powerful support of your gospel has made up for much of the malignant abuse A.G.G. and Company have been showering on your head of late.... I feel sure that we have now entered on a new phase in this war, thanks first and foremost to your plain speaking in the *Daily Mail*.[124]

Northcliffe replied to Charles St. John Hornby of W. S. Smith's, "It is like you to write me so nice a letter. As regards abuse, I am a pachyderm."[125] Charles M. Lincoln of the New York *World* extended "heartiest congratulations upon the great thing that you did, and I can assure you that there is a very widespread recognition in America of the service which you perform."[126] W. F. Bullock, the *Daily Mail* New York correspondent, reported that "you have immensely enhanced the reputation of your newspapers in this country & I predict that when you next visit the States you will be toasted as the one man who was able to wake England up & who in waking her up did not count the cost to himself."[127] Perhaps Northcliffe valued most the many letters sent from the troops in the field thanking him for his help.

Sir John French was not among those who supported the press lord's course. Though he had wished to publicize the munitions shortage in defense of his own role, he was aghast at Northcliffe's direct assault on Kitchener. It was already widely considered that his disclosures to Repington were most disloyal to the war secretary, and French worried that he would be held responsible.[128] However, French had his defenders. Many people, including H. A. Gwynne, editor of the Conservative *Morning Post*, thought him only a pawn of Northcliffe. Gwynne warned Brinsley Fitzgerald, "don't you see that the Harmsworth people are only using Sir John."[129] Nevertheless, the field-marshal's instigating role in the press campaign cannot be denied. Though French may not have been well served by his friends, his months-long correspondence and personal discussions with Northcliffe and others constitute conclusive evidence. Philip Magnus considered that on the matter of munitions, "Kitchener's obtuseness…cannot excuse the underhand methods of intrigue which Sir John French permitted himself to employ against his chief."[130] To protect his position as commander-in-chief, French undoubtedly used the shells shortage as a screen for planning and execution blunders of his own.[131]

To straighten out the muddled shells situation, Lloyd George accepted the new post of minister for munitions in the coalition government. The 26 May *Daily Mail* declared that "the appointment of Mr. Lloyd George to this new office meets a great many of the criticisms of the *Daily Mail* and we think it will satisfy the country." In a note to the Welshman, Northcliffe described his place in the government as the "heaviest responsibility that has fallen on any Briton for 100 years."[132] Outside of this selection, however, the press lord had little cause for celebration at the membership of the new government. Contrary to his wishes, Asquith remained prime minister and the Liberals predominant. Kitchener stayed at the War Office, while Fisher's resignation was accepted. Although Churchill left the admiralty (where Balfour was installed), he remained in the cabinet at the duchy of Lancaster.

Bonar Law, somewhat surprisingly, accepted the colonial office. In one other positive step from Northcliffe's point of view, Haldane was replaced as lord chancellor (by Buckmaster) and left the government. The Northcliffe press had attacked both Churchill and Haldane, but had been especially brutal to Haldane, whose ties to Germany were unceasingly trumpeted. The *Daily Mail* found most useful Haldane's reported remark about his college days in Germany, which he called his "spiritual home."[133]

With little else to cheer about, the Northcliffe newspapers put their hopes in the new minister for munitions. The 18 June 1915 *Daily Mail* editorial, "The Truth and the Result," credited Lloyd George's candor with improving labor's attitude toward the war. It also surveyed the situation in which the country found itself in the eleventh month of the struggle:

> Mr. Lloyd George's frank speeches, his blunt and straightforward interviews and the ever accumulating evidence of letters and reports from the front which we have published, have shown our Army to be struggling... against heavy odds because it has been supplied with the wrong kind of shells....Victory, then, depends above all, on rapid output of shells and machine guns and munitions and our swift organization of fresh armies by national service....
>
> Hitherto a mere fraction of the nation—the British Army—has been fighting a whole people, and a people organized to the highest pitch, inspired with a fanatical hatred of British freedom and determined to devastate Great Britain, massacre its people and lay its greatness in the dust. The hour has come when this dismal state of affairs is to end and the British nation is to line up active and resolute behind its army.

By mid-June it had become readily apparent that Northcliffe's attacks on Kitchener were not without merit. Sir William Robertson Nicoll, editor of the *British Weekly*, confided to the press lord, "People are beginning to surmise that there is something wrong about K. and I do not see how it will be possible for him to escape. But a great many people will stick to him as they did to Buller. I see already a great and growing reaction in your favour."[134] Lord Esher, no friend of Northcliffe, later admitted: "No detached mind could call in question Lord Northcliffe's choice of the higher expediency. He believed that Lord K. was standing in the way of a freer development of our manufacturing resources for the production of the munitions of war; therefore Lord K had to be bent or broken, because he was unquestionably...covering with his high authority the blind complacency of his subordinates at the War Office. This seemed the plain common sense of the matter then, and there is no evidence that it is less so now."[135]

Since its formation the coalition government of May 1915 has been attributed to various causes. At the time, as A. G. Gardiner's columns show, at least in some quarters the press agitation was given prominent place. However, since the publication of *Politicians and the War* in 1928, Lord Beaverbrook's analysis, which gave the resignation of Lord Fisher from the admiralty first place and downplayed the press role, has taken precedence.[136] Asquith himself gave equal weight to both Fisher's resignation and the shells situation.[137] In his book *1914*, Field-Marshal French claimed that the shells crisis brought the downfall of the government.[138] This self-defense by French goes too far, but Repington's 14 May article, by influencing Lloyd George, can be said to have triggered the sequence of events that led to a coalition government. The die was already cast when, the next day, Lord Fisher's resignation gave final impetus to the end of the last Liberal government. The subsequent public attack on Kitchener by Northcliffe in the *Daily Mail* served to strengthen the war secretary's position and doomed any chance that Lloyd George would take the War Office in May 1915, ensuring that he concentrated his formidable talents completely on munitions. The press lord's action also emboldened others to voice challenges to what remained of the Kitchener myth of infallibility.

In the aftermath, neither Northcliffe nor his press claimed responsibility for the coalition Government. The *Daily Mail* of 26 May credited the change to "the failures of Sir John French's appeals to the War Office for... high-explosive shells and to the resignation of Lord Fisher on account of disagreements with Mr. Churchill." In response to charges in the House of Commons by John Dillon, an Irish Nationalist M.P., that the actions of the *Daily Mail* had led to the downfall of the government, the paper responded on 9 June that "what caused the formation of the new Government was the revelation that our men were hampered by the lack of an unlimited supply of high explosive shells... not any articles in the *Daily Mail*."

Perhaps the most important factor in the fall of the Liberal government was the failure of the Allies to have any significant success in the war. Winston Churchill later wrote that without the power of the Liberal party and Parliament to counteract the "tireless detraction" of the press "there remained... as the reply to remorseless depreciation, only victory in the field. Victory would have carried all before it, but victory was unprocurable."[139] The string of 1915 disasters on the Western Front and at the Dardanelles resulted in unrest among the Conservatives, which was finally voiced by their leader, Bonar Law. With Bonar Law and Lloyd George both convinced of the need for change, Asquith was forced to act.[140]

Nevertheless, the newspaper campaign Northcliffe carried out against Asquith and various members of his government from the beginning of the war to May 1915 must be given some credit for shaping the new situation. Although not the most important factor, continuing press revelations in the months leading up to May 1915 fostered a climate of unrest which made a government change possible, and, when added to the many military failures, inevitable. It has been suggested by several historians that the press campaign over the shells cleared the way for Lloyd George and the new ministry of munitions.[141] If there was a "conspiracy" to unseat Asquith, the historian Bentley Gilbert has written, it was Northcliffe that began it, not Lloyd George.[142]

The conflict over the shells has been seen by writers and historians as an important stage in the battle between an old and a new way of warfare and the effect of total war on a Liberal state and its government.[143] In 1921 Lord Esher commented,

> The Shell Controversy may have some historical value.... It was undoubtedly a contest between the older and newer conceptions of carrying on a great war. It throws light upon the archaic methods of the State when faced with such a crisis as that of 1914, and the want of flexibility and adaptiveness of its public servants....
>
> Finally, by becoming the watchword of faction, this dispute became the historic ensign for the legitimate ambition of a man [Lloyd George] who was destined to lead the people of England with such fire and vigour that their fleets and armies were ultimately to achieve what in May 1915, seemed beyond achievement.[144]

Having successfully aided Lloyd George's arrival at the ministry of munitions by the attacks of his press, Northcliffe turned his attention to the matter of conscription, the most contentious battleground of freedom versus control in British society.

FOUR

"A Very Hard Nut to Crack"
The Conscription Question,
July to December 1915

IN THE SUMMER OF 1915 THE OWNER OF THE *DAILY MAIL* FOUND his influence revived along with his newspaper sales. He was widely credited with bringing down the old government. Winston Churchill later wrote of his enhanced stature,

> The furious onslaughts of the Northcliffe Press had been accompanied by the collapse of the Administration. To the minds of the public the two events presented themselves broadly as cause and effect. Henceforward Lord Northcliffe felt himself to be possessed of formidable power. Armed with the solemn prestige of *The Times* in one hand and the ubiquity of the *Daily Mail* in the other, he aspired to exercise a commanding influence upon events. The inherent instability and obvious infirmity of the first Coalition Government offered favorable conditions for the advancement of these claims. The recurring crises on the subject of conscription presented numerous occasions for their assertion.[1]

Although they might profess otherwise, anxious government officials curried Northcliffe's favor. General Sir Ian Hamilton, who became the target of the *Daily Mail* and *The Times* over Gallipoli, recalled a visit to an "administrator" who was "admonishing me as to the unsuitability of a public servant having a journalistic acquaintance when, suddenly, the door opened; the parlour maid entered and said, 'Lord Northcliffe is on the phone.'"[2] Sir Frank Swettenham, head censor of the Press Bureau, complained to General Haig in August that "all the leaders of the political parties were afraid to interfere with the Press. Lord Northcliffe wrote what he liked in consequence, and *The*

Times kept aloof from any agreements which the other London dailies might make with the Prime Minister."[3]

The major issue over which Asquith sought to make newspaper agreements in the last half of 1915 was conscription.[4] The *Daily Mail* began to call for compulsion during the spring press agitation over shells, but it was summer 1915 before Northcliffe overcame his last fears of the political consequences and committed wholeheartedly to conscription as the fairest course and the one that would prove Britain's resolve to her Allies. In his view, unless Britain demonstrated her determination to France and Russia by instituting compulsion, one or both might make a separate peace with Germany. Before the war, he had supported the calls of Lord Roberts and the National Service League for compulsory service. After the death of Roberts in late 1914, the organization's leadership passed to Lord Milner, who was reluctant to criticize the government and speak out in the first year of the war. Second only to conscription as a national issue of concern in the fall of 1915 was the situation in the Dardanelles. As Northcliffe was a "westerner," against the campaign from the beginning, the reports of failure that reached London only increased his anxiety. He appealed to a wide range of political figures, in and out of the cabinet, over the question. In October the eyewitness report of an Australian journalist stimulated increased government activity concerning the Gallipoli campaign. However, before conscription and the Dardanelles came to the fore, other matters, including relations with the new government and propaganda, held Northcliffe's attention.

Though the press lord's prestige may have been enhanced, bitter opponents remained, in and out of the government. The businessman F. S. Oliver, a supporter of Lord Milner on conscription, called for "the internment and physical dissolution of Northcliffe."[5] He suggested to L. S. Amery that Northcliffe and Asquith should be disposed of together and prescribed the method: "You will need a swift and large motorcar, a box about 7 ft long and 3 ft square, a carpenter with some screws, three bottles of Perrier and a cold ham. You will then captivate both Squiff and Northcliffe, and float them off into a minefield in the estuary of the Weser."[6] The relentless criticism and hostile tone of Northcliffe's newspapers brought several officials to consider action against him in the fall of 1915. The attorney-general, the home secretary and the Foreign Office, each separately gathered evidence aimed at the *Daily Mail* and *The Times*.[7]

On 15 July 1915 Northcliffe celebrated his fiftieth birthday. The Associated Newspaper employees gave their chief a luncheon at the Ritz.[8] In a speech afterward he told the assembly that he intended "to continue his policy of criticizing the government till such a time as we apply ourselves as scientifically as Germany to carrying on the war."[9] He added that "If only all this munition problem had been tackled six months ago, things would have been in a very different state." Northcliffe's spirits were high. Only two months after copies of the *Daily Mail* and *The Times* had been publicly burned, circulation had more than recovered. A few days after his birthday, the press lord made his fourth visit to the front. Notes from this journey and his other trips were later expanded into *At The War*, published in 1916.[10]

With the exception of the minister for munitions, the coalition government received no "honeymoon" period of respite from criticism. The *Daily Mail*, which now declared itself "THE PAPER THAT REVEALED THE SHELL TRAGEDY," kept up its "Truth Will Out" campaign in July. For example, the paper quoted Earl Curzon's House of Lords declaration that "it is not unfair to speak of this country being in grave peril."[11] It called as well for "More Truth" about the Dardanelles, demanding that "the public ought to know. They should not be further chloroformed."[12] After Lord Haldane spoke out at the National Liberal Club in defense of General Von Donop and seemed to suggest that Lloyd George should also share some of the blame as he had been part of the shells committee since October 1914, a series of *Daily Mail* articles furiously attacked Haldane and any ideas of bringing him back into the government.[13] The last page of the 20 July *Daily Mail* was made up of pictures of German prisoners under the headline "HUNS FROM LORD HALDANE'S SPIRITUAL HOME." The next day's issue trumpeted Lloyd George's triumph in settling the Welsh coal strike.

Austin Harrison, owner of the *English Review*, sent Northcliffe a letter of praise for his "splendid" *Daily Mail* leaders attacking Haldane and praising the minister for munitions.[14] The press lord replied that he was off to have another "peep" at the war, but before he left he would try to meet with the minister for munitions and suggest that the Welshman bring in men of business "to put his office straight."[15] Northcliffe saw in Lloyd George a dynamic alternative to Asquith. Though they differed over strategy and the drink question, both men believed there must be a more vigorous effort to mobilize the nation's resources.[16] To that end Northcliffe fed information to the Welshman. In August his intelligence resources obtained information, which Lloyd George requested, about Swedish iron and coal going to Germany.[17] The press lord kept up the flow of censored letters from the front as well.[18] In the fall of 1915 the two men also shared the belief that some sort of compulsory national service must be instituted.

Besides Lloyd George, several other government insiders also communicated with Northcliffe. Prominent among these men was the attorney-general, Sir Edward Carson, who in the press lord's estimation, was second only to Lloyd George in ability.[19] Carson was one of the very few nonsoldiers to whom Northcliffe deferred on war matters, and he could also intimidate the press lord—a rare talent. Carson had not agreed with the *Daily Mail* attack on Kitchener, principally because of the bad effect he felt it would have on morale. He told its proprietor, "if public confidence is shaken in him there will be no one left in whom they will repose it.... who else will the public trust at the present moment I cannot imagine."[20] Besides Kitchener, the two men corresponded and met over varied war issues including German propaganda in France, conscription, and the Dardanelles. In response to Northcliffe's letter lauding his entry into the government, Carson replied, "It was kind of you to write me.... The work will be very heavy and anxious. Like yourself I have always had misgivings about the Dardanelles, but being a mere outsider I could not estimate the Pros & Cons. It will be a very anxious consideration for us all."[21] The press lord also shared his fears that France might be enticed into a settlement:

> German agents, aided by a large number of French people, are circulating the motto, "Germany will fight to the last German and England to the last Frenchman."...
>
> The French people do not believe that we are making an effort, and I respectfully urge that it is possible that before we are aware of it pourparlers may be going on between the French radical socialists and the Germans. General Joffre has said he will shoot, without trial, any French Deputy concerned in such negotiations, but it is a fact that the majority of the French people are very weary of having the Germans in their midst, and that, after another winter in the trenches, the Germans may succeed in their desire to make a separate peace with France.[22]

In August, after the Suvla Bay landing brought matters to a crisis, Carson joined the government's Dardanelles Committee, which oversaw war policy. About Gallipoli, Northcliffe asked Carson, "Is it not wise to discuss this disastrous expedition in my newspapers.... the Germans are intimately informed of our impending catastrophe. *Can nothing be done to minimise it?*"[23]

Northcliffe's erstwhile antagonist, Reginald McKenna, replaced Lloyd George as chancellor of the exchequer. Though he continued to loath the press lord, McKenna replied courteously to his note of congratulations that it "helps to relieve me of the anxiety I feel at undertaking the Exchequer at a moment like this."[24] The chancellor enrolled the press lord's publicity expertise for the tremendous task of raising funds to finance the unprecedented demands of the war. The 22 June *Daily Mail* included several exhortations for the "People's War Loan." The next day the two men met personally.

Northcliffe helped to persuade McKenna to engage the advertising agent Hedley Le Bas, who had been working on army recruiting since before the war began, for the loan campaign.[25] To encourage fund-raising among workers, the *Evening News* began running a contest that paid a premium to those holding certain numbered loan vouchers. The press lord wrote to McKenna that "If the Treasury Officials would have the wisdom to shut their eyes to a slight lottery element in such schemes as that of the 'Evening News' you would be able to raise exactly as much money as you wanted. The working class have no chance of speculative investment at all, and that is why so many of them bet."[26] He also sent McKenna requested information on French loan methods and asked, "When are you going to tap the hidden hoards of India?"[27] The loan was successfully subscribed.

Lord Curzon, the Conservative former Indian viceroy, was another new cabinet member with whom the press lord and his newspapers were in contact.[28] Northcliffe sent Curzon, who had been made Lord Privy Seal, examples of censored letters, and complained about shortages in supplies for "Kitchener's armies" at home.[29] Lovat Fraser of *The Times* also met with the new minister and kept his chief informed of their discussions. Curzon supported Walter Long's proposed Registration Bill, a stride in the direction of compulsion.[30] In a 30 June editorial, "Getting Ready to Begin," the *Daily Mail* called the National Register a "first step towards organizing our human resources." The next month the National Registration Act passed and 15 August was declared Registration Day, on which all citizens aged fifteen to sixty-five were required to report their names, occupations, employer, and any war work skills.[31]

While progress was being made toward organizing manpower, in 1915 official British propaganda continued to follow often conflicting direction from the Foreign Office, the Admiralty and the War Office. Northcliffe was certain that the British were not being vigorous enough in their publicity efforts. He was contemptuous of the amateur efforts of the Wellington House propaganda bureau under C. F. G. Masterman and warned Arthur Balfour, the new First Lord of the Admiralty, that "the poison spread from Berlin... should be more carefully considered" and "cannot be competed with by an ordinary Government department, but needs watching by a small staff of experts."[32] The owner of the *Daily Mail* reported his own intelligence concerning German activity in Holland to Sir Edward Grey and suggested that the foreign secretary meet with Geoffrey Robinson to discuss a series of articles "on the burden we are bearing in the war," which he proposed to translate into several of the most useful languages for dissemination abroad.[33] The press lord funneled other information gathered by his agents to the government through Lord Murray of Elibank, including news of internal German conditions and war production and the pessimistic report of an American military attaché on the Russian front, which praised the enemy effort.[34]

The situations in the United States and in Russia continued to trouble Northcliffe. The censorship and delays caused by the distance between Petrograd and London severely hampered communications with his correspondents. The press lord complained to Hamilton Fyfe in Russia that the censor killed an "immense amount of matter," but that he put his *Daily Mail* reports before the cabinet so that "nothing was wasted."[35] He found it lamentable that the British public did not understand the "feelings of the Russians" and had "no knowledge of the great humiliations" they had suffered. The Petrograd correspondent of *The Times* passed along that Britain's eastern ally appreciated his proprietor's attempts to publicize Russian sacrifices, but added that their army had not received promised British munitions which, it was claimed, had forced the withdrawal from Galicia.[36] Northcliffe replied that Russia needed to supply more news so that the Allies, and the Americans, could better realize her predicament. He wrote that it was "vital that the allies should know about each other. It is equally essential that American sympathy should be with Russia."[37] If it were possible, the same letter continued, he would travel to Russia personally to persuade Britain's ally to provide more publicity to counteract German propaganda flooding the United States such as "horrible invented films of Russian atrocities in East Prussia."

In the final months of the year, Northcliffe's correspondents warned of a Russian domestic crisis that, from September, in their estimation, bordered on revolution.[38] On the other hand, despite Russian retreats, Wilton considered the military state of affairs to be somewhat improved. However, he reported that there continued to be a lack of rifles, so much so that by the next spring only one and a half of the four million new recruits would have weapons. The correspondent of *The Times* also informed his chief that he was making up a pamphlet on England's efforts for distribution to the Russian troops.[39]

From the United States, Northcliffe received numerous requests for his views on the war and a possible peace settlement. He replied to William Charles Reick of the *New York Sun* that he had already given a statement to George Harvey for the United Press, but promised he would "write something at some future juncture of the conflict."[40] Thomas Curtin, in America for the *Daily Mail,* informed his chief that accusations were rampant that the Irish, Canadians, and Australians were doing Britain's fighting and that the Americans were not getting the details of what Britain was doing in the war.[41] The press lord supplied an introduction for Ralph Pulitzer to Surgeon-General Melis of the Belgian army that suggested he be given a tour.[42] "We have had a hard fight," the chief proprietor of *The Times* wrote to his Washington correspondent, Arthur Willert, "but amidst all the abuse the staff has been splendidly loyal. Hard words break no bones, and we are beginning to get the shells. Conscription is going to be a very hard nut to crack, but we will crack it."[43]

Certain that the coalition government would have to be pressured into implementing compulsory service, in mid-August 1915 Northcliffe launched a major push for conscription. The 16 August *Daily Mail* published a "Manifesto" in support of national service which included a proconscription form to be filled out and mailed to the government. The same issue also criticized the "unfairness" of the National Register, because it lacked any regulatory power over "slackers." In the following weeks *Daily Mail* articles and editorials hammered away at the subject. The 28 August editorial, "Hush! Don't Mention Compulsion," attacked Liberal press calls to wait for a government lead on the question. On 5 September a full-page headline declared "Women of England Demand National Service." When Parliament reconvened 14 September (after a six-week recess), the paper challenged it "to be bold, to be honest, to be national," and to pass compulsory service.

The newspaper campaign targeted government and public opinion, but also forced the hand of Lord Milner, and his National Service League. When the coalition government failed to bring in conscription, Milner had begun planning a campaign of his own.[44] Four days after the *Daily Mail* published its "Manifesto," the League also called for universal service of all able-bodied men.[45] Northcliffe assured Milner that his press would give all aid possible to the campaign and added he was

> extremely glad that you have decided to join your forces to our little manifesto, and arouse the country to the fact that we shall be faced with a separate peace on the part of Russia or France with Germany unless national service is adopted by this country. Last night I received the following telegram from "The Times" correspondent in Petrograd, "Further delay will imperil alliance."...
>
> Count Beckendorff [the Russian ambassador] to-day told the Foreign editor of "The Times" that he believed that the putting into force of National Service in England would satisfy Russia and greatly hearten her.[46]

The press lord's support proved a decidedly mixed blessing. Angered that he had been compelled into what he considered premature action, Milner told John St. Loe Strachey, editor of the *Spectator*,

> I don't know that I should have chosen this moment to make a move, but our hands were forced by Northcliffe, because it was quite impossible, once the question had been raised in this acute form, for the National Ser-

vice League to look on indifferently. The most extraordinary psychologi-
cal phenomenon I know is the man, not uncommon though, who apparently hates Northcliffe more than he loves England, and would prefer to
see the country ruined to letting N. make a journalistic "scoop."

I am convinced that the only thing to do now is to try and rally everybody, whatever their past opinion or future programme, for the one single
purpose of winning this war.[47]

After the king, with whom Milner had been staying, expressed his displeasure
over the campaign, Milner prepared a written explanation (probably for his
royal host) of his action, in which the role of the press played a prominent
part. He reported that

A great deal of fuss has been made about the "Northcliffe" agitation....
Personally I discouraged it for all I was worth, foreseeing that, as Northcliffe is a "red rag to a bull" not only to the Liberal but to a large section of
the Unionist Press, the fact of him making himself prominent in the agitation for National Service would create a reaction against it.

As a matter-of-fact this is just what has happened. Almost the whole
Press—the *Morning Post* is almost the only exception—has joined in the
hue and cry against Northcliffe.... papers like the *Daily News,* the *Daily
Chronicle,* the *Nation* & the *Star* have thrown themselves furiously into the
anti-Northcliffe agitation with the obvious intention of using the unpopularity of Northcliffe to damage the cause of National Service....

Under these circumstances it becomes impossible for those who honestly believe that the adoption of National Service ... is essential to avert
defeat, to sit still and do nothing.[48]

As the historian Alfred Gollin has noted, the fact that this document spends
so much time on press matters underlines the powerful position of the newspapers in this period. With the politicians either muzzled in the government
or simply not speaking out, the press carried on the public debate.

Though Asquith remained set against conscription, the ferocity and the
duration of the war had led other Liberals to overcome their traditional antagonism to compulsion. Since the previous November Lloyd George had realized some form of national service was needed.[49] His spring 1915 Treasury
Committee activities in regard to munitions drove him closer to the Conservatives on the issue.[50] By August the Welshman viewed conscription as the
only way to replace the skilled laborers he wanted back from the army.[51] Another Liberal with impeccable credentials, Commander Josiah Wedgwood,
M.P., became something that would have been unthinkable before 1914—an

ally of Northcliffe over this issue. The two corresponded about a growing parliamentary party of officers in opposition to the government that included Frederick Guest, former ADC to Sir John French.[52] Much to Asquith's displeasure, from the end of June, Guest raised the national service issue in the Commons.[53] His group became known as the Liberal War Committee.[54] Sympathetic Conservative backbenchers were only too happy to let Liberals take the fight to their own leader.

Colonel Harry Lawson (later Lord Burnham and proprietor of the *Daily Telegraph*) attended a dinner with Guest at which the planned House of Commons conscription campaign was discussed. Lawson later recorded that he had pointed out to the group (which included Milner, Wedgwood, and Repington, among others) in "plain language" that they had blundered badly in starting a press war. *The Times* and *Daily Mail* campaign, in his view, antagonized "not only the Radical press but also the Labour journals and the Labour party. That being so they had done everything they could to defeat their object to start with."[55] Lawson also emphasized the importance of Kitchener to the gathering. The war secretary remained unconvinced of the wisdom of conscription despite the efforts of such persuasive men as Milner and L. S. Amery to change his views.[56]

A week later Lawson had lunch at 10 Downing Street with Asquith. The prime minister voiced his appreciation for the "splendid patriotism" of the *Daily Telegraph*. He also pointed out Kitchener's unconvinced attitude on the question and asserted that, in his opinion, Milner was out of touch with the public and "always wrong." Lawson recorded that the prime minister

> said that the harm done by the Harmsworth combination in the press was unspeakable. No more unpatriotic action had ever been taken by any section of Englishmen.... He knew of the dinner at which I had been present, given by...Guest... and he ridiculed the men who were conducting the agitation. I pointed out to him that they drew their strength entirely from the Harmsworth papers, and that the sinister figure at the back of the whole of this agitation—as in many other ways—was...Repington... who supplied the M.P.s with their figures and arguments.... Asquith...to use his own words,..."had put the fear of God into Sir John French" when he was in France on the whole subject of press agitation, and he did not mean to allow this method to be carried on with impunity.[57]

Soon after the formation of the coalition, Asquith had written the king that future press transgressions were to be put in the hands of the public prosecutor with full power "to suppress by executive action offending newspapers without previous prosecution."[58] In September, the attorney-general, Sir Edward Carson, pondered action against both *The Times* and the *Daily Mail*.[59] The *Daily Mail* offense was found in the 7 September article, "Recruiting by Blackmail," which decried "sneaking and haphazard compulsion under the guise of 'moral pressure.'" *The Times* misstep came 10 September in the article "The Government and the Pink Forms," which protested the "fresh campaign of private pressure." When the evidence was found too weak to take to court, F. E. Smith, who had been consulted in the matter, wrote Carson that he wished the government had had a case.[60]

Because of his highly placed army connections, Charles à Court Repington, the military correspondent of *The Times*, remained an invaluable source for the proconscription forces. He wrote to Northcliffe about the Liberal attacks,

> I see that the Manchester Guardian declares that there is no chance of conscription being adopted & says that the military case against it is overwhelming because the War Office has…more men than it can supply and send to the front.
>
> By this I presume it means more men than the W.O. can arm. This is true but it makes an overwhelming case against the War Office & not against conscription. A case against conscription can only be made out when proof is given that voluntary service can supply the men needed. The General Staff have been consistently & deliberately prevented from telling the Cabinet how many men are needed for this purpose.
>
> …The Government shun all inquiry, & keep the General Staff at arm's length, because they know that if there was an inquiry, & if the views of the *best men* on the General Staff were given to the Cabinet the whole imposture would be exposed.[61]

Northcliffe suggested that "one or two members of the General Staff speak to individual members of the Cabinet, like Lloyd George, on the points you raise."[62] Repington replied that "conscription must come. It is merely a question of when the Government will tell the people the whole truth.… The General Staff cannot go behind the backs of their superiors. I fancy that Lloyd George knows the situation well enough."[63] On 6 October Northcliffe met for lunch with the Welshman at Milner's Great College Street residence. Afterward he sent Milner a note of thanks and "regretted much that you were not there. A great deal of important information was elicited which you ought to know."[64] At a meeting soon thereafter with Northcliffe and Repington, Lloyd George told the two men he wanted a small war cabinet and that the large cabinet was "useless."[65]

While the conscription campaign was ongoing, revelations concerning the Dardanelles operation came to the attention of the cabinet. Charges of official mismanagement and neglect were made in a damning report by the Australian journalist Keith Murdoch. General Sir Ian Hamilton, the commander at Gallipoli, had allowed Murdoch to visit the Anzac (Australian and New Zealand) zone on an inspection of postal arrangements for the Australian government.[66] The journalist had been shocked by the squalor, sickness, and depression he saw during a brief visit to the Australian beachhead.[67] His dire report, addressed to Andrew Fisher, the Australian prime minister, was finished in London in late September. This document pointed out the extremely tenuous position of his countrymen and indicted Hamilton and the British for ignorance and incapacity in their treatment of the Anzac forces.[68] Murdoch's United Cable Service office was located in Printing House Square. When he told his harrowing story to Geoffrey Robinson, the editor of *The Times* had Murdoch repeat his information for Sir Edward Carson.[69] A copy of the report was also given to Northcliffe, who discussed it with Lloyd George. The press lord wrote to Murdoch that he would

> not be able to rest until the true story of this lamentable adventure was so well known as to force immediate steps to be taken to remedy the state of affairs.
>
> The matter has haunted me ever since I learned about it, and I was glad to hear from Mr. Lloyd George that your letter had produced a good result in regard to one thing, although I do not know exactly to what he referred.
>
> Merely the minor part of your statement, to the effect that the men are being sent out with summer clothing is enough to indict the state of muddle which is existing.[70]

Lloyd George, who preferred an operation in Salonika to the Dardanelles, passed the document on to Asquith. The prime minister, without allowing Hamilton to defend himself against its accusations, had it printed and circulated to the members of the Dardanelles Committee.[71] This was before them when the decision was made to send either Haig or Kitchener for a direct inspection of the situation.

Murdoch, who met with a parade of British officials, wanted government action, not public disclosures. He told Northcliffe that a plan to organize Australians in London for a protest to the government was "mischievous" and he hoped "there will be nothing done to give the idea that Australasians are whining because they are hurt. Strong official action would be very much more preferable in the interests of my country."[72] The evacuation of the Dardanelles, Northcliffe and others believed, would be the wisest course. The press lord asked Carson's support for this policy:

> Since, many months ago, I communicated with you (and long before, with some of your colleagues), the appalling waste of splendid life to no purpose has continued. Even since I saw you a few days ago, I have had further news of fresh horrors.
>
> The Indian Mutiny made a mark on public memory for fifty years. It requires no imagination to realise that the Dardanelles tragedy, which the Australians and New Zealanders are determined to reveal to the world, will for all time be a theme of universal discussion.
>
> I am now assured that the men can be got away with the loss of only 2,500. The public know nothing about the expedition, and are still hopeful and confident. The head of the largest discount association in England told me on Thursday that he and his colleagues were convinced that victory was near at hand.[73]

The blundering in the Dardanelles, added to Britain's lack of support for Serbia, led Carson to resign from the government. *The Times* first reported this development on 12 October. Over the next few days, in spite of attempts to keep him in place, he remained adamant. Before the official announcement of Carson's departure, *The Times* rose to his defense on 18 October, declaring that "No resignation is tolerable at this stage except in a man who has foreseen a long series of blunders into which the want of a policy had led us, and has striven to warn his colleagues and has failed. That, we must assume, is the case of Sir Edward Carson." When the official announcement was made the next day, *The Times* called his resignation "a political event of the first magnitude—none the less because for the moment it seems likely to stand alone."

The *Daily Mail* went even further. Its 19 October editorial, "The 22, A Conspiracy of Silence," asserted that Carson's resignation was "plainly due to his independence and refusal to accept any policy of drift," and charged that the Cabinet had "for fifteen months ... by the suppression of news, completely deceived the democracy as to the course of the war." The editorial continued that "We say here plainly, and we take the responsibility for doing so, that it is not true, as every German knows and every Turk knows, that we are on the eve of a great victory in the Dardanelles. It is not true that the Germans have shot their last bolt in Russia. It is not true that there is evidence of any decline in Turkish morale." The government should not fear telling the people the truth, the paper asserted, because if only a portion of the truth were known, it would elicit a torrent of support for national service. The jeremiad ended with the dire warning that "when the people know the extent to which they have been duped and deceived by the 22 politicians supposed to lead us, a violent cataclysm will most surely arise for which English history has no precedent for two hundred and fifty years."

Northcliffe continued this apocalyptic view of events in a 21 October conversation with Sir George Riddell "full of prophesies and criticism."[74] The press lord catalogued the incompetence of the government over the "scandalous" management of the Gallipoli campaign, the "muddled" Balkan negotiations, the lack of a "proper military plan," the "neglected and mismanaged" defense of London, the "serious" condition of affairs in Russia, and the fact that the recent offensive in France had been "the most costly victory ever secured by British arms."[75] As a result, Northcliffe predicted, the government would be out in three months, followed by a "Committee of Safety" of a few leading men (including Carson and Lloyd George) and then a revolution. He threatened a public exposure of the state of affairs in his newspapers, adding, "No doubt they may prosecute me, but I shall not mind if they do. When the story of the Gallipoli campaign is published the public will be aghast. Carson will probably state the case. He is an able man."[76]

This vision of events was somewhat premature, but had more than some truth in it for Lloyd George and Carson, whose resignation and opposition represented one more step in the procession toward the replacement of Asquith a year later.[77] A week after Northcliffe's conversation with Riddell, the *Daily Mail* called for a small war council composed of the military heads, an air minister, and perhaps three others.[78] The paper quoted Napoleon, who once said, "a nation of lions led by a stag (by which he meant a politician) would be beaten by a nation of stags led by a lion. It never occurred to him that a nation of lions might be led by a committee of stags. In this war we are discovering only too painfully that he was right and that a Cabinet of 21 Ministers, all but one civilians, cannot conduct successful campaigns." After Carson left the government, Northcliffe continued to send him letters of warning, particularly concerning Anglo-American relations. The press lord expected a strong American reaction to the British blockade when Congress next met, and forwarded Willert's letter to that effect. When the former minister replied that he felt Britain made "too many concessions, not too few," to the Americans, Northcliffe promptly explained that it was not the "nature of the blockade," but the "shilly-shallying" and "cavalier treatment of American ships" that had caused the irritation.[79]

In late October General Sir Charles Monro was sent to take the Dardenelles command from Hamilton. Monro was an avowed westerner who agreed with Northcliffe's view that the operation should be ended. He recommended withdrawal to Kitchener and forecast the cost as high as 40,000 casualties. The war secretary traveled to the Dardanelles in November for a personal view. While Northcliffe continued to attack Kitchener bitterly in his private correspondence, he had learned the futility of public criticism. Now he ordered his newspapers not to advertise Kitchener's activities. Letters to Marlowe and Robinson condemned any "booming" or "puffs" of the secretary for war.[80] The press lord informed Robinson that "Lloyd George assures me that this man is the curse of the country. He gave me example after example ... of the loss of life due to this man's ineptitude.... He is the creature of publicity and lives by publicity." In the same vein, Northcliffe wrote to Lord Murray of Elibank, who had been a defender of Kitchener:

> I feel particularly guilty about Lord K. as the myth was invented by one of my writers, George Steevens, in his "With K. to Khartoum," and my newspapers have been accused by the Radical Press of having suggested to the Government that he should be employed at the outbreak of the war.
>
> The public impression is that Mr. Asquith has paralyzed the efforts of Lord K. My opinion is that Lord K. was the Cabinet's old man of the sea. If the Government knew about newspapers and advertising—which they do not—they would realize that Lord K was purely the creation of publicity, and as soon as his poster is off the hoardings and he is "kept out of the news," as the Americans say, he will cease to trammel action....
>
> A friend of mine in the War Office told me that it was the opinion of the W. O. that more work had been done at last Friday's War Council meeting than for months. He is only a minor official... but things do percolate even in that dense atmosphere.[81]

Kitchener's November inspection tour of the Dardanelles took him out of the country for some time. While he was absent the government further undercut the war secretary's powers by appointing Sir William Robertson Chief of the Imperial General Staff (CIGS). Robertson became the government's chief military advisor and overlord of the army command in France.

Sir John French, Northcliffe's former ally in the shells agitation, also felt his position slipping away. Relations between the two men had cooled.[82] The newspaper campaign against Kitchener, Asquith's warning about the press, and French's worries about his deteriorating prestige all contributed to the change. In July Riddell recorded that Northcliffe told him that French "has sealed his doom."[83] Lloyd George's confidant added to his diary, "I suppose he has declined to continue his association with Northcliffe." The Battle of

Loos in September and October proved to be the final failure for French. Sir Douglas Haig took command of the British forces on the western front in December 1915.

When Kitchener returned from his inspection, the government decided on evacuation. This was carried out with an almost miraculous lack of casualties. The *Daily Mail* characterized the withdrawal as a government admission that the operation had been a "stupendous blunder."[84] The 21 December editorial charged that "too late is written in letters of fire upon the record of the Government. We were 'too late' in aiding Belgium, we have been 'too late' to save Serbia," and "we sent our expeditionary force to the Dardanelles 'too late.'"

The final months of 1915 also marked the death throes of British voluntarism. By October 1915 recruiting was almost exhausted. Over three million men, including the patriotic and adventurous cream of British manhood, already had volunteered.[85] Asquith, however, continued to delay conscription. A War Policy Committee under Lord Crewe was appointed to consider the question. In a supplemental report, its Labour party member, Arthur Henderson, called for a final voluntary effort to demonstrate to the working classes that all alternative methods had been tried.[86] Many labor leaders continued to denounce conscription as a Northcliffe scheme.[87] Asquith and Kitchener managed to convince Lord Derby to lead the final voluntary push.

Derby was a great landed aristocrat, a remnant of a previous era, dubbed the "King" of Lancashire. In the first year of the war his record in recruiting stood second only to Kitchener's.[88] On 5 October 1915 he was put in charge of what would prove to be the last government effort to raise the men needed by the army before resorting to compulsion.[89] Under the "Derby Scheme" all men between the ages of eighteen and forty-one whose names appeared on the recent National Register would be asked either to enlist or to "attest" their willingness to serve with the armed forces when called.[90]

Since the spring of 1915 Northcliffe had been in touch with Derby on manpower questions. Among the topics they discussed was recruiting in Ireland, which the press lord believed largely untapped. Northcliffe discussed manpower in his place of birth with Colonel Eustace Jameson, the director of Irish recruiting, who informed him that Derby had been keen on a plan to tour Ireland, but had been diverted from this course by Kitchener.[91] The war secretary's hostility killed all suggestions to extend the Territorial reserve system to Ireland. Hedley Le Bas, who had made a recruiting tour, told Northcliffe that Kitchener, like most Englishmen, was ignorant of conditions in Ireland and that the 80,000 Irish who had enlisted "might easily have been doubled if the military authorities had handled the recruiting question on businesslike lines."[92]

In addition to his belief that Irish recruiting was being bungled, the press lord also considered it criminal that married men were being taken while many bachelors remained untouched. His refusal to publish appeals aimed at married men in his newspapers and his attacks on the policy angered the government. The prime minister's wife, Margot, who loathed Northcliffe even more than did her husband, confided to St. Loe Strachey, editor of the *Spectator,* that "Northcliffe should be crucified. *Quite* entre *nous*...Northcliffe cd [sic] have been arrested & imprisoned...for glaring cases of stopping recruiting."[93] Strachey responded,

> Your letter has amazed and depressed me more than anything I have heard of late. If, as you tell me, the Government have proof that Northcliffe was engaged in a conspiracy to stop recruiting...it was their absolute duty to arrest him and bring him before a court under the Defence of the Realms Act. To accuse them of not having done this appears to me to be an accusation of the greatest dereliction of duty....Why should your people give Harmsworth a protection and a privilege which is not given to some penny-a-line journalist who makes a mere technical infringement of the Defence of the Realm Act?...I have never been able to understand why Harmsworth had the influence he seems to have over the Liberal party.[94]

Though Northcliffe wanted conscription, Derby's pledge to seek out the remaining unmarried men prompted him to offer his assistance to this final voluntary effort which both likely believed would ultimately fail. Their goal was to supply badly needed men for the army, by whatever method possible, and they realized that the campaign brought conscription closer, no matter the result.[95] The 18 October *Daily Mail* profiled Derby and congratulated him for his "Single Men First" declaration. Northcliffe wrote to him, "I am going to help your scheme as much as I can—and I think I can help it."[96] Derby gladly accepted the offer and a confidential 23 October letter asked the press lord's aid to arrive at the number of recruits for which the plan should aim.[97] To support the effort, Northcliffe suggested a press bureau be set up.[98] Derby liked the idea and replied that he would look into it. The press lord also recommended Hedley Le Bas's advertising skills for the cause.[99] After Derby complained that Lord Selborne's protection of agricultural laborers was depriving him of the "biggest source to which I look for recruits," Northcliffe looked into the problem of agricultural exemptions and urged that Selborne modify his remarks on the subject.[100] A few days later, Derby sent a private note that he now thought he would be able to challenge any "starred" exemption, even agricultural workers.[101]

Both men felt a strong public statement from the prime minister was needed to make it clear that single men would be taken before married men and that this would be the final voluntary effort if it failed. Derby wrote to Northcliffe on 31 October that he was "anxious about what Asquith will say on Tuesday. Unless he says that this is the last effort of voluntary recruiting and adds that unless young men come forward voluntarily in sufficient quantities . . . older men and married will not be taken until the younger men have been taken compulsorily, the scheme will fail."[102] Surprised that there was any possible question about Asquith's not making a "definite statement," Northcliffe suggested that Derby threaten resignation, "otherwise the onus will fall upon you, which would be a grave piece of injustice. . . . A firm ultimatum from you will, beyond question, bring about the desired result."[103] The next day Derby replied that he was "completely in the dark" as to what Asquith would say but that "he knows what my opinion is and what I think is essential should be said to secure success, and I should not hesitate for one minute in resigning unless I have a clear assurance on the two points of importance I named to you."[104]

On 2 November Asquith pledged in the House of Commons that married men would not be taken until after the single men had been drawn. The next day's *Daily Mail* editorial, "Mr. Asquith's Reply to 'The Daily Mail,'" pointed out that the speech responded to three things "constantly pressed on him" by the paper. These were that compulsion would be implemented if Derby's scheme failed, that single men would be taken first, and that a War Council would be set up. On 11 November, Asquith authorized a further statement on recruiting that clarified questions regarding his earlier speech. Derby declared that Asquith's latest utterance "seems to me very far reaching on the subject of compulsion if the voluntary system fails. I somehow think that as a matter of fact we shall have a success. . . . Really the week after next will be the critical time. It is practically the last week and anything that you can do in your papers to help me to stir up some sort of excitement I should be very grateful for."[105] "I will do my damnedest to make your scheme succeed," Northcliffe replied. "I quite realize that the week after next is the critical time. I think that the Prime Minister's declaration is splendid."[106] The 12 November *Daily Mail* repeated Asquith's "Cast-Iron Pledge" to the married that single men who failed to come forward by 30 November would be taken first by compulsion. The paper was heartened by the announcement of a War Council to be made up (in the absence of Kitchener) by Asquith, Lloyd George, Bonar Law, McKenna, and Balfour. It noted, however, that Balfour had a lot of work to do—particularly the air defense of London.

In the last few weeks of the Derby campaign (which was extended from 30 November to 11 December), the *Daily Mail* kept up the cry. The 5 December edition noted that despite the fact that "Lord Derby has done all that man can do," the single men had not yet come forward in the numbers needed, but pleaded that voluntarism might yet be saved by their swift action. On the final morning, the *Daily Mail* exhorted single men to "JOIN FIRST THING TODAY."[107] A pictorial displayed the "Closing Scenes in the Great Recruiting Campaign." At its conclusion, except as a delaying strategy for the Asquith government, Derby's "Great Campaign" proved a bust. Despite the best efforts of many people, including Northcliffe, it ultimately produced only 340,000 men, well short of the goal of 500,000. The disappointing results made it evident that voluntarism could no longer fill the manpower needs of the nation. Also, for the government to keep its pledge to the married, compulsion would have to be aimed first at single men.[108]

In the ensuing weeks of political turmoil over this issue, Northcliffe stayed in close touch with Lloyd George, to the decided discomfort of many of those around the minister for munitions. C. P. Scott, editor of the *Manchester Guardian,* recorded that on Sunday 12 December he met Northcliffe and his wife before lunch at Walton Heath, Lloyd George's residence. Scott agreed with J. L. Garvin of the *Observer,* who felt the Welshman had "suffered from his recent intimate association with Lord Northcliffe."[109] After the press lord met with Lloyd George and Carson the following weekend, the 21 December *Daily Mail* called the Welshman's "Too Late" speech of the day before in the Commons (which revealed that in May the Germans were making 250,000 shells a day while the British made 2,500) "the gravest indictment that has yet been drawn against the Government."[110] Frances Stevenson, Lloyd George's secretary and mistress, wrote in her diary that the "chief thing that these Liberals objected to was D.'s [Lloyd George] association with Lord Northcliffe...for Northcliffe is not trusted."[111] Neither was her future husband. Many Liberals were undoubtedly angered by Lloyd George's support of conscription and his perceived alliance with the owner of the *Daily Mail.* Their cooperation, however, lasted only as long as it suited both their aims. A cabinet crisis, which included a resignation threat from Lloyd George if compulsion was not brought in, came to a climax in the last few days of December. Kitchener agreed at last that unmarried men should be conscripted and a bill to that effect passed in January 1916. Asquith once again proved his political skill by holding together the coalition—with the sole resignation of Simon.[112] The *Daily Mail* declared "The End of the Voluntary System. And Sir John Simon."[113]

While Northcliffe had been supporting the Derby scheme, the government had been preparing evidence against him to lay before the cabinet. The head of the Foreign Office Press Bureau, increasingly frustrated with the many uses the enemy made of the attacks on the government by Northcliffe's newspapers, complained to J. C. C. Davidson, Bonar Law's assistant at the Treasury, that "practically the whole of his time was taken up in counteracting the influence and effect of *The Times* in allied and neutral countries."[114] In cooperation with the home secretary, Simon, the Foreign Office Press Bureau prepared a secret report for the cabinet, *The Northcliffe Press and Foreign Opinion*, which detailed their use as anti-British propaganda in Germany and neutral countries like America.[115] This document, apparently laid before the cabinet in November, listed extracts from German papers quoting *The Times* on topics from blockade failures and recruiting to the Dardanelles campaign and Lord Kitchener.[116] The summary charged that:

> From the beginning of the war articles by the Times military correspondent have been regularly quoted in the German press. Since June, however, these have been supplemented by the Times leaders, which are now generally quoted at length and commented upon, and the use of which forms an important part of the enemy's propaganda, not only for the keeping up of the spirits of his people at home, but for displaying our efforts in an unfavorable light—magnifying his own—abroad. Every extract which appears in this section has been sent to neutral countries, to all the smaller papers in Constantinople and Bulgaria.

Turning to neutral countries like America, the report indicted Northcliffe for playing into the hands of German propagandists by attacking the cabinet. As evidence it reproduced the "exact" text of a cable sent by Northcliffe for reprint in the *New York World:*

> Have not seen reports to which you refer as to political troubles here. My own individual opinion is that our present executive of twenty-two members totally unsuited direction of war. Believe we shall have Government by small committee reasonable time. These opinions are expressed almost every day in my own newspapers much more forcibly than I care to state them in a foreign country. The really serious aspect of affairs here is that, owing to censorship, this democracy knows practically nothing about the course of its own war. Many people here are buying American newspapers to read the war news. As soon as our people learn the facts, I am convinced they will demand some such drastic change of government here as I have outlined above.

The Northcliffe newspapers had also been personally critical of Simon. The 11 October *Daily Mail* editorial, "Half-Truths," repeated the attacks of Lord Selborne on Simon's censorship policy, which kept the French and Dardanelles news from the people. The same issue reported, in a full-page headline, "BELGRADE TAKEN BY THE GERMANS." An accompanying map, titled "The Road to India," infuriated the government, which considered prosecution.[117] The Liberal press was also outraged. *The Star* of 12 October charged that "If the Kaiser had paid £100,000 for that pro-German map it would have been worth it."[118] At the end of November, Simon apologized in a letter to *The Times* for accusations he made that the newspaper discouraged Britain's allies, particularly Russia.[119] The *Daily Mail* of 26 November noted "The Attack on the Northcliffe Press." Two subsequent unfriendly articles in *The Times* resulted in a seven-hour-long assault by Simon in the House of Commons on 30 November, but his own unpopularity mitigated its effect.[120] Clementine Churchill, who kept her husband Winston informed while he served in France, wrote to him that the attack would "have been very damaging if it had not been made by a prig and a bore."[121]

However, Simon was not without support. The king had his secretary, Lord Stamfordham, write a letter of thanks to the home secretary for speaking out against the "dangerous influence of the Northcliffe Press."[122] Mrs. Asquith asked Strachey for "high-toned notes on Sir J. Simon's terrible indictment of the Times & d. Mail" and worried about the loyalty of those frightened of *The Times*.[123] "England has ignored Northcliffe too long," she complained. "He is a public danger and would be tolerated in no other country but ours."[124] Calls were once again heard in the Commons for the government to seize *The Times* and make it an official organ for the remainder of the war.

The Times of 1 December responded that "If Ministers themselves would attack the Germans with half the energy they devote to *The Times* they would be a good deal nearer to winning the war." That morning's *Daily Mail* denounced Simon's House of Common's attack on Unionist newspapers whose only crimes were to call for a more vigorous prosecution of the war and more shells. The editorial, "A Lawyer at War," noted that,

> In his speech, which was simply a rehash of articles from radical newspapers, Sir John Simon made much play with the excellent and accurate map which we published on October 11 ... entitled "The Road to India." ...
> Does Sir John Simon pretend that that map has not been largely proved to be accurate since it was published? Is it not known to the whole world that the Germans have practically cleared the way to Constantinople? Does Sir John Simon deny that German activities in Persia are based on an attempt to reach India? Sir John Simon says the publication of this map encourages the enemy and depresses the neutrals.

The enemy knows exactly where he is every day of the war, and neutral countries are plentifully supplied by the German Press Bureau with... reports, the general accuracy of which are not denied by British Military authorities.... To suggest that our Foreign Office is to be blamed is, it appears, rank treason.

What really encouraged the enemy, the paper concluded, was radical wobbling over conscription, not maps that told the truth. A separate article in the same issue proudly listed the achievements of the *Daily Mail* campaigns for more shells, the ministry of munitions, single men first, the national register, smaller cabinets, and the War Council.

With storm clouds once again gathering about his head, Northcliffe received letters of support. "Judging from the newspapers there seems to be no question that before long you will either be an earl or assassinated," wrote Mary Roberts Rinehart from America. "The feeling in this country as to what you are doing and the stand you are making is generally favorable. I have not as yet seen your motives or your patriotism impugned, although that has happened to almost every British statesman."[125] Valentine Williams sent a message as he passed through England on the way to Boulogne:

> You are used to the raging of the gentiles & I am perfectly confident that you will be a match for Simon & the rest. But I am afraid you will feel the underlying motive of the speech which is to impugn your patriotism in the eyes of the public.... you know better than anybody else that your fault — or crime — in the eyes of the cabinet radicals is to have looked farther than they, to have been right where they have been wrong, to have brought home to them & to their... admirers the full responsibility of their unpardonable acts of commission & omission.
>
> Obviously they are out after us and I hope we shall not give them an opening — otherwise I think Simon has dug his own grave. Did you see the *Chronicle* this morning? A *Liberal* paper calling for the muzzling of the press?[126]

Despite the desires of some officials, notably Sir John Simon, the cabinet refused to ban or prosecute Northcliffe's newspapers.[127] Measures were taken against others, however. On 6 November the *Globe*, an ultra-Conservative evening paper, was suppressed by the government under DORA regulations against publishing "false statements tending to depress His Majesty's subjects and give comfort to the enemy."[128] In a Guildhall speech at the Lord Mayor's Banquet soon after, Asquith denied that the suppression raised the question of the freedom of the press, because, he said, the *Globe* had spread a "malignant lie ... after it was contradicted on the highest authority." He then went on to compliment the patriotic self-restraint of the press during the war, "with two notorious exceptions," —an unspoken reference to *The Times* and the *Daily Mail*.[129]

By January 1916 Northcliffe could count some successes. Even though he viewed it as a year too late, conscription for single men had been passed. Moreover, the Dardanelles had been evacuated and at less cost than anyone could have dreamed. Those in and out of the government who wished to see him silenced were disappointed. He and his press remained unmuzzled. However, as the new year began, Northcliffe's October 1915 prediction to Riddell proved false. Three months after Carson's resignation, Asquith remained in power. The prime minister had survived the conscription storm as he had the shells controversy. Consequently, in 1916 Northcliffe continued his criticism of the Government's prosecution of the war.

FIVE

"No More Shilly-Shallying"
Air Power & Conscription,
January to June 1916

AT THE BEGINNING OF 1916 NORTHCLIFFE EXCHANGED NEW YEAR'S
greetings with several correspondents. "I think we may fairly congratulate
ourselves on the results of the year's work," John Walter wrote to him about
The Times. "The paper has aroused an astonishing amount of jealousy, but no
doubt posterity will properly appreciate the extraordinary services it has rendered the country during the past year."[1] From America, Arthur Brisbane
called for the press lord to conserve himself for a postwar role:

> The war is like a forest fire, destructive and horrible. It has little to do with
> the real life of the world, and I hope that this fire in Europe will not burn
> you up and your energy. Such men as you will be needed especially when
> the war is over and the period of reconstruction comes.
>
> When you look back at our war in America—which was brutal and big
> for one country, you can see that the really important work of the nation
> was the work AFTER the war.
>
> Don't give all that you have now and wear yourself out. Save some-
> thing for the work that will begin—I hope—next Spring.[2]

Northcliffe's view of the task ahead in the new year was reflected in the
1 January 1916 *Daily Mail* editorial:

> As a nation we have been slow to awaken to the new world that is being
> hammered out of this war. We have been backward in grasping all this
> prodigious convulsion means.... We have been tardy in summoning up all
> our powers of vision and energy and resolution....

But now, thank Heaven, it is beginning to be understood. It has been the work of 1915 to tear the scales from the nation's eyes.... after sixteen months of war it is at last possible to say that the consciousness of what is at stake is penetrating into every British home and mind.

However, the newspaper noted, the politicians, as usual, lagged behind the public: "But what is true of the country as a whole is not equally true of every section in it....The politicians for the most part stick to their habit of talk and their habit of party....What the nation hopes is that in 1916 there will be no more shilly-shallying.... For all the British people the watch-word of the New Year should be Economy.... The message of 1916 to the politicians is, Trust the people." To overcome the military stalemate in France, the paper called for tightening the naval blockade and using air power to go "over, if we cannot go through the German walls." A final recommendation was that "new brains" were needed, capable of applying themselves to the situation of 1916.

To those who called for Northcliffe to take public office he replied that he considered the outside position of press critic vastly superior. When Repington was approached to stand for a House of Commons seat, he sought his chief's confidential advice.[3] Northcliffe's reply summarized his view of service inside government:

You asked me about a candidature for Parliament. My thought of that sort of thing, and one by which I guide my own career, is that in fighting Governments (for that, alas, has to be our position at present) it is best to choose one's own battlegrounds, and I hope that I can say, without lack of modesty, that in my opinion the pages of my newspapers form far better entrenchments from which to deliver one's attacks than the floor of either House of Parliament.

In my own case if I go down to the House of Lords I find the enemy well entrenched on the Government benches, whereas from Printing House square or Carmelite House I am able to bombard him every day with good result.

As Military Correspondent of "The Times" you are unique. As one of six hundred and seventy members of the House of Commons you become simply one of the leg-pulled and wire-pulled back benchers.

Nothing will induce me to let the enemy choose my ground for fighting him.[4]

Lloyd George appeared sympathetic with this view in early 1916. In response to Repington's articles calling for concentration on the western front in support of Sir William Robertson and the general staff, the minister for munitions told Sir George Riddell that during the war the press "had performed the function that should have been performed by Parliament, and which the French Parliament had performed."[5]

In the first six months of 1916, the air war and compulsion took up the majority of Northcliffe's efforts, but, as usual, his interests were widespread and also included finance, the food problem, and Ireland. He wrote H. W. Massingham, editor of the *Nation*, in January 1916, about feared daylight air raids on London, manpower, and finance. He pleaded with Massingham to "urge compulsory thrift on McKenna and the instant provision of high powered fighting aeroplanes for defensive purposes."[6] The *Daily Mail* called for "Compulsory Thrift to Pay for Compulsory Service."[7] The 10 January issue asked, "When is the Economy Going to Begin?" Convinced the Germans would soon bombard England with their more powerful fighting aircraft, Northcliffe had his newspapers call for an increased and coordinated air defense. The 14 January *Daily Mail* considered the probability of daylight air bombardments and the futility of guns against "aeroplanes flying at perhaps 80 miles an hour and twelve thousand feet up." The 22 January editorial congratulated the Liberal *Manchester Guardian* for having the courage to contradict government denials that air superiority had been lost to the German Fokker aircraft.[8]

The press lord also approached members of the government directly. "I am assured by people who know the state of our air defences," he warned Andrew Bonar Law, at this time colonial secretary as well as Conservative leader, "that we have nothing capable of meeting the raids which will come as certainly as this letter will arrive at your house. I do not know what will be the attitude of the people in face of the great death roll that is sure to follow such raids."[9] Bonar Law directed him to General Sir David Henderson, who was in charge of the Royal Air Corps, the army branch of the air service.[10]

Eighteen months into the conflict, British air power remained divided between the War Office and the Admiralty, with resulting confusion and jealousy as to the responsibilities of each.[11] From the Parliamentary debates, Northcliffe assumed the Admiralty was in charge of London's air defense.[12] He was informed, to the contrary, by Bonar Law that it was "entirely in the hands of General Henderson."[13] The press lord warned the colonial secretary that "from private information from Germany I understand we are to be attacked very vigorously in the air as soon as the weather is propitious."[14] The *Daily Mail*, now "THE PAPER THAT DEVELOPED AIRMANSHIP," stepped up its air campaign. The 2 February editorial, "Too Late With the Aeroplane," chronicled the ten-year history of the newspaper in championing air power. Over the next week, the paper suggested keeping the Germans busy with raids on military targets in their homeland and asked, "Who is Responsible?"[15] The 10 February edition blamed the division of the air service between the army and navy for allowing the air raids on London. In the face of this harsh newspaper criticism, Bonar Law arranged for Henderson and the press lord to discuss the question. The meeting between the three men did not leave Northcliffe much impressed with Henderson, whom Bonar Law defended.[16] The *Daily Mail* described Henderson as "chiefly known for his 1914 statement that 'for airships to drop bombs on London would be quite opposed to the ethics of war.'"[17]

In a *British Weekly* article, "Work for Lord Northcliffe," Sir William Robertson Nicoll called for the government to use the press lord's expertise by appointing him air minister.[18] This would serve the dual purpose, Nicoll argued, of disarming the government's chief critic and showing what he could do. In response to this suggestion, Lloyd George told his press confidant, Sir George Riddell, "Northcliffe would not be a success. He has no experience of acting with equals. He would be especially handicapped in a cabinet of twenty-two.... he is best where he is."[19] The *Daily Mail* called for an air minister "instantly" and replied to Nicoll's suggestion of Northcliffe, "that there are men better able than he is to undertake the task; and, furthermore, that he could not conscientiously take part in a government that is fighting a defensive rather than an offensive war."[20] The press lord sent Nicoll a note of thanks for his "kind article," which painted a gloomy picture of Britain's position:

> Things have gone from bad to worse since our last conversation about the war. Among the worst features is the breakdown of our Intelligence Department in regard to Germany. There is great and disquieting activity at Kiel.
>
> As to the Flying Corps at the front, the official communiques are lies. Our men are out-engineered by the Germans, and the loss of life and destruction of morale are appalling. The British public have no powers of deduction otherwise they would realize that we, the British, have had no air raids on Germany for a very long time owing to this fact.[21]

In addition to the dangers in the air, Nicoll also urged Northcliffe to take up the cause of Lord Fisher, who was conducting a clandestine campaign against Balfour's leadership at the Admiralty.[22] The press lord feared the Germans were about to unleash their navy from Kiel for a blow at Britain, for which the fleet was not prepared. However, he had become frustrated with Fisher's devious methods and was not sympathetic to Nicoll's appeal for aid. He told Nicoll that

I do not think it is wise to take up the claim of Lord Fisher in a newspaper.

I am a believer in Lord Fisher, but genius is always odd and one of his oddities [is] indirectness. If things are as he states, and I believe them to be so, he could...make a discreet...speech in the House of Lords, which would arouse the nation and bring it to his side....

I fear newspaper intervention might prevent the very thing we wish.

As to myself; I have no desire or ambition other than to...assist through my newspapers, and I do not believe there will be any change in the administration of affairs until the nation has experienced the sharp shock of catastrophe.[23]

In late February Lord Derby was put in charge of a cabinet committee to coordinate the Royal Air Corps and the Royal Naval Air Service.[24] He soon asked Northcliffe's aid in his new task.[25] The press lord responded,

I am just leaving for what I believe will be a very interesting visit to the French army, but I shall be most glad to talk over the subject of aircraft when I return. I have been intimately connected with it since 1908 and *know* that you are surrounded by a number of incompetent people in high places who will most assuredly let you down. In questions of life and death one cannot mince words.

The lying from headquarters in France conceals a lamentable state of affairs. Unless you privately get at the truth from the actual flying men and not from the people on top you will unknowingly incur a responsibility of unspeakable dimensions. Some of the horrible facts are getting known. I suggest you see Lord Peel and Sir Charles Nicholson, the Liberal member for Doncaster. They know a little.

The Farnborough establishment should be at once put in the hands of a person like Sir William Lever, Lord Devonport, Sir Richard Burbidge, of Harrods, or Guy Galthrop, of the North Western Railway. The whole air service is chaos.

Please excuse plain words. I have only one desire and that is to win the war, and we are not winning it.[26]

Derby took some of this advice, conferring with "actual" airmen, as well as Peel and Nicholson. From them, he told Northcliffe, he "learned a good deal."[27]

The *Daily Mail* reacted to Derby's appointment in the 24 February editorial, "Lord Derby and the Air Services. What Will He Do with Them?" The paper pointed to his limited record on the question and called for the matter "*to be dealt with now*." Derby's only recorded speech on the air war called for the public and the press not to talk about the air raids. This was something the *Daily Mail* declared it could not do:

We can neither accept this advice nor ask our readers to accept it. And for this reason. This country is governed by public opinion. Ministers have proved time after time—they have even confessed—that they do nothing until they have been pushed and prodded by the Press or the public. They have steadfastly declined to use any initiative of their own.... It is unfortunately necessary to press the Government hard and to keep on pressing it....Whatever the rest of the Press may do, the *Daily Mail* will not repeat the mistake of thinking that things may safely be left in the feeble hands of flabby officials and platitudinous politicians.

In March, after only a month on the job, Derby resigned from his duties on the Air Coordination Committee. He had tired of presiding over endless squabbles between inflexible army and navy officers and was also frustrated because he had no power to force action. His letter of resignation advocated a combined air service to Asquith.[28] Though the prime minister thought its creation would only increase problems, in May he approved the appointment of an Air Board. The new enterprise was headed by Lord Curzon, who had had little useful work to do since joining the cabinet and had called for some sort of supervisory air agency since Derby's departure.[29] His appointment was greeted by the 13 May *Daily Mail* editorial, "The Wrong Man. What Does Lord Curzon Know About Aircraft?" The new board also ran into problems with Arthur Balfour and the Admiralty, who feared infringement in their sphere. Nonetheless, the Air Board proved useful, though Curzon's abrasive manner added to the complaints of his colleagues.[30]

Despite his earlier contrary advice to Repington, Northcliffe's depth of feeling over the air issue brought him to make an extremely rare appearance in the House of Lords. On 23 May 1916 he rose to speak during a debate on the air service.[31] As always he called for more speed in the matter and hoped that "this somewhat shadowy Board must develop into an Air Ministry." He urged Curzon to encourage inventors by setting up a separate Board of Inventions, and manufacturers by giving government financial assistance. His final recommendation was that the government increase provision for the training of flying men.

At the same time he battled for improvements in the air war, Northcliffe also crusaded against what he saw as the remnants of dangerous German influences in England. Since the first months of the war, the *Daily Mail* had called for the closing and confiscation of German interests, particularly banks. The press lord feared powerful hidden forces were protecting German-owned businesses and urged McKenna to take action against them. The chancellor of the exchequer replied that he would gladly close the banks if only given the authority.[32] On the same question, Northcliffe confided to Sir Edward Carson: "For some reason, and probably because of influence behind the scenes, the Government have declined to allow the publication of the list of German firms in England, with the result that many people are trading with these firms in ignorance of their nationality. As you are no doubt aware, very strong influence is brought to bear by the Germans to prevent the publication of these names. There can be no other reason for the secrecy. The matter is not of the pinprick order. It is really a very big question."[33]

The press lord made his sixth visit to the front in late February, this time at the invitation of the French government. He once again enjoyed the adventure. Henry Wickham Steed, foreign editor of *The Times,* accompanied him. Steed was impressed by Northcliffe's physical stamina and his "cheerfulness and patience under discomfort."[34] When the French military authorities stopped the pair's progress toward Verdun, Northcliffe appealed directly to Prime Minister Briand and they were soon allowed to continue.[35] Their automobile's overheating radiator had to be filled repeatedly with snow from the roadside, and the two were forced to share a crust of bread for dinner at Bar-le-Duc amidst a multitude of refugees from Verdun. The pair completed their journey to General Pétain's Headquarters in a French army lorry. Steed described his proprietor's view of events as "the public eye in miniature."[36] With his aid, Northcliffe sent home dispatches, published internationally, on the great battle which praised Pétain and the French army.[37] The horrors he witnessed at Verdun deeply affected Northcliffe. He returned to England in so agitated a state that his family and friends were concerned for his health.[38]

The possibility that France might make a separate peace because of the bloody toll of the war constantly worried the press lord. He sent the former French premier Georges Clemenceau, a fellow newspaper man who also backed a vigorous prosecution of the war, a letter that warned of the pacifist leanings of some of the British members of a Parliamentary committee arriving from London for consultations:

> I write in English because my French is not that of the Acadamie and your English is so excellent.
>
> I was very pleased to see by this morning's "Times" that you are to be one of the Anglo-French Commission. So far as the British delegates are concerned, more than one of them require very careful watching. The choice has not been well made. There are a few people here who do

not like the vigorous prosecution of the war, and by a curious misfortune they have pushed their way on to that Committee.[39]

Clemenceau shared this letter with Lord Bertie, the British ambassador in Paris.[40] Northcliffe was cheered to hear that *Le Matin* planned to publish a page in English because he felt it would aid understanding between the two allies. He wrote to M. Le Roux at the paper, "It is essential that in the future France and England should be very closely bound together. We must have the Channel Tunnel and we must have international marriages.... As to that subject ... I understand there is considerable activity already in the Pas-de-Calais."[41]

The press lord continued to monitor relations with Britain's eastern ally as well. The Petrograd correspondent of *The Times* accompanied a group of Russian visitors to England and reported on the visit to his chief.[42] Northcliffe also granted an interview to the Russian *Bourse Gazette* which had published articles attacking both British policy and himself. He explained to his correspondent in Petrograd that he was more interested in the Russian paper's circulation than its policies. "We sell the Times' service to Hearst's American newspapers because we wish to appeal to those who are hostile to us," he cabled Wilton. "What is the use of preaching to the converted."[43]

In 1916 keeping France and Russia in the war also concerned the foreign secretary, Sir Edward Grey, and the CIGS, Sir William Robertson. In February Grey sent both allies a complete list of Britain's contributions to illustrate the country's sacrifices.[44] The Foreign Office also endeavored to improve its propaganda measures in allied and neutral countries. Robertson knew very well that one clear path to convincing France and Russia of Britain's commitment lay in increasing her manpower contribution. Once in operational control, the CIGS decided that Kitchener's timetable had to be moved up to 1916 and to do that more men would be needed than could be supplied by present methods.[45] When conscription for single men was put into force in the first months of 1916 it had soon became apparent that the manpower supplied would be insufficient. Asquith followed his usual pattern of delay in the face of insistence from Robertson, Lloyd George, and others that conscription must be widened to include married men.

Many of those with spouses who had attested under the Derby plan, believing they would not be taken until all single men had been "combed out," found themselves called to the colors.[46] Letters of protest from the men and their wives flooded the *Daily Mail*. Incensed that his press had come under criticism because of its support of the Derby plan, Northcliffe had the complaints sent to him. Because of Derby's 1915 pledge to look after them, the press lord considered Derby still to be responsible and told him so in no uncertain terms.[47] Derby replied that the letters should not be forwarded because he no longer had anything to do with the matter.[48] In his view, the tribunals processing the complaints now had the sole responsibility of handling any problems.[49] The *Daily Mail* assailed Derby in its 26 February editorial, "The Married Men Problem," which also criticized the large numbers of exemptions granted to single men.

Despite all attempts at explanation, for months Northcliffe continued to be bitter about the broken promise to him and the married men. In March, the *Daily Mail* continued to call for "Fair Play" for the married men.[50] When Derby requested they talk over the misunderstanding, the press lord countered:

> I do not see that any good can come from discussing matters.
>
> You made a promise to me which you have broken. You told me that you would not for a moment think of remaining with a Government that did not keep its word. On the strength of that promise I used the whole strength of my organization to help a scheme in which I did not believe. The best I can do for you is to suppress the violent letters about you that are reaching us every day — many from Lancashire.[51]

Derby found it hard to reconcile Northcliffe's position with *The Times*, which said it was Derby's duty not to resign, writing to him, "Perhaps some day...I shall be able to prove to you...that I am not as black as you paint me."[52] The press lord remained adamant, explaining that the article appeared in his absence and that the writer did not know of his "private pledge to me" and his "pledge to the people whose homes are about to be broken up."[53] Derby had his defenders against the attacks of the *Daily Mail,* including St. Loe Strachey in the *Spectator.* He wrote to Margot Asquith, "I am glad to see you liked my defence of Derby and the Government in the matter of the pledges. It literally makes my blood boil to see the dishonourable accusations brought by the Northcliffe Press. In my opinion the Government and Derby acted perfectly squarely all the way through."[54]

The spring conscription campaign gave Northcliffe his initial opportunity in 1916 to support the army, in the person of Sir William Robertson, who called for the government to act on the manpower question.[55] The *Daily Mail* described the government's inaction as "Fiddling While Rome Burns."[56] The 11 April editorial called for "Equality of Sacrifice" and went on, "We Must Have Compulsion." Labeling Asquith "the world's greatest virtuoso in dilatoriness," the paper urged him to make up his mind because the country could not afford to wait and see any longer. That day's "Message from the

Chief" predicted that the latest "vigorous" *Daily Mail* appeal for compulsion "will, I am sure, have great effect on our wobbly rulers." On 17 April the editorial, "How to Lose the War," described Asquith's suggestion for calling up eighteen-year-olds as a "miserable half-measure" and called for a "war opposition ... to give material for an alternative Ministry and put an end to the paralyzing effect of the disastrous Coalition."

These attacks on the government brought charges that Northcliffe had a personal grudge against Asquith. He addressed this in a letter to Massingham:

> You did me an injustice in last Friday's "Nation" in suggesting that I have some personal vendetta as regards Mr. Asquith.
>
> ...I distrust Mr. Asquith because he obviously distrusts himself. I do not know him well, but my belief is that he is too kind. Nobody is punished, and among many other blemishes there is little sense of the need for celerity in any Government Department.
>
> ...compulsion would not have been necessary had the matter been properly handled. Even now, though we may get scientific recruiting, there is no sign of scientific utilization of the men recruited. We have an immense army of non-combatant soldiers in France and in England. There is probably the same proportion at Salonika and in Egypt.
>
> ...The young men in the Army Pay Department in France should be sent to the front, and their places taken by some of the hundreds of middle-aged men who write to me, and probably to you, asking to be allowed to do something to help the war. Or their places might be taken by women. That is only one example of man waste.
>
> ...Fifty thousand men are required by May 27th. If the Government will give me permission, I will guarantee to go to France and get them in Rouen, Abbeville, Havre, G.H.Q. and elsewhere.
>
> There is talk of shortage of labour for unloading ships. Let the Government do what the French do—use the German prisoners for the purpose. German prisoners so working to whom I spoke at Cherbourg were happy and cheerful. Arbeit macht das Leben süss.[57]

Others supported Northcliffe's course. Lord Milner praised his efforts for conscription on 18 April in the House of Lords.[58] Austin Harrison of the *English Review* advised the press lord to back candidates who would oppose Asquith. His 20 April letter continued, "Asquith has fudged again & it is clear from the press that he will ... keep the Coalition together. The real reason of this is fear of you—jealousy. They fear if the Coalition falls you may be asked to form or join a Government, & they would rather lose the war than see you in office."[59] In reply Northcliffe suggested that Harrison, himself, become a candidate and downplayed the government's fear of his own influence. As to his personal ambitions for power, he asserted, "I am not likely to exchange the strength of my printing presses for the powerlessness of the portfolio."[60] He repeated this sentiment to Sir John Willison, *The Times* correspondent in Canada, adding, "Unless we can get rid of Asquith, Kitchener, Balfour, and Bonar Law we shall lose the war."[61] Bonar Law held an equally low opinion of the press lord. When he and Riddell discussed a vicious attack in the Liberal *Daily News* on Lloyd George, which Riddell put down to his cooperation with Northcliffe, the colonial secretary appraised the owner of the *Daily Mail* as an unprincipled opportunist who was "quite unreliable and altogether wanting in stability."[62]

H. G. Wells, who represented the living voice of the science that Northcliffe wished to see applied to the manpower question and the war in general, was among those who lauded the press lord's efforts. He wrote in April to congratulate the owner of the *Daily Mail* for "playing a supremely useful part in goading on our remarkable Government."[63] He also prophesied salvation through revolution by the 1930s and continued that "there is nobody in the country with the imagination, the instruments, and the prestige for revolution except yourself. The war has brought you into open and active conflict with the system as it is." Northcliffe urged Wells to

> go and look at the little part of the war in France and Flanders. The French are celerity itself. ...
>
> By June their man power will have reached its zenith, and they expect us to pay our share of the blood tax, which up to the present we have not done. Germany will do all she can to make a separate peace with Italy and France, and if we persist in putting only a third of our army in France into the firing line, and keeping one million five hundred thousand men in England, as we are, France will be entitled to ask us how much longer we are going to continue our leisurely war with Germany on her territory.[64]

The same letter also explained the method of his attacks on the government over conscription and other questions, and professed his lack of personal ambition:

> I find the only way to get anything done is to attack the coalition incident by incident, muddle by muddle. If the armies already raised were scientifically used there would be no need of compulsion at this juncture, quite apart from the million and a half men in khaki in England. Havre, Boulogne, Rouen, Calais, Abbeville and environs are alive with soldiers doing civilian and women's work. It makes one['s] blood boil to know that

while France has called up boys and men of fifty, our Army Pay Department is packed with young men doing the clerical work of girls.

I am very much with you as to the future, though I see it probably not as clearly as you do. It is not unlikely that the war itself may produce within the next few years something approaching a revolution....

I have no ambition in this matter, and am not likely to give up the strength of my presses for the powerlessness of a portfolio.

The *Daily Mail* campaign for conscription continued into late April and linked the problem to Britain's unwieldy cabinet system. The editorial of the 29th, "The 23 Scandal. How Much Longer?" called for a concentration of power in as few hands as possible, noting "there is no instance in history of a war being successfully conducted by a large committee." More important than the press in extending conscription was Lloyd George's threatened resignation and pressure from Bonar Law. In this latest political crisis, Asquith once again conceded and survived in office. Compulsion was extended to all able-bodied men between eighteen and forty-one in May 1916. The 3 May *Daily Mail* hailed "Compulsion at Last."

At the same time Parliament grappled with the conscription issue, German submarine attacks and the needs of the war combined to cause scarcities in many items, including food.[65] For years Britain had imported much of her food supply and now relied on the Royal Navy to get staples through. It was not until a year into the war that the government began patriotic calls for conservation.[66] By 1916 food queues were common and a source of alarm to many, including Northcliffe. That year's poor harvest made necessary the adoption of more severe measures. The 4 May *Daily Mail* discussed the nation's "Food Problems." The government asked the press not to publicize the food issue; however, Northcliffe had little faith that the politicians could cope with the problem. He informed Wells,

You probably know that last week they summoned all the Editors of the country to a conference, to ask them not to mention shipping and possible food shortage. At the same time they issue appeals for economy, one of which you signed. Time after time exactly the same course has been followed with the same result.

We are heading now towards a distinct food shortage. One strong man who would order the people to eat less would effect the desired result — or it might be achieved by a very rigorous campaign of publicity by speech and newspaper. As it is, we shall drift on, come around to the old accusations of plots and conspiracies and when too late adopt some hastily contrived economic machinery.[67]

1916 also saw a reawakening of the Irish problem, which had been over-shadowed by the war. The executions carried out by the British in the after-math of the bloody April "Easter Rising" centered in Dublin only created martyrs and radicalized Irish opinion in favor of Sinn Fein, which had not been involved in the insurgency. The rash British action also brought cries of indignation from the American government and public, and further compli-cated relations with the most powerful neutral. In the aftermath, Northcliffe's brother, the Liberal M.P. Cecil Harmsworth, traveled to Ireland.[68] Cecil wrote his older brother from Dublin, whose ruined streets he compared to the aftermath of a zeppelin raid. His letter commented that "the view here seems to be that, whatever scheme of provisional govt is adopted, a large body of troops should be kept in the country. It is generally believed that popular sen-timent has swung around in favor of the Sinn Feiners."[69] Cecil also noted the "curious feeling of pride in the devastation" and recommended that the Irish Territorial troops should be disarmed. Lloyd George was enlisted to tackle this latest Irish crisis. The *Daily Mail* loudly applauded the choice, calling the Welshman the "handyman of the Coalition."[70]

In Northcliffe's view, Ireland's problems could not be solved until eco-nomic conditions in the country were improved. He returned to this theme again and again for the remainder of the war. During this period the press lord met often with Lloyd George. On 27 May Riddell recorded in his diary that "L.G. never tells me about his meetings with Northcliffe, but I am sure they are in daily contact."[71] Cecil Harmsworth called this time "a period of something like friendship between them—they were collaborating for a settlement of the Irish problem."[72] The press lord attempted to bring together Lloyd George and William Murphy, owner of the influential Irish news-paper, the *Daily Independent.* Though Murphy traveled to London for meet-ings, he remained inflexible.[73] Unfortunately, at this time, like so often before, the problem proved insoluble.

At midyear 1916 Northcliffe held a dim view of the Allied military situ-ation. He instructed his papers to concentrate on Ypres and Verdun, which he believed would both likely fall. The same message also commented on the 31 May naval Battle of Jutland, which had been called, at first, a triumph: "I am convinced we have overdone the cry of victory in the North Sea Battle. If we have sunk the ships we say we have, why is it that neither the Dutch nor the Danes have picked up one single sailor from any ships other than those named in the German official statement. . . . The perspective at the moment should prominently include Ypre[s] and Verdun, and after the fall of these we must prepare for an immense peace campaign by Germany."[74] Jutland may have been no great victory, but the German fleet never again challenged the British in any force. Ypres and Verdun both held.

The press lord's opponents continued to discuss how best to counter him. Strachey wrote to Margot Asquith,

Northcliffe is certainly most tiresome, but how to deal with him is a very difficult matter. I had no hesitation in going for him in regard to K., but I, like you, was disgusted to see how none of the rest of the Press took the point.

The real difficulty about Northcliffe... is the fact that so many members of the Cabinet not only are unwilling to stand up to him, but actually court him and ask him for his support. Therefore, when one denounces him for trying to pull the Government down, his people laugh at one and say, "This is all very fine, but if Northcliffe is really a public danger as you say, why are Cabinet Ministers hand in glove with him?"

Of course, Northcliffe has done immense mischief with the French... and give[n] the impression that we have sacrificed France to England.[75]

The problem of what to do with Lord Kitchener was finally settled by the fortunes of war. Sent on a mission to Russia in June, his cruiser, the *Hampshire,* struck a mine and sank with almost all hands. On hearing the news, Northcliffe reportedly proclaimed, "Providence is on the side of the British Empire after all."[76] The press lord saw the event as a golden opportunity to turn out Asquith. When Lloyd George was offered the War Office, Northcliffe advised against acceptance on the grounds that it would "give the Government a new lease on life and that it will be impossible to turn them out."[77] The Welshman had long been dissatisfied with Asquith and considered resignation. However, he was unable to resist the War Office, even with the reduced powers that Kitchener had lost to Sir William Robertson, which Lloyd George tried, unsuccessfully, to regain.[78] The *Daily Mail* announcement of 7 July was much more subdued than that which had greeted the Irish appointment six weeks before.[79] Though disappointed, Northcliffe did not burn his bridges. Maurice Hankey, secretary of the War Committee, recorded in his diary that the press lord and Churchill were among the first to call on the new secretary at the War Office.[80]

Northcliffe's relations with Churchill deteriorated further when he told him outside Lloyd George's office, "I suppose you have come after LG's job."[81] The remark was made in jest, but Churchill took it in earnest. He returned a statuette of Napoleon which the press lord had given him. In a letter which gave his side of the incident, Northcliffe remarked to Lloyd George that Churchill's reaction "must be a matter of health."[82] The press lord had the statuette sent to Blenheim Palace by messenger along with an apology.[83] "I am sorry that you took such a chaffing remark so seriously [sic]," he wrote to Churchill, "I had no desire whatsoever to hurt your feelings.... I ask you to accept an expression of my regret for having said it."[84]

Robertson and Haig made a powerful military combination with which the new secretary for war had to contend. The CIGS had close relations with Repington, to whom he fed information backing his western strategy and the idea that politicians should not meddle in army affairs.[85] The commander-in-chief resisted newspaper aid. Since his experience in the Sudan with Kitchener, Haig had felt only disdain and revulsion for the press. He likened Sir John French's 1915 alliance with the newspapers and Northcliffe to "carrying on with a whore."[86] Robertson attempted to change his attitude, writing him in June, "I am sure things would be much better if we got the press on our side.... My idea is that we ought to send out, on your invitation, 4 or 5 of the big newspaper Proprietors e.g. Northcliffe, Burnham etc for a few days to some part of our front."[87] Haig replied that the present was not an opportune time for a visit of the proprietors as secret preparations were underway for a new offensive. This operation on the Somme would prove the most bloody battle of the war for the British, after which nothing would be the same.

The first six months of 1916 had shown mixed results for Northcliffe's attempts to "tear the scales" from the eyes of the nation and the government concerning the sacrifices needed to defeat Germany. He felt the Air Board only a shadow of the powerful Air Ministry required for a maximum effort. However, the extension of conscription did promise to supply the army with the men it called for, if only the politicians could be kept out of the way. With Kitchener out of the picture, Northcliffe felt a renewed confidence. In the second half of 1916 eliminating government interference with the general's prosecution of the war became his obsession. This struggle between the government "frocks" and the Army "brasshats" dominated the next six months and helped to topple the Asquith government.

SIX

"Asquith's Head on a Plate"
The Fall of Asquith & the Rise of Lloyd George,
July to December 1916

THE BATTLE OF THE SOMME BEGAN DISASTROUSLY FOR THE BRITISH
cause on 1 July 1916 when the unprecedented artillery barrage that preceded
it failed to clear away the German defenses. The British suffered more than
50,000 casualties on that single day—with only meager gains to show for
their sacrifice. As the toll mounted over the following weeks and months, Sir
Douglas Haig stubbornly continued the bloody frontal assaults. The Somme
marked a new direction in Haig's relations with the press, which, he realized,
could be useful in explaining that the campaign was not a failure, despite the
dreadful human wastage.

Three weeks into the battle, at the commander-in-chief's invitation, the
press lord arrived at St. Omer, the British headquarters.[1] This tour marked
his first substantial discussions with Haig.[2] Sir Douglas took twenty minutes
from his pressing schedule for a talk alone with Northcliffe before they shared
lunch with General Lancelot Kiggell, Haig's chief of staff, and General John
Charteris, his head of intelligence. The commander-in-chief recorded in his
diary that he "was favourably impressed" with the press lord's "desire to do
his best to help win the war. He was most anxious not to make a mistake in
anything he advocated in his newspapers, and for this he was desirous of
seeing what was taking place. I am therefore letting him see everything and
talk to anyone he pleases."[3] Northcliffe described Haig in his journal as "a
quiet, determined, level-headed, easy mannered, blue-eyed Scottish gentleman with a Scottish accent, neither optimist or pessimist, the kind of man
who sets puzzles for Prussians."[4] The men attended church services together
two days later, and the chief proprietor of *The Times* requested that Haig
report anything in the paper not to his liking.[5]

From St. Omer, Northcliffe toured bases at Abbeville, Rouen, and Havre. He visited hospitals on behalf of *The Times* Red Cross fund, inspected the Central Training School's recreated trenches at Havre and was particularly impressed by an immense recycling station, noting in his diary, "*nothing wasted.*"[6] During his stay, he also saw General Rawlinson of the Fourth Army, General Trenchard of the Royal Flying Corps, Sir Julian Byng, commander of the Canadian troops, and General Birdwood, commander of the Anzac forces.[7] The press lord met with Haig again for lunch on 2 August, just before a trip to the Italian front. Haig commented on Northcliffe's enthusiasm and the fact that he was "very anxious to do all he can to help to win."[8] Enthralled both by Haig and by the improved conditions he saw on his visit, Northcliffe pledged his complete support. He recorded in his journal that Haig "showed me his plans. Each time I see him I am convinced of his qualities. We talked of the wobble of politicians."[9]

The politicians soon received Northcliffe's appraisal. He sent Lloyd George, the secretary for war, a glowing report which described a demoralized enemy and renewed British confidence. He found "no comparison whatever with the state of affairs in August 1916 and the state of affairs at any other time at which I have been to the war."[10] The press lord strongly urged Lloyd George "to spend at least two weeks with the army....You will find yourself in the midst of an organization which...is as well nigh perfect as it can be." Lord Derby, by this time under-secretary for war, received a similar letter of praise.[11]

The Welshman did not agree with Northcliffe's adoring assessment of Sir Douglas Haig and the army. He viewed the Somme as a larger repetition of the Neuve Chappelle and Loos failures. Appalled at the British casualties, his aim was to reduce the carnage in France and Flanders—if necessary by diverting troops elsewhere or holding them in Britain.[12] This difference of opinion developed into a serious rift between the two men. St. Loe Strachey commented to Margot Asquith in August that "I am glad to hear that Ll. G. is now no longer keen about working with Milner, Northcliffe and the rest. Long may he remain so. Northcliffe is really absurd and I think the more he is ignored the better."[13]

Winston Churchill and F. E. Smith, the attorney-general, agreed with Lloyd George's view of the Somme offensive as a costly failure. On 1 August Smith placed before the cabinet a memorandum by Churchill to that effect. The same day Northcliffe wrote to the war secretary from France, "any wavering now will cost us eventual losses beyond calculation, alarm France and hearten a depressed Germany."[14] Rumors soon spread that Lloyd George, Churchill, Smith, Bonar Law, and others were conspiring both to relieve

Haig and to form a new government.[15] This spurred Northcliffe and others in the press to new heights of praise for the generals. In response to an 8 August piece in *The Times* by its chief proprietor, which described conditions at the front as "perfect" and warned that nothing should be touched, Lloyd George told Sir George Riddell that the press lord had been "got at" by the soldiers and was "all wrong this time. Things behind the lines require to be vastly improved."[16] The Welshman traveled to Paris on 10 August and asked Arthur Lee, one of his parliamentary secretaries, to have Northcliffe contact him so that he could "put him straight."[17] The press lord, in turn, told Lee that Lloyd George was almost as unpopular with the army as Churchill, that he had "fought battles on his behalf all along the line," and urged Lee to convince his chief to remedy the misapprehensions on both sides with a long visit with the army in France.[18] Northcliffe further warned Lee that even though Lloyd George had been "the life and soul of the war... if he continues to appear to side with the intriguers we must expect people to say that 'birds of a feather all flock together.'"[19] Government interference with the army troubled Northcliffe. "I go off to Italy with a heavy heart in this matter," he told Geoffrey Robinson at *The Times.*[20]

On his way to Italy, which had joined the Allied cause in May 1915, Northcliffe first stopped in Paris for a luncheon with Lord Bertie, the British ambassador.[21] Bertie recorded in his diary on 6 August that the press lord "criticized Asquith, not Lloyd George" and that he believed German firms in England and their sympathizers were "endeavoring to create an *atmosphere* of peace. It will take at least two years' more fighting to crush Germany and obtain a peace such as we ought to have, so as to prevent a renewal of the war in a few years time."[22] To sample neutral opinion, after Italy Northcliffe visited Switzerland and Spain. He was back in France on 9 September with Haig, to whom he reported that Spain "was full of Germans and the whole Press is anti-British."[23] Northcliffe and Henry Wickham Steed, foreign editor of *The Times,* stayed two days with the British army. Haig recorded their anxiousness to be of service "in any possible way."[24] In an 11 September letter, the commander-in-chief told his wife that Northcliffe described Lloyd George as "a shirt-sleeve politician" who always does "whatever he (Lord N.) advises!"[25]

In his discussions with Haig, the press lord had included his thoughts on propaganda as a weapon of war against the German army—particularly the use of airplane-dropped leaflets that recounted the excellent conditions among the prisoners held by the Allies. Northcliffe was delighted to find, at last, a military leader who did not dismiss his propaganda plans. General Charteris, as head of intelligence, became the press lord's propaganda liaison with the army. He told Charteris that,

After reading a number of German soldiers letters given to me by the Germans themselves in No. 4 Hospital, Versailles, at the end of September 1914, I sent this scheme to Lord French through Colonel Swinton, but nothing came of it. Later, I put it before General Henry Wilson, but he told me that after all it was a minor matter—the thing was to kill Germans, with which I agreed; and he also told me that the French would break through the German lines last June; so that his calculations regarding an early victory may have also led him wrong in his conclusions regarding propaganda.

I am very sure that had the Germans such an asset as we possess in the good treatment of our German prisoners, both in our hospitals and in our camps, they would deluge our army [with] its propaganda....

With my knowledge of the psychology of the Germans, I believe this bombardment of the German mind is almost as important as the bombardment effected by guns.[26]

To produce a state of mind in the German army favorable to surrender, the press lord recommended to Charteris that the British scatter by airplane copied German letters home, as well as pleasant photographs of conditions in English camps. He underlined that to obtain proper results a continuous effort, day in and out for months on a huge scale, would be needed and suggested that the whole thing be placed in the hands of one alert man, who would do nothing else. Two weeks later Charteris responded, "We are getting on with the dropping of letters and pamphlets on the German side of the line; quite possibly in consequence of that ...we have had the biggest batch of deserters coming over together since the beginning of the war. It is not very big, only 10 in all, but they came together, and therefore it is encouraging."[27] From France, Northcliffe sent Geoffrey Robinson at *The Times* a copy of his propaganda plan and his views on the Battle of the Somme: "Let me once more say that what is taking place on the Somme must not be measured by metres. It is the first time we have had a proper scientific attack. There are no complaints of bad staff work, no complaints of lack of ammunitions, no muddling.... If we wrote communiques as well as the Germans, we would lay much more stress on the German losses, which are *known* to be immense."[28]

During the September visit Northcliffe was shown the preparations for a second great offensive planned to begin within days. On Haig's recommendation that he view something called a "tank," he revisited General Sir Julian Byng at Canadian headquarters. Expecting storage devices, Northcliffe and Steed were understandably surprised (and at first inclined to laugh) at the "rumbling caterpillar leviathans."[29] Steed described his chief's personal experience with one of the vehicles. "Northcliffe tried to enter one of them by the manhole on the top; but as his girth was some inches larger than the hole, he stuck midway and had to be hauled down to the inside by the feet while I sat on his shoulders above. Getting him out again was an even harder matter, though presently he emerged minus some buttons."[30] After some initial success in the 15 September offensive, the tanks either suffered mechanical failures or bogged down, but showed the promise of this innovation. The 16 September *Daily Mail* hailed the "Great Successes on the Somme" and noted the new methods and weapons being used, particularly "a new type of heavy armoured car" and the "tactical use of aeroplanes and their remarkable feats of machine-gunning." In the following months, Northcliffe kept in close touch with Haig through his personal secretary, Sir Philip Sassoon. "I must write to you how much we all liked the Times leader of the 18th," Sassoon announced in a 19 September letter. "It must have made people realise for the first time the true significance of our victory of the 15th — the C in C was quite delighted with it."[31] The press lord also continued his correspondence with Charteris concerning publicity, recommending that several important American journalists be shown special treatment.[32]

The criticism of Lloyd George and others could not dent Northcliffe's renewed faith in the army. "The war is going splendidly," he declared in a letter to the Australian journalist Keith Murdoch. "We have thrown up a military genius at last in Haig and he is blasting his way into Germany by the only possible means."[33] John Evelyn Wrench recorded that the press lord "lunched with Briand, the French premier, who also believes in Douglas Haig, and said to Northcliffe, '*Sir Douglas 'Aig est le seul général qui fait ce qu'il dit!*'"[34] The press lord found the British civilian authorities less praiseworthy, particularly concerning military exemptions. September messages to his employees asserted that "we are doing good service to the country, on the Man question" and called for the continuation of the campaign "against the tribunals and exemptions. I find that medical exemptions have been given to young men who, in the French and German armies, would be in the trenches."[35]

When Lloyd George visited the front in September he failed to take Northcliffe's advice to spend time with the British rank and file and make himself known as something other than a politician. Though he stayed two weeks, most of his time was spent in Paris or with senior officers far from the front.[36] Sassoon complained to his press ally that the Welshman was rude to the French, would not follow any of the plans made for him and, in general, "did not make a favourable impression either in the British or French army."[37] "If *this* is the man some people would like to see P.M.," Sassoon continued, "I prefer old Squiff any day with all his faults!"[38]

The secretary for war was well aware that Haig had taken the place of Kitchener as the embodiment of the army to the nation and that open criticism would be politically dangerous. He also realized that Haig had the backing of the bulk of the British press, including Northcliffe. In order to gain more evidence for his case, Lloyd George arranged to have Sir John French sent to the Continent, ostensibly to study French artillery practices. Sir William Robertson, the Chief of the Imperial General Staff in London, approved French's inspection tour, even though he knew that Lloyd George was attempting to sway the cabinet toward a war strategy different from that of the general staff.[39] When Northcliffe later heard rumors that General French was criticizing Haig "at the Court and elsewhere," he had Repington warn him that the result would be bitter attacks in his newspapers.[40]

Though Northcliffe and Lloyd George differed on strategic questions, they nevertheless stayed in contact. Both men worried about the effect in Britain and abroad of what they considered defeatist talk of a negotiated peace with Germany. The Americans continued to offer mediation through President Wilson's personal envoy, Colonel House. In late September, the press lord urged the war secretary to give a statement to Roy Howard of the American United Press, who had stopped in London on his way to Germany.[41] Lloyd George took his advice and their conversation, published internationally, became famous as the "Knock-Out Blow" interview.[42] In it the Welshman made it plain the Allies intended to fight to the finish and would not agree to a compromise peace. The 29 September *Daily Mail* printed the interview and congratulated the war secretary for his "straight from the shoulder language that Americans appreciate." This bold and unauthorized statement by Lloyd George bolstered home and Allied morale and sent a clear signal to the Americans and the Germans. It gained him, however, only a brief reprieve from Northcliffe's ire.

In October the intrigues against the army came to a climax. Against the advice of such "westerners" as Robertson, Lloyd George called for increased numbers of troops for Arabia and the Balkans, particularly for the support of Rumania, which had joined the Allies in August and whose position was dire.[43] In the first few days of the month, Northcliffe met with Derby to discuss the problem.[44] At this time he told Sassoon, "You are dealing with people, some of whom are very thick-skinned, others very unscrupulous, but all afraid of newspapers. It was urgently necessary that they should be told...'Hands off the army.'"[45] On 4 October the press lord had Repington assure Robertson that he would support him. The following day's *Daily Mail* editorial, "Comb Out or 45. The Chief of Staff Speaks Out," supported Robertson's call for "more men *now*."

Sassoon and Haig were kept informed with regular Northcliffe letters containing "News from the Home Front," by which the press lord meant the battle against the politicians. A 6 October note from Sassoon commented, "the Chief [Haig]...was especially interested in your 'News from the Home Front' & most amused at the title. I am glad that things are quieting down in that region of the war, but it is an enemy that wants watching every instant of the day and night—but so long as you are watching we can feel quite unruffled out here."[46] Northcliffe responded with a further report. "I send you a few little jottings from the Home Front.... the Cabinet...are a pack of gullible optimists—'detached cynics' Leo Maxse calls them, who swallow any foolish tale. There are exceptions among them and they are splendid ones, but the generality of them have the slipperiness of eels with the combined vanity of a professional beauty.... Quite a number of them, as you know, have plans in their pockets for winning the war."[47]

At a London Aldwych Club press luncheon on 9 October, Northcliffe spoke out on the dangers of government interference with the army and the possibility of an unfavorable negotiated peace.[48] He also railed against the pacific influence of Lord Haldane.[49] Cecil Harmsworth called the ovation received by his brother on the occasion one that "would not be accorded, I think, to any of our statesmen with the possible exception of Ll. G."[50] News of the address reached the Continent. Sassoon heard "what a magnificent speech you made at the Aldwych" and asked for a copy. His letter went on, "It is very heartening for all out here to know how much they can rely on you for support and encouragement."[51]

On 10 October the strategic differences between the secretary for war and his military advisors developed into an open breach. Completely out of patience, an angry Lloyd George called for an Allied conference to save Britain's "prestige" and "honour" and to keep Rumania from becoming another disaster like the fall of Serbia.[52] Robertson notified Lloyd George in writing that if his views were ignored he "could not be responsible for conducting this very difficult war under these conditions."[53] Northcliffe offered his help and urged Robertson to take his case to the prime minister. The chief of staff replied, "The Boche gives me no trouble compared with what I meet in London. So any help you can give me will be of Imperial value."[54]

After Northcliffe heard from Repington that Robertson could not sleep because of Lloyd George's latest "interference," he made a personal visit to the War Office. A letter to Sassoon described his confrontation with the Welshman's secretary, J. T. Davies, in which the press lord told Davies that he could no longer support the war secretary and that:

if further interference took place with Sir William Robertson I was going to the House of Lords to lay matters before the world, and hammer them daily in my newspapers. This may seem a brusque and drastic thing to do, but I think I know the combination I am dealing with better than you folks who are so engrossed in your splendid and absorbing task....

I have heard nothing since, because I am in the country, but Geoffrey Robinson tells me that General Robertson says that matters are better. I also heard that Winston has been going about libeling me in extra vigorous style, which is a good sign.

...I am a believer in the War Secretary of State to a very great extent, but he is always being egged on by Churchill, the Attorney General and other little but venomous people.[55]

Northcliffe continued that he had taken the further step of securing support in the House of Commons, through his brother Cecil, to organize a "force sufficiently strong to end these antics." Additionally, the press lord sent word to Asquith that he could not support the government unless the military chiefs were allowed a free hand.[56]

Lloyd George used Northcliffe's outburst as an opportunity for a counter-stroke against Robertson over the issue of official leaks to the press.[57] In a strongly worded reply to Robertson's ultimatum, Lloyd George stated that he refused, as war secretary, to play the part of a "mere dummy." His rebuttal made particular reference to Northcliffe's confrontation with Davies.[58] Though the War Council did agree to limit communications with the press, Lloyd George found himself fighting a losing battle over strategy. He was forced to bide his time in his conflict with the generals and their press allies.

The Northcliffe newspapers backed up their proprietor's pledge to Robertson. Coining the alliterative slogan "*Ministerial meddling means military muddling*," the 13 October *Daily Mail* reminded the country of the Antwerp and Gallipoli blunders and declared that the government should limit itself to supplying men. That day's "Message from the Chief" declared, "If we continue to grind into the public mind the horrible fact that political interference means an increase in the death roll of our army, Sir Douglas Haig and Sir William Robertson will not be worried as they are at present. This was a scandalous attempt to weaken the Army in France at the moment of Victory— an attempt to send our soldiers on mad, wild expeditions to distant places." Repington congratulated his chief for the *Daily Mail* stand against Lloyd George's efforts to drain men away from the western front and called again for him to take a "watching brief" in the government.[59] "I watch the Government so closely," Northcliffe replied, "that I do not think they will be able to do anything very suddenly. Moreover they talk. Personally I think if I were to join them I should lose what little influence I have. The people would never tolerate a newspaper owner being a member of the Government."[60] Repington disagreed, responding, "I think that our people will tolerate anything to win the war, and prefer that power and responsibility should be combined. However you are the best judge of what is possible."[61]

The campaign against government interference hit home. On 14 October Lloyd George told Riddell that Northcliffe was "taking up a strong line against him and is endeavouring to make friends with Asquith," who planned to "leave him severely alone."[62] The Welshman also said that the press lord's vanity was "colossal, that he wants to be a Dictator," and that he did not intend to be "dictated to." At a dinner two days later Riddell warned of a conspiracy between Northcliffe and the generals to get rid of the Welshman.[63] Lloyd George complained to Repington that the *Daily Mail* attacked him even after he bowed to the generals and accepted conscription for men aged forty-one. He said Northcliffe was "like a flea; he hopped about and you never knew where to catch him."[64] In late October, the war secretary told Riddell that "even the Almighty formed a Trinity. Northcliffe is a Unitarian. It is a poor sort of religion."[65] A few days after this, Lloyd George complained to Lord Burnham, proprietor of the *Daily Telegraph*, that the owner of the *Daily Mail* was "mad with vanity." He went on that the press lord had threatened to "turn him out" if he sent troops to Salonika and that Northcliffe was "not a man I should care to go out tiger shooting with; and after my experience, I would not go out with him on a rat hunt."[66] Burnham felt the general staff were using Northcliffe as they had the year before against Kitchener.

Although Northcliffe and Lloyd George bitterly disagreed and tempers flared on both sides, the two men needed each other. The press lord knew that the Welshman represented the best, perhaps the only, realistic alternative to Asquith. For him this fact overrode their other differences, including war strategy. Lloyd George in turn realized the power over public and private opinion that Northcliffe wielded. He was not a man to let disagreements override political practicalities.[67] In an attempt to wean Northcliffe from the generals, the war secretary urged him to talk with Albert Thomas, the French munitions minister. After they met the press lord reported to Sassoon that

> The object of the meeting was to convince me that military direction of the war is not always for the best, and that had the soldiers been obeyed, Paris and Verdun would have been lost: that soldiers always say a thing is impossible.
>
> I told him that so far as the Battle of the Somme is concerned—which to me is the crux of the war—I could not support any interference with the soldiers, and I gave him a good deal of information about our political geniuses and their various well-meant but ignorant schemes of strategy.[68]

Though support of the army was widespread, there was opposition to Northcliffe's campaign against government interference, and he feared that the politicians would mobilize press support. Hedley Le Bas warned of a possible anti-Haig campaign in Burnham's *Daily Telegraph*, "the line of attack will be, that in view of the reckless manner in which he has sacrificed his men on the Somme, he has proved himself incompetent."[69] Northcliffe alerted Sassoon that the *Daily Telegraph* and the *Observer* had joined forces for an attack on the army. He requested that "a remonstrance" should be sent to Major Waldorf Astor, owner of the *Observer*, on the attitude of his paper, "which he absolutely controls, with regard to the Army."[70] "Now that almost everyone has lost someone in the war," the press lord continued, "it is very easy to arouse criticism." He feared the "great many gloomy people about" whose "feelings can easily be worked upon."

National gloom was understandable when, at the end of the Battle of the Somme in November 1916, the British had precious little to show in exchange for their 400,000 casualties. The war again struck home for Northcliffe when another nephew, Vere, Rothermere's second son, was killed in the fighting that month.[71] Haig, despite mounting criticism over his seeming disregard of British lives, survived as commander. Northcliffe's support helped ensure that he stayed in place. The battle did have other results. The Somme and Verdun campaigns took a physical toll on the German army and affected its morale. If they did not before, the Germans now realized that the British, with their conscript army, were a serious military power. In addition, at home, the Somme brought more open criticism of the Asquith government.

In November the political situation surrounding Asquith began to fragment. On the 8th the Nigeria debate in the Commons revealed the serious division in the Unionist ranks and threatened the position of Andrew Bonar Law.[72] In the middle of the month Lloyd George began (through Sir Max Aitken) negotiations to meet with the Conservative leader. The men finally came together, with Sir Edward Carson, on 20 November to formulate a plan for a small War Council that would be presented to Asquith. Carson, like Northcliffe, was a devoted westerner and wanted Asquith removed. At this point Bonar Law and Lloyd George were less willing to act so drastically.

Largely because of his feud with Lloyd George over strategy, during November Northcliffe was shut out of the inner circle of political intrigue, but at the end of the month Geoffrey Robinson worked to involve him.[73] Robinson visited Arthur Lee with the aim of patching up the differences between their chiefs. He reported that Lee "thought it a pity that L.G. and Northcliffe had not for some time been on speaking terms. I told him that there was not very much in this, and that so far as I knew, Northcliffe ... was quite alive to L.G.'s great qualities and desire to win the war."[74] The efforts of Robinson and Lee succeeded; however, Lee complained at the time to his wife, Ruth, of the danger of being caught between Lloyd George and Northcliffe, that "It is all very well this going about like a Dove of Peace, with an olive branch in one's beak, but one is apt to get taken for a bloody pigeon and get shot at by both sides."[75] In the first days of December, Robinson's chief regularly visited the War Office while, at the same time, Lloyd George attempted to persuade Asquith to agree to a small War Committee. Lee reported that their meetings on December 1 (before and after Lloyd George saw Asquith) went well and thought it critical that the two men work together in the crisis.[76] He considered the press lord "with all his faults" a "national asset" and one of the three biggest men in the country along with Carson and Lloyd George.[77] The Welshman questioned the reliability of the press lord's support. He had told Lord Burnham at breakfast on December 1 that an "alliance with Northcliffe is something like going for a walk with a grasshopper."[78]

To the press lord's growing frustration, Lloyd George did not share complete details of the crisis; however, he conveyed enough to ensure his support.[79] *The Times* of 2 December 1916 called the political crisis "The Turning-point of the War" and demanded a small cabinet that would rid the country of "worn and weary" men such as Grey, Crewe, Lansdowne, and Balfour. That day's *Daily Mail* editorial, "The Limpets, A National Danger," warned that "government by the 23 men who can never make up their minds has become a danger to the Empire."[80] Pointing to a long list of failures, the paper called for "idle septuagenarians" like Balfour and Lansdowne, as well as "semi-invalids" like Grey, to be replaced.[81] Another meeting between Lloyd George and Northcliffe resulted in that day's *Evening News* placards proclaiming "Lloyd George Packing Up!"[82]

To bolster Derby's questionable resolve, Northcliffe informed him that, "We are receiving some thousands of letters weekly attacking Asquith, Grey, Balfour and Co. The public see that their inaction is losing the war. Many of these letters mention your name in hope ... with it those of Lloyd George and Carson and also — if I may say so with modesty — with mine, though I have no intention of leaving my printing presses for office."[83] Derby invited Northcliffe to come around for a talk, and added that "Ll. G ... is coming here to see me first thing tomorrow, so I suppose the explosion has taken place. I had hoped the P.M. ... would have climbed down, but I suppose he has not — my course is quite clear — if Ll. G goes — I go — I back him through thick and thin — he really is out to win this war. I don't think any support of an individual in or out of Parliament is comparable to what the press can give & I am sure you will give him all the support in your power — Even if you won't — to use your own words — 'leave the printing press for office.' "[84]

On Sunday 3 December Lloyd George and Asquith met and, in Lloyd George's view at least, came to a suitable agreement about a small War Committee. Unlike Northcliffe, the Welshman did not wish Asquith to resign. That day's *Weekly Dispatch* revealed "Mr. Lloyd George's Proposal for a Small War Council," the interviews and meetings of the day before, and the positions of Asquith, Balfour, and Bonar Law. Cecil Harmsworth recorded in his diary of 3 December that "Alfred has been actively at work with Ll.G. with a view to bringing a change."[85]

Other newspapers may have been better informed in the first week of December, but none carried the weight of *The Times*, whose editorial of the 4th, "Towards Reconstruction," contained delicate information that seemed to point to Lloyd George as the source. This was widely believed to have been written by Northcliffe, but was actually penned by Geoffrey Robinson with information from Carson.[86] Regardless, Northcliffe must have seen and approved it in advance. Both men feared a patched-up settlement that would leave Asquith in place. *The Times* disclosure, written with what has been called a "calculated offensiveness," discussed the ongoing negotiations and revealed the prime minister's capitulation, in the face of "Mr. Lloyd George's stand," to create a small War Council.[87] According to *The Times*, Asquith was to be reduced to figurehead status. Infuriated, the prime minister wrote to Lloyd George that "Such productions as the first leading article in today's 'Times,' showing the infinite possibilities for misunderstanding and misrepresentation of such an arrangement as we discussed yesterday, make me at least doubtful of its feasibility. Unless the impression is at once corrected that I am being relegated to the position of an irresponsible spectator of the War, I cannot go on."[88] Lloyd George's response was conciliatory: "I have not seen the 'Times' article. But I hope you will not attach undue importance to these effusions. I have had these misrepresentations to put up with for months. Northcliffe frankly wants a smash. Derby and I do not. Northcliffe would like to make this or any other arrangement under your Premiership impossible. Derby and I attach great importance to your retaining your present position — effectively. I cannot restrain, nor I fear influence Northcliffe."[89]

After consulting with Reginald McKenna and others hostile to Lloyd George, the prime minister decided to test his strength by attempting to reconstruct the government, rather than give in to the Welshman's demands. Before Asquith called on the king, Edwin Montagu, the minister of munitions, found him very angry about the "Northcliffe article."[90] Montagu had seen the press lord at the War Office the day before *The Times* assault, assumed he had gotten the information from Lloyd George, and almost certainly shared this with the prime minister.[91] He urged Asquith "not to be put off by the Northcliffe article; he had never paid any attention to newspapers, why should he give up now because of Northcliffe?" Asquith replied that it was because the article "showed quite clearly the spirit in which the arrangement was going to be worked by its authors."[92] On 5 December Montagu again pleaded with the prime minister not to give a victory to Northcliffe. He listed three factors that had led to Asquith's changed position. First was Northcliffe and *The Times* article; then the advice of McKenna, Runciman, and Grey; and, finally, disagreements with Lloyd George as to personnel — particularly Carson. About Northcliffe he wrote,

> It is lamentable to think that you should let him achieve the victory that he has long sought. He wanted to drive you out; he alone is fool enough not to believe in you. His efforts were resisted by Lloyd George, by Bonar Law, by Derby, by Carson, by Robertson. Using information that he had no right to obtain, he sees a chance of success, takes it and is successful. He published that article to wreck the arrangement and you have had to let him do it. I do not say that this was avoidable, but I say that his personal victory in this matter is a matter of the deepest possible chagrin to me.[93]

The plea continued, "Lloyd George sent for me this afternoon and I spent some time with him... he wanted to work with you. He did not want a victory for Northcliffe." The next day Montagu addressed a similar message to Asquith's private secretary, Maurice Bonham Carter.[94]

After Asquith failed at reconstruction and resigned on 5 December, the king turned first to Andrew Bonar Law, as the leader of the opposition.[95] When this attempt failed, Lloyd George, who had overcome his own reluctance in the face of Asquith's affronted change of heart, began negotiations with the disparate political groupings whose support was needed to form a government. *The Times* described the situation as being "in the melting pot."[96] Robinson recorded in his diary that during a visit to the War Office he found Derby wavering and Lloyd George "asked me if I saw Northcliffe to convey to him that it did not help him when the Daily Mail and the Evening News assumed too intimate a knowledge of his actions and intentions. Also that too much vituperation of individuals was not so useful as insistence that the whole system of Government was unsound and could not win the war."[97]

Despite the Welshman's plea, the *Daily Mail* of 6 December 1916 described the outgoing government as "The Haldane Gang" and recommended that the country "Let Them All Go!" Other headlines applauded Lloyd George for his stand against "A Torn Up Promise" and for fighting until he got his War Council. The "Germans Fear Mr. Lloyd George, The Allies Like Him," and "The Empire Trusts Him," proclaimed the *Daily Mail*.

That day's *Evening News* also declared "The End of the Haldane Gang." Cecil Harmsworth recorded on 6 December that "the London Liberal daily papers are full of denunciations of Northcliffe, whom they regard as the arch-wrecker of the Asquith Govt. There is truth in this of course, but not all the truth."[98]

A. G. Gardiner's *Daily News* and other Liberal journals trumpeted warnings of Northcliffe's evil influence from the beginning of the cabinet crisis. The 2 December edition foresaw doom for "any Government which lives by the sanction of a press dictator." On the 5th it stated that the enemy was "looking for a rupture not less cheerfully than Lord Northcliffe is working for one, and if that gentleman were the ally of the enemy he could not be doing more priceless service to them than he is doing at this moment." A 7 December *Daily Chronicle* article, "The Press Vendetta, Tyranny and Torture," claimed Asquith had been too lenient in allowing the yellow press to attack him and his allies and now, the "new Ministry, however constituted, will have to deal with the Press menace as well as the submarine menace; otherwise Ministries will be subject to tyranny and torture by daily attacks impugning their patriotism and earnestness to win the war."

While this war of headlines was carried out, the political negotiations continued. In Northcliffe's view, the Foreign Office and its blockade policy were especially in need of new leadership. He was disturbed to hear that Arthur Balfour might be removed from the Admiralty—only to be made foreign secretary. The *Daily Mail* and the *Evening News* called for the exclusion of Balfour and his cousin, Robert Cecil, from the new government.[99] Robinson recalled a conversation with Lloyd George about his efforts to form a new government. "Pointing to the placards about 'A Bad Balfour Rumour' which the Evening News was already displaying in Whitehall, he said that Northcliffe really must give him a chance. He had great difficulties in forming a Government at all. Northcliffe had always purported to believe that he, L.G., was the man to run the war, and he must let him do it in his own way. It would be time to speak if the thing was a failure after six months."[100] The press campaign failed. Lloyd George needed Balfour to cement Unionist support, and he accepted the Foreign Office. Robert Cecil remained in place as under-secretary and blockade minister. The press lord, however, was not completely without influence in the construction of the new government. He was instrumental in ensuring that the businessman Sir Albert Stanley was appointed to the Board of Trade.[101] Northcliffe also aided Lord Devonport in attaining the new position of Food Controller.[102] The historian Alfred Gollin viewed Milner's inclusion in the War cabinet as, in part, a friendly gesture to the press lord.[103]

In order to form a government, it was necessary for Lloyd George to give assurances concerning his relationship with Northcliffe. He promised the

Unionists on 7 December that the press lord (and Churchill) would not be included.[104] One of Lloyd George's pledges to a Labour party delegation was that he and his government would not give large newspapers preferential treatment and that he would treat "Lord Northcliffe in exactly the same way as he would treat a labourer."[105] The Liberal home secretary, Herbert Samuel, recorded in his diary of 7 December that he visited Lloyd George at the War Office and declined a request to continue as home secretary. During this meeting, Lloyd George blamed McKenna and Northcliffe, "each in his own way, as responsible for this smash."[106] On 7 December Lloyd George became prime minister and the next day moved to 10 Downing Street. The new five-member War Cabinet included the prime minister, Lords Milner and Curzon, Bonar Law, and Arthur Henderson (Labour).

Despite Northcliffe's repeated protestations that he did not choose to become a minister (including a 7 December *New York Times* interview in which he defended his own course and stated he would not join the cabinet), his considerable vanity must have been wounded when Lloyd George did not at least offer him a place in the government that he believed he had helped to make possible. He was also undoubtedly informed of the promises concerning him that Lloyd George had made to the Unionists and to Labour. In Lord Beaverbrook's account of events, when Lloyd George offered conciliation, Northcliffe declined a proposed meeting, telling Beaverbrook that "Lord Northcliffe sees no advantage in any interview between him and the Prime Minister at the present moment."[107] Damaged pride best explains his refusal. *The Times* of 8 December gave a statement that Northcliffe preferred "to sit in Printing House Square and Carmelite House." However, two days later Sir Maurice Hankey reported that, during a visit to Lloyd George's home to discuss the formation of the cabinet secretariat (which would play an important future role), he overheard the new prime minister in "a long talk on the telephone with Lord Northcliffe, whom he seems to funk."[108] Whether flea or grasshopper, Northcliffe remained too important to ignore.

Asquith gave a speech to a Liberal party meeting at the Reform Club on 8 December in which he commented on his reasons for resigning and revealed his bitterness toward the press.[109] He openly admitted that *The Times* article of 4 December was a precipitating factor. Strachey commented to Margot Asquith that her husband's

speech at the Reform Club meeting was splendid on the side of magnanimity, but...I think he made a very great mistake in letting the world know, even though it was true, that what determined his action was the leading article in the "Times." Honestly that does not seem to me to be the way to keep the Harmsworth Press or newspapers in general in order.

There is nothing that a newspaper likes so much as to be told that it had brought down a powerful Ministry. It feeds its vanity, and what is worse, gives the public in general a wholly exaggerated belief in its powers. What . . . Northcliffe wants above all things is to create prestige for himself and his papers and to make himself dreaded by politicians. . . . There was always danger from this kind of attitude and it has been increased a hundred-fold by recent events. I hear whispers of the Harmsworth "terror" on all sides.[110]

The 9 December *Daily Mail* proclaimed the new government "A Ministry of Action At Last" and reveled in "The Passing of the Failures." A page of photographs showed the outgoing ministers with accompanying captions across their chests, including Asquith ("Wait and See"), Grey ("Belgium, Serbia, Bulgaria, Greece, Rumania"), and McKenna ("German Banks Still 'Winding Up'"). Though Sir John Simon had left office over conscription in early 1916, he was also displayed with a "No Compulsion, Down with Daily Mail" slogan. Haldane ("My Spiritual Home Is Germany") and Churchill ("Antwerp & Gallipoli") were also presented. Northcliffe ordered this feature and congratulated the newspaper's picture department, with which he was often at loggerheads, on the results.[111]

The 9 December *Daily News* countered that the country must choose between newspaper "Placards or Parliament." Gardiner commented, however, that there was

> one advantage which Mr. Lloyd George's Government will have over its predecessor. It will be subject to a friendly organized and responsible criticism which will aim at sustaining it and not destroying it. The fall of the late Government and most of its failure were due to the absence of such a criticism. It became the target . . . of a ruthless and uncritical press campaign which appealed directly to the passions of the mob against the authority of Parliament. . . .
>
> I see that in the "Times" yesterday it was announced that Lord Northcliffe preferred sitting in Carmelite House and Printing House Square to sitting in the Cabinet. Mr. George knows what that statement means. The country knows too. It means that having destroyed one Government Lord Northcliffe is going to exercise the powers of a dictator over its successor. Let that threat be dealt with at once. If it is not, if the real power is not in the Cabinet, but in Carmelite House, this country is lost.

For once Gardiner was partly correct. Northcliffe was ready to aid, at least the new men in the government. He instructed his employees at Printing

House Square, "We must do our best to get the new ministers known, and thus strengthen their position in the country."[112] How long the press lord would continue his support became the question.

The members of the new British government found themselves promptly barraged with advice from Carmelite House. Northcliffe wrote Sir Albert Stanley at the Board of Trade recommending men of business like Alfred Butt, who was "trained by Sir Richard Burbidge of Harrods and now runs 22 music Halls," and Claude Johnson of Rolls Royce, a "fine organizer."[113] He also volunteered to give up any of his own people that Stanley might want. Northcliffe congratulated Carson for taking the Admiralty, writing, "I was told by telephone yesterday from the War Office that you had again sacrificed yourself and taken charge of the Admiralty. I have been a little overworked lately, but the news has come as a tonic and I feel ten years younger since I heard it."[114] His letter then proceeded to give a lecture on the blockade, attacking the slackness of the Admiralty and the paucity of ships used, the interference of the Foreign Office, and the tricks of the Prussian officials in the United States in providing blockade-runners with false papers.[115] The new prime minister also received advice for his first policy address:

Here is another suggestion with which to spoil your speech to-morrow.

I suggest a short, affectionate, direct message to the men in the trenches at all the fronts: to the armies behind the armies: to men of the Grand Fleet, and destroyers, trawlers and mine sweepers: to the doctors and nurses, and others who will occur to you.

I suggest something that would be a direct link between the Prime Minister and these people—something so crystallized that it can be used over and over again in English, French, Australian, Canadian, New Zealand, South African and home papers, not, of course, forgetting the munition workers of both sexes.[116]

The *Daily Mail* applauded Lloyd George's House of Commons address the next day which proclaimed that, before there could be peace, Prussian militarism must be destroyed, and pledged to mobilize the nation under Neville Chamberlain, the new director of National Service.

Northcliffe's enemies feared his influence on Lloyd George. Strachey attempted to alienate the two in his *Spectator* articles. He wrote to Mrs. Asquith: "My great desire, though I admit it is a rather hopeless task, is to free Lloyd George from the Northcliffe influence, which I think thoroughly injurious. I tried…to drive a wedge between Northcliffe and Lloyd George by praising Lloyd George for his courage in standing up to Northcliffe in regard to Balfour and Bob Cecil, and I am sure I was right in doing so. That, however, was not a popular thing to do with either the Lloyd Georgeites or the North-cliffites.... one may be pretty sure one is right if one gets abuse and has made enemies of both sets of combatants."[117]

On 10 December the *Weekly Dispatch* published Northcliffe's United Press article, "Fashioning the New England," printed worldwide.[118] In this piece, the press lord reviewed the progress of the war and roundly praised Lloyd George for his courage, even though he admitted the two had often been on opposite sides of vital issues. The article described the Welshman as a "human dynamo" whose "every erg of energy is focused on the immediate task at hand. He combines the persuasiveness of the Irishman with the concentration of the American and the thoroughness of the Englishman." For this occasion, Northcliffe broke his own rule about newspaper prophecy. To those who asserted that the new government and Lloyd George would not last, he declared, "I believe that he will be at the head of the Government that wins the war: that brings a settlement of the Irish question and maintains that essential factor goodwill between the people of the English speaking nations of the British Empire and the people of the United States."

Across the Atlantic, the newly re-elected Wilson administration watched the December political upheaval in Britain with dismay. The 1916 presidential election had been won with a pledge to keep America out of the war. Sentiment coincided most closely with the Liberalism of Asquith and Sir Edward Grey, not Lloyd George, who was considered a reactionary.[119] Colonel House, Wilson's close advisor and his agent for peace negotiations, wrote to the president that he was watching British developments closely and predicted that if the "Lloyd-George-Northcliffe-Carson combination succeed in overthrowing the Government and getting control," England then would be under "a military dictatorship" and there "will be no chance for peace until they run their course."[120] Nevertheless, Wilson continued his attempts. In response to a tentative German peace move, the American secretary of state, Robert Lansing, sent identical notes to Britain and Germany asking them to state their war aims.

Northcliffe found the prospect of a negotiated peace unthinkable, but not wishing to offend Wilson, he tempered the response of his newspapers. The 22 December 1916 "Message from the Chief" remarked that the "only criticism I make is that President Wilson's note was not leaded....The note was the most important thing in the paper."[121] The same day, the American ambassador in London, Walter Hines Page, wrote to Lansing that the British felt the struggle was "a holy and defensive war which must be fought to a decisive conclusion to save free government in the world" and that they were angry because the note seemed to place the Allies and the central powers "on the same moral level."[122] He went on that Northcliffe had assured him that his papers would continue to say "as little as possible," but that "the people are mad as hell." The press lord advised Lloyd George that the "delay in the British reply to Wilson is all to the advantage of Germany."[123] In 1917, the Welshman ensured that Northcliffe would have an opportunity to directly affect Anglo-American relations.

Since December 1916 (and particularly since Lord Beaverbrook published his 1932 account of the fall of Asquith) many participants and commentators have offered their opinions of the role of the press and of Northcliffe in the episode.[124] These have ranged from a complete disregard for newspaper influence, to those Liberals and supporters of Asquith who saw a conspiracy between Lloyd George and Northcliffe that overthrew the Government. Although Beaverbrook denied that Lloyd George gave any detailed information to Northcliffe in visits to the War Office in the first days of December, he did, however, admit the press lord's "great influence ... on the development of events ... in denouncing the inefficiency of the Asquith Government and in interpreting and focusing the popular judgment in this matter."[125] The former head of the Press Bureau and lord chancellor, Lord Buckmaster, hardly an admirer of Northcliffe, was one of those who felt that the press, and particularly the owner of the *Daily Mail,* contributed substantially to the fall of Asquith.[126] In his judgment, the press lord was being protected by forces within the government from the time of the Shells Scandal and after:

> It was plain during the whole of the time of my control of the Press Bureau that many of the more powerful newspapers had support and encouragement from within the Government which rendered the proper execution of my duties extremely difficult. On more than one occasion, when strong measures should have been taken with newspapers like the "Times" and the "Daily Mail," my efforts to exercise against them the powers conferred by the Defence of the Realm Act were defeated from within.... it was plain that there were people anxious to secure newspaper support.... I believe this immunity which papers controlled by Lord Northcliffe, by some means or other, contrived to obtain was a prominent factor in the aggregate of events which produced the final catastrophe.[127]

More recently, J. M. McEwen has correctly pointed out that it was not only the Northcliffe and the Conservative press that attacked Asquith in December 1916—his former staunch Liberal supporters had largely deserted him as well.[128] McEwen concluded that it is "doubtful" Lloyd George would have become Prime Minister when he did, in December 1916, without the aid of the press.[129]

From the evidence it appears that Northcliffe and his newspapers should be given more credit than they have generally received for the demise of the Asquith government in December 1916. Whether or not the press lord wrote *The Times* article of 4 December, which triggered Asquith's reneging on his agreement with Lloyd George, the belief of Northcliffe's involvement proved decisive. Asquith's anger over the supposed collusion with Northcliffe combined with Reginald McKenna's advice to provoke the prime minister to fight the humiliating terms Lloyd George presented. Perhaps in his Reform Club speech a few days after he left office, Asquith used Northcliffe as a convenient excuse to cover his own political miscalculations; however, as Strachey noted at the time, it was an unwise admission of the press lord's power.

In the longer view, more important than *The Times* piece was the eighteen-month campaign the Northcliffe press had carried out against the government, practically acting as the opposition since the spring 1915 shells agitation. Unlike the many voices that deserted Asquith only at the end, their condemnations in early December were only marginally more strident than they had been since early in the war. The cumulative effect of Northcliffe's personal and newspaper campaign against the government helped to wear down Asquith's resistance and left him a bitter man. Asquith's refusal either to compromise with Northcliffe (as Lloyd George did) or to have the government muzzle his attacks finally cost him. The failed Somme campaign and the unrest among the Conservatives forced the politicians to act at last, as had similar forces in May 1915 when the coalition government was formed. The most remarkable attribute of the Asquith coalition may not be that it fell in December 1916, but that it lasted as long as it did.

At the end of 1916, Northcliffe had more reason to be pleased than at any time since August 1914. At long last Asquith and most of his muddling cronies had been toppled. The dynamic Lloyd George now led a small War Cabinet that promised to get on with the war in an efficient and energetic manner. The press lord felt himself to be at the height of his power and influence, and many others saw him as Lloyd George's political godfather. A few days before Christmas, Valentine Williams sent a note. "You have gone another stage forward with the war since I saw you last and I think it will probably prove the most important—Mr. Asquith's head on a plate is the most acceptable Christmas present you could have given the Empire!"[30] If there were remaining problems, such as the survival of a few political leftovers like A. J. Balfour and Robert Cecil, these could all be dealt with in 1917. The important thing was to support the army and win the war. Unfortunately, the new year would not progress very far before Northcliffe once again found himself in conflict with his government and its leader, Lloyd George.

SEVEN

"To Tell the People of America the Truth"
The United States Enters the War,
January to May 1917

TWO AND A HALF YEARS OF WAR HAD MADE CONDITIONS IN BRITAIN increasingly grim. The war effort, combined with German submarine activity, brought severe shortages. Food supplies were seriously endangered. Britain's financial reserves had also reached precarious depths. The military leadership came under increased criticism as well—the Admiralty for its submarine and blockade policies and the army for the horrendous casualty toll and its perceived failure to use the civilian talent that now made up the bulk of its men. By 1917 few families were left untouched by the loss of a loved one. However, the increased German submarine activity had one positive effect from the British point of view. Germany's response to President Wilson's request for war aims at the end of 1916 (made to the British as well) was a statement that neutral mediation was not required and a declaration soon after that on 1 February 1917 all vessels bound for Britain would be subject to unrestricted submarine attack.[1] Unless Germany relented, America's full-fledged entrance into the war seemed certain.

The most immediate problems for Britain were food and finance. The 9 January *Daily Mail* described the "Food Crisis" as yet another legacy of the "wait and see" Asquith government. Northcliffe urged Lord Devonport, the food controller, to implement strict rationing. According to private information he had from Germany, the press lord reported to Devonport that the submarine campaign would increase greatly as soon as the enemy could get their latest submarines, being built all over Germany, into the water. He also had information from the United States that the movement in favor of a food embargo was growing. This would mean that the army in France would not be properly fed, and, he told the food controller, "improperly fed soldiers cannot fight. Surely we should stop the consumption of meat at once, so that this awful possibility will be avoided."[2] Northcliffe was concerned that Sir Edward Carson was not keeping Devonport up-to-date on the submarine sinkings, which, he warned, "have so much to do with your work."[3] The *Daily Mail* regularly addressed the food issue, but not always as seriously as its owner wished. The 6 February "Message From the Chief" noted that the paper, "was good today, but I am not throwing any bouquets at it on its handling of the food question. Food and the loan are the two most important things of our time. Even now the public do not seem to realize that the British and German empires are involved in a starving match."[4] Concerning the latest War Loan, Northcliffe told Sir George Riddell that he believed the "arrangements for raising the loan had been mismanaged."[5] He predicted further that "unless L. G. displays greater powers of organization he will be displaced before the war ends."

The press lord passed along to Bonar Law, now chancellor of the exchequer, a scheme for raising funds by Alfred Butt, who was aiding Lord Devonport.[6] Since Kennedy Jones had done such a good job publicizing the previous War Loan, Northcliffe suggested to the chancellor that he head a Bonus Bonds organization with bonds to be sold by any shopkeeper.[7] Bonar Law responded that he thought "the public & the Press need a breathing space," but that he was very much obliged "for consistent & most powerful support which you gave to the loans."[8] Northcliffe's enemies noted his efforts. In "The Loan and the Mobocracy," the 17 February *Daily News* warned,

No one can be indifferent to the attempt which is being made to set up a mob dictatorship over Parliament and to drive every self-respecting man out of public life....
   The object is to destroy the authority and power of Parliament.... as for the House of Lords, Lord Northcliffe has made only one speech in it and he is not likely to repeat the experiment. He has no use for Parliament and is leading the mob against that institution. He is engaged in establishing government by the Press. That is the instrument which will make him master of our destinies.... But to accomplish his purpose Lord Northcliffe must get rid of the men who represent the dignity and authority of Parliament in the public mind. Hence this avalanche of vulgarity and insult.

Though Northcliffe protested again and again that he did not want government office, the calls for him to serve continued. Some even prophesied that he would lead. Hedley Le Bas predicted that, "before the end of the year I am convinced you will have taken up your abode in Downing street. I find the members of the new government are very unhappy and I am sure they are going to have a short life."[9] "Heaven forbid that I should ever be in Downing street," Northcliffe answered. "I believe the independent newspaper to be one of the future forms of government. Some of my friends say it is not a responsible method... to rule. Let them try newspaper ownership and find out."[10] His letter to Le Bas also touched on propaganda in America, a constant subject. He told Le Bas, "I expressed my views on the propaganda, which you will see in the 'Daily Mail' tomorrow morning, called 'Make it Simple.'"

With America believed to be on the verge of joining the Allied cause, propaganda in the United States came to the fore in early 1917.[11] From August 1914 until the United States joined the war in April 1917, the British and the Germans were locked in a propaganda duel over American opinion.[12] British efforts since September 1914 had concentrated on counteracting German publicity, with the aim of ensuring America's continued sympathy for the Allies. Charles Masterman was appointed director of the War Propaganda Bureau at Wellington House in London. He brought together there an impressive array of British writers and journalists. The Masterman bureau aimed its literate, low-key, and covert efforts at the American elite, mainly on the East Coast. Sir Gilbert Parker, a well-known author of the time, directed the effort aimed at the United States. Northcliffe believed the British preached to the converted and that the mass public had been dangerously overlooked. He also had an understandable prejudice toward newspaper propaganda that Masterman and Parker did not share.[13] If the United States joined the war, a different sort of British appeal would be needed, one that would ensure that the British received their fair share of American aid and would help to mobilize the new partner for the struggle.

The British ambassador to the United States, Sir Cecil Spring Rice, a diplomat of the old aristocratic school, considered it likely that his country would send another representative to explain the position of the Allies. His greatest fear was that this would be Northcliffe, the "incarnation of all he disliked in the twentieth century."[14] Spring Rice also believed that, at its chief proprietor's direction, *The Times* had printed a personal attack on him.[15] Colonel House, Woodrow Wilson's close advisor, had met Northcliffe and been entertained at Sutton Place during his trips to Europe on the president's behalf. House recorded that when Spring Rice called for lunch on 2 January he was "disturbed over the thought of the British Government sending someone to this country to explain the views of the Allies. He said it must necessarily be an Englishman because the French spoke the language so indifferently. Northcliffe, he thought, would be an impossibility because among other objections he had 'brain storms.' Northcliffe would be glad to hear this — for it is the brain storms that Spring Rice is subject to that make Northcliffe so antagonistic."[16] Spring Rice suggested Asquith or Lord Bryce for the job, to which House answered that he saw no need for anyone at present. House also noted that Frank Polk, the counselor of the American state department, thought well of Northcliffe coming over, or "anybody who could take back word of the pro-ally feeling in this country, thereby setting England right."[17]

The press lord received complaints from the United States concerning the British ambassador, and there were rumblings in early 1917 for Spring Rice's recall. However, some in America, such as the prominent Chicago businessman Samuel Insull, feared the action might be regarded as a propaganda victory for the Germans.[18] At the Foreign Office, Robert Cecil agreed with Insull (whose telegram Northcliffe had sent him). Cecil commented to the press lord that Spring Rice got mixed opinions but that he "has some great merits" and "is also very impressed with the great danger that … a British Ambassador runs if he appears to interfere at all in domestic American matters."[19] House was told by his British Intelligence confidant, Sir William Wiseman, that Northcliffe, Carson, and Curzon all wanted Spring Rice removed. In a letter to the president, House admitted that Spring Rice was "temperamentally unfit," but considered him "infinitely better than any Northcliffe product that might be sent over to replace him."[20] The press lord vacillated on this issue. He told the writer Eden Philpotts that, "I get very different views from English people about our Ambassador at Washington.… what is lacking there is a propaganda department."[21]

The subject of propaganda in America consumed Northcliffe. He reported to Lloyd George the "disconcerting reading" that the last American mail had brought. He warned that steps must be taken "to hearten the pro-Allies in the United States, or we shall have a food embargo, which is what the Germans are working at. What we are winning by projectiles we look like losing by lack of propaganda."[22] He continued that the prime minister's recent interview in *Everybody's Magazine* by Isaac Marcosson, one of America's leading journalists, was "the best thing that has happened for us. It is read in every village in the United States and was immensely advertised." Northcliffe believed Marcosson's pen could benefit the army as well. He recommended to General Charteris that the journalist be invited to GHQ for an interview with Haig. The press lord hoped this would help remove from the American mind the idea that the British were looking on while the French were fighting.[23]

Frustrated with what he perceived as government bungling in America, Northcliffe dispatched Pomeroy Burton, the manager of his Associated Newspapers, on a fact-finding trip in late 1916. Burton reported back at the end of January 1917 with a scheme for war publicity in the United States.[24] Calling the whole English "so-called propaganda scheme" wrong, Burton enclosed a memo that laid out his plan for a "War Intelligence Department, Or, Special War News Service."[25] The special aim of the new department would be to perform the *"vital duty of keeping millions of neutrals correctly and promptly informed about the progress of the war*—the developments of the war to be shown in their true light, with their exact significance made clear." By utilizing the direct and improved facilities he proposed, American journalists would be able to get the facts for themselves, and, for the first time, "be able to tell the people of America the truth, and the whole truth, about the war."[26]

Northcliffe shared Burton's report with Lloyd George and Milner, who attempted to recruit the press lord's services for a propaganda department designed to coordinate the many conflicting government efforts. Unlike Asquith, Lloyd George believed that properly handled publicity could be very valuable, particularly in America.[27] Once he became prime minister, serious attempts were made for the first time to strengthen and coordinate the British propaganda effort. The writer John Buchan, who had been serving in France on Charteris' Intelligence staff, was chosen to head the new department, but only after it had been offered to several notables, very likely including Northcliffe.[28] Before Buchan's appointment became official, the press lord wrote to Lloyd George, through his secretary, J. T. Davies, that:

> unless the new department has absolute power and is responsible to the Prime Minister or Lord Milner, it will be a sheer waste of time. I should be most willing to serve under Mr. John Buchan and bring a small useful staff with me, but I suggest two things:
> (1) That the department has absolute power.
> (2) That it is not necessary to hire a Hotel for it. Four decent sized rooms in the Automobile Club would be enough for a long time.
>
> A wicked member of the Reform Club said yesterday, I understand, that the large bath at the Automobile Club would be used for the washing of all the new Government's dirty linen.[29]

Despite this offer, Northcliffe never joined Buchan's organization. He did, however, become a member of a propaganda advisory committee made up of newspaper notables, which was created at the same time to offer assistance.[30]

Buchan was made director of a new Department of Information, headquartered in the Foreign Office, on 9 February.[31] Northcliffe appeared to be pleased with the choice, notifying Charteris that the new appointment was "good news" and that Buchan "understands the Army point of view, and will, I trust, get rid of our appalling cumbersome Press Bureau."[32] Buchan was inclined to make greater use of newspapers and film than his predecessor,

Masterman, and it was a priority of his department to keep American opinion informed. He, therefore, took Northcliffe's suggestion to supply British papers to those American journals that did not already get them.[33] In addition to more news for the United States, under Buchan's direction the British also increased the scale of their effort. A British Information Bureau was set up in New York, and numbers of American newspapermen were invited to visit Britain and the front. The newly enlarged staff distributed a much larger quantity of less high-minded material than previously employed.[34]

At the same time that British propaganda was being rearranged, Lloyd George continued his struggle with the army. With Lord Derby at the War Office, military strategy remained securely in the hands of Sir Douglas Haig and Sir William Robertson. Northcliffe arrived on New Year's Day at GHQ where he met again with Haig, who repeated his argument that all possible men and material should be concentrated in France.[35] In full accord, the press lord promptly traveled to Paris, where he met with Lloyd George and Lord Milner over the matter and threatened, once again, to turn his papers against the government. While in Paris, Northcliffe also urged Clemenceau, the opposition leader, not to allow Briand, the French premier, to divert more men to the Balkans.[36] Haig recorded in his diary that he spoke to the press lord again on 5 January about the danger of Lloyd George's interference and that although Northcliffe had "much confidence in Milner and thinks he holds sound views on strategy... N. is determined to keep Lloyd George on right lines or force him to resign the Premiership."[37]

The next day the press lord revealed his doubts about Sir William Robertson to Haig, telling him, "You call him Wully. I think 'Wooly' [sic] would suit him better because he is not firm enough."[38] Haig commented in his diary following this entry that, "there seems to be some truth in this opinion because the British forces are not yet being concentrated at the decisive front, i.e., France."[39] In mid-January Northcliffe and Repington rejoiced at news from Robertson that, at the Rome Allied Conference, General Cadorna and the Italians refused to send any men to Salonika in the face of strong French pressure.[40] This, at least temporarily, halted efforts to reinforce the Balkans.

Britain's Allies were also feeling the strain of two and a half years of war. The amounts of munitions and other supplies sent to the eastern front never satisfied the Russian demands, and the British feared the defeat or withdrawal of her giant partner would free all the might of Germany to be hurled against the west. While planning was ongoing for the new propaganda department, Northcliffe told Charteris, "I have done my utmost. Ill-luck seems to drag our footsteps in as much as Lord Milner, who had the matter in hand, has gone to Russia."[41] Milner headed a mission, with Sir Henry Wilson as military representative, that traveled to Petrograd in January to appraise the deteriorating military and political situation and make recommendations to the British government as to how best to aid the troubled giant.[42] Milner's report, given to the cabinet on 6 March was pessimistic concerning both the political and administrative situations. Wilson was more optimistic in his opinion of the Russian army, but Russia refused to coordinate major military support for a proposed offensive in the west planned for 1917 under the leadership of the French commander, Robert Nivelle. Milner had not foreseen the March revolution which followed his visit by two weeks. The abdication of the czar and the rise of a provisional government, which the British immediately recognized, brought further concerns. Some British optimists hoped the revolution might bring a new efficiency to Russia, as had happened in 1790s France, but by the end of March such dreams of an improved war effort were dashed by the reality that military and industrial conditions had grown worse, not better.[43]

Robertson and Haig, never sanguine concerning the planned Nivelle offensive, felt that without Russian support such an action would be dangerous. Further, Robertson warned, in the event Russia left the war, the Allies would lose their numerical superiority and all forces would have to be concentrated in France to face Germany.[44] Whatever the doubts of his generals, Lloyd George wanted a victory before the British public wearied completely of the war. The charming and optimistic Nivelle persuaded the Welshman and his French counterparts that he had found a way to break through the German lines and secure victory. An Anglo-French offensive was planned for no later than 1 April.[45]

While this strategic debate raged, Northcliffe passed along to Haig, through Charteris who was visiting London, information about "the rising tide of criticism, due to casualties and perpetual French propaganda."[46] To counteract this, the press lord recommended to Sassoon that Marcosson be allowed to interview his chief. The owner of the *Daily Mail* had taken Marcosson to Lloyd George so that the journalist could share his views on the failure of British propaganda in America with the prime minister.[47] Northcliffe told Sassoon,

> It is an amusing sidelight on the mind of the politician that in talking with Lloyd George the other night Marcosson told the [him] that it was a great pity that the Americans knew nothing of the Chief of our Army, whereupon Lloyd George at once provided him with an introduction to Nivelle. Marcosson came to me later puzzled at the incident, and I had to explain the circumstances to him.
>
> …I am not at all anxious about the eventual result, though I am not pleased with the present situation. The internal situation of Germany, as

described to me by one of my spies who got back to England yesterday, is desperate. I am quite sure that you will begin to find a difference in the German soldiers rations.... They are writing back complaining for the first time. The soldiers in reserve are not getting anything like enough.[48]

Sassoon replied that he would ensure that Marcosson saw his chief and that he found Lloyd George giving an introduction to Nivelle "very amusing." Sassoon added that the prime minister "seems quite determined to see no good in the poor British Army! What you told me about the German rations quite confirms what we get & the fact that they have stopped all leave may well be to prevent the soldier returning to find terrible destitution in his house."[49]

At the same time, Northcliffe warned Repington about the "very dangerous" complaints being made to Parliament that the army was not properly using civilian brains.[50] The press lord was "all for stopping civilian interference with the operation of war," but he could see how the army wasted brains.[51] His own secretary, Price, who attended to what was "probably the largest and most complicated private correspondence in England," had been assigned as a junior clerk under Colonel Hutton-Wilson, "an amiable mediocrity in charge of the press arrangements in France with no knowledge whatever of the subject." The press lord feared a coming public movement that would "shake the army to its foundations, unless the brains that the country has given to the war are used."[52] However, a letter to the journalist Leo Maxse defended Haig's position, admitted the great difficulty involved in picking out talent and protested against the injustice of the "strongly growing anti-Haig party in England," stating that the commander was "paying for the blunders of his predecessors. The agitation is no longer confined to Churchill & CO., as I happen to know."[53]

Seeing "rocks ahead," the press lord sent warnings to Haig and Sassoon that listed the commonly heard grievances that civilian brains were not being used, that preference was given to regular army officers over those from the dominions, and that casualties were needlessly heavy in comparison with the French.[54] In reply, Haig sent thanks "for the very generous way you have supported me & championed the cause of the armies in France" and defended his generals, particularly Plumer.[55] The commander-in-chief called the accusations that casualties were out of proportion to the French, "based on ignorance of the facts." Far from being in the hands of the "same generals," he listed new men like Horne, Plumer, Allenby, and Gough. As to nonutilization of "civilian brains," Haig asserted that the army "really have succeeded in getting hold of a large proportion of talent," and put down the problem as "another of the penalties we have to pay for... not having had an organized

Nation before the calamity of war fell upon us!" As far as the lack of advancement for dominion soldiers, the commander claimed there were more appointments open than there were capable dominion officers to fill them. Haig concluded that the army "must expect criticism, and if it enables us to improve our arrangements I welcome it." He offered gladly to step down if there was a "great leader" to take his place; "meantime I do my best and have a clear conscience."[56]

In 1917 Northcliffe's varied activities in support of the British war effort resulted in direct enemy retaliation. On 25 February German destroyers shelled his favorite home, Elmwood, on the coast of Kent near Broadstairs. The next day's "Message from the Chief" reported:

> the paper was nearly deprived of its chief Proprietor last night—a source of mingled feelings among the staff.
> At 11.30 my house was lit up by 20 star shells from the sea, so that the place was illuminated as if by lightening. Shrapnel burst all over the place, some of it hitting the Library in which these notes are prepared every day, and killing a poor woman and baby within 50 yards of my home and badly wounding two others. The bombardment lasted from 6 to 10 minutes, according to various estimates, and was the result of a Destroyer raid. The Authorities have no doubt that my house was aimed at and the shooting was by no means bad. I understand that the destroyer was three miles out.[57]

Herbert Wilson, the chief leader writer for the *Daily Mail*, was "horrified" to learn that "what I have always dreaded had happened but that you had mercifully escaped."[58] He begged Northcliffe "not to risk your life.... The Germans know perfectly well that you are the soul and heart of this war, and that if you were put out of the way the various puppets now in office would probably run and make peace." In addition to shells, German propaganda also took aim at the press lord. He corresponded with Sir Reginald Brade at the War Office about flyers from Switzerland that solicited subscriptions for a German *Anti-Northcliffe Daily Mail*.[59]

Undaunted by the attacks of the enemy, Northcliffe continued to campaign against British waste in material and manpower. A particular target was Neville Chamberlain's National Service Department.[60] For example, a letter to Stanley called its publicity department's leaflet scheme "grossly wasteful" and "involving the use of much labour."[61] The press lord complained directly to Frederick Higginbottom, at the offending department, that offers for free advertising from periodicals, including his own Amalgamated Press, had been turned down.[62] Higginbottom replied that he had remedied the situation and had met with Northcliffe's Fleetway people, as well as representatives of other periodicals.[63]

To organize civilian workers properly, the press lord felt some manner of compulsion was needed.[64] However, Lloyd George and the war cabinet feared a repetition of the turmoil the country had suffered over military conscription and the strikes that would surely follow.[65] Chamberlain wanted his department to be the arbiter of the conflicting claims on manpower.[66] This had been part of Lloyd George's original December 1916 scheme for the National Service Department, but the military refused to cooperate with any plans that would divert men from the fighting. The Department was also soon in conflict with the ministry of munitions. The prime minister, busy with other concerns, did not press the issue. Chamberlain felt he had been betrayed, and left without instructions, organization, or authority to carry out his job.[67]

To make matters worse for the director-general of National Service, the Northcliffe newspapers cried out for compulsion and battered his department and his leadership unmercifully. For example, the 8 March *Daily Mail* editorial, "Muddled National Service," protested the chaos at the organization. The Chamberlain family rallied to Neville's defense. In a letter to their sister, Hilda, brother Austen repeated a friend's description of Northcliffe as a "foxy toad," which he found "a terrific combination of abusive epithets."[68] In Neville Chamberlain's view, the otherwise inexplicable Northcliffe vendetta arose from the ongoing quarrel between the press lord and the prime minister over compulsion.

Numerous complaints about Chamberlain were lodged with the prime minister by the press lord through Lloyd George's secretary, J. T. Davies, and also through Riddell. Northcliffe warned Davies that it was "worth going into these matters, because they are the cause of grumbling about the Manpower Department, which the Asquithians hope will bring down the Government. I know nothing of Mr. Chamberlain: the only things of his that have come to my notice have been blunders."[69] He wrote Riddell, who had the prime minister's ear,

> I am beginning to think that the man who is going to drag him down is Mr. Neville Chamberlain....
>
> You are, I am sure, as interested as I am in seeing that our Prime Minister remain where he is. I cannot believe that he will survive with Muddled Man Power ... a thing that affects every household in the country, and we are snowed under with complaints ... which, out of our desire to support the new Government, we are not printing.

My people say that I have the faculty of finding out the weak spot in organizing. Mr. Neville Chamberlain's department is at present a very weak spot.[70]

The press lord also asked Davies to arrange a meeting with the Welshman to give him news about "a good many of the prevalent muddles—the things that breed discontent and eventually bring down Governments. Many of them can be put right very simply."[71]

In late March, Northcliffe again warned Lloyd George of "the great pool of labour now being formed by Mr. Chamberlain, apparently with the object of drowning the Government."[72] A few days later, the 2 April *Daily Mail* announced that the government had appointed Lord Milner and Arthur Henderson to a "strong Committee" to look into National Service. That day's editorial, "High Time for an Enquiry," noted that after three months of "card-indexing, typewriting and advertisement the mountain of officialdom" at the department had produced a "very insignificant mouse."

An April article in Rothermere's *Sunday Pictorial* called for Northcliffe to take over National Service. Lord Cowdray, who had recently been named president of the Air Board, assumed the press lord would soon replace Chamberlain. He sent a message to Northcliffe that he hoped the new post would not require all his time and that he could still lend a hand in air matters.[73] Northcliffe replied that he "had nothing to do with the little leading article.... I do not believe the matter can be put right without compulsory powers, limited only by the authority of the War Cabinet. The delay is making the matter more and more contentious, as I can see by reading reports of meetings of workers throughout the country."[74] Unable to come to an understanding with Lloyd George, or quell the criticism of the Northcliffe press, Chamberlain left his post in August. He returned to Birmingham nursing a bitter hatred of both men.[75]

The shortages that struck the nation in 1917 included newsprint. After the February 1917 War Loan drive, Northcliffe complained to Sir Albert Stanley at the Board of Trade about the unnecessary waste of tons of paper by huge government posters and newspaper advertisements.[76] He suggested to Sir George Riddell that they approach Lloyd George together about the paper problem.[77] He also came into conflict with other newspaper proprietors over the issue. Waldorf Astor's *Observer* proposed the confiscation of paper stocks by the government. At a 2 March conference between a number of proprietors and Stanley to discuss the issue, Northcliffe reported to *The Times* employees that even the Liberal "Mr. Cadbury…was opposed to Colonel Astor's suggestion for the confiscation of paper stocks, and remarks were made about Astor wealth."[78] The government had contemplated confiscation, but the meeting stopped the plan. Lloyd George sent his personal assurance that "nothing more would be done."

Nevertheless, the Northcliffe press was forced to cut back further on the size of its publications and to raise prices. The chief proprietor of *The Times* warned that "not an ounce of paper has reached this country for three weeks. We are all living on the small supplies within the country. Nor is there any chance of paper coming in as the Germans are deliberately trying to destroy the British Press by sinking every boat containing Norwegian pulp and paper."[79] The 5 March *Daily Mail* editorial, "The Paper Crisis," regretted the lost readers due to the half-pence price increase and asked its customers to share with their friends. Northcliffe informed Stanley that, to aid the paper stocks problem, the *Daily Mail* was initiating a new "no returns" policy.[80] All of his newspapers were instructed to use greater brevity, smaller type, and to save space whenever possible.[81]

Lord Devonport's efforts to control the waste of food also displeased Northcliffe, who had been instrumental in his appointment. The 28 February *Daily Mail* called for action by Devonport and insisted that stricter rationing was wanted. For publicity, the press lord suggested using periodicals. He wrote one of the food controller's deputies, Winton Thorpe, that "Lord Devonport can get his orders carried out by housewives throughout the country without compulsion, food tickets or any other form... by using the domestic periodicals which have for years given recipes every week. The thing could be organized very simply, and without any expense to the government, whose wasteful advertising in other departments amounts to a scandal."[82] Northcliffe continued that the "sale of these periodicals amounts to millions, and they are also passed from hand to hand." He urged Thorpe to see George Sutton, the manager of Northcliffe's Amalgamated Press, on the subject "and get the thing done." The press lord wrote directly to Devonport that he hoped he would not mind "a candid friend saying that the lack of action in your department is causing criticism throughout the country very damaging to the Government.... If you could but realize how anxious the whole of Great Britain is to be ordered to do things, I am sure you would be drastic.... Sir Edward Carson told me that the navy cannot protect the public's food."[83] The 23 March *Daily Mail* gave a grave food warning in a full-page headline that "No One Must Buy More Than 14 Day's Food." The next day's headline warned that there would be a "Shilling Loaf on Monday."[84] Press criticism, particularly by Northcliffe, stung Devonport. He told the American journalist Marcosson during an after-dinner conversation that his friend Northcliffe was a "strange person. He got me into the Cabinet and now he is moving heaven and earth to get me out."[85] When told of this, the press lord remarked that "Devonport seemed to have lost all his business sense the moment he got into the Cabinet."[86]

Public criticism of the Admiralty mounted because of the food shortages and other hardships caused by the German submarine blockade. Northcliffe told Sassoon that the "public is already crying out for a change at the Admiralty... though I am sure that the Navy and Carson are doing their utmost, but democracies are fickle things — bad to go to war with, and when a war has been on for a long time and every family has lost a relation, food doubled in price, businesses closing down every day, food restrictions, and taxation enormous, the democracy naturally spends most of its time criticising."[87] Admiralty censors killed a *Daily Mail* story on the use of decoy vessels, Britain's most effective antisubmarine weapon. Northcliffe sent the piece to Carson and warned, "It is possible that if the public do not hear more about the Navy they will demand unwise changes.... Such narratives are in the nature of advertisements of the Navy, of which we hear so little. Out of sight, out of mind."[88] Though Carson was sympathetic, he replied that there were "some things that if published would help the enemy, and perhaps the most important of these is our use of 'decoy' vessels of all kinds.... the First Sea Lord and the war staff regard it as vital that the doings of these... should be kept as secret as possible."[89] However harmless the narrative seemed, Carson continued, "the details it contains would be of immense value to the commanders of enemy submarines, and would give them an insight into our methods which would go far in increasing our difficulties — already so grave." On 8 March the press lord presided at an Aldwych Club luncheon at which Carson spoke about the submarine problem.[90] Commenting on the gathering, Lord Fisher, the former First Sea Lord, told Lord Lambert that "Northcliffe has fixed on Carson as his new Prime Minister judging from his effusive praise of Carson at Aldwych."[91] The press lord had tired of Fisher's refusal to make public his criticisms, and the *Daily Mail* reflected his annoyance from early 1917. Lord Fisher noted in his letter to Lambert that the paper recommended that he should never be allowed office again.

When German aeroplanes dropped bombs at Broadstairs, near Northcliffe's home in the Isle of Thanet, he wrote to Carson about the raids, which had driven people away:

I am not an amateur strategist, but I do understand something about Air work, and was for some years hammering the aeroplane at the heads of the Army and Navy, who reluctantly adopted it.

The cause of the Broadstairs raid, which has had a bad effect here... was faulty signaling. There are not enough look out points....

I watched the gradual building up of the Air Service here, and I know that it needs a shake-up in the form of an inquiry at which there are independent and non-service inquirers engaged.

It is little short of a scandal that after two and a half years an enemy aeroplane should be able to arrive here where we have probably fifty machines, on a sunny morning. The machine was undoubtedly sent for photographic purposes.[92]

Northcliffe's letter coincided with talks Carson was having with Commodore Godfrey Paine, the director of the Naval Air Service. Carson replied to the press lord that he was having his suggestions considered, but told him that, "in the judgment of my expert advisers it is almost impossible to stop a single enemy aeroplane from reaching our shores."[93] The same was true, he continued, for the Germans, who could not stop British "aeroplanes at Dunkirk from attacking Zeebrugge three or four times a week," despite powerful German antiaircraft gunnery defenses and large numbers of "aeroplanes for intercepting raiders." Carson informed Northcliffe that the bombing at Broadstairs had, in fact, been in retaliation for one of these British raids.

During a personal visit to the Admiralty over the matter, the press lord spoke to the First Sea Lord, Sir John Jellicoe, who brought Commodore Paine to hear the grievance.[94] Jellicoe gave Northcliffe a statement from Sir John French, who had been made Commander of Home Defence, that the air situation in the Isle of Thanet was satisfactory. In the version recorded by Carson's biographer, when Northcliffe confronted Paine, the "peppery" commodore replied that the "Naval Air Force was not in the business of protecting the houses of private citizens in the Isle of Thanet."[95] The press lord reported to Carson,

> You will remember that Sir John Jellicoe handed me a statement by Lord French that air matters were all right at Thanet.
>
> Remembering that Easter 1915 Lord French invited me to stay with him in BRUSSELS at Whitsuntide [7th Sunday after Easter] 1915, I do not place too much reliance on his statements.
>
> The matter about which I spoke is one that I thoroughly understand, and I know that Sir John Jellicoe is wrong. I hope that he is not misleading you on other matters....
>
> I hope that you will not think that I am trying to teach my grandmother to suck eggs, but watching events in a very tiny part of our sphere of naval operations for two and a half years, I have never seen any sign of prevision....

I do hope that you will not mind my frankness, but I do not suppose that you are aware of the amount of gossip that is going on about the navy generally.[96]

Carson responded angrily that, "I do not like it to be suggested that Sir John Jellicoe may be misleading me, as I have the most complete confidence in him." He fully realized that "there have been, and are likely to be, many misrepresentations and rumours to the detriment of the Navy, but all I can do is to satisfy myself that the naval experts here are the best I can procure & that everyone here is working to the best of his ability and of that I am certain."[97] Northcliffe was quick to explain that he did not mean to say that Jellicoe was deliberately misleading Carson, but that he was relying on French, who knew little of the matter.[98]

Northcliffe also volunteered his aerial expertise to others. He told Lord Cowdray, recently named president of the Air Board, that "I have been mixed up with aviation since its inception, and know something of the Monsters of the Aerial Deep who you will encounter in your work."[99] Cowdray gratefully accepted the offer and agreed that "No one has done more for aviation than you nor can anyone be of equal service."[100] He asked Northcliffe to act as chairman of a committee designed to look into and report on commercial aviation matters. He told the press lord that his involvement would "ensure that it did its work effectively & comprehensively. Commercial aviation would be sure of development & years of possible delay would be avoided." Replying that he was glad Cowdray had not forgotten about commercial aviation, Northcliffe told him that he would "be glad to do anything you ask me to do—especially if I may choose some of the members of the Committee myself."[101] Happy to have this pledge of help, Cowdray replied that the work would begin within two months.[102] Accordingly, in late March, the press lord assumed the chairmanship of the new Aerial Civil Transport Committee, his first official post of the war.[103] Sir Arthur Pearson, former proprietor of the *Daily Express*, sent a note of delight at hearing of Northcliffe's appointment. Pearson expressed the hope that this "first official position which you have cared to accept will...only be a prelude to others of even greater importance. I wish they would get you to settle the Irish question."[104]

In March 1917 Northcliffe took a public stand on Ireland. The visit of the Dominion prime ministers, he believed, offered an exceptional opportunity. He wrote to Geoffrey Robinson at *The Times*, "This is the golden moment for a Settlement. From a conversation with Sir Robert Borden [Canadian prime minister] at Brighton last friday night I inferred [that] the Dominion Prime Ministers over here have little to do beyond inspecting their own troops. It is a question not of weeks but of days to get this Irish Question settled."[105] At a Saint Patrick's Day speech to the pro-Nationalist Irish Club in London, the press lord revealed his proposals to "remake" the troubled isle. He told his audience that he chose to address his remarks to a club composed of those with whose political views he was not in accord because he believed it a "waste of time to talk to those with whom one agrees" and because he "was born in Ireland" and "should have some of your national pugnacity."[106] "No one whose earliest associations in life go back to a salmon leap on an Irish river," he said, "can be indifferent to the welfare of that beautiful, but badly managed country." In his opinion, Ireland was at an urgent moment in her history. All the other Allied countries were gaining a substantial war bonus in the form of industrial legislation, better economic conditions, and other benefits. He asserted that only industrialization, and the better jobs it would bring, would make a lasting settlement possible.

In the view of the press lord, there had been much "nonsense talked in the past of the non-suitability of Ireland for industrial enterprise." After studying the matter he believed the same changes could be made such as had occurred in Spain or that he had been personally associated with in his own operations in Newfoundland. "Though Ireland does not have black coal," he asked, "what about the white coal of her rivers?" He believed the "ambitious and adaptable" Irish people would work hard if given the right opportunity. Those to whom land ownership had been granted worked "with the same diligence on their farms as the French proprietor does." He saw this as abundant proof that the Irish worker, given proper incentive, would be as industrious as those Irish in the United States. Declaring himself an optimist about Ireland, Northcliffe traced the wrongs or injustices in Ireland to "the great fact that Irish industry, progress and agriculture have been sacrificed to the Free Trade principle."[107]

Turning to the question of Irish self-government, Northcliffe called "unanswerable" the argument that this department of the British government had been badly managed. Though the British system was, in his opinion, the very best in the world, in Ireland it had not been as adaptable as in other parts of the Empire and "strangely neglectful" in sharing industrial development during the war. The press lord called for a new approach, while admitting that no government would please everyone. His plan would begin with a personal investigation into Irish affairs outside the passion and discussion of "bygone" wrongs that plagued Parliament. The inquiry need not take place in Belfast or Dublin. He could suggest half a dozen quiet Irish towns where calm deliberations could be made and witnesses speedily drawn from all parts of Ireland. Northcliffe ended his talk with an entreaty to his Northern friends to consult with their countrymen and to point out to the British government that, for Ireland to play her proper role in the war, "fresh development" and "Irish happiness" were needed. Looking to the future, the press lord pointed out that, in order to appeal to the world after the war, Ireland needed to take her proper place now.

The owner of the *Daily Mail* took personal charge of his newspaper's coverage of his declaration. The journalist Michael MacDonagh was assigned to cover the event for *The Times*, and this report also appeared in the *Daily Mail*.[108] Northcliffe wrote to Geoffrey Robinson at *The Times* that "Last night I talked with a great many Irish people—mostly, of course, of the Sein Fein variety. Quite a number of them had come over specially for the meeting. They seemed to be more hostile to the Irish Members than to Carson. What took place privately was more interesting than the formal speech making. I had rather a job to get them to drink the King's toast, but, with a few exceptions the whole room rose."[109] He instructed Thomas Marlowe at the *Daily Mail*, "I am sorry to burden the Paper with the speech that I made on Saturday night but it is part of a plan that I have to try and get some sort of an Irish Settlement. I want you, therefore, to give the space to it on the Turn-Page, the report being as given by *The Times* representative, whose version I shall correct myself."[110]

Northcliffe also tried to rally the concerned politicians. The day after his speech, he advised the Irish M.P., T. P. O'Connor,

I spoke in public to some Irish people last night and in private to others.

I am bound to say I do not think that you Irish members are popular with them. I heard your company described as "saft," lazy and too fond of talking. One little group expressed the opinion that you should all be pensioned off—a remark that was received with applause!

…I mean to work as hard as I can for some sort of Settlement. Rome was not built in a day, and I can see nothing worse than the present state of affairs.

The golden days of the visit here of the Dominion Premiers are passing rapidly. They are the men who can do this thing for us.

Having taken my stand on this matter, I mean to go on with it privately, as I am not in the least desirous of placing another political personality on the back of an overburdened public.[111]

This attempt by Northcliffe to shape an Irish settlement sank below the waves as did all such wartime endeavors. It received little attention in Britain, but was noticed and applauded in the United States. Pomeroy Burton cabled that his chief's Irish statement had made a strong impression, and the 21 March 1917 *Chicago Tribune* commented:

Lord Northcliffe, before the war, had three cardinal points of opposition to the liberalizing forces in Great Britain. He was opposed to Lloyd George because Lloyd George embodies all the Liberal plans which the Tories feared—the extension of state socialism, the taxation of great fortunes and unearned increment, the nullifying of the aristocratic veto, etc.

As the most brilliant and vigorous defender of aristocratic government Northcliffe also was opposed to women's suffrage and to an Irish settlement which would do justice to the Irish.

The liberalizing effect of a democratic war, fought by the people for causes they adopt, has made Northcliffe reverse on all three issues. He made Lloyd George Prime Minister, the creation was his as near as it could be that of any one man. He may try later to unmake the present government, but the record stands now as a reverse of policy for Northcliffe.

He adopted women's suffrage because of the wonderful work of the British women for the nation, because of the way in which they came forward. If they were citizens, as they proved they were, they had to be recognized as such.

He says now something must be done for the Irish, probably not because of sentimental reasons but because the consequences of English blundering in Ireland are so sadly revealed against the consequences of British wisdom in South Africa.

War is a loss, but not a dead loss.

As it became only a matter of time until the United States joined the Allied cause over the continued German submarine campaign, Pomeroy Burton continued his publicity work in America. He sent his reports to Northcliffe and to John Buchan's Foreign Office propaganda branch. Burton wrote to his employer on 16 March that he was "convinced a hundred times over of the urgent necessity for vigorous work in this field, to make up for past neglect and to fortify our position whether the war ends soon or not."[112] He felt he had "made a very satisfactory start" and had little doubt that by the time he got back from a tour of the west he could "formulate a clear and workable plan." In his opinion, President Wilson had so far "talked much and done little, with the result that the country is totally unprepared in every direction." However, Burton reported that the "strongest executive men in the country" were already at work formulating important plans and that he had been in "conference with several of them."[113]

On 6 April 1917, mainly in response to German submarine sinkings of her merchantmen, the United States officially entered the war. Even so, the Americans were careful to designate themselves as "Associates," not Allies. The *Daily Mail* praised Wilson's 2 April War Address as "the most tremendous monument of the war" and compared it to "Lincoln's great speeches for its gravity and pathos."[114] Two days before the official declaration, Northcliffe forwarded to Lloyd George a telegram he had received from Burton with a request from Howard Coffin, of the American Council of National Defense, asking British aid in America's mobilization effort. Telling Lloyd George that Burton had gone to the United States "at the wish of the Foreign Office," Northcliffe's cover letter continued, "If speedily acted upon it will give the American government an idea of our national promptitude and also bring us all sorts of help quickly."[115] The prime minister replied the same day, that "we are sending over immediately a very strong mission to America to deal with all the subjects referred to in Mr. Pomeroy Burton's cable; but in addition to those topics we are anxious to get the American cooperation in the matter of American shipping and food supplies. I agree with Mr Burton that there is nottime [sic] to lose."[116] The mission Lloyd George mentioned was headed by Arthur Balfour.[117] Northcliffe sent the foreign secretary a congratulatory note on 5 April and, six days later, advised him that "America is a land of pitfalls for English people. Twenty-one visits have convinced me that it needs a great deal of knowing."[118] About this time, the press lord later told his wife, he refused an offer from Lloyd George to go to the United States as ambassador in place of Spring Rice.[119]

On 11 April 1917 Burton forwarded a request from the U.S. Federal Trade Commission (FTC) concerning Northcliffe's paper mills in Newfoundland. Since a recent order in council had forbidden all shipments to Europe, except food and munitions, the FTC asked if the press lord's paper supplies could be rerouted to the United States for the use of small papers throughout the country hard hit by shortages. They were prepared to pay a reasonable price and to publicize this "magnanimous act."[120] In reply, Northcliffe asked Roy Howard whether, in return, the FTC could supply coal, sulphur, and felt wires to his port of Botwood, Newfoundland. He offered to supply a large quantity of mechanical sulfide pulp and added that he had people on the spot who would be able to handle the whole transaction.[121] After some delay, Howard cabled the FTC's approval of the deal.[122] Burton also asked, for Howard Coffin, what "practical" workers were coming with Balfour, requesting their names and the war work branches they represented.[123]

Burton's wide-ranging activities in America caused confusion and criticism that was relayed to his chief. Northcliffe instructed him to confine himself to his original propaganda mission and to make any other inquiries through the Foreign Office.[124] Nevertheless, Burton continued to send requests from U.S. officials. A 17 April cable asked for information on English price controls of staples such as wheat, sugar, cotton, wool, cattle, and hogs.[125] Frustrated with his somewhat overzealous employee, Northcliffe ordered

Burton back to England after he sent his propaganda report.[126] Burton's report, dated 20 April, asserted that Wellington House and the War Office, Foreign Office, and Admiralty "might have saved a lot of money by doing nothing—the results would have been the same."[127] He also listed an impressive number of Americans, including notable writers and film stars, that had been enlisted for the British publicity effort.[128] Despite Northcliffe's order, Burton managed to remain in the United States and sent further reports in May that recorded that he had successfully put his plans into the hands of the Americans.[129]

Although heartened by the entry of the United States, Britain still faced critical problems, most prominently the worsening food situation.[130] In the face of mounting submarine losses, the food controller initiated stricter rules, to the applause of the *Daily Mail*, which called for bread rationing.[131] The newspaper described the situation as "very grave" and called for the submarines to "be dealt with as they have not yet been dealt with by the Navy."[132] It also called for food consumption to be cut down "within the strictest limits." The *Daily Mail* praised Lloyd George's speech of 27 April concerning the submarine peril and heaped blame on the "Old Gang" for their past negligence, as well as their present "mockery and jibes."

Three days after the United States joined the war, the delayed Anglo-French assault under Nivelle was launched, despite the criticism of Haig and Pétain and the fact that the Germans had withdrawn to a more defensible line. The 11 April *Daily Mail* editorial, "The Battle of Arras, Haig's Great Results," poured praise on the field-marshal for his "consummate generalship" in the new Allied offensive. However, Nivelle's strategy was soon countered by the enemy, and the push collapsed along with the fragile morale of the French army.[133]

The renewed losses caused problems in Britain as well. Northcliffe sent a warning, through Charteris, that Haig's enemies in the government were "endeavouring to turn the newspapers against him. The newspapers are under so many restrictions, chiefly at the hands of the Admiralty, that they are rather sensitive."[134] Repington wrote to Northcliffe about the army man-power problem. He had met with Robertson and General Sir Auckland Geddes, the director of recruiting at the War Office. Geddes reported that he had "only the drafts to make good the casualties of a fortnights hard fighting."[135] A few weeks later, after a tour of the front, Repington sent his chief an alarming report. "The one dominating question is that of men. Everyone of our staffs implores us to push the man-power question. We are short and we are going to be very short....We are also short of horse & many guns promised have not come, having been given away to French, Russian, Italians & so on....We seem to be doing badly with the submarines, but I suppose the navy is still sacrosanct & above all criticism."[136] Within days this final prediction would prove wrong.

Though Northcliffe had been reluctant to do so before, the unrelenting losses to the submarines and the resulting food crisis finally moved him to unleash his newspapers on the Admiralty. In May the *Daily Mail* was filled with dire warnings of the submarine menace and caustic criticism of the navy. The 2 May editorial, "Behind the Scenes at the Admiralty, Too Much Civilian Control," complained that the Admiralty was "not a Board of Strategy, but mainly a Board of Supply." The sea lords were kept too busy worrying about their own departments to spend time on larger concerns, the paper argued, and the fact that there were five civilians on the board made it practically "a branch of the Civil Service."

The paper also became increasingly strident in a series on the interrelated food problem. The 9 May editorial, "IF," repeated the call for compulsory measures and warned of Lord Devonport's "grave responsibility" if his voluntary system failed. The next day's editorial, "Hardships Yet Unknown," quoted the recent statements of several ministers, including Lloyd George and Curzon, on the peril, commenting that "wait and see had obvious dangers as a food policy."[137] Editorials in the following weeks attacked the wobbling of the food controller, called for sugar to be rationed, and asked, "When Is Lord Devonport Going to Begin?"[138] The 26 May issue identified "The Three Enemies, Hindenburg, The Submarines, and the Profiteer." The paper hailed Lloyd George's good news of improved figures in shipping losses, but noted that there were no accompanying disclosures on sinkings of enemy submarines. "To win this war," the journal continued, the "Navy has first of all to sink submarines.... Haig has meanwhile to drive Hindenburg from Northern France and Belgium," and the country had to deal with a third enemy, "not the least dangerous of all," the food profiteer.

As his newspapers opened fire on the Admiralty, Northcliffe distributed information from America to members of the government. Arthur Willert, *The Times* correspondent in Washington, cabled that Congress was procrastinating and that the executive was not yet organized or giving the necessary leadership.[139] Willert's chief passed this information along to the prime minister. The press lord also received a cable from Garet Garrett, managing editor of the *New York Tribune*, which warned that the possibility of Germany winning the war had not "penetrated" the "American intelligence."[140] To wake up the people, Garrett wished to "caste the truth upon them" and asked for Northcliffe's help to "tell us in your own forcible language" what the situation really was and "how long England can stand destruction of tonnage at this rate." Garrett asked for exact numbers, if possible, concerning how much tonnage England had left available for food importation, what her "absolute necessities" were, and "how serious your foods shortage already is." This was needed, Garrett argued, for the Americans "to understand the vital necessity of dropping everything else and attending solely to war's business." He added that "only the truth can stir us to action" and that America "must have it immediately by all means."[141] In response to this, Northcliffe notified Balfour in the United States that "American newspapers cabling me asking whether the submarine menace really serious. They state that United States cannot be impressed unless it knows the facts. Could you urge Foreign Office to allow me to give the facts which I know."[142] He then proceeded to write a series of articles for the *New York Tribune* on the lessons that America should learn from Britain's experience.

At this time, Lloyd George considered who would succeed Balfour in America. The foreign secretary recommended Sir Edward Grey. Rather than send another diplomat, the prime minister and the war cabinet were inclined to appoint a businessman to organize the British supply and financial arrangements. Robert Cecil notified Balfour in America, through his secretary, Eric Drummond, that when Grey was suggested, the war cabinet responded that a "different type of representative was required at this juncture. They are anxious to get someone who will help to organize America for war."[143] Cecil cabled further that "The Prime Minister wants to send a businessman. I believe, though he has not said so to me, that he is thinking of sending Northcliffe. I could not make myself responsible for such an appointment & if he presses it I shall tell him so & beg that he will wait for your return so you can approve it."[144] Balfour was horrified at the idea. He replied to Cecil that to "send a commercial man or Northcliffe might in my opinion have an unfortunate effect on the present and future relations of the two countries and I earnestly trust that no such decision will be taken until I have the opportunity of explaining situation here, which perhaps Cabinet hardly appreciate."[145]

Unaware of the discussions concerning him, at the end of May Northcliffe wrote to Repington that he was kept busy with his Civil Aerial Transport Committee duties.[146] At the same time, the *Daily Mail* prophesied a future "Invasion by Air" of massed German bombers, quite unlike the latest "mere baby-killing expedition."[147] However dire his newspapers made the situation seem, Northcliffe reported in a more encouraging letter to Lady Ripon that

General Pershing...will be in London next week, though this is not generally known. The first United States army will consist of 40,000 men — not much, but it is a beginning. They will join the French forces.

As for the Government, I think it is in a stronger position now than it has been for some time. Lloyd George's vitality is astonishing. As you

know, he and Lord Milner constitute the government, the rest of the cabinet being more or less ciphers as regards the war....

The submarines have not been doing well just lately—from the German point of view—that is, up to last Saturday. I have not seen the figures
since.[148]

On 29 May the Civil Aerial Transport Committee published a visionary *Private and Confidential* Memorandum (signed by Northcliffe as chairman), which
called for further study of such postwar questions as the role of the government, air mail services, aerial law, and meteorological investigations.[149]
The next day, the press lord agreed to head the British war mission to the
United States.

This appointment (and its acceptance) was not so surprising as it might
appear from first glance. Rumors had been circulating since the beginning
of the year that Northcliffe might be asked to go on some sort of American mission, and in April an offer apparently was made by the prime minister. Both men realized the extreme urgency of organizing the United States
for war, and both agreed that British publicity there must be strengthened. The prospect must have appealed to Lloyd George on several counts.
First, the press lord had the expertise needed to organize both the business
and the publicity sides of the mission. In addition, the Welshman was well
aware of Northcliffe's varied experience of the United States, his reputation
there, and his belief in its absolute importance. A final, and perhaps decisive,
factor was that the press lord's loose-cannon activities had been a constant
irritation to the prime minister, and the mission would remove him for an extended period.[150]

Before approaching the war cabinet, Lloyd George first gained the support confidentially of Bonar Law and the heads of the departments with
which Northcliffe would have to cooperate.[151] Rather than chance an almost
certain denial from President Wilson, the Welshman gained U.S. approval
from the American ambassador Page, who knew Northcliffe well. One final
personage remained to be consulted, the foreign secretary, Arthur Balfour,
still on his mission. When contacted, he immediately cabled his strong disapproval, although Lloyd George apparently withheld this information from his
colleagues and Northcliffe.[152] After thus preparing the ground, the prime minister pressed his choice on the war cabinet. Maurice Hankey, its secretary,
wrote in his diary of 24 May,

Interesting discussion at morning War Cabinet on subject of the articles
on the submarine question in The Times and Daily Mail and all the
Northcliffe Press, which supply most valuable propaganda to the enemy,

who makes full use of it. Ll. G. very angry about it, which amuses me, as before he became Prime Minister he could talk of nothing except "telling the people the truth." He is now trying to persuade the War Cabinet to send Northcliffe to America to co-ordinate the purchases, transport arrangements, etc. of the various Depts. This, of course, is really a dodge to get rid of Northcliffe, of whom he is afraid. I am certain N. will not accept it, even if he is asked.[153]

Hankey was mistaken. Although the two men had an appointment scheduled for the next day, Lloyd George called Northcliffe to an urgent meeting on the night of 30 May. When he described the American mission as "vital" and in need of someone with credentials only Northcliffe possessed, the offer was accepted.[154]

Many reasons, besides the considerable persuasive powers of the prime minister, can be listed for the press lord's change of heart since his April refusal. As Lloyd George must have known when he made the offer, the task combined two of Northcliffe's wartime passions, America and propaganda. Also, in May the mission no longer included onerous diplomatic duties, and by the end of that month the submarine peril appeared to be abating. Further, Northcliffe had already taken a step toward breaking his vows not to join in the government by his duties with the Civil Aerial Transport Committee. Perhaps the most important factor was that, after almost three frustrating years of criticism from the sidelines, the press lord was at last ready to assume a more substantial role in the war. Too old to serve in the military, he was limited to criticism, however influential, while younger family members died of their wounds. He felt each loss deeply. Whatever his previous doubts and fears, once he accepted, the decision seemed to have a calming affect, as though some inner tension had been released. Hankey noted in his 31 May diary that Northcliffe "was very quiet and restrained, and much pleasanter than I found him before."[155]

The announcement of the appointment was met with astonishment and anger in most British circles. The friends of Balfour were particularly incensed when *The Times* called Northcliffe the "Successor to Mr. Balfour." The Liberal M.P. Colonel David Davies, one of Lloyd George's close supporters, told the Welshman it was "a damn bad appointment" and a "gratuitous insult to the Americans" that would "raise a devil of a storm in the liberal party, which is just what you want to avoid.... Here it will be said that you are afraid of the Harmsworth Press....We shall soon have a Government of the Harmsworths, thro' the Harmsworths, and for the Harmsworths."[156] The prime minister defended the choice to C. P. Scott, whose allegiance it had shaken, on the grounds that "Dr. Page when consulted had welcomed the idea" and that "it was essential to get rid of him. He had become so 'jumpy' as to be really a public danger and it was necessary to 'harness' him in order to find occupation for his superfluous energies. I had to do this ... 'if I was to avoid a public quarrel with him.'"[57]

A cartoon that appeared at this time in *London Opinion* showed Carson and Lloyd George celebrating Northcliffe's absence, with the caption, "If Asquith had conceived such a splendid idea, he would have been Prime Minister still!"[58] However convenient and restful it was for Lloyd George to have Northcliffe out of the country, the prime minister must also have believed that the man who was his chief press critic and ally could also perform his duties suitably. Organizing the effort in America was too vital to Britain for Lloyd George to have acted otherwise.

EIGHT

Deeds and Words

Chairman of the British War Mission to the United States, June to November 1917

BY MID-1917 THE ALLIES HAD ALREADY PURCHASED VAST QUANTITIES of materials in the United States, where thousands of foreigners worked in another powerful (and legally neutral) sovereign nation, overloading the country's factories with orders. The British apparatus in place was "officially unofficial" in order to circumvent the strictures of international law concerning the construction of a supply base in a neutral country.[1] When the United States openly joined the war, Britain, France, Russia, Belgium, Italy, and Japan all sent envoys to "state their needs and to discuss the best means of cooperation."[2] The British were therefore in immediate competition for supplies and financial assistance with the other Allies, most prominently the French, who sent a delegation under René Viviani, later headed by André Tardieu.[3] Many Americans viewed the French more favorably than the British, a tradition that stretched from Lafayette and George III to the more recent Irish and suffragette issues. Britain's wartime blockade and economic blacklist policies had also raised the ire of American business interests. German propaganda broadcast with some success the notion that the French continued to do most of the fighting in the trenches, while the British held men back.

America's entry brought to an end many of the wartime conflicts between the two countries; however, one major stumbling block to complete cooperation survived, the Irish question. Before 1917 the Wilson administration, partly because of political pressure applied by a large Catholic Irish-American community, had urged Britain to come to a settlement over home rule. The increasing importance of the United States as the chief supplier of money and material to the Allies made the British government acutely sensitive to this issue.[4] British overreaction to the April 1916 Easter Rising in

Dublin exacerbated the problem. After April 1917, the heads of each of the succeeding missions, starting with Balfour, had to address this question with the American government and with the moderate Irish-American leadership.[5] Partly to soothe U.S. opinion, Lloyd George proposed, and then convened in July 1917, an Irish Convention to seek a solution to the problem.

Since his first trip in 1894, Northcliffe had visited the United States twenty times by 1917. Few in Britain matched his knowledge of America. On the U.S. side of the Atlantic, he was regarded as a powerful figure whose rise to greatness seemed more American than British. Arthur Willert, *The Times* correspondent in Washington, wrote that, even before the war, his chief was "a hero in American newspaper circles" and "to the American public a figure of immense, though undefineable, extra-constitutional powers."[6] The press lord's informal dress (usually a blue serge suit, soft white collar, red checked tie and gray soft hat) and equally informal manner aided his general popularity and the ease with which he could work with the Americans, particularly the business leaders. His style was in marked contrast to Arthur Balfour's starched-linen, frock-coated formality, which had led the foreign secretary to be described in the American press during his visit as "an interesting survival."[7] Nonetheless, Balfour's preceding British mission prepared the ground for full cooperation and provided a sound base on which Northcliffe built.[8]

There was initial American hostility to the idea of the British sending any follow-up to Balfour. When Woodrow Wilson learned from Colonel House, his closest advisor, of Northcliffe's possible appointment to the new position, he telegraphed House that the "action mentioned in your letter of yesterday would be most unwise and still more unwise in the choice of the person named."[9] During the period of neutrality, Wilson had made contact with British Liberals sympathetic to his "Peace without Victory" campaign (announced 22 January 1917, just before the Germans began unrestricted submarine attacks).[10] Among these men was Northcliffe's most bitter critic, Alfred G. Gardiner of the *Daily News*. In January 1917 Gardiner poured poison in the ear of the American public in a scathing *Atlantic Monthly* article.[11] In it, he attributed to Northcliffe "ambitions ... Napoleonic in scope," along with "no loyalties to anything except the wind that blows at the moment." It was therefore understandable that Wilson considered Northcliffe, like his American press counterpart, William Randolph Hearst, just another "troublemaker."[12] On 4 June 1917, Wilson wrote to his secretary of the navy, Josephus Daniels, that "I don't believe in Lord Northcliffe any more than I do in Mr. Hearst."[13]

Lloyd George had stressed the urgency of his mission to the press lord and had told him, falsely, that Balfour requested he leave immediately. Consequently, after accepting the position on Wednesday evening and being hurriedly briefed in the next two days, he departed Saturday morning, 2 June, on the U.S.M.S. *St. Paul*, with only a valet.[14] His ship and Balfour's crossed in the passage.[15] Lloyd George thus presented the foreign office and the United States with a fait accompli that both were forced to accept. The terms of reference that listed Northcliffe's duties were broad enough to leave him some flexibility of action.[16] His primary task, the control of British operations, included the recruiting of British citizens, and the manufacture, purchase, and transport over land and sea of all supplies. The instructions gave him full authority to reorganize the independent and often conflicting treasury, Admiralty, War Office, ministry of munitions, ministry of shipping, and ministry of food missions already in place in order to "prevent overlapping and secure better results." He was granted direct access, as needed, to the prime minister or the heads of these departments, with the power to resolve their conflicting claims. The issue of publicity was not addressed in the mission terms; however, they did include the establishment and maintenance of the "friendliest possible relations, not only with the United States authorities, but also with the representatives of our Allies." The aim was to promote cooperation and to avoid competition, which only resulted in price increases. One additional instruction of note stated that Northcliffe was to "keep the British Ambassador at Washington generally informed of the main lines of his action," and was to "profit by the Ambassador's advice and assistance, whenever these may be required." Unfortunately, this would prove difficult.

Both Northcliffe and Lloyd George knew the appointment would be attacked by those who saw him as "a menace to public life."[17] Numerous British newspapers ridiculed the choice, including the *Daily Chronicle*, the *Morning Post*, and Gardiner's *Daily News*, in which an article proclaimed that the appointment was a "humiliation" to the country.[18] However, the press lord received some press support, including that of Leo Maxse at the *National Review*, who called him "the man for this Mission."[19] In Parliament, Andrew Bonar Law explained Northcliffe's nondiplomatic duties to a hostile House of Commons. Curzon defended the appointment against a "malignant" speech in the House of Lords by Buckmaster, which questioned, among other things, *The Times*'s declaration that Northcliffe "succeeded" Balfour, the nature of his duties, and the power given him to contact the prime minister directly.[20] Curzon's defense claimed that the press lord did not "succeed" Balfour because their missions were completely different. Buckmaster wrote to Gardiner that if "this is so the Times deliberately lied."[21] *Punch* commented on the parliamentary debate that "It has been interesting to learn that his lordship 'will have the right of communicating direct with the Prime Minister'—a thing which, of course, he has never done before."[22]

Northcliffe was well aware that by sending him to America, the prime minister hoped to muzzle the criticism of his newspapers and their support of the army. Henry Wickham Steed, foreign editor of *The Times*, later commented that "one of the reasons which induced Mr. Lloyd George to ask Northcliffe...was a wish to utilize his knowledge of America...while removing his influence from the military wrangle at home. If so, Mr. Lloyd George was mistaken. Before Northcliffe started, he left general instructions to the editors... to 'back the soldiers.'"[23] The *Daily Mail* kept Field-Marshal Haig's name before the public. The 9 June editorial celebrated "Haig's Triumph, The Victory at Messines."[24]

Other instructions to his newspapers included a 7 June "Message from the Chief" that announced his departure and instructed the *Daily Mail* and its associated papers not to publish "one line of criticism of the United States... only those who know the Fenian, pro-German and anti-English pressmen in America can realize the minute efforts they make for anti-British attack."[25] To further prevent any "distorted account" being published in American newspapers, the press lord sent J. T. Davies, Lloyd George's secretary, a press release with his own version of the mission objectives.[26] When the statement appeared in the 7 June *New York Times*, House wrote Wilson that he was sorry Northcliffe was coming. He had believed Balfour's telegram to his Government had "headed him off," and now feared his visit would "stir up the anti-British feeling here that at present is lying dormant."[27]

Some Americans were cheered by the news. Two days before Northcliffe arrived, Roy Howard of the United Press cabled, "We are delighted to have you with us. We are a bit fed up on British and French compliments and are sorely in need of word from someone who knows... enough to frankly tell Americans what a rotten demonstration we are making of our much talked about speed and enterprise. We have been so completely lulled into a state of asinine self-satisfaction that nothing short of a kick in the hip-pocket will establish our sense of proportion. Hoping you are bringing the kick with you."[28] The *St. Paul* docked at New York on June 11.

After first considering whether "to let him run amuck," Colonel House and Sir William Wiseman, the British military intelligence officer who kept an eye on Northcliffe during the mission, conspired to surround him with people who would "keep him straight."[29] These included Arthur Willert, who joined the mission. House sent his immediate greetings and asked the press lord to call on him if he could be of assistance.[30] Northcliffe sent thanks the same day for this offer, to which he replied, "I shall not hesitate to avail myself."[31] The colonel informed the president that he had asked Wiseman to advise the press lord not to talk through the press and not to "attempt to force his opinions upon our people."[32] Nevertheless, Northcliffe immediately launched a personal public relations campaign, hosting almost daily luncheon parties in his suite at the Gotham Hotel. Willert wrote that "nothing would ever convince him that publicity was not part of his duty."[33]

The new head of the British War Mission was a magnet for the American press. Following a brief session with journalists at his hotel suite, a 12 June 1917 article in the *New York Sun* described Northcliffe as "a maker and unmaker of ministries; furious critic of slovenliness and incapacity and certainly regarded at home as the most powerful figure in British public life outside a responsible Ministry... in this country to take up his duties as Head of the British War Mission... a post assigned to him because a man of extraordinary energy and executive capacity, as well as tact and accurate understanding of the American people was needed to coordinate the activities of the various British war commissions." A *Brooklyn Daily Eagle* interview soon after noted how the press lord was "bringing the realities of war and Germanism home to us...here was one who had seen what the Germans had done — who had heard the stories from the lips of those who had suffered."[34] George Harvey, a friend of Northcliffe and editor of the *North American Review*, dubbed him the "Man of the War" and the "electric engine of the armies of democracy."[35]

However, as always, Northcliffe had his critics, in the press and elsewhere. In the 16 June *Daily News*, Gardiner reacted to a *New York Tribune* article that credited the press lord with the fall of Asquith by proclaiming it "only amusing as an illustration of the game which the Newspaper Potentate plays with the public of two worlds." On the same day *The New Republic*, an American weekly review sympathetic to Gardiner, asserted that Northcliffe had been sent to the United States because "he exercised an enormous influence on British opinion" and the British government "rejoiced at the opportunity of installing him in a public office situated in a foreign country."[36] Two weeks later the same journal offered to send "William Randolph Munsey" (a combination of William Randolph Hearst and Frank Munsey, the two primary newspaper bogeymen of the American Left) to England in Northcliffe's place.[37] By the standards of diplomats like Lord Hardinge of Penshurst, the permanent under-secretary at the Foreign Office, the socializing and the amount of publicity Northcliffe generated were disreputable. Hardinge later described Northcliffe as "a business hustler" who "hoped to effect some big *coup* for his own glorification."[38]

Since his mission had no diplomatic status, Northcliffe needed the cooperation of the British ambassador at Washington on matters of protocol and had been instructed to seek his advice. Unfortunately, the hostility of Sir Cecil Spring Rice represented a real impediment. While en route Northcliffe had already notified the prime minister that he was disturbed by reports of Spring

Rice's interference and that, although he would attempt to "work with him in every way," if he found him to be "a man of small parts inclined to make mischief" he would return.[39] At his arrival in New York, in stark contrast to Balfour's reception and to Northcliffe's fury, no one from the British embassy greeted him.[40] He sent an angry cable to the prime minister that if conditions did not improve, he would return.

Determined to get on with his job, Northcliffe put aside his anger and traveled to Washington. At this time he confided in his mother, to whom he wrote almost daily, that his four days in America seemed like four weeks. The letter went on that, "It is barely more than a fortnight since I resolved that it was my duty to make this great sacrifice & I have had to adjust and readjust my view of the tremendous task I have in hand.... The American Govt is very nice to me. *They are a mighty people these Americans & will end the war.*"[41] On 15 June, with Spring Rice, the press lord called on several members of Wilson's cabinet. Josephus Daniels, the secretary of the navy, recorded that during their interview Northcliffe criticized the British for withholding information on submarine activity and called the censorship "stupid" because the knowledge withheld would "stimulate both patriotism and sacrifice."[42] Daniels was also a member of the American government's Committee on Public Information (CPI), which had been organized in April under the reforming journalist George Creel. The CPI's main task was to persuade the American public, which had supported neutrality, to a view of the war consonant with Wilson's moral vision of a crusade to "Make the World Safe for Democracy." Though Northcliffe thought this idealism naive at best, for a time the CPI shared his view of the harm caused by repressive censorship and also espoused the idea that publicity should be honest and seek to educate, rather than mislead, the citizenry.[43]

Besides Daniels, Northcliffe and Spring Rice also visited Counselor Frank Polk at the state department. Polk reported to House that his two British visitors "were polite to one another, but it is easy to see that they are not close friends."[44] That evening, the press lord and Spring Rice had a tense encounter at the British embassy before a formal dinner, in which the diplomat raised the personal attacks he believed *The Times* had made upon him. Only the arrival of the French ambassador prevented Northcliffe from storming out. His first mission report to Lloyd George recounted this confrontation with Spring Rice, describing him as "an odd person ... either overwrought by the strain of the war," or "not quite right in the head."[45] After their altercation, the press lord reported further that Spring Rice then told him that "we have got to work together, whatever we may feel about each other." The Ambassador, nevertheless, carried out a campaign of petty obstruction that hindered mission efforts.[46]

The first meeting between the new chairman of the British mission and Woodrow Wilson took place on 16 June 1917.[47] In a letter to his wife, Northcliffe described the president as "a determined looking gentleman with whom one would not care to be in antagonism, he is about as tall as I am, more slightly built, very quiet in his manner, compresses more meaning into a few words than any other American I have met, uses more American in his speech than I had expected, is I believe with his family quite a hermit, is always surrounded by a bodyguard of detectives, does not entertain privately, bears his worries remarkably well, is quite humorous and amusing and, incidentally, the most powerful individual in the world."[48] Three days after the meeting, House wrote to the president that "you charmed Northcliffe in your few minutes talk with him....I have heard from many directions of his enthusiastic praise of you. You seem to have been a revelation to him. I am glad you treated him so kindly for he has shown a desire to work in harmony with everyone."[49] Willert reported to Geoffrey Robinson at *The Times* that Northcliffe "has started well. He has made a good impression. He was expected... to do all sorts of indiscreet things. He has instead lain low and... his conversation with officials has been tactful and to the point. The President, who had expected a political ogre...has expressed himself to be agreeably surprised."[50]

A cable to the prime minister from Northcliffe described his reception by the president as "cordiality itself." The message also recounted, however, that Wilson and several of his advisors complained of a lack of submarine news. Before they could expect their own people to sacrifice, they argued, it was necessary to demonstrate the severity of the conditions under which Britain suffered.[51] Numbers of Americans thought the British exaggerated the submarine peril, the report continued, or still believed they had been tricked into the war. Others objected to "joining a bankrupt concern." The press lord added that the Irish were more powerful than he had thought and that he was meeting with a number of their leaders. He concluded by assuring Lloyd George that he would do all in his power to work with Spring Rice and that "no effort at conciliation on my part will be lacking, even if my personal dignity suffers."[52]

In part because of the friction between himself and the ambassador, Northcliffe established his own office at 681 Fifth Avenue in New York, away from the diplomatic scene in Washington, where Charles Gordon, the mission vice-chairman, eventually took command of the office.[53] As the center of American finance, journalism, commerce, and railways, New York also made a more practical site from which efficiently to discharge mission business.[54] The office was staffed largely with people from the *Daily Mail* in order "to secure reliability and prevent the leakage of confidential information."[55]

The major official challenges Northcliffe faced involved finance, organization, and supply. Publicity in the United States, which he considered of equal value with these other areas, the press lord assumed on his own. The area in which he was least experienced and prepared, the realm of international finance, soon superceded all other concerns because three years of war had left Britain almost bankrupt. On 28 June Balfour cabled House that the British were "on the verge of a financial disaster which would be worse than defeat in the field. If we cannot keep up exchange neither we nor our allies can pay our dollar debts. We should be driven off the gold basis and purchases for the U.S.A. would immediately cease and Allies' credit would be shattered."[56] Northcliffe was sent a similar message and, because Spring Rice was out of Washington, was instructed to take matters in hand and call on the president if necessary.[57] After conferring with House as to the wisest course of action, the press lord traveled to Washington. On 30 June 1917 he met with Wilson again, this time concerning Britain's desperate financial situation.[58] The president directed him to the secretary of the treasury, William Gibbs McAdoo.[59] Northcliffe called his visit to the treasury (and his overall job) "an urgent begging mission of colossal scale."[60]

Stunned by the immense sums requested, $200 million a month, the Americans asked for facts and figures from the British government to back up its dire predictions of financial collapse and to insure that the supplies requested were absolutely necessary. Northcliffe shared with House and McAdoo the information sent in reply. By the middle of 1917, he informed them, Britain had spent £3.71 billion on the war and had loaned almost £1 billion to its Allies, some of which had to be spent in Britain. He estimated that the British had already disbursed perhaps $5 billion in the United States.[61] The press lord spent several days in mid-July at Magnolia, the colonel's Massachusetts retreat. While discussing the financial situation, House informed the president that he found Northcliffe surprisingly modest in admitting he had been "thrust into a situation of which he knows next to nothing, and he frankly seeks advice."[62] At the same time, the press lord complained to Lloyd George of America's ignorance of Britain's tremendous sacrifice, blaming whoever was "responsible for the suppression of this information" for rendering "our position here, as beggars on behalf of the British nation, most difficult."[63] He also asked for "better support and quick action at home."

Efficient responses to Northcliffe's many requests were handicapped by constant problems and delays in his communications with Britain. In July, he made special arrangements with John Waterbury of Western Union to give his cables round-the-clock priority.[64] C. J. Phillips, one of his secretaries, returned to Britain to coordinate communications with the government and was installed at the Foreign Office. Geoffrey Dawson (formally Robinson) and other of Northcliffe's employees kept him up-to-date on European developments with regular reports from London.[65] These were often shared with House. Dawson's 26 July memo spoke of the poor conditions in Russia and France, ending with a personal note that the "Govt are thoroughly appreciative of all your work."[66]

On 10 August Northcliffe cabled Bonar Law at the exchequer that he was again to spend the next four days with House, "through whom I have been able to effect much more good than I have achieved at Washington."[67] The press lord considered the quiet and unassuming House the "power behind the throne" and the most important American figure after Wilson.[68] During this visit to Magnolia, Northcliffe told the colonel that British resources were exhausted, and that unless the United States could meet "our expenses in America," it would only be a matter of days before "the whole financial fabric of the alliance would collapse."[69] House explained the political difficulties that had to be overcome for the administration to obtain from Congress the $400 million Britain requested.

McAdoo complained to House that he was "somewhat confused by the number of people who are undertaking to speak for Great Britain."[70] He added that the British needed a "big man over here" to deal with the financial crisis. He could not yet judge "how practical" Northcliffe was on matters of finance, but he struck McAdoo as "a man of great energy and purpose." The press lord realized his limitations in the realm of international finance, but he was, at the time, the biggest man the British had on the scene. He knew that the Allies needed to coordinate their monetary requests and worked closely with Tardieu, his French counterpart. The good relations Northcliffe established with McAdoo and Tardieu proved invaluable. The three men managed to arrange $185 million in American credits, which temporarily averted the disastrous possibility of a suspension of the loans. Tardieu later wrote that without "means of payments in dollars...the Allies would have been beaten before the end of 1917. America's entry in the war saved them. Before the American soldier, the American dollar turned the tide."[71]

While he helped to solve the immediate crisis, Northcliffe realized that assistance was needed for the further immense and complicated loan arrangements that still remained to be made with the United States. The Americans also called for a separate full-time British financial liaison. In discussion with House, it was decided that Lord Reading would be the best choice to take over the financial end of the mission's duties. Reading, the Lord Chief Justice, had previously negotiated a 1915 Allied loan agreement with the United States.[72] Northcliffe underlined the seriousness of the need in repeated cables to his government. The appointment was delayed for several reasons. Despite Northcliffe's cables, the government worried about how he would react. Bonar Law questioned whether there were not already too many Englishmen in America, and would have preferred a Unionist. Reading had also recently been attacked in some newspapers for his financial dealings, and there was still on him the taint of the Marconi scandal.[73]

In addition to treasury negotiations, under Northcliffe's control the war mission included Admiralty, purchasing, munitions, food, shipping, and War Office groups. These were further subdivided into separate departments, twenty-eight in all.[74] Part of his job was to streamline the operation and reduce duplication and waste. He wrote to George Sutton, the manager of the Amalgamated Press operation, that the opportunities for slashing staff would have appealed to Rothermere, but that he was going to proceed carefully.[75] The procurement of munitions was put under the control of Charles Gordon, who represented the mission in Washington as director general of war supplies.[76] After Gordon's appointment the British also began to handle their own purchase arrangements, which had previously been negotiated by J. P. Morgan & Company.[77] A new purchasing department was formed under Henry Japp, which by the end of August carried out all arrangements, except for wheat.[78] One other notable addition to Northcliffe's team in the United States was Colonel Campbell Stuart, a Canadian officer who had been assigned to the British embassy in Washington. Stuart assisted the press lord for the remainder of the war and afterward helped manage his publishing businesses. In total the mission employed 10,000 people in the United States and Canada and spent $10,000,000 a day. These colossal expenditures resulted in Northcliffe being called the "World's Champion Spender" in American newspapers.[79]

Food supplies for Britain, which had been cut to the bone by the submarine campaign, for a time had priority over even munitions. Northcliffe notified the prime minister that he was seeing members of the American cabinet personally, but that the "slow passage of the food bill and lack of power of requisition, with other difficulties, make for delay."[80] Special arrangements finally were made to insure both supply and railroad transportation to ports.[81] The press lord met with Herbert Hoover, head of the American Food Administration, over the matter. He was impressed by the wide powers given Hoover, who, Northcliffe told the prime minister, was a sincere friend of the Allies, but was discontented with British policy.[82] Hoover complained that high food prices in the United States were successfully used by German propagandists because the war was not yet understood in America. By September the British food situation had improved somewhat, partly because the convoy system had brought submarine losses to manageable levels. This innovation, which grouped merchantmen for their voyages under the protection of destroyers and other antisubmarine craft, had first been experimented with in April. Northcliffe had not been impressed with his own experience with the system crossing the Atlantic in June, but by summer's end, he had come to appreciate it. He continued, however, to think that the shipping losses, though reduced, remained at excessive levels and that the prime minister foolishly downplayed the threat.

At the same time Northcliffe dealt with the loan and food crises, he also gave attention to pressing shortages in oil, steel, and metals. At Lloyd George's direction, he appealed to House and to Josephus Daniels for 200,000 tons of oil to prevent the "immobilization of the fleet."[83] Over the next month, he saw Daniels several times concerning the oil problem. The two also discussed Britain's needs in plate steel and ship construction.[84] The press lord was able to secure six tankers for the British. For the oil to put in them, as he often did, he cut through the government red tape and met directly with industry leaders. In this case, a visit with A. C. Bedford, the president of Standard Oil and chair of the American Petroleum Committee, got the Royal Navy its requirements, although at a high price.[85] Northcliffe later wrote to Page in London about the oil situation. He told the American ambassador that to convince Bedford, he allowed him to read his government's urgent and secret telegram. After reading it twice, Bedford responded, "If it can be done it will be done."[86] Northcliffe added, "You can imagine the panic at No. 10 if they had known I disclosed that cable to the oil controllers." On 5 July he informed the prime minister that relations with the embassy were improved and that "we are slowly arriving at solution of all anxious matters, except copper and steel plates, but we have had a very hard time of it."[87]

Northcliffe blamed his problems in obtaining copper and other metals partly on the Irish, who, he explained to Lloyd George, "hurt us in all sorts of ways that are not apparent in England. Apart from their power in the press they have much to do with various metals used in munitions."[88] The Irish leaders the press lord met were skeptical about the Irish Convention, and he found American newspapers "strangely silent" on the issue. Franklin K. Lane, the American secretary of the interior, told him that the settlement of the Irish question would mean a 10 percent increase in war activity.[89] Northcliffe urged the prime minister to publicize the Convention with interviews in the American press. He warned the Welshman that little was known of the matter and that the "Sinn Feiners describe it as an English trick."[90] "A personal statement by you on the eve of the Convention," Northcliffe added, "would reveal to the United States Government and people that [the] Sinn Feiners are determined to make trouble at any cost and are not sincere in their desire for Home Rule." By this time, the press lord felt he had made some improvement in relations with the Irish-Americans. He told his friend

Page that he was heartened by his splendid reception in Boston, whose press, though largely Irish-controlled, "spread itself over me in a most handsome fashion."[91]

Replacements for the shipping tonnage lost to German submarines was also vital. When the United States requisitioned ships being built in American yards for Britain, Northcliffe attempted to halt the loss. At his mid-August Magnolia visit with House, shipping also had been on the agenda (as well as other matters, including propaganda). Afterward, he reported to the prime minister that the new American shipping controller, Edward Hurley, was instilling more enthusiasm into the effort.[92] Two days later, the press lord complained to Lloyd George that the prime minister's recent speech had contradicted the seriousness of the submarine situation, thereby depriving the British of the appeal they had been making against the proposed confiscation of their ships, as well as damaging the American effort to build more destroyers.[93] Northcliffe also remonstrated to Josephus Daniels about the prime minister's utterances, which led Daniels to wonder if Lloyd George had "interned" his critic in America.[94]

By August, Northcliffe's genuine efforts to do his best overcame House's earlier apprehensions. The colonel cabled Wiseman (in England to consult with the government) that the press lord was "doing good work and is getting along well with everyone."[95] In fact, House began to feel duplicitous because he deliberately withheld information and had so much contact with the British government behind Northcliffe's back.[96] The colonel also was careful in what he disclosed because he knew Northcliffe's confidants included members of the political opposition, such as Theodore Roosevelt. Northcliffe saw the former president several times during his visit, but realized that, although immensely popular in the country, he was an enemy of the Wilson administration. In London, Wiseman discussed Spring Rice's interference with the government. He informed House that the "tendency" was to support the press lord and that, in fact, there were calls for Northcliffe to be made ambassador.[97] After discussing the matter with House, the press lord cabled Wiseman that Spring Rice should be given a long leave of absence, not dismissed, because "people would say that Northcliff [sic] had done it."[98]

Meanwhile, the mission chairman cabled his government that "in regard to the imminent confiscation of ships...whatever is done should be done quickly," suggesting that an urgent protest should be lodged with the president.[99] British prospects for retaining the ships appeared dim; however, Northcliffe continued to work through House to salvage at least a portion of them. On 25 August 1917, he pleaded with the colonel that the seizure would "create a very bad impression in Europe.... Is there not some possible compromise?... My instructions are to point out that my Government will keenly feel the blow, which will be a very serious one for England, if these ships are taken over by your Government."[100] The press lord petitioned Edward Hurley, the chairman of the United States Shipping Board, who agreed with Hoover that ignorance of the American public concerning the war handicapped all their work.[101] Despite the press lord's best efforts, most of the ships were ultimately seized.[102] Though he failed in this instance, Northcliffe otherwise performed well under difficult circumstances as head of the British supply effort. Regardless of the reasons for his controversial appointment, he turned out to be a capable choice.

After many weeks of delay because of political wrangling in Britain, Lord Reading arrived in September as chief financial negotiator.[103] Anxious that no "jar from England should mar his very difficult work," Northcliffe was put in the ironic position of pleading with the government to muzzle British press hostility to Reading.[104] Soon after his arrival, House wrote to Lloyd George that the "coming of the Lord Chief Justice has already resulted in good. Lord Northcliffe is helping to make his visit a success."[105] The press lord informed Henry Wickham Steed at *The Times* in London that the Americans had become the "complete masters of the situation" as regards the Allies. He continued that, "if loan stops, war stops."[106]

With the financial negotiations in Reading's expert hands, Northcliffe was freed to concentrate on publicity. He wrote home that, "for the sake of our position at the Peace Conference and our position in American History, it is essential that we should be better known here."[107] The press lord blamed the censorship and unnecessary British secrecy for American innocence. A letter to his family in August complained that the "ignorance about the war is absolutely colossal and lack of knowledge of our tremendous effort and mighty sacrifice deplorable. If there is ever any hanging from lampposts, those who are responsible for our form of censorship should be the first to be strung up."[108]

The entrance of the United States made it possible for the British to be less secretive in their publicity efforts. During Balfour's mission, an office for the purpose was opened in New York, headed by Geoffrey Butler, who became the "adviser and mouthpiece of the Mission."[109] Buchan's Foreign Office Department of Information had official responsibility for British publicity in the United States and kept a wary eye on Northcliffe's activities, mainly through Butler. The Foreign Office worried that too visible a British campaign would outrage an already suspicious Wilson administration and wanted propaganda restricted to a limited role in support of its diplomacy. Northcliffe (and the prime minister) believed it could be used independently.

In the press lord's view, the new relationship with Britain's "Associate" merited the removal of the constraints under which British publicity had been handicapped. He did not fear being honest with the public and believed that the message of British sacrifice must be broadcast more forcefully and widely to the Americans. Northcliffe wrote home that his tales of British suffering were often considered so much "hot air" and that he cudgeled his "brain how to get round the difficulty, how to make these people realize the immensity of our sacrifice."[110] Another letter recorded that the press lord told one American of the "glories of our Guards regiments. He was under the impression that they had been guarding Buckingham Palace and doing work of that kind."[111] During his August stay at Magnolia, Northcliffe reported that the Colonel told him, "you must stress the part the English are playing.... we simply cannot get money for the English till they have made a more effective approach to the people of the United States."[112]

To spread his message, Northcliffe used whatever methods made themselves available. American journalists competed with each other to publish his views on the war, and he also wrote or authorized numerous additional pieces.[113] In June Roy Howard broached the subject of articles for his United Press. "When you decide the time is ripe," cabled Howard, "please declare us in.... I hope you won't waste your big shells on small circulations.... I realize more than some stay-at-home American editors the size of the job of arousing Americans."[114] To counteract what he considered his government's dangerously optimistic proclamations about the submarine losses, the press lord gave Howard a series of interviews which, while complimenting the "American Spirit," and efforts in the air service, warned of the lack of ship building because of the hiding of the truth concerning German submarine activity.[115]

Some of Northcliffe's writing caused official consternation, on both sides of the Atlantic, and at least one piece was edited by the censorship. The most controversial Northcliffe article appeared in the October 1917 edition of the American journal *Current Opinion*. This directly challenged President Wilson's idealistic explanation for American participation in the war that the CPI, the administration's propaganda branch, broadcast to the country. Though Northcliffe had great admiration for Wilson, he did not believe appeals to idealism would be as effective as appeals to self-interest. Consequently, he asserted that "the motive which brought the United States in was not sympathy for any other nation, was not desire for gain, was not an abstract fondness for democratic as opposed to autocratic government: it was self-interest, self-preservation, self-respect. The American People are not fighting to make the world safe for democracy, but to make the world safe for themselves."[116] House recorded in his diary that Northcliffe could get in "serious trouble should the President chance to see" the *Current Opinion* piece.[117]

The colonel discussed the press lord's indiscretions with Reading and Wiseman, whose job it was to keep Northcliffe from making such statements.

Wiseman cabled Sir Eric Drummond at the Foreign Office that Northcliffe "cannot keep his hands off propaganda, and is even now engaged in writing a series of articles for American magazines which criticize the President and have given some offence in that quarter. He is convinced that he is doing it in the best interests of the country, and simply cannot see that no British official ought to write articles of any kind, still less of a controversial nature."[118] Though he agreed with Wiseman at the time, Arthur Willert later defended Northcliffe's campaign, writing that "the annoyance it caused the government was trivial compared to the good it did the country. Northcliffe to the public was not a high official behaving improperly, but a great British newspaper magnate, telling what the war meant in striking and intelligible language."[119] Despite the press lord's occasional misstep, House considered that "he does what he promises and he rings true," and wondered "how well we analyze him. There must be more to him than his critics see.... I must confess he is a puzzle to me."[120]

Woodrow Wilson was aware that Northcliffe was constantly promoting Britain's interests, with an eye on war aims and the peace settlement.[121] However, in this instance, the president either did not notice or, more likely, chose to avoid the controversy and did not directly answer the press lord's challenge to his view of the war. At least one Liberal American journal, however, did respond. In an article titled, "Lord Northcliffe, Benefactor," the 1 November issue of the *Nation* sarcastically thanked the press lord for enlightening the United States and remarked that "Mr. Wilson will, we are sure, take this noble Warwick's rebuke to heart and give us soon a revised interpretation of American war motives and policy."

In addition to his written appeals, Northcliffe also carried out a speaking campaign. He was uncomfortable before an audience, his voice was rather weak, and he spoke from notes. However, with practice he improved and gained confidence from the enthusiasm of the crowds he faced. His early talks in America emphasized several themes: the enormity of Britain's contribution (that had been masked by the censorship); that the war would be a long one; and the immediate need for the United States to mobilize all her resources to help the Allies overcome the Prussian menace.[122] One of his first engagements came in late June, before a Player's Club luncheon in New York hosted by the American writer, Isaac Marcosson, whose introduction declared that, "no Englishman knows us so well."[123] On this occasion, Northcliffe expressed the hope that newspapers and magazines would now be able to "deal frankly with the war," and denounced the censorship as a grievous blunder. However, cognizant that his position was vulnerable to criticism, the press lord trod lightly at first. For example, in early July he addressed the Washington Press Club, but did not allow his comments on censorship and spies to be reproduced in the press, much to the chagrin of those waiting to pounce on any miscue.[124]

Northcliffe's first opportunity to voice his opinions before a large crowd came on 21 July 1917, during British Recruiting Week, to a rally of 14,000 at Madison Square Garden in New York. Although his speaking voice was not powerful enough to reach the whole hall, he received an enthusiastic reception.[125] The next day's *New York Times* reported that another of the speakers, Alexander Humphries, "voiced the enthusiasm of the audience by exclaiming—I wish to God we had in this country a Lord Northcliffe. We need one perhaps more than Great Britain did."[126] The press lord's recruiting activities also led him to make a speech at AT&T headquarters that was "radiated" over the entire system. He told his mother that he had the "amazing experience of talking to ten American towns, distant from New York between 500 and 3000 miles. I was also the first man to have a telephone receiver at each ear and to hear on the right the waves of the Atlantic and on the left the waves of the Pacific."[127]

After the success at Madison Square Garden, the press lord spoke at almost every city he visited. In a September trip to Atlantic City, he shared the podium at the National Chamber of Commerce convention with Herbert Hoover. Reportedly, four thousand had to be turned away.[128] Northcliffe told the enthusiastic crowd: "I am here because I have been a continual eyewitness of the war on its various fronts. At the war, behind the battle line and in the most serious part of the war—the home front, the battle with the politicians.... It is obvious to anybody...that war is no longer a question of a few hundred thousand in gay uniforms and on prancing horse; it is a matter of whole nations in arms and supported by every business effort.... This is a war of engineers and chemists as well as soldiers.... It is essentially a businessman's war...that requires the brains of men of business."[129] A week later, the press lord addressed the American Bankers Association, also in Atlantic City. He exhorted the audience to "Pull Together!" against Germany and called for the "massed battalions of finance, to bring up your reserves and simply smother him with all arms, big guns and small, subscriptions of a million dollars and subscriptions of a hundred dollars."[130]

At the same time, Northcliffe prodded his government on various other publicity matters. Tanks previously sent over had been a great success.[131] He asked Sir Eric Geddes at the Admiralty to go one better and to supply a captured German submarine for propaganda use in the United States.[132] Geddes had the outer shell of a German mine-laying submarine brought over. Postcards of it were given to paying visitors. When an Italian Air Corps flyover made a great impression in Washington, Northcliffe requested of Lord Cowdray, at the Air Board, that the British counteract this with some sort of show of their own.[133] To appeal to the sympathy of the Americans and to demonstrate British sacrifice, he asked through Butler for one-armed or one-legged veterans to talk at functions. The request specified English officers, not "colonials or Kelts [sic]."[134] The press lord also cautioned his government about the effects of the ongoing "America First" propaganda campaign that he felt had "already resulted in the confiscation of our ships and aeroplanes." He feared the loans as well could be "cut off without much warning."[135] The growing war fervor in the United States threatened British supplies; however, it also quieted Irish-American criticism of Britain, now America's partner in the conflict, at least as long as the Irish Convention continued to meet, as it did through the rest of 1917.[136]

Perhaps Northcliffe's most notable U.S. propaganda success came in his late October tour of the American Midwest, an area with a large German-American population, which the British considered to be a hotbed of pro-German sympathy.[137] Burton and others had warned Northcliffe of the special need for publicity in this region for years, and he had heard the same sentiment from American passengers on his voyage over. Burdened with his official duties, Northcliffe dispatched Geoffrey Butler to Chicago personally to appraise the situation.[138] A month later, the press lord wrote to Page in London, that "the Middle West and the West feel neglected by England, and they are neglected."[139]

The press lord hoped a major British military or political figure could be persuaded to undertake an American tour. He had two men in mind for the job—Lloyd George and the South African general J. C. Smuts, who had been brought into the highest British councils. The dynamic prime minister was an obvious choice, and Northcliffe had suggested a "whirlwind" tour in June. Two months later, to counteract French publicity, he again broached the idea. Dawson reported to his chief that the premier wanted to come, adding "it is his true *role,* and in some ways the day-to-day business would go on better without him."[140] Soon after this, the prime minister told Dawson that he would like to go, but his colleagues were against it.[141]

In June 1917, Lloyd George had included General Smuts in a newly created War Policy Committee designed to oversee the entire war effort.[142] Northcliffe regarded the South African as a perfect authority to comment on imperial affairs in the United States, and asked Smuts to undertake a tour to explain Britain's plans for Germany's possessions after the war to the "no-annexation" Americans.[143] The press lord told the prime minister that, "unless we send Smuts here to conduct proper propaganda, Americans will not understand why it is essential we retain those colonies."[144] Smuts agreed that a propaganda campaign was needed in the United States, but felt that at the present, while the fate of the small nations in Europe was still "in the balance," it was an awkward time for publicity in regard to the German colonies and that such efforts would be considered "selfish imperialism."[145] The press lord continued to hope that Smuts would come at some later date. He wrote to him that the "task of propaganda work among one hundred million people scattered over so vast a continent is not an easy one and requires time."[146]

When no other suitable arrangements could be made, Northcliffe took on the challenge himself. During the tour, which began in Detroit, the press lord gave "advice to everyone from big industry down to housewives."[147] One of his first tasks was to appease an angry Henry Ford. The American industrialist felt insulted by British handling of an offer to supply, at cost, 6,000 of his new and inexpensive agricultural tractors for the food production ministry. Dawson explained to his chief that S. F. Edge, a former representative of Ford's British competitors (and presently attached to the ministry of munitions), had done everything in his power, including the staging of unfair tests, to attack the American machines.[148] As a result, Ford refused to allow any Englishmen into his factories. The press lord told Winston Churchill, who became munitions minister in July, that Ford had twice put him off, but that he would gladly go to Detroit and "eat humble pie."[149] Thomas Edison, an acquaintance of both men, finally arranged a mid-October meeting at which the misunderstanding was laid to rest.[150] Northcliffe toured Ford's plant and even took a turn behind the wheel of one of the tractors in a plowing demonstration.[151]

The first Midwest speech was made to a capacity crowd at the Cleveland Armory on 22 October. Northcliffe was introduced by Myron Herrick, a former governor of Ohio and ambassador to France, as "England's most powerful man," whose "fearless courage had saved the situation for the Allies."[152] The press lord's address rallied support for the second Liberty Loan and called for more ships, while warning of the continued strength of Germany. As an eyewitness to the war, he also condemned the "malicious" rumors that the British were holding back troops and that there would be an early peace.[153] Herrick told Northcliffe privately that he considered it "little short of criminal that the British Government does not realize the need for propaganda in this country."[154]

While in Cleveland, Northcliffe also gave an interview to Kate Carter of *The Press*, aimed at the female audience. He appealed to American homemakers to conserve food, using sugar as an example of a habit which only "brings on all sorts of trouble," like diabetes, so that doing without it was actually a "benefit not a sacrifice."[155] Carter described the press lord for her readers as having "none of the manner or appearance of the movie, stage or best-seller Englishman. There's no monocle, no drawl. His manner of speech is crisp and jerky, clear, forceful. The words and phrases he uses are American." A letter home described his itinerary for the following days as "in length something like … a trip to Brindisi, Petrograd, Stockholm and back; but each visit is an urgent necessity."[156]

Chicago was Northcliffe's next destination. He spoke at the University Club to a thousand leading citizens, to whom he repeated the points he had made in Cleveland. In response to German attempts to frighten the American public with threats to sink troop ships, the press lord reassured his audience that the convoy system now in place was effective, and pointed out that almost no Canadian troops had been lost in the crossing.[157] Surrounded constantly by burly bodyguards, behind whom he could hardly see, Northcliffe toured the Chicago naval installation and met with Josephus Daniels. On 24 October he was guest of honor at a Chicago Chamber of Commerce meeting. After a wheatless and liquorless dinner, his address again underlined the vital need for ships. The *Chicago Tribune* commented that "Lord Northcliffe's most valuable contribution to the war discussion … undoubtedly was his insistence on the vital importance of our ship program … the neck of the bottle through which our strength is to be poured into Europe."[158] The *Chicago Herald* declared that "Lord Northcliffe knows. For over two years in England he led the fight against the murderous inertia of red tape and the suicidal policy of 'wait and see.' … He has seen with his own eyes the red reckoning of the war.… Probably no other man in this country today knows so well the necessities of his nation … necessities to be supplied by America or not at all. We can accept his statements … as facts and his conclusions as sound."[159]

The next day, Northcliffe arrived in Kansas City, where he spoke to a luncheon meeting of leading newspapermen from Kansas, Missouri, Iowa, Nebraska, Oklahoma, and Arkansas. The press lord told his fellows that they had misled their readers by emphasizing news that Germany was weakening and by slighting discouraging reports. Dubbing the press lord, "The British Kingmaker," the 26 October *Kansas City Star* called his criticism "just," and agreed that it was dangerous to create the impression that Germany was weak. The same day's *Kansas City Times* editorial, "Lord Northcliffe's Warning," praised the frank language he used to convince those who doubted the seriousness of the war. The paper added that, "Lord Northcliffe has unmasked for us the true face of war and has bidden us to accustom ourselves to look upon it. It is something perhaps no American could have done, and for that reason it should make all the more sober the reflections with which the warning is received, for it comes to us paid for with a price by disillusioned England while we are yet unscathed." That evening, to a record audience at the Knife and Fork Club, Northcliffe pointed out the Allied mistakes that had prolonged the war and that he hoped the United States would avoid.[160] He called for ships so that the American army would not be "marooned" in

France without supplies, and "tore to pieces" the idea that there would be an early peace.[161] He also predicted that the men on the battlefields would dominate the postwar world, asserting that the privates and the officers had been bound together in a "brotherhood of blood" which held "clean cut ideas of capital, labor and the other issues paramount in the public mind today."

At his next destination, St. Louis, Northcliffe praised the enthusiasm he had found on his tour to yet another capacity crowd at a Chamber of Commerce luncheon.[162] His address emphasized the concentrated efforts of businessmen needed to win the war, as well as the sacrifices of all Americans — men and women.[163] In a newspaper interview he saluted the American effort in providing men and training facilities for them, as well as the progress made in aviation. However, he again warned of the shipping shortage, the problems of supplying a huge Army in France, and predicted a long war that would require mandatory food conservation.[164]

In Dayton, Ohio, Northcliffe's final stop of the tour, he presented Orville Wright with the Albert Medal in recognition of his accomplishments in aviation.[165] Though Northcliffe believed much more remained to be done, the vast potential he saw in the Midwest heartened him. Josephus Daniels wrote in his diary that the press lord returned to the East Coast "happy over the splendid spirit of the patriotic West."[166] In a 1 November *Daily Mail* article, the "Middle West's War Spirit," Hamilton Fyfe recounted the warm welcome given Northcliffe and the enthusiasm he had witnessed.

It would be impossible to measure accurately the effect the Midwest tour achieved. The increased war spirit reflected in the newspapers until the end of the conflict can be assigned to many causes, including other Allied speakers and the work of the thousands of "Four Minute Men" the CPI dispatched to all parts of the nation to arouse enthusiasm for the war. They, like Northcliffe, made emotional and practical appeals that did not always agree with Wilson's view. However, one gauge available for the achievements of the Midwest expedition, and his overall campaign, can be found in the appraisals of his American and British contemporaries. Edward Hurley, chairman of the United States Shipping Board, wrote to the press lord, "I want you to know that I sincerely believe that your being in America during the most trying period of the war, making speeches throughout the country, had more to do with arousing the interest of our people than any other thing I know of….We did not realize the seriousness of the situation until you presented it to us."[167] Mary Roberts Rinehart, the American writer the press lord helped reach the western front in 1915, recorded that "no better man could have been sent" and that "he roused a fighting spirit which was enormously valuable."[168] Sir Robert Borden, the Canadian prime minister, wrote to him that, "your work in the United States has been crowned with great success and

I was especially interested in learning something of your wonderful tour in the middle West...which cannot fail to be attended with immense advantage to the cause we all have at heart."[169] Geoffrey Butler, who had been horrified when he first heard Northcliffe was to come to America, advised Buchan that the press lord's "many personal friends and profound effect which he recently created in the Middle West must after a certain time make themselves felt as facts that cannot be overlooked."[170]

The successful unofficial propaganda campaign Northcliffe carried on in the United States undoubtedly helped educate America as to the true nature of the war and the immense sacrifices Britain had already made. His publicity campaign also marked a shift away from defensive and subdued methods to a more offensive strategy. Eustace Percy, at the British embassy during Northcliffe's tenure, reflected the official Foreign Office view of Northcliffe's activities. Percy later wrote that, though he liked the press lord well enough, in his Midwest tour, Northcliffe had "trodden on just a sufficient number of sensitive toes to confirm the wisdom of Spring-Rice's indomitable silence."[171] The press lord began in America the struggle with Balfour and his diplomatic minions over propaganda that would continue in 1918 on an official level. However, Northcliffe would never again be so personally involved in the effort.

While the press lord did valuable work in the supply and financial realms, his unique talents shone most brightly in the public relations campaign he carried on in the United States from June to November 1917. No other British figure of the period possessed the same combination of knowledge and skill to awaken the Americans to the challenge they faced in 1917 and 1918. The mission represented a period in which Northcliffe's power was coupled with enormous responsibility. He accepted the challenge Lloyd George presented to him in order to "traffic...in deeds not words," and he carried out his many responsibilities admirably.[172] However, his words may well have been the most important contribution to what Northcliffe called "the most important task of his life."[173]

By the fall of 1917, his strenuous duties and the unaccustomed American heat had taxed even Northcliffe's abundant energy and stamina. With the mission on its feet and running smoothly, he proposed to return to Britain in November for a short visit, and suggested his brother, Lord Rothermere, act as a temporary replacement.[174] A week after the Midwest tour ended, the press lord sailed for England. Lord Reading eventually succeeded as head of the War Mission in February 1918. He also took the British ambassador's post, eliminating the squabbling that had marred Northcliffe's tenure. Arthur Willert wrote of the different contributions of the two men that Reading "could not have contributed to the awakening of America as Northcliffe did,

Northcliffe could not have assisted the American government to take advantage of the awakening as Reading did, and no professional diplomat could have performed either task."[175]

Even though some of his activities had caused concern in official British circles, before his departure Northcliffe received a message from Lloyd George:

> I wish...to thank you for the invaluable work you have done in the United States as head of the British War Mission. It was an appointment requiring exceptional tact and vigour and the War Cabinet desire to express to you their complete satisfaction....They would also like to congratulate you on the great energy and effect with which you have striven to explain what Great Britain has been doing and the needs of the Allies to the American public, and the successes of your efforts to combat attempts of the enemy to sow dissension between the people of the U. S. and Great Britain.[176]

The press lord left the United States on 3 November and arrived in London nine days later. He would not cross the Atlantic again until after the war.

Northcliffe returned to Britain at the peak of his wartime popularity and influence, his work in America widely acclaimed. To the amazement of many, he had shown that he could fulfill duties of the highest responsibility and importance. Had he wished it, almost any government position might have been his for the asking. The year had begun with predictions that its end would find him resident in Downing Street. In mid-November 1917, the press lord returned to challenge the present occupant, David Lloyd George.

NINE

"Pegasus in Harness"
Politics & Propaganda,
November 1917 to April 1918

NORTHCLIFFE RETURNED FROM THE UNITED STATES WITH GRAVE MIS-givings about the British political situation. Over the preceding months he had received disturbing reports of unrest, gloom, and weakness at home. The "virile" American atmosphere left him impatient with his government, including the prime minister, who, during the press lord's absence, had enjoyed a partial respite from Northcliffe's newspapers. Without its owner's stewardship, compared to the previous years, the campaigns in the *Daily Mail* lacked vigor.[1] The Northcliffe journals, however, continued to support the generals, even though their chief was increasingly disillusioned with the western strategy of attrition. Lloyd George complained that since 1916, the press lord had been "the mere kettledrum of Sir Douglas Haig, and the mouth organ of Sir William Robertson."[2] The standoff between the prime minister and his contumacious generals continued, partly because press support made it politically impossible to replace them.

With his leadership secure, Haig had gained approval for yet another offensive, which began 31 July 1917 in Flanders. The British Army soon found itself mired in nightmarish mud created by a combination of rain and shelling.[3] The commander-in-chief, however, pressed his generals to keep up the attacks, while being less than honest about casualties and results. Based on army information, the newspapers printed stories of British success.[4] In November, as the battle slogged toward its end, once again little progress had been made while the British Army suffered grievous casualties.

Allied setbacks made it possible for Lloyd George to enjoy one victory over the generals. At Rapallo on 6–7 November, in the aftermath of the Italian military debacle at Caporetto, the Allied leaders agreed to set up a Supreme War Council at Versailles to superintend the general conduct of the war.[5] The prime minister appointed Sir Henry Wilson, who had been his unofficial advisor for some time, as the British military representative to the Council. Theoretically, unity of action had been established and a step taken to curb the power of Robertson and Haig. On his way home, the prime minister made a speech in Paris to publicize the Rapallo agreement. The address underlined the grave errors of the past to demonstrate the need for a Supreme Council to coordinate Allied efforts.[6] In addition to his army problems, Lloyd George returned to London to find turmoil over manpower and over the creation of a unified air ministry. The *Daily Mail* compared the need for an "adequate and effective air service," to the shells emergency of 1915.[7]

This was the charged atmosphere that greeted Northcliffe on 12 November when he reached London. Leo Maxse, editor of the *National Review*, wrote that, "Indeed you are welcome. You come in the nick of time—every kind of folly is being perpetrated by the village idiots who misgovern this great country."[8] The day of his arrival, Charles à Court Repington, military correspondent of *The Times*, asked to see him as soon as possible about the "Allied staff created at Paris contrary to the desires of our leading soldiers at home and abroad, and contrary to the public interest."[9] The press lord, however, agreed with Lloyd George that coordination was needed. The 14 November *Daily Mail* declared its support for "unified control and the establishment of a permanent military council," although it disagreed with Lloyd George's assertion at Paris that the German line was "an impenetrable barrier" and his criticism of the "appalling casualties" of the Somme.

Northcliffe's greatest worry at this time was that relations with the United States would be mismanaged. On the voyage home, he wrote,

> the value of the American Giant to the Great Cause depends entirely on how it is used by those who direct the war. Wealthy beyond dreams in Man Power, Machine Power, Money Power, Food Power, Steel Power, Copper Power, Oil Power, Cotton Power, Inventive Power and Enthusiasm, he is being confused by the conflicting demands of the Allies. Generous, but ignorant of the war, he has been giving with both hands. So far little harm has been done. But the Giant must insist on cooperation, system and foresight on all our parts unless, he, like Russia, the other Giant, be wasted. The Inter-Allied Conference is the first sign that he is getting impatient.[10]

A few days before his departure, Northcliffe told the American secretary of the navy, Josephus Daniels, that he was going to London for the Allied meetings (which would include Colonel House), but that he "feared there would be no commanding figure, with initiative."[11]

House arrived in London a few days before Northcliffe, and the two worked closely to keep the prime minister on the proper course.[12] On 14 November the press lord briefed Lloyd George on American preparations, particularly their air services. He telephoned House that the prime minister wished him to join the cabinet, but that he declined to join "so spineless a body" and to be put in a position where he could not criticize.[13] The press lord also confided that when he returned he instructed Lloyd George to write the colonel immediately so they could have dinner the same night, even though the two already had an appointment on the following day. "It is common knowledge," recorded House, "that N treats LG as if he, the PM, was subordinate and speculation is rife as to when the worm will turn."[14]

After the prime minister told House that he did not believe he would go to the Paris Inter-Allied Conference, the colonel and Sir William Wiseman decided to "read the riot act to LG."[15] At House's suggestion, Wiseman phoned Northcliffe that if Lloyd George did not go, the colonel would advise the French government to call it off. This, Wiseman went on, would have a "disastrous effect throughout the Allied countries and would exhilarate Germany." The press lord agreed and, with Wiseman, had lunch with the prime minister to discuss the situation.[16] At this 15 November luncheon the men also spoke of the planned air ministry and who would head it.[17] Since Northcliffe had called for such a unified organization for years, the position must have been very appealing. Whether Lloyd George actually offered the job or not, the press lord apparently left the prime minister with the impression that he would take the post.[18] House met with Lloyd George that evening and agreed to delay the Paris conference one week.[19] The colonel recorded that he now had "Reading and N, LG's closest friends, working to force the PM to coordinate the work we have in hand. N delights in this. He is as eager as a hound on a trail. Today he refused another offer from George to become a member of the Cabinet. He wished N to become Minister of the Air services."[20]

It was in this environment of intrigue between Northcliffe and House to pressure Lloyd George into more active cooperation that on 16 November, four days after his return, *The Times* published its chief proprietor's letter (dated the day before) to the prime minister.[21] This public declaration, which the Welshman claimed he had not seen previously, took the ministry to task for continuing to make the same mistakes concerning the censorship, the control of sedition, and other needed compulsory war measures that the more "vital" Americans and Canadians had already enacted and that the Northcliffe press had been supporting for years.[22] The letter condemned the government's obstruction and delay, such as the postponement of Reading's mission, and the "absurd secrecy" that masked the ongoing British efforts in America. The press lord also blamed the British failure to counteract German propaganda as partly responsible for Allied "tragedies" in Russia and Italy. Instead of being punished, the letter charged, those responsible for the many blunders had been retained and even elevated. *The Times*'s missive concluded with a warning that unless there were "swift improvements in our methods here, the United States will rightly take into its own hands the entire management of a great part of the war. It will not sacrifice its blood and treasure to incompetent handling of affairs in Europe."[23]

The most embarrassing disclosure in *The Times* for the prime minister was Northcliffe's public refusal of the air ministry, which the two had discussed privately. Despite Lloyd George's "repeated invitation," the press lord declared, he "could do better work" if he maintained his "independence" and was not "gagged by a loyalty that I do not feel towards the whole of your administration."[24] Lord Cowdray, majority owner of the *Westminster Gazette* and head of the Air Board, had led the reconstruction work in the preceding months for the new ministry and had assumed he would be its head.[25] Cowdray immediately resigned and never forgave Lloyd George, which only inflicted further damage to the already fractured Liberal party.[26]

This public attempt by Northcliffe to jolt the government into action constituted an egregious breach of gentlemanly and political etiquette. Austen Chamberlain and Sir Edward Carson condemned him.[27] Carson attacked the action publicly and asked Northcliffe why "he did not speak in the House of Lords where he could be answered."[28] Lloyd George golfed with Sir George Riddell the day after the letter was published and told him that Northcliffe could not be relied upon, that he had "no sense of loyalty and there is something of the cad about him."[29] The Welshman also believed the press lord was "angling for the Premiership." However, a week later, Lloyd George informed Riddell that Northcliffe had apologized for improperly mentioning the air post in his newspapers.[30] Regardless, the premier was too thick-skinned to allow his personal feelings to intrude in political calculations, and the press lord remained too powerful a force for a politician in Lloyd George's precarious position to alienate.

American opinion in the main backed Northcliffe's position. Arthur Brisbane cabled that "Everybody has read your letter declining Cabinet position with great interest. What you say about America is true. America should be kept enthusiastic and effective in the war. There must not and will not be any further situations like the Russian and Italian."[31] Willert wrote to his chief concerning the speculation "as to whether you are going into our Cabinet."[32] The 16 November *Chicago Herald* expressed gratification that Northcliffe "who knows both British and American methods sees by comparison how efficient

America's preparations are and stimulates a renewed determination to make greater efforts by his tribute." The same day's *Chicago Tribune* justified Northcliffe's "criticisms of efforts at home on ground that it will prove a stimulus to inertia." Geoffrey Butler reported to John Buchan from New York that Northcliffe had been attacked in the anti-British *Evening Post* and the pro-English *Globe* and that the suggestion was abroad that the press lord and the prime minister were "working together for political ends." This, Butler commented, "shows you at present the situation is quite inchoate."[33] He also passed along that the New York *World* printed a cartoon entitled "Balancing the Books," which "provoked much mirth ... showing Roosevelt and Northcliffe writing on both sides of a ledger, the one writing 'America is always wrong,' the other 'England is always wrong.'"[34]

Among the British critics of Northcliffe and Lloyd George was John St. Loe Strachey, the editor of the *Spectator*. He wrote to Asquith, now the de facto leader of the House of Commons opposition, that the Welshman was dangerous and should be removed because of his Paris speech. He urged Asquith to move a vote of censure in the Commons, which would "kill two birds with one stone, i.e. knock out Lloyd George and reduce Northcliffe to his proper proportions."[35] In the debate of 19 November, Lloyd George successfully parried the questions of Asquith and others by reversing himself and stating that the Supreme Council would have no executive power.[36] The next morning's *Daily Mail* praised Lloyd George for squashing the "Asquith Crisis."

The same day Northcliffe's letter was published in *The Times,* House and Lloyd George had lunch with the royal family. The two men joked about the prime minister's predicament with the press lord. House spoke of "how perturbed we were when we heard he was coming." Lloyd George replied, "of course you know why I sent him," and went on that he had noticed that, "before he left, N was doing much more talking, and I expected every day to have to recall him."[37] When House asked if Northcliffe was to return to the United States, Lloyd George replied, "I hope you will ask for him because I would like to send him. I would even be willing to take Roosevelt for a while in exchange, although," the Welshman added, "not permanently."[38] Afterward, House saw Northcliffe, who criticized the British lack of efficiency and said that Balfour and Bonar Law should be gotten rid of, along with the First Sea Lord, Jellicoe, whom the press lord referred to as "the man who ran away from a sea fight" at Jutland.

While still in America, Northcliffe had told Josephus Daniels of his unhappiness with the inactivity of the British navy. Under Jellicoe's leadership, he said, the navy was "not accustomed to fighting & had no real engagement since Nelson's day."[39] In October, *Daily Mail* criticism led Jellicoe to demand that Sir Eric Geddes, the First Lord of the Admiralty, seek charges against the newspaper. Geddes brought the matter to the attention of F. E. Smith, the attorney-general. As had been the case many times before, the articles were found objectionable, but not illegal.[40] When Northcliffe returned the campaign resumed. He complained personally to Lloyd George and Carson that the Sea Lord should be removed. Jellicoe finally resigned under pressure Christmas Day, 1917. His account of the dismissal included as a factor Northcliffe's influence on the prime minister.[41] The Marquess of Milford Haven (formerly Prince Louis of Battenberg) wrote to Jellicoe, "I cannot find words to express my disgust and indignation....We are ruled by journalists and lawyers."[42]

On 20 November Lloyd George and the War Cabinet met with the British and American Missions at 10 Downing Street. At this conference, House noted that Northcliffe railed against the "stupid and useless" censorship to which he paid no attention himself, adding that "the British Gov dare not interfere."[43] The colonel commented that the press lord "certainly is an unruly member. LG wants him back in America because he wishes to get rid of him here. N also insists on going to the inter-Allied conference at Paris, and he handles himself just as if he were dictator of England, and, in a way, he is, for the government are afraid of him."[44] Lloyd George appraised Northcliffe's performance at the conference to Riddell as "not a success. His observations were really very poor. He made the worst show of anyone present. I was surprised, and so were all of us. He is a strange creature. He came to Carson and referring to Carson's speech in which he castigated Northcliffe unmercifully, remarked, 'Well, I deserved it. I don't complain.' Carson was amazed and told me he thought N an extraordinary peronage [sic]."[45] When the king and House met the same evening, the colonel recorded that his royal host was "full of N and his dictatorial assumptions. He asked me to find out quietly, without using his name, whether the PM intended to let N go back to the US.... I told him I was ... certain N would return to America whether the PM desired it or not." House dined with Lloyd George afterward, and they also talked of Northcliffe. In the colonel's opinion, the prime minister was "evidently afraid of him and unfortunately, N knows it."[46]

Before attending the Paris Conference Northcliffe was rewarded, on 24 November 1917, for his American efforts by being elevated a step in the peerage, from baron to viscount. Wiseman reported to House that the king had talked of Northcliffe in a "denunciatory way. However, he was compelled to make N a viscount the next day. He must have done it with a wry face."[47] Reading explained to Wiseman that despite Northcliffe's recent attack, Lloyd George had neither the Liberal, Labour, or Conservative members behind him, but, that he did have a majority of the newspapers (if

Northcliffe's were counted). With an election impossible for the time being, it was therefore necessary to "placate" him in every way possible, including the appointment of Rothermere as air minister, which was announced in the 27 November *Daily Mail.*[48]

The British delegation departed for Paris on 27 November in what L. S. Amery called Lloyd George's "Noah's Ark" train.[49] Those aboard, more than a hundred in all, included Northcliffe, Milner, Balfour, Reading, Geddes, Robertson, and Sir Henry Wilson. After some preliminaries, on 1 December meetings at Versailles began between Lloyd George, Clemenceau, Orlando, and Colonel House. During the talks, House recorded, the prime minister was "constantly ridiculing N. He again asked if I would not agree to take N back if he would agree to let Roosevelt come to England. I replied that I had learned to like N and that he could send him to America and we would welcome him."[50] At the conference, the colonel and Northcliffe discussed whether returning to America would be wise. House advised him to "travel back and forth at intervals, and not remain long enough in either place to lose touch with conditions."[51] Northcliffe told House this coincided with his own view. The two men also spoke of the necessity of someone being near Lloyd George. The press lord thought that, while he had courage, at times the prime minister "hesitated to do necessary things" and worried too much about politics.[52] House was disappointed in the results of the Paris talks. He returned to the United States disheartened by the "utter lack of virile unity of purpose and control" he found in Europe.[53] Before departing, he sent Northcliffe a note of thanks for the assistance and cooperation he had given, "with characteristic energy and generosity the value of which it would be hard to estimate."[54]

While the Paris conference was ongoing, Lord Lansdowne, a distinguished Conservative elder statesman, had a letter published in the 29 November *Daily Telegraph* that called for negotiations with Germany for a reasonable compromise peace.[55] Lansdowne had originally submitted this to *The Times,* but Dawson refused to print it, fearing it would damage the effectiveness of the first meeting of the Supreme War Council scheduled within days.[56] This decision angered Northcliffe, who was in Paris at the time, but was nevertheless accused of violating traditional policy by keeping the letter out of *The Times.*[57] The press lord told Lloyd George in Paris that he would have published it, side by side with a "stinging leader."[58] The 30 November *Daily Mail* declared, "If Lord Lansdowne raises the white flag he is alone in his surrender." *The Times* commented that "the letter reflects no responsible phase of British opinion ... in all the Allied countries it will be read with universal regret and reprobation."[59] To stop any sympathetic growth of pacifism, Bonar Law responded for the government. He declared on 1 December that the letter was "a national misfortune" and that a "peace made on this basis would be nothing less than defeat."[60]

Northcliffe agreed wholeheartedly. He called for the word "Pacifism" to be dropped out of the *Daily Mail* "almost entirely. I have been in Europe nearly a month and have never met such a person....Virile people like the Americans...do not understand...our 'lack of backbone' in these matters. This lack adds to their long confirmed belief that we are 'effete.' We shall have some serious trouble with the United States before the end of the war. Let us do our best to postpone it. Let us not confirm the impression rubbed into them by the 15,000,000 Irish and German Propagandists that 'England will fight to the last American.'"[61] Louis Tracy, on the mission staff in New York, wrote that, "Lansdowne's letter created the worst possible effect here. It was most bitterly resented by all loyal Americans. Your description of it as a symptom of paranoia was hailed cheerfully as the 'right dope,' but I trust you will persuade the government to suppress any further outbreaks of the disease."[62]

After the adjournment of the Inter-Allied Conference, Northcliffe visited the front. On 4 December, at the invitation of the American commander, General Pershing, a special train took the press lord and other delegates to view the troop preparations of the United States.[63] Northcliffe reported to Cyrus Curtis, proprietor of the Philadelphia *Ledger,* that he had the great pleasure of "seeing the New England troops guarding fair France. Need I say how great an encouragement this is, not only to our splendid Ally, but to old England."[64] On the trip, Northcliffe and Pershing discussed the transportation problems involved in bringing over the American army and how best that army could be utilized. The press lord argued in favor of Lloyd George's recent proposal to House that some units be incorporated into the British Army.[65] Except in an extreme emergency (and then only temporarily), Pershing was absolutely opposed to having his troops serve under any other flag. He told Northcliffe that none of the colonial forces were used in that way and that "no people with a grain of national pride would consent to furnish men to build up the army of another nation."[66]

When Northcliffe also called at British general headquarters, Charteris, Haig's head of intelligence, recorded that the army's press ally "was very strong in his condemnation of the Government, much impressed with American methods as opposed to ours, and bubbling over with the importance of his own mission and full of himself. Unfortunately, D. H. was too pre-occupied to respond and Northcliffe was rather wounded in his self-esteem."[67] Haig had good reason for preoccupation. Battlefield developments in France, after appearing bright, had recently foundered. In the first few days following the 20 November push at Cambrai, the British army had made impressive gains. The 22 November *Daily Mail* called the assault a "Splendid Success" and a full-page headline proclaimed, "HAIG THROUGH THE HINDENBURG LINE." Unfortunately, the momentum of the British spearhead of 400 tanks was soon reversed when reserves were not brought up fast enough either to exploit the breakthrough or to halt the German counterattack. By the time Northcliffe visited GHQ the gain was lost, although Haig apparently chose not to share this information. A national celebration of ringing church bells prompted by overenthusiastic reports of victory soon turned into anger and disillusionment at the suppression of news on the following reversals.[68]

Cambrai proved the final straw that broke Northcliffe's previous solid support of the generals. By mid-December, at the same time he pressed the authorities about manpower, the press lord complained to Haig's secretary, Sir Philip Sassoon, that "in some quarters it is asked, what is the use of sending out men to be 'Cambrai-sed.'"[69] Besieged by criticism of the army, Northcliffe told Charteris that the government felt it had been misled and "that the suppression of the news from Cambrai is causing uneasiness that will undoubtedly bring about outbursts of public feeling.... I am convinced that unless examples are made of those responsible and changes at once made in Headquarters staff the position of the Commander-in-Chief will be imperiled."[70] In the following days, the Northcliffe newspapers began a campaign aimed at Robertson and his western strategy. *The Times* of 12 December featured the article, "A Case for Inquiry," which called for the punishment of those culpable for Cambrai. The next day the *Daily Mail* followed suit. Meanwhile, Northcliffe defended Haig, who, he felt, was being misled by his incompetent staff. The press lord warned Sir Douglas, through his secretary, Sassoon, about the intense popular resentment which was spreading to Parliament.[71]

As Northcliffe returned to the familiar ground of crusading newspaper owner, the chances of his returning to the United States dwindled. "The only possible solution of the leadership of the Mission," the press lord informed Reading in late December, was that "it should be incorporated with your work. When you come back to England I will take charge of it.... I congratulate myself that the organization is well constructed."[72] He had been asked to organize the London end of the War Mission and wrote to Andrew Caird, with the mission in America, that he was "glad to stay for other reasons. This Government is always on thin ice, half of it just as wobbly as it has always been.... I watch these people vigilantly day and night."[73] Wiseman cabled House that he believed Reading would soon replace Spring Rice and that Northcliffe probably would not return "at present."[74] When Spring Rice was recalled, Louis Tracy reported from New York that Northcliffe had received the credit. According to Tracy, a "man the other day coined a verb about the situation. He said that if someone did not behave himself, 'Northcliffe would Spring-Rice him.'"[75] A final decision was made in January that, while Reading returned, Northcliffe would stay in London.[76]

Remaining in Britain also allowed the press lord to continue his efforts to promote an Irish settlement. He instructed the *Daily Mail* not to mention the question because he did not wish to "injure some negotiations I am making."[77] Northcliffe used his press connections in this regard. John Healy of the Dublin *Irish Times*, who visited the press lord in London, attempted to arrange a peerage for his chairman to assure the paper would take the proper line after the reports of the Irish Convention were published.[78] Northcliffe wrote to Healy that he was "hopeful that we can get something done about Home Rule. If Ulster had any conception of the delay which has been caused in the United States through Irish hostility or apathy she would not fail to make the proper sacrifice."[79]

In January Sir Edward Carson resigned from the government to avoid possible conflicts with the ongoing Irish Home Rule talks.[80] The 22 January 1918 *Daily Mail* hailed the "Public Spirited Resignation," which left Lloyd George a free hand in the negotiations. Northcliffe's suggestion to Carson that Ulster come to an accommodation, prompted a reply that it would not be easy, after loyally supporting the war for three years, to tell the people of Ulster that the best way they could help would be "to agree to submit to a Govt. that you loathe and hate. This is your reward."[81] A message to the prime minister called for a bold stroke on the question, without which, Northcliffe was convinced, there could be no settlement.[82]

In late February Lord Decies reported the deteriorating situation in Ireland, including a breakdown in law and order, to the press lord and asked him to put the matter before Lloyd George. Decies wanted a new executive for Ireland to replace the present administration, which, in his opinion, had allowed the country to "drift."[83] Healy agreed that the state of affairs was "exceedingly bad" and proposed to Northcliffe that if the latest attempt to restore order failed, Decies should be given "careful consideration" for the viceroyalty.[84] Northcliffe felt Ireland was being "stirred up by German money" and deferred to Healy's expert judgment in the matter, while promising Decies that he would speak to the prime minister as soon as possible.[85]

Besides Ireland, the situation in Russia was also troubling. Despite the 15 December 1917 armistice signed by the Bolsheviks and Germans at Brest-Litovsk, Wilton, Petrograd correspondent of *The Times,* cabled his chief that Russia was "still the greatest factor in the war." He urged the immediate shift of Allied support to the anti-Bolshevist forces including "our friends" the Cossacks, Ukrainians, and Siberians.[86] A message two weeks later asked why *The Times* and the *Daily Mail* were "booming" the Bolsheviks and discouraging the pro-Ally forces in Russia.[87] Over the following months the British government negotiated unsuccessfully with both the Bolsheviks and their opposition, in the hope that some eastern pressure could be maintained on the enemy.[88]

In January 1918 the continuing attacks of the Northcliffe press on Robertson caused the military correspondent of *The Times* to tender his resignation. Repington did not share his chief's disillusion with the generals, and he felt Northcliffe had "tied himself to L.G.'s chariot wheels."[89] *The Times*, charged his resignation letter to its manager, had assumed a "subservient and apologetic attitude" toward the war cabinet in "neglect of the vital interests of the Army."[90] However, at the same time he sent the press lord a note thanking him for his courtesy during their association.[91] Always looking for allies against Northcliffe, Strachey commiserated with Repington:

> It is obvious...that you could not have gone on after the Northcliffe Press opened its guns upon Robertson and Haig. I don't pretend to understand the whole depths of the intrigue, but I feel pretty well convinced that Northcliffe and his entourage are out for the Premiership. The fact that he performs the "nolo episcopari" stunt only convinces me the more that he desires to be Prime Minister.... Of course a great many people will say that it is absurd and that I am fighting a shadow, but from many indications I have had, I deem this not to be the case.... I hope you will agree with me that though we won't have Northcliffe, we must get rid of L.G., or at any rate get rid of him from the seat of supreme power.[92]

Repington replied that he "most heartily" agreed with Strachey "in your views about Lloyd George and Northcliffe. I think they are a curse to the country. I have no doubt myself, though I have no direct evidence, that they are directing this odious campaign against the high command and I can't think why the Army Council does not take up Northcliffe, Marlowe and Fraser and have them shot."[93] Repington soon found more sympathetic employment with the *Morning Post* and became the most outspoken adversary of his former chief's attacks on army strategy.

Though accused of attacking the commander-in-chief, Northcliffe attempted to shield Haig's reputation in his newspapers. For example, Lovat Fraser noted in a précis of his article, "Things Hidden," which called for the truth about Cambrai, that he had "completely eliminated points which tell against Haig."[94] This 21 January attack on Robertson, but perceived by many also as an assault on Haig, described western strategy as "the strategy of the stone age" and called the theory of attrition "ridiculous."[95] Articles in the following week kept up the pressure. They asked more questions about Cambrai and, for the first time, accused the general staff of blaming the politicians or a lack of men for their own failures.[96]

Voices in the press and Parliament rose in defense of Robertson, among them the *Morning Post*. The chief of staff wrote the editor, H. A. Gwynne, a note of thanks in which he lamented what a "d____d disgraceful position for a Government to be in, to have to resort to such vile and unmanly tactics to get rid of those they don't like."[97] In the House of Lords, Northcliffe's old adversary, Lord Buckmaster, condemned the attacks and asked why they were not stopped if the government disagreed with them.[98] In a letter to Asquith's secretary, Sir Maurice Bonham-Carter, Strachey asserted that, "L. G. has begun his campaign to get rid of Robertson, and I suppose ultimately Haig, and is using the Northcliffe Press as the instrument."[99] The *Daily Mail* campaign following Cambrai, its owner gleefully noted, was "getting plenty of free advertising" in the other newspapers, which reminded him of the "good old days of the shells."[100]

Lloyd George, who wished to replace both Haig and Robertson, was incensed at Northcliffe's attack because he feared it would only rally support for them.[101] General Smuts, in France testing the waters for a change, noted the renewed support for Haig. In Parliament, the Unionist War Committee passed a resolution that called on the government to condemn the Northcliffe press. The prime minister urged the press lord to suspend his campaign and told Lord Stamfordham on 22 January that he "could have taken him out and shot him."[102] Lloyd George was also considering shifting Milner to the War Office in place of Lord Derby, who was very staunch in his defense of Robertson. He told Amery that Northcliffe's clamor had made it "impossible to sack Robertson or Derby for some time to come."[103]

At the same time Lloyd George refrained from making changes at the War Office, the resignation of Carson in January 1918 presented an opportunity to reorganize propaganda, which had been under his nominal control. Buchan wrote to Northcliffe that the department required a new head who could "get things done."[104] He suggested that it needed either to be made a ministry or to be put under someone in the war cabinet, adding that no one would be "half as good as yourself."[105] On doctor's orders, Northcliffe was resting at Elmwood. Since he had caught a chill in Liverpool on the return trip, his health had been poor. He informed Lord Ribblesdale, who had questioned his duties in the House of Lords, that he would like to lunch with him, but that his doctors had ordered him away to rest for ten days.[106]

Lord Beaverbrook, to whom Lloyd George entrusted the propaganda reorganization, approached Northcliffe with the new government plan.[107] Despite the Welshman's anger over the anti-Robertson campaign, Beaverbrook had pointed out to the prime minister that "a friendly arrangement" with the owner of the *Daily Mail* was vital to his administration, since he had no party and depended upon the support of the press.[108] The premier needed little persuasion. He had come to believe that propaganda was the troublesome press lord's true talent. Harnessing his energies would also have the added benefit of keeping him too busy to meddle elsewhere.

In the discussions with Beaverbrook, Northcliffe again refused to consider cabinet office in order to stay independent and to continue his criticism.[109] He did agree, however, to take over foreign propaganda if Beaverbrook took office as chancellor of the duchy of Lancaster, with overall control of British propaganda. He also gave Beaverbrook assurances of his loyalty to the prime minister. Beaverbrook told Riddell, "Whether I can rely on the guarantees I don't know. I expect to lose my life in a deadly scrap with Northcliffe which is sure to come sooner or later."[110] Riddell responded that Northcliffe would keep his word, but warned that "if new circumstances arise and you disagree with him, he will become your enemy. He has no give and take such as most men display when dealing with friends and associates." It was agreed that Northcliffe would report directly to Lloyd George and would assume the job at his request.[111]

However, for the next ten days the prime minister delayed in appointing Beaverbrook to the Duchy (mainly because of royal objections). The resultant climate of rumor, which reminded him of what had happened when he went to America, prompted Northcliffe to withdraw in a letter to Beaverbrook, who sent Lloyd George his own resignation the same day.[112] This action spurred the Welshman to go ahead with the appointment despite the king's disapproval. After further negotiations, Northcliffe was brought back into the fold. He accepted a more limited job as head of propaganda in enemy countries on 13 February, while Beaverbrook became head of the renamed ministry of information.[113] Northcliffe agreed to send the prime minister a monthly report on his activities.

The newspapers announced the appointment on 18 February. Once again there was confusion about Northcliffe's exact position. In response to a report that Bonar Law had stated that Northcliffe had been appointed minister of propaganda, the press lord lectured his staff that this "should have been telegraphed or telephoned to me. As a minister I should be a member of the government, which, with this wobbly ministry in power, would mean the virtual extinction of the 'Daily Mail' as an independent newspaper, for you would be obliged to support me in this government."[114] Nevertheless, rumors soon spread that the press lord was moving into rooms adjoining 10 Downing Street.[115]

The day after he accepted responsibility for enemy propaganda, North-cliffe wrote to the prime minister that a "bold stroke" was needed to settle the army question.[116] Though he longed to rid himself of Robertson, Lloyd George told Hankey that the newspaper campaign had made it impossible, as "all the world would say that it was done at Northcliffe's dictation."[117] Despite this, a few days later Robertson was replaced as CIGS by Sir Henry Wilson. Lloyd George finally had all he could take of Robertson's intransigence and gave the king a choice between himself and the CIGS.[118] Haig, unwilling to sacrifice his own career for Robertson, supported the prime minister. When Lord Derby, out of loyalty to Robertson, threatened to resign, Haig advised him to stay in office. The field-marshal recorded in his diary that Derby accepted his advice, adding that, "If he left, Lord North-cliffe would probably succeed him. This would be fatal to the Army and the Empire."[119] The *Daily Mail* of 18 February, now "THE SOLDIER'S FRIEND," announced Northcliffe's appointment and supported the choice of "Ugly Wilson" to replace Robertson. The newspaper called on Wilson to use the brains in the army, allow only trench-experienced men to order attacks, comb out the army behind the army, promote able new men of nonmilitary backgrounds, and stop undue elevation of cavalry officers. The "riddance of Robertson ought to do good," Northcliffe reported to Lord Rosebery, "as also the changes on Haig's Staff."[120] Notable among the alterations was the reassignment of Charteris, who wrote that after this time, Haig "was unwilling even to meet with Lord Northcliffe."[121] The commander-in-chief, like his predecessors in the press lord's esteem, found he could not control his troublesome newspaper ally.

Though his newspapers began to attack the generals, the press lord wanted it made clear that his publications supported the average soldier, who, he believed, would decide the next general election and run the nation after the war. He wrote to Charles Beattie, *Daily Mail* night editor, demanding to know why "the 'Soldier's Friend' was omitted from the issue of Monday the 4th. It does not seem possible to get into the minds of the people at Carmelite House that this item is of vital importance to the paper and the Army."[122] He explained to Marlowe that he had "called the paper 'The Soldier's Friend' for a deliberate purpose, and we ought to make it the Soldier's Friend by giving the soldiers news of all kinds. We do not do so. The Soldier's department of 'Answers' is now the backbone of the paper. Your nocturnal Scotsmen have not the imagination to look very far ahead and see the importance of the soldier vote."[123]

The fall of Robertson, added to the inclusion of Northcliffe and Beaverbrook in the government, caused considerable unrest in Parliament. Lord

Esher reported to Haig that the prestige of the prime minister had received a "severe shock" and that the "powers of the Amalgamated Press are greater than those of the Inquisition. The King blasphemes, but does not resist. He like everyone else, is terrorized by Northcliffe."[124] Esher went on that, although the hostility in the Commons was widespread, "no one dares to attack openly except a few more or less insignificant MPs." This situation changed a few days later, when Austen Chamberlain spoke out in defense of the power of the Commons, as opposed to the press power, which he considered an "insidious menace" to the government.[125]

During the 19 February debate on the army estimates, Lloyd George successfully defended his administration over the replacement of Robertson, whose views, he said, unfortunately had proved "incompatible" with British and Allied war policy.[126] Chamberlain used the occasion to call the press attacks on army and navy officers both "deplorable" and "cowardly." He urged the prime minister to "cut away the root of evil" by severing his connections with Northcliffe, Rothermere, and Beaverbrook. The functions of government and the press, he declared, were antithetical to one another and could not be combined. Members of the Commons were not allowed to make speeches contrary to the policy of the government or to attack its personnel, noted Chamberlain; therefore, the newspaper owners should not be allowed to print hostile articles.[127]

Chamberlain had expressed the long pent-up feelings of many in the Commons. He was widely congratulated for his remarks, and he followed up with letters to Lords Curzon and Milner, urging them to "take action inside the Government."[128] He was disappointed in their lack of response. Milner thought he was "barking up the wrong tree."[129] Others were more willing to act. Walter Long, the colonial secretary, considered resignation, but Chamberlain counseled against this because he did not wish to see Lloyd George's government fall, only to see the press lords out of it. Among the rank and file, the Unionist War Committee passed another resolution, this time in support of Chamberlain's position.[130] In response to this rebellion, Frederick Guest, the chief government whip, canvassed the strength of the government and advised the prime minister to tread carefully while standing by his friends and his appointments.[131] To act in accordance with the resolution, he noted, Lloyd George would have to dismiss all the press lords, "as none of them would resign." Beaverbrook and Rothermere, Guest believed, would continue to support the government up to, and through, the next general election. "Northcliffe," Guest said, "may do anything."[132] Milner recommended that, in the face of the strong feeling in Parliament, there was nothing to be done except "to lie low till the storm blows over.... The less people hear or see of Northcliffe, Beaverbrook (certainly the most unpopular name of all)...the next few weeks the better."[133]

When Chamberlain made his comments in Parliament, Northcliffe was deeply involved in a newspaper crusade over the food question, which continued to be one of Britain's major problems. The next day's "Message from the Chief" dismissed the political stir: "the Parliamentary 'criselet' being now over, let us get back to pigs and potatoes and rationing."[134] In March, Northcliffe informed Reading in America that "a further move has been taken in the discussion about the alleged press domination. Austen Chamberlain is starting the matter again in the House of Commons. He is absolutely like a bear with a sore head since his brother was ejected and he has lost office."[135] The press lord reassured Reading that, although a number of Britain's leaders, such as Carson, were getting "rattled" about the war, the prime minister was not one of them. Northcliffe reported that there were the "customary intrigues" against Lloyd George in Parliament, of which the country took no notice. He understood there was a plan to have a general election in October, a long time away in wartime, but ventured that when the election came, the prime minister would sweep the country and "eliminate a great many parliamentarians whose only desire is to unseat him."[136] He worried that the Welshman did not take care of his health, describing him as "whiter and older looking than even when you left."

Lloyd George made no answer to Chamberlain's February remarks about the press lords until 11 March, when he responded in the House of Commons. The prime minister defended his choices by saying that every Allied government had the press represented and that Beaverbrook, Rothermere, and Northcliffe were highly qualified for the posts they had been given.[137] Further, Beaverbrook and Rothermere had given up "all direction of their papers" when they accepted their duties. As for Northcliffe, since he held "no Ministerial office," he had not been asked to give up control. Northcliffe, the Welshman declared, "in addition to being a great news organizer," had made a "special study during the War of conditions in enemy countries" and was therefore invited to take charge of that department. "No man better qualified for that difficult task could," in Lloyd George's opinion, "be found in the Empire." Despite the prime minister's assurances, Chamberlain remained unconvinced that the press lords were not a danger. Later in the same debate, he pointed out the great amount of confidential information available to these representatives of the press and the constant temptation to make use of it in their journals.[138] He voiced his regret that they had not resigned or, alternatively, that Lloyd George had not "seen his way to make a clean cut and sweep away once and for all the whole atmosphere of suspicion and of intrigues which it has engendered." The *Daily Mail* dismissed the debate as "a shocking waste of time."[139]

As the parliamentary storms of February and March passed, the enemy propaganda operation settled down to its work. It became known simply as Crewe House after moving into Lord Crewe's Curzon Street mansion.[140] Wickham Steed, Northcliffe's advisor on foreign affairs, convinced his chief that the new department should concentrate its initial efforts against Austria-Hungary, the enemy's weak link.[141] The two men formed an effective combination. While Steed formulated the details and traveled into the field to implement them, Northcliffe fought on the home front against Foreign Office and war cabinet objections.[142] The press lord's wartime propaganda activities (most often directed at America) had already brought him into conflict with the Foreign Office, and from February 1918 he intruded his "amateur" efforts into Europe, becoming even more of a threat to traditionalists.

Steed's plan for Austria-Hungary required the British government to state plainly that British war aims supported the liberation of the peoples of the Dual Monarchy and its break-up. War aims had been a bone of contention for some time.[143] In recent months, the Lansdowne letter also had called for Britain to state her aims, which made Lloyd George hostile to the idea. However, when it was revealed that the negotiations going on at Brest-Litovsk between the Bolsheviks and the Germans included such topics as self-determination and open diplomacy, the prime minister felt it necessary to speak out in response.[144] Because the continuing manpower comb-out was causing considerable friction among British workers, Lloyd George hoped a public declaration of unselfish principles would help calm the waters and counter Bolshevik appeals to Allied workers to join a worldwide revolt.[145] Further than this, it was hoped they would justify "not merely the continuation but the intensification of the war effort."[146] The speech was also designed both to reassure Britain's Allies that they would continue to be supported and to appeal directly to the peoples of the Central powers with the argument that it was their governments that stood in the way of peace.[147]

The prime minister declared his war aims before a trade union conference on 5 January 1918, a few days before Wilson made public his Fourteen Points. The speech called for the restoration of Belgium, reparations for her recovery, the reestablishment of the "sanctity of treaties," a territorial settlement based on the ideal of self-determination, and the creation of "some international organization" to limit armaments and diminish the probability of war. Lloyd George called for an independent Poland, but stated that "the break-up of Austria-Hungary was no part of our war aims," while at the same time declaring, "we feel that, unless genuine self-government on true democratic principles is granted to those Austro-Hungarian nationalities who have long desired it, it is impossible to hope for the removal of those causes of unrest in that part of Europe which have so long threatened its general peace."[148] In *The Times* of 7 January, Steed called Lloyd George's proclamation "the most important State document issued since the declaration of war."[149]

Balfour, the ever-cautious British foreign secretary, did not believe explicit war aims were in Britain's best interests. He had consistently advised delay in the matter, hoping a separate peace could be arranged with Austria without revealing Britain's diplomatic hand.[150] Already personally hostile to Northcliffe, Balfour was less than receptive to his 24 February letter that asked the government to declare its policy toward the "various nationalities composing the Dual Monarchy."[151] Two courses of action were possible for the British, according to the press lord. The first, to work for a separate peace with the existing Hapsburg aristocracy, had been tried and had failed. The head of enemy propaganda declared it high time to try another policy. This involved breaking the power of Austria-Hungary, "the weakest link in the chain of enemy States," by supporting and encouraging all anti-German and pro-Ally people and tendencies.[152]

The most effective propaganda weapon, Northcliffe asserted, would be for the Allied governments and President Wilson to insist upon "democratic freedom" for the races of Austria-Hungary on the principle of "government by consent of the governed."[153] However, the ultimate aim of Allied policy should be, not to form a number of small states, but to create a non-German confederation of Central European and Danubian States.[154] The territorial promises made to Italy in the London Convention of April 1915 constituted a stumbling block; however, recent civilian unrest and military reversals had made the Italian government more amenable to compromise. On all sides, Northcliffe asserted, the time seemed ripe for a speedy implementation of his plan.

Balfour replied, two days later, that Northcliffe's "very lucid memorandum raises...the fundamental problem of the Hapsburg Empire," and promised to put the question before the cabinet.[155] He offered his own observation that the two alternative policies were not mutually exclusive. In Balfour's view, "everything which encourages the anti-German element...helps to compel the Emperor and the Court to a separate peace, and also diminishes the efficiency of Austria-Hungary as a member of the Middle-Europe combination." In either case, argued Balfour, "the earlier stages of that process are the same, and a propaganda which aids the struggle of the nationalities, now subject either to Austrian Germans or to Magyar Hungarians, towards freedom and self-determination must be right, whether the complete break-up of the Austrian Empire or its de-Germanisation under Hapsburg rule be the final goal of our efforts."[156]

Northcliffe's response, drafted by Steed, warned that the Italians believed a strong offensive against their country would be launched within the next two months. To weaken this offensive, or to turn it into a defeat, Allied propaganda must begin at once. While the press lord agreed that the two policies he had listed "may not be mutually exclusive," it was "very important that one or the other of them should be given absolute precedence."[157] Otherwise, it would place Northcliffe in an awkward predicament. He wished his department's efforts to be based on Allied and British policy. For this reason, he urged the war cabinet not to delay its own decision, and to obtain a verdict from France, Italy, and the United States as quickly as possible.

No official reply appears to have been made to this last request; however, after war cabinet discussion it was agreed orally that Northcliffe's department could go on encouraging the anti-German and pro-Ally elements in the Dual Monarchy up to the point of promising independence.[158] Though dissatisfied with this answer, the press lord decided to carry on. For the campaign, Steed had Northcliffe obtain the services of Dr. R.W. Seton-Watson, whom Steed called "the best official expert on Austria-Hungary."[159] Steed and Seton-Watson became codirectors of the Austro-Hungarian section of Crewe House.[160] After some problems with the Foreign Office, the pair traveled to Italy, the base of propaganda against Austria-Hungary, where the Pact of Rome between Italy and Yugoslavia, which modified the territorial promises made to Italy, was adopted on 7 March 1918.[161]

As his propaganda plans made some progress, Northcliffe was less than happy with the *Daily Mail* war coverage in France. Hamilton Fyfe, who had been returned to the field to address this problem, wrote that he was sorry his chief did not like the latest articles, but explained, "My view is that people at home, & the men out here, want to read about the little, every-day incidents of Army life & are sick of reading War with a W unless there is something really big on, which there probably will be very soon now."[162] Fyfe was certainly correct that something "really big" was about to happen.

On 21 March 1918, the German army, reinforced by divisions freed from the Russian front, began a massive assault in an attempt to end the war in France. British casualties in the first few days of this attempt to split the British and French armies were reported to be 150,000. The *Daily Mail* called it the "Greatest Battle of All" that would decide whether the British would be "Free Men or Slaves."[163] Over the following weeks, daily reports followed the conflict. General Pershing recalled that he spoke to Northcliffe in London on 24 March about the German advance and found him "almost unable to speak of it, so many of his friends had lost relatives."[164] The same day the press lord wrote to Bullock in New York that "we are at the beginning of the great battle which may decide the future history of the world for some centuries. I do wish that our American friends were quicker. Those I know here use very violent language towards their own Government. Every man available will be wanted."[165]

Meanwhile, in an attempt to blunt the Austrian offensive expected 10 April, millions of leaflets and other appeals were distributed across the Italian front by airplane, rocket, special rifle grenade, and contact patrols.[166] Northcliffe gained permission from the war cabinet, preoccupied by matters in France, for the propaganda literature to proclaim the independence of the "subject races."[167] Gramophone records in the "no man's land" between the trenches played Czech, Slovak, and Southern Slav songs to stir the national aspirations and pride of those serving the Austrians.[168] The desertions and disaffection stimulated by this nonviolent barrage were substantial factors in delaying the planned Austrian offensive.[169] Subsequent military intelligence credited the campaign with forcing the Austrians to replace some front-line regiments with more trustworthy troops.[170]

While some success was achieved in Italy, the military crisis in France brought calls for Northcliffe to withdraw his support of the government before a premature peace was made. With the storm "steadily rising," Leo Maxse wrote, "I do most earnestly hope that you as a man who have [sic] rendered such conspicuous service during the war will reconsider your present disposition to back up Lloyd George and Co. as from all accounts they are as least as capable as Squiff and Co. ... of going off around the corner, thoroughly rattled as the P.M. frequently is, and making a suicidal peace with the Boche.... There would appear to be hardly one stout heart in the War Cabinet, all of whose members I am told were gibbering at the recent crisis."[171] "I often hear remarks like those in your letter," Northcliffe replied, "but I never hear the names of any persons with whom to replace the present Government."[172] Maxse wrote again a few days later "as a friend" who was deeply concerned that the press lord was so "intimately identified with the Lloyd George Government, backing it up... and treating the War Cabinet as a sort of God Almighty, whereas it contains... four or five of the biggest b____ f____'s in the country." Maxse had feared this would happen from the time Northcliffe went to America, which, he said, "was Lloyd George's only object in offering it to you."[173] In response, the press lord repeated his request for the names of those he should support, and Maxse could only offer Robertson. Signing his letter "Beavercliffe," Northcliffe retorted that when Maxse found a "dictator who is not afraid of the politicians, I shall support him."[174]

Others suggested that Northcliffe take a more important role. J. Hugh Edwards, M.P., told the press lord that on a recent speaking tour of the north his name was acclaimed on every occasion it was mentioned. "I assure you," Edwards wrote, "that there are legions of us who feel that you ought to be in the

War Cabinet at so critical a time in our history."[175] Beaverbrook later commented that, in this crisis, Northcliffe held himself in reserve for duty as an emergency premier should the British be driven from the continent and the Lloyd George government fall.[176] However, there is no evidence to support this contention and it seems unlikely.

The German advances in France made it vital that American units be pressed into battle with the British and French. The gravity of the situation was underlined by Haig's April 12 "Order of the Day," that "Every position must be held to the last man.... With our backs to the wall and believing in the justice of our cause, each one of us must fight on to the end."[177] In the emergency, General Pershing had agreed to lend men to the cause, but only until the end of April. Pomeroy Burton sent Northcliffe a memo from France concerning Pershing's reticence to commit American troops further. The press lord forwarded this to Lloyd George.[178] Burton urged the government to appeal to President Wilson that the Americans would be needed for the duration of the battle.[179] Lloyd George cabled Reading in Washington that "It rests with America to win or lose the decisive battle of the war.... the President must overrule at once the narrow obstinacy which would put obstacles in the way of using American infantry in the only way in which it can be used to save the situation."[180] Intervention from Washington ensured continued American troop support.

Back in Britain, the dire military straits had cast a pall over the nation and its leaders. The House of Commons was in "utmost gloom," Cecil Harmsworth recorded in his diary. There was "not merely anxiety," but "stupefication and bewilderment at the hurried and confused retreat of our glorious army—just as if they were so many Italians or Rumanians."[181] As had happened throughout the war, military reversals brought changes in the government. To invigorate the War Office, Lloyd George removed Derby in mid-April and installed Lord Milner.[182] Rumors spread that Austen Chamberlain was to be brought into the war cabinet.[183] In response, the *Daily Mail* warned against the appointment of an "ineffective mediocrity" whose career had come to an end in the Mesopotamia failure.[184]

In the midst of the crisis, to promote Irish support, a renewed effort was made for a settlement. Northcliffe's 16 April message to *The Times* employees revealed his view of the pending Irish negotiations and the Chamberlain rumor:

> If this be true a more cynical job could hardly be perpetrated, nor one more calculated to discourage the Allies. At this moment the Germans are advancing on the Channel ports, and the strongest men in the Empire are wanted for the War Cabinet....

If he is appointed I shall not, after the passing of Home Rule, be able to continue giving the great support of my newspapers to the Government which I now do — often with a twinge of conscience. I have so notified the Prime Minister.

The War Cabinet is feeble enough at present.... the addition of Mr. Chamberlain would bring this Government down back to the level of Mr. Asquith's.[185]

After the choice was made official, the *Daily Mail* editorial, "How to Lose," attacked the government for playing politics in this time of crisis with "party maneuvers to placate tariff reformers."[186] On the other hand, the *Yorkshire Post* marked Chamberlain's selection as "a personal triumph for him over the Harmsworth influence; but more important still, it indicates that Mr. Lloyd George has determined openly to ignore it."[187]

Worried about the absence of Lord Milner's stabilizing influence from the war cabinet and the possibility of secret peace negotiations, Northcliffe consulted him. "I feel anxious at your disappearance from the War Cabinet," the press lord wrote. "Recent events have made me distrust the Prime Minister. He was asking for my support of the Home Rule Bill through my brother Cecil, who is one of his Secretaries, but did not mention the Cabinet change. I greatly fear that such a secret habit may some day find us face to face with a secret peace negotiation."[188] Northcliffe also warned of the "purely artificial agitation being attempted to bring back Robertson," which had no public support, nor any backing from the army. The only support seemed to be unsigned letters to the *Morning Post* and *Star*. He told Milner that he brought the matter up only because he had "personally found that the Prime Minister and his secretaries are prone to be affected by spurious Press manifestations of this kind." Milner reassured Northcliffe that, "I do not altogether like the *methods* of the Prime Minister. But I do not think any influence I have with him will be lessened by my not being in the Cabinet. I have no fear of his engaging in secret peace negotiations. And despite great defects wh.[*sic*] we all realise, I believe he is the best man we have to see us through the present intensely critical time."[189] Milner agreed that the agitation to get Robertson "put back as a sort of military dictator is quite artificial. Wilson is, in my opinion, a far abler man & much better [suited] to be Chief of Staff.... the prejudice against him...wh.[*sic*] that unprincipled scoundrel, Repington, has done his best to foster is steadily disappearing."

The "vote catching bargain with Mr. Chamberlain," the exclusion of Milner from the war cabinet, and Lloyd George's lack of resolution over Ireland combined to rouse Northcliffe to tender his resignation.[190] He wrote his brother Cecil that the prime minister "will not trick me again. I am getting away from all connection with him. It will not matter to him because he will have the full support of the 'Daily Telegraph.'"[191] Lloyd George did not respond directly. Beaverbrook acted as intermediary in negotiations to keep Northcliffe in place, at least temporarily. Recuperating at Elmwood from influenza and bronchitis, the press lord suggested to Beaverbrook that Sir Campbell Stuart, already doing most of the work as vice-chairman, become head of the London headquarters of the British War Mission.[192]

At Beaverbrook's insistence, Northcliffe agreed on 19 April to stay another month, only because "certain matters are pending which render it unwise for any sudden change to take place."[193] However, he asked to see the prime minister about the matter. The minister for information replied that Lloyd George

> expressed himself in the strongest possible way to the effect that it was quite impossible for you to give up your duties as things stand now. He said he was aware that the Italian Mission was now making good progress and was sure that it would prove successful. He was sending you a copy of the report on Austria, obtained presumably from our secret agents there, and felt certain that when you read it you would want to go on with the work.
>
> After this expression of opinion I did not hesitate to say that I felt certain you would agree to remain in control.
>
> As to the British War Mission in London, the Prime Minster is very anxious to have a personal talk with you before coming to a definite decision. When you are well enough to come up to town will you go and see him?[194]

Northcliffe responded that, unfortunately, his doctor would not hear of his leaving Elmwood until the bronchitis had disappeared, and further, that he had "not the least intention of continuing with the Departments mentioned for longer than the period I named.... I want to get away from any connection whatever with this alleged War Cabinet, in order that I may say what I think of it.... Will you please let the Prime Minister know of my decision at once, as I propose making a public statement on the matter, but do not wish to embarrass him unnecessarily."[195]

After Lloyd George sent a note (along with the promised evidence of the value of his work) that if the German offensive could be stopped as the British military chiefs hoped, Austria might "fall to pieces" once again, Northcliffe relented.[196] Under the circumstances, the press lord agreed to stay until a replacement could be found, but notified the prime minister of one important condition:

Though no binding assurances have been given, or engagement entered into, a very precise impression has been conveyed, under my responsibility, that this country, at least, favours a policy of Liberation of the Hapsburg subject races with a view to their constitution, in the event of an allied victory, into a non-German polity, or Danubian Confederation.

I, therefore, regard myself as entitled to be informed and consulted before any steps are taken, direct or indirect, public or secret, that might involve a departure from this line of policy.

It is not only a question of consistency in our methods, it is also a question of keeping faith with the representatives of the Hapsburg subject races who are being encouraged to fight on the side of the Allies for the liberation of their own peoples and for the Allied cause in general.[197]

In 1918 the Allied cause faced the greatest peril since the first months of the war. The crisis seemed to invigorate Lloyd George at the same time Northcliffe's own health and vitality waned. Not since December 1916 had the prime minister shown the political mettle he displayed, first in finally replacing Robertson and then installing Austen Chamberlain in the war cabinet— the last despite the howls of Northcliffe and others. Once again Conservative support proved more attractive than that of the press, and failures on the battlefield brought political changes at home.

The period after Northcliffe returned from America marked his greatest political moment of opportunity, had he wished to make an attempt to seize the reins of power. In *Men and Power,* Lord Beaverbrook saw Northcliffe as "the real victim of his own rash act" when he publicly turned down the air ministry in November 1917.[198] The diminutive press lord, destined to outlast all his great contemporaries, described with his usual drama Northcliffe's "rise and fall" in the six months from June to November 1917 as "unprecedented in political history."[199] Beaverbrook underestimated how far Northcliffe had already come by June 1917 and exaggerated the consequences of his letter six months later in *The Times.* The aftermath of his attack brought no fall. On the contrary, he was advanced a step in the peerage. The press lord continued his London duties with the American mission and soon added the tasks involved as head of propaganda in enemy countries. Had Northcliffe seriously sought cabinet rank, it is probable that Lloyd George, to keep him appeased, would have agreed. Commenting both on Northcliffe's unwillingness to join the cabinet and on those who saw him as "the man" needed to lead England, E. T. Raymond wrote that "Pegasus will not work in harness, and it would be madness to give him the reins."[200]

Those who believed that the owner of the *Daily Mail* aimed for the premiership misjudged him. While the thought of leading the country to victory over the German foe must have appealed to his considerable vanity, Northcliffe prized the freedom to criticize more than government rank. He wanted action, not power. Dawson commented, "Poor dear St. Loe Strachey solemnly writes...warning the country against 'a Northcliffe ministry.'... he gravely publishes letters discussing the likelihood of such an event. If he had an ounce of common sense he would realize that Northcliffe has neither the desire nor the power to form a ministry, but that this kind of pompous controversy gives him precisely the position which he enjoys and which Strachey detests."[201] The press lord told a publishing colleague, "I have no desire to be Prime Minister. I have twice refused Cabinet rank because I believe that I can be more useful in my present position as an independent critic. A good many of our radical friends want me in the Government in order to shut me up."[202]

Northcliffe's chief task in the rest of 1918 would be to turn his propaganda against Germany and then to consider what kind of a peace Britain could hope for in the aftermath of years of total war. H. G. Wells, as usual, had a grander vision. He wrote to the press lord,

> Our government is mentally stale. The German is equally stale. Hardly anyone seems to have a clear purpose....You seem to me — I'm not flattering you at all — in a position not only unique now but unique in history — for giving the lead into a new state of world politics.... the future is for the man who has the courage to be new. Your Ministry can be such a little bureau for scattering handbills among the Enemy troops or it can override the Foreign Office exactly as the Ministry of Munitions stepped over the Ordnance department. With your press instrument also available you can put on a hoarding before the whole world the outline of your settlement that would smooth German imperialism, catch the Emperor Charles into its purpose, unite the Atlantic and Mediterranean... & secure the peace of the world.[203]

This sort of challenge might have been met by the Northcliffe of 1914–17, but in 1918 it proved too much to carry out.

TEN

"Great Propaganda"
From War to Peace,
May to November 1918

IN THE SECOND HALF OF 1918, NORTHCLIFFE TURNED MORE AND MORE
to propaganda as a bloodless method to stem the German tide until sufficient
American force arrived to ensure victory. Though he put greater faith in
propaganda than in Haig, the press lord continued to support the army because he believed the Allies must destroy the Germans on the ground before
the war could be safely concluded. In his view, a compromise peace would
merely interrupt, not end, the conflict. By May, the deteriorating military
situation had created a politically dangerous climate, which was ignited on
the 7th by publication in *The Times* and other newspapers of a letter by General Sir Frederick Maurice, who had been relieved only recently of his duties
as director of military operations.[1]

The Maurice letter accused Lloyd George and Bonar Law of misleading
statements about army strength in France, and the furor surrounding it grew
into a debate on the general direction of the war. The accusations culminated
in a confrontation with Asquith in the Commons which turned into a triumph
for Lloyd George.[2] The 10 May *Daily Mail* editorial, "Squashed! Mr. Asquith
and General Maurice," trumpeted the victory. Further articles recounted
"Another Old Gang Fiasco" and "General Maurice's Dud Bomb." To Lord
Reading in America, Northcliffe commented that he had "no doubt read
of the ridiculous attempt of the Old Gang" to unseat Lloyd George, and that
when it came to a "show down" in the House of Commons it was obvious
the prime minister had overwhelming support. In the press lord's view, the
Welshman was "complete master of the country if he only knew it."[3]

At the same time, Northcliffe's propaganda department turned to the
main enemy, Germany. Ordered by his doctors to Bournemouth for a rest

cure, the press lord nevertheless stayed in close communication with his charges. In light of the achievements against the Dual Monarchy, Lloyd George sent a note that he felt "sure that much can be done to disintegrate the *moral* [*sic*] of the German army along the same lines" and that he would "watch with great interest future developments."[4] His letter did not mention the condition the press lord had laid down in late April, when he agreed to continue his work, concerning government policy toward Austria-Hungary. "I have as yet received no assurance from you," Northcliffe reminded the prime minister, "that I shall be kept informed and consulted before any steps are taken, direct or indirect, public or secret, involving any departure from the policy I have adopted with the full consent of the Government in my Propaganda work."[5] Despite repeated inquiries, this assurance was never given.

While he supported the prime minister as the best available hope for British victory, the press lord believed Lloyd George's preoccupation with the House of Commons and politics left him too little time for the real business of the war. He wrote to Beaverbrook at the ministry of information that Lloyd George needed "one shrewd man at his side," such as Northcliffe had in every department of his businesses.[6] He went on that the Welshman was "so heavily engaged in seeing the wrong people and has such a overworked personal staff" that he never heard of many real problems. The press lord felt it the duty of his newspapers to give needed criticism. He lectured the staff of *The Times* on 7 May that "we are doing the Prime Minister a disservice by continually purring about him. He is a vitalizer, but no organizer. He will neither reform himself nor appoint strong men to help him."[7] The chief proprietor informed Dawson a week later that, in his opinion, the paper lacked "independence."[8] He added that *The Times* had been very noncritical for months, and he did not wonder that it was regarded as a "Government organ." Dawson's chief reminded the editor that he had "kept out of the Government partly in order that it may not become such." Turning to his propaganda effort against Germany, Northcliffe complained that the "most urgent matter which I have in hand...cannot be decided except by the Prime Minister.... I am now waiting for weeks for a decision as to whether I am to distribute propaganda over German lines by aeroplane or not? As it is, he is being bluffed by the Germans. The Prime Minister could settle the matter in five minutes."[9]

The War Office propaganda arm had used airplanes successfully since 1915.[10] The superiority of the British in this area led the Germans to declare the activity contrary to the laws of war. Beginning in 1917, convicted British pilots were incarcerated, not as prisoners of war, but in civilian jails. In the face of this policy, the British government halted the flights and threatened retaliation. However, the other Allied powers continued using airplanes. Incensed at his government's pusillanimity, Northcliffe wrote to Beaverbrook, "it is incredible that we should be ... the only nation which ignobly is afraid to drop propaganda into enemy lines by aeroplane."[11] He blamed the prime minister for refusing to reverse the decision of the army council. "I am handicapped," he declared, because Lloyd George, "always has one eye on Mr. Asquith and one on the Government. We can get nothing done. The Germans are afraid of our propaganda. They want to come to an arrangement with us to stop it."[12] Northcliffe also held Lord Milner responsible. He wrote to the secretary for war on 8 May suggesting that the British consider reprisals against German pilots. Milner replied that the threat of reprisals already had gotten several British soldiers released from prison and that, though British flights had been suspended, the government held itself "free at any moment" to resume them.[13] The press lord complained to Balfour at the Foreign Office, "We are greatly handicapped by the fact that, though the enemy are using aeroplanes for the distribution of Propaganda, we are not allowed to do so except on the Italian front."[14]

Northcliffe's personal effort was limited by a series of illnesses, including bronchitis, influenza, and laryngitis, that plagued him in this period and led him to put Sir Campbell Stuart, the deputy-director, in day-to-day charge of Crewe House operations until he could recover.[15] Stuart acted as chair of the propaganda committee meetings until October and handled organizational and administrative duties while others, such as Steed, saw to the propaganda details. H. G. Wells was persuaded to direct the campaign against Germany.[16] Wells believed that some sort of world government was necessary and had promoted the idea of a League of Nations. When the two men met at Crewe House to discuss propaganda, Wells reported that Northcliffe told him, "You want a world revolution.... Isn't our sitting here social revolution enough for you."[17]

Wells had sent Northcliffe a plan for German propaganda before he officially joined Crewe House.[18] His scheme called for four simultaneous approaches: one underlined German responsibility for the war, another emphasized the probability of defeat, a third pointed out the waste and loss involved in continuing the war, and the fourth proposed a "League of Free Nations" as a nobler replacement for the German dream of world domination. Wells dubbed the last appeal the "Great Propaganda." This plan for world organization, meant to change Germany by luring the population away from dreams of "Berlin-Baghdad" and "Mitteleuropa," became the cornerstone of the campaign.[19] Crewe House strategy for Germany was refined in a special 31 May meeting of the committee for enemy propaganda. A Wells memorandum called for a "clear and full statement" of the war aims of the Allies, including an international congress or "League of Nations," to be used as "the standard of their activities."[20] He blamed the present disaster on the German ruling classes and called for "the sharpest distinction" to be drawn between Germany and "its present Junker Government" in all British propaganda.[21]

The Crewe House scheme for Germany was submitted to Balfour in a 10 June 1918 letter from Northcliffe, which called for the Allies to "put in the forefront" their ultimate objectives and the use they would make of victory.[22] The propaganda plan offered both an element of fear (in a continued blockade) and an element of hope (that peace might be achieved by renouncing their military goals). To further the element of hope, Northcliffe called once again for a redefinition of Allied war aims, which, he asserted, "have been defined too loosely to be comprehensible to the Germans." Also, there had been apparent inconsistencies which made it possible for enemy writers to misrepresent the aims as "dictated by imperialistic ambition ... involving annexations and indemnities." If the real object of the Allies was to establish a world peace that would preclude war, it seemed necessary that the separate aims, such as the restoration of Belgium, the liberation of Alsace-Lorraine, and the establishment of civilized government in Mesopotamia and Palestine, should be put forward as essential points in the general scheme for the settlement of world politics on a basis which would remove the causes of future wars.[23] Northcliffe was well aware of the great practical difficulties that were bound to arise as soon as an attempt was made to give "formal expression to the general idea of a League of Free Nations." However, he believed it was most urgent that some statement should be put forward at the earliest possible date because this would in effect be an offer to the Germans of conditional peace. If accepted, Germany would be able shortly after the conclusion of the war to come into the new society of nations. If refused, the war would have to continue, while it was made clear to the German people that the "privilege of admission to this society would inevitably be postponed for a period proportional to the length of time that they continued the war."[24]

Balfour replied that he was in general agreement and would bring the letter before the cabinet, but he noted that it made no mention of the German colonies.[25] Northcliffe answered that he had "no settled views" on the colonies, except that they should not be returned.[26] He added, however, that since Germany was responsible for the war, the Allies were entitled to demand "restitution, reparations and guarantees as preliminary conditions of any peace settlement." At the 25 June meeting of the committee for enemy propaganda, Wells reported that the effort against Germany remained handicapped by the failure of the British to declare any official policy. He complained that his subcommittee was provisionally going ahead with its work, but was embarrassed by the "scores of foreign policies being followed in this country by different people with conflicting and possible disastrous results."[27]

Crewe House also had responsibility for propaganda against Bulgaria.[28] Here again, Northcliffe asked for a clear and comprehensive Balkan policy from the government as a precondition of success. Any solution would need to include a definition of the competing claims of Bulgaria with Serbia, Greece, and Rumania. Without this, he argued, "any propaganda in Bulgaria would resolve itself into a competitive bargaining between the Allies on the one hand and the Austro-Germans on the other."[29] The press lord asked Balfour for a reply as soon as possible so that he could send a mission to Salonika to start the work. This was done after Balfour replied that he agreed with the "general ideas underlying your policy."[30] Beaverbrook also asked Northcliffe to take over propaganda in Russia, which the press lord declined after discussions with his staff convinced him that it was more than they could handle and, although large parts of it were occupied by the German army, it was not an "enemy country."

Crewe House did agree to accept responsibility for Italian propaganda, which had been handled by the ministry of information. Steed added this to his other duties.[31] Since Italy was an Ally, Balfour worried that the activities of Crewe House might damage relations between the two countries. The foreign secretary wrote to Northcliffe that he was "anxious about reports of Steed's attitude toward the Yugo-Slavs at Versailles *despite* an FO briefing."[32] Steed reportedly attacked the Italian government, which if true, Balfour felt, would have an "unhappy effect" on Italian relations. The Foreign Office notified Sir Rennell Rodd, the British ambassador in Rome, of the changes in propaganda procedure.

On the battlefront, the German army once again came within forty miles of Paris. The 10 June *Daily Mail* editorial, "The Battle for Paris: Mr. Clemenceau's Heroic Lead," recounted the struggle, while the newspaper planned for evacuation. George Curnock reported to his chief that arrangements had been made to transfer the *Daily Mail* office to Nantes if need be; however, he added that it was "not believed here that Paris will fall; but it is anticipated the Boche will endeavour to get near enough the next time to bring the city under a naval gun bombardment and treat it like Rheims and Amiens. In such an event there would be a great exodus. Already 1,600,000 have gone."[33] As in 1914, the Allies stiffened before Paris and began to drive back the enemy the next month.

In Northcliffe's estimation, to accept anything less than total victory would be an unpardonable sin. June revelations of peace initiatives at Russia's expense, led by Milner, reached him via Steed and Clifford Sharp, *The Times* correspondent in Stockholm.[34] Sharp also reported that Lloyd George was trying to convince British socialists such as the Webbs to sacrifice Russian territory to Germany. He believed that others in the government, including Curzon, Bonar Law, and Beaverbrook were simply "afraid." With no politician having the stomach to lead, Sharp turned to *The Times* and Northcliffe. He told Steed that he had "never been a Northcliffe enthusiast, but I am certainly leaving England with the feeling that amongst those in high places he more than any deserves the confidence of those of us who mean to see things through."[35] This episode destroyed the press lord's former staunch faith in Milner, and he began to speak of his German connections as he did those of Haldane.[36]

Both Northcliffe and Steed believed that any peace that gave Germany a free hand to exploit the vast resources of Russia would only mean a future, more powerful, attack on the west by a regenerate enemy. The 21 June *Daily Mail* carried the article "Watch Lansdowne and Others," which declared that any ministers who made a peace that allowed Germany "a free hand in the East" would "deserve to be ... hanged by their indignant fellow countrymen ... who would not suffer the war to end in so shameful a betrayal." When this blast brought only silence from the government, Northcliffe told Steed that "We've hit the bull's eye!"[37] The reported clandestine negotiations, added to the prime minister's refusal to reconstruct the government on lines which he approved, led Northcliffe to belittle Lloyd George, as well. He told Dawson that the "difficulty of dealing with our Prime Minister is that you never know what he is up to. He is oblique, evasive and Welsh. In dealing with President Wilson, as I did for six months, one had a feeling of absolute confidence in the man. The one endeavors to cajole; the other commands. One is an intriguer; the other has no comprehension of such mental perverseness."[38]

On the propaganda front, when no action had been taken by mid-June on the question of dropping leaflets by airplane, Northcliffe renewed his plea to Milner that propaganda against Germany was being "severely handicapped" because balloons were not satisfactory substitutes.[39] Colonel Hankey responded for the war cabinet that, to the contrary, the general staff were holding up the use of planes because balloons had been "such a conspicuous success, it has not been considered right to subject our airmen to the risk of reprisals, with which they are still threatened in this work."[40] Wells wrote to Northcliffe that he wished the press lord was healthier so he could take hold "as only you can do of the whole ... Propaganda situation."[41]

The director of propaganda against Germany reported the continuing disorganization, waste, and internecine conflict in Britain's publicity effort and ascribed the cause to the absence of a definite scheme of action. For propaganda to be effective, in his view, there must be the clearest most emphatic statement of its leading ideas, "known to all the organization and accepted and loyally adhered to by everyone."[42] It also must be the policy of Lord Beaverbrook's organization and *The Times*, Wells argued, because from a foreign point of view, *The Times* still spoke for England. Additionally, Wells reported, the National War Aims Committee, the official duties of which were to combat socialism and pacifism in Britain, often contradicted the efforts of Crewe House.[43] He discussed this committee with Frederick Guest, one of its members, and found that its anti-German activities, assisted by Northcliffe's *Evening News*, supplied the enemy with valuable propaganda material. Wells complained to the press lord that at the same time Crewe House sent out leaflets that called attention to the "great future that lies before a regenerate Germany[,] provided it regenerates," the *Evening News* made daily demands for German internments.[44] "This campaign to insult and repudiate everything German," he added, "grows and grows. It is an infernal nuisance to us." Wells did not see how Crewe House could be "anything but ineffective and a little absurd until the War Aims Committee and the section of the press that goes beyond it, are made to toe the line that we have drawn." Unless there was better teamwork, he warned, the war was "going to end in a worse muddle than the muddle that begot it."[45]

Northcliffe answered Wells's many criticisms point by point. First, as to control of propaganda, he stated that his commission was direct from the prime minister and not Lord Beaverbrook, who, he was not sure, "had any knowledge of organization."[46] The press lord agreed to see Beaverbrook as soon as he was well enough and promised to show him Wells's letter. On the question of Germans in England, Northcliffe disagreed completely and would "intern every one of them who had been naturalized within five years of the outbreak of the war." As to the National War Aims Committee, he stated that he had "no authority over it" and considered it "a scandalous series of jobs." The press lord traced the overall problem back to Lloyd George:

> The whole of these difficulties could be settled if the Prime Minister were a man of business, which he is not. If he would summon into a room these miscellaneous propagandists whom he has allowed to multiply and would deline their territories and functions, we should get a move on. That is not the way of our gifted orator. Flashing about Europe like a dragonfly, from Edinburgh to Taranto and from Versailles to Downing Street, with one eye on the war and ... the other on Mr. Asquith, he has no time, even if he had the executive ability to achieve practical results.[47]

If given a free hand, Northcliffe told Wells, he would deluge the German people by airplane with "all sorts of American and English views, whether I agree with them or not." He had asked *The Times* to publish the "great

Socialist Manifesto," although he did not agree with much of it, but, nevertheless, he hoped to send it into Germany.

Wells also devised a Socialist Manifesto for use in Germany and agreed with Northcliffe's assessment of the National War Aims Committee. He reported that it seemed "to be a pretty costly organization for doing nothing. The worst thing about it is that it has no War Aims at all."[48] He was largely in agreement with Northcliffe concerning airplane propaganda, but felt "the matter" should be chosen very carefully. He sent the press lord a report from Adastral House, the War Office propaganda office, where, he said, "Dr. Chalmers Mitchell is doing some very effective work."[49]

As Northcliffe's health improved in July, preparations began for a general election based on the newly enlarged franchise.[50] The widespread industrial unrest during the war had convinced the press lord that the new electorate would not support a government made up of the same old Conservative faces that presently surrounded Lloyd George. He feared revolution would follow the return of such an old-fashioned and reactionary crew. The press lord also believed that the armed services vote would be crucial. Since it was expected that the poll would be held before the end of the war, newspaper coverage of the campaign would be critical for the soldiers overseas. He backed a redistribution of land to returning veterans who wanted it, and lectured his employees on the question.[51]

Also in early July, ongoing disagreements with the Foreign Office led Beaverbrook (not for the first time) to tender his resignation. Since its creation, the ministry of information had sought a free hand for its propaganda activities overseas and had asked for access to the intelligence files of the Foreign Office, War Office, and Admiralty. Balfour considered this a crude violation of his dominion, and his department bedeviled Beaverbrook with endless delays and other obstacles.[52] In the latest incident, Lord Hardinge, the permanent under-secretary, interfered with a propaganda effort aimed at Japan. Besides Italy, Northcliffe dealt with enemy countries; consequently, his department was not subject to the same degree of conflict with the Foreign Office. He felt the ministry of information was doing good work, especially in Canada and America, and wrote to Beaverbrook that, "While I think it might be wise to defer your resignation in the hope of improving relations with Lord Hardinge I shall support you if he continues to play the enemy's game by opposing propaganda."[53] The press lord told C. J. Phillips at the Foreign Office that Beaverbrook had drive but was "apt to regard all permanent officials as fools."[54] Even so, he believed it was not "beyond the wit of man to devise a solution by which the Foreign Office can work with him."

Northcliffe sent Balfour a letter supporting Beaverbrook's position, while stating that he, personally, had "received every help and courtesy" from the

Foreign Office in his own work.[55] Despite their previous differences, he added that Balfour should be in the war cabinet so that misunderstandings, such as the War Office asking him to do things contrary to the wishes of the Foreign Office, would not occur. Balfour replied that he also felt their relationship to have "been of the pleasantest" and that he was content to leave all details of propaganda to Beaverbrook.[56] However, the foreign secretary went on, it was "obviously impossible to have two Ministries responsible for Foreign Policy; and this is a position into which, under the existing system, we are easily left."

When Beaverbrook and the Foreign Office could not come to terms, Lloyd George became involved. Northcliffe told him that:

> The dispute between Beaverbrook and the Foreign Office is undoubtedly delaying propaganda and lengthening the war....
>
> My experience of our Ambassadors is that they have no comprehension of propaganda, which is, of course, a highly complicated system of advertising, and no part of their training.
>
> Beaverbrook told me that he had been offered some situation in the Foreign Office, but that it would deprive him of any influence that he had.... Beaverbrook's propaganda work has been, in my opinion, a great success.
>
> ... If my doctor would allow me to use my voice I could settle this dispute, which is more unfortunate than may appear on the surface.[57]

Beaverbrook reported to his colleague on 11 July that, "Nothing has developed since I saw you on Saturday. The Prime Minister, Mr Balfour & Lord R. Cecil made a great attempt to settle the matter on Tuesday afternoon—but I don't think we made any real progress. Settlement means subjection so far as I am concerned."[58]

As Beaverbrook grappled with the Foreign Office, Northcliffe went on with his own effort to persuade the War Office to amend its airplane policy. He told Beaverbrook that he had been "in communication with Lord Milner and Sir Maurice Hankey about the humiliating confession of fear of the Germans which we have manifested by acceding to their will that we should not use aeroplanes for propaganda."[59] He enclosed a letter from Hankey suggesting that Beaverbrook should intervene, and sent an extract "from the Italian wireless" that demonstrated "the effective way in which the aeroplane can be used as compared with the doubtful meanderings of the balloon." On 12 July Beaverbrook supported Crewe House with a memorandum to the war cabinet on the issue.[60] Five days later, he informed Northcliffe that the government had agreed to allow a resumption of airplane propaganda. Delighted to hear that the war cabinet had, finally, rendered it possible to carry out "efficient" propaganda in Germany, the head of enemy propaganda told Beaverbrook, "I am sure that we shall now be able to get to work, but the incident makes one despair of the brains of G.H.Q."[61] He suggested that Adastral House, the War Office propaganda branch doing the same work, become a part of the department of propaganda in enemy countries.[62] Beaverbrook agreed and recommended this to Milner.[63] Unfortunately, because of further disagreements, the war would be in its final days before the use of airplanes was resumed.

In mid-July, Wells was angered by the dismissal of a young Crewe House assistant, who, it had been discovered, came to Britain from Germany at age thirteen.[64] He complained to Northcliffe that his "most useful assistant" had been "swept away...by this infernally indiscriminate anti-German wave."[65] In the same letter, Wells again pressed Northcliffe over the cooperation of his newspapers. "Lord Northcliffe of Crewe House has sent Mr. Balfour a very remarkable document," said Wells, "embodying his conception of the Allied War Aims. Will he not now induce Lord Northcliffe of Printing House Square and Carmelite House to insist upon that document becoming the guiding memorandum upon foreign affairs of the Times, the Daily Mail and the Evening News?"[66] The press lord answered abruptly, "Let me say at once that I entirely agree with the policy adopted by my newspapers, which I do not propose to discuss with anyone. I have not wandered about Prussia for two years without learning something, and if you will wait you will find that I will unearth much sinister and alive Prussianism in England."[67] Wells replied that he was "sorry that you insist on being two people when God has only made you one. I cannot, for my own part, separate 'The Evening News' from Crewe House while you remain one person."[68]

This was only one incident in an ongoing dispute between Northcliffe and Wells over the treatment of Germans in Britain and proposals for the postwar period. The distance between the conciliatory and punitive positions of the two men finally led to Wells's resignation. In response, the press lord wrote to him, "I cannot say how sorry I am that you have deprived Crewe House of your valuable services, and I want to thank you for laying the foundation of the great work that will be carried on, now that we have, at a length, been given permission to use the aeroplane.... I hope you will not resign from our Committee. All committees need stimulus and criticism."[69] Hamilton Fyfe was appointed to take over German propaganda.

Wells's reasonable view of the alien question was in the minority. Every setback in France inflamed the British public over the matter. Northcliffe instructed Dawson that, "in view of the forthcoming Debate about the Germans in England, I should very much like a strong article distinctly disasso-

ciating ourselves from the Gov in their flabbiness in this and other respects....
if you watch the provincial newspapers, you will see that almost every small
body is passing Resolutions about the Germans in our midst."[70] The press
lord again criticized *The Times* for being too friendly to the government and
for being known in the country as a government organ. "I declined to join
the Gov," he told Dawson, "because I wanted to keep my independence and
get things done.... So long as Sutherland continues to tell Lloyd George
that 'The Times' will dance to any tune he plays, so long will he continue his
covert negotiations with Haldane, Webb, MacDonald and others."[71] Northcliffe notified the *Daily Mail* staff that "We must continue to develop the alien
propaganda. I hear on excellent authority that certain Home Office officials
are determined to protect their friends."[72]

In addition to taking action against the aliens in Britain, Northcliffe believed the German nation should be punished after the war by economic
sanctions. While his official propaganda declared that these might be tempered if the enemy gave up its plans for world domination, the *Daily Mail*
more closely reflected his own view that it was impossible to return to "business as usual" after the war.[73] The prime minister also wielded the economic
weapon, declaring in early August that the longer the war, the sterner the
sanctions would be.[74]

At the same time, questions were raised in the House of Commons concerning the extravagant practices of the businessmen at the ministry of information.[75] Stanley Baldwin, M.P., joint financial secretary to the treasury,
defended Beaverbrook for the government. He sent Northcliffe a note the
same day that he was very glad that the press lord's name was not mentioned
in the course of debate, "as I was most anxious that nothing should be said
about your propaganda work in the House at present."[76] Northcliffe publicly
praised Beaverbrook in a letter to the editor of *The Times*. Privately, he sent
the minister of information a "friendly but frank letter about last night's suspicion arousing debate:"

What was said in the House of Commons by more or less irresponsible people is being said everywhere, and by responsible people, and various evil rumours are being spread, chiefly, I believe by members of your
old gang.

I gave you the best support I could in my newspapers this morning as
I promised you I would, but I cannot continue that support unless you
help me by cleansing your dud ridden establishments....

You have done a great deal to improve your Ministry—more than
your critics know, but the war winning is being hampered by your reten-
tion of numbers of men who are just as inefficient as the people in the

Foreign Office & Home Office, whom I am continually prodding. I do not suppose a day elapses upon which we do not receive some complaint about your Ministry....

On the broad question of reform, I suggest that you free your Ministry from criticism and make it efficient by firing everybody who is not a propagandist. To suggest that Company Directors are propagandists is to suggest that they can advertise, and as you know, very few of them can....

Those who are critics of inefficiency in government must themselves be efficient.[77]

Beaverbrook's defense was equally frank:

There seems to me a misunderstanding on the main question. It is chiefly the men who I have inherited from the old regime who might be described as "propagandists," though of course I have got rid of some and added others. The business men are almost entirely the people brought in by myself because of the muddle in administration that the "propagandists" were making.

Their position and influence has been distorted out of all relation to the facts....

I am really a victim of attacks from the Radical Press, not because I have employed officials of this type, that is a mere red herring across the trail, but because I stand in relation to Germany for the whole policy that the "Times" and the "Daily Mail" support and the "Westminster" and the "Daily News" detest....

Journalism, business and politics are all propagands [*sic*] in one of their aspects. But the trouble is that this particular problem of national propaganda is entirely new, and there are no experts on the matter as a consequence. One simply has to take people who have been concerned in one or other of the professions of which propaganda is a part.[78]

In July and August the German army's last hopes for military victory collapsed when the Allies, unified under Marshal Foch, attacked and caught them off guard. Afterward, General Ludendorff always called 8 August 1918, the "Black Day of the German Army."[79] However, even those closest to battlefield developments predicted the war would last well into 1919 or longer, with the Germans entrenched on a shorter line in fierce defense of their own soil. Allied planning and strategy were made on that basis, despite ongoing rumors of peace. Northcliffe agreed with those who thought that the war would last at least another year. He sent his nephew Esmond Harmsworth,

Rothermere's only surviving son, a note predicting that, though the war would be long, it would "end with the total dispersal of the German tribes."[80]

On the publicity front, Northcliffe called for an Inter-Allied Propaganda Conference.[81] He notified Lloyd George that he had summoned representatives of the governments of France, Italy, and the United States to London to confer with his department as to how their activities could best be coordinated.[82] The conference, attended by forty Allied members, began in London at Crewe House on 14 August. During its three days of sessions, which focused on Germany, the participants shared information and created a permanent London Inter-Allied Enemy Propaganda Council to unite the efforts of the Associated powers.[83] Northcliffe also proposed to the prime minister that one consolidated organization, to be called the British War Mission, should act as an umbrella for all his responsibilities.[84] He wrote that he would "be glad to accept the Chairmanship of this Mission" to carry on his work which, in his opinion, was "daily growing in importance."[85] Lloyd George approved this change.

At the same time, rumors spread that Northcliffe and Rothermere were planning to replace Lloyd George. The prime minister put some credence in a report to this effect that he had from Milner. Sir George Riddell, who had dinner with the press lord on 12 August, disagreed and noted that Northcliffe "seemed quite friendly to L. G."[86] Perhaps the prime minister believed there was a threat from the press lords because of the discussions he had with them concerning the coming election. Northcliffe told one of his *Daily Mail* employees, Andrew Caird, in January 1919 that since the previous August he had "conducted a campaign regarding the General Election. The original plan was that the Prime Minister should go to the country on his own, forming a Government of 'All the Talents' and Parties beforehand. I was asked to join it, but declined."[87] This account gains plausibility from the Welshman's sounding of his advisors in August 1918 as to whether they thought Northcliffe's inclusion would strengthen the war cabinet, which, he told them, he had reason to believe the press lord was "very anxious to enter."[88] The response was unanimous that the press lord would be unpopular and a difficult man with whom to work. Riddell recorded that Lloyd George agreed with this assessment and then stated that Balfour or Reading would be more useful.[89]

Beaverbrook asserted in *Men and Power* that, in "the middle of 1918," Northcliffe made a bid for power, using Reading and himself as intermediaries with Lloyd George. The demand, according to Beaverbrook, was that the chief proprietor of *The Times* should become "Lord President of the Council in a Lloyd George–Northcliffe administration. He would in effect, divide Downing Street with Lloyd George, and he would keep Fleet Street for himself."[90] The refusal of the Welshman and his colleagues was supposed to have been passed on to Northcliffe by Sir Campbell Stuart, who had accompanied him to Scotland and stayed in touch with London by telephone. No other account substantiates this claim.[91] Beaverbrook also asserted, in the obituary he wrote for Northcliffe, that in the dire military situation of mid-1918, the press lord was holding himself back so that if Britain was expelled from the Continent and the Lloyd George Government fell, he could form a "die-hard" administration to carry on the war effort. Whether real or imaginary, all these plans soon were made moot by the improving military situation, which strengthened the hand of Lloyd George.

On 16 August Northcliffe hosted a Printing House Square luncheon at which he addressed 150 overseas press representatives. Also present were the prime ministers of Canada, Australia, and New Zealand. The speech ranged over a variety of topics, from the loyal support of the Dominions and the colonies to the dangers of "Lansdownism" and a negotiated peace.[92] Northcliffe estimated British casualties at 900,000 for the year. Cecil Harmsworth recorded that his brother "challenged the censorship again and spoke out against fatuous official reticence."[93] The *Daily Mail* reported that he spoke "the plain truth" that the "only peace worth having, the only peace that can be durable and effective, is a peace imposed on Berlin, and in Berlin, by the Allies."[94] Any other solution, in Northcliffe's view, would be a compromise that would merely interrupt the war.

Evidence of the effectiveness of Crewe House mounted. In reply to a cable from Northcliffe on the anniversary of his first visit to Magnolia, House had written in July that he was "reading today in our cable dispatches from neutral countries nearby Germany how much they were disturbed by 'the propaganda which Lord Northcliffe is directing against us. The English are doing more to defeat us in this way than the armies in the field.' This is the greatest tribute one could have."[95] The British director of naval intelligence informed the enemy propaganda committee that he had "undeniable evidence" that its propaganda in Austria was having an effect and was "gaining in power." He added that "he wrote in order that the efforts ... might not slacken."[96] Though still limited to the use of balloons, in the June–August period, 7,820,367 leaflets of all kinds were distributed over the German lines.[97] Enemy newspapers called for a similar campaign in retaliation.[98]

As their battlefield position deteriorated, the military leaders of Germany also acknowledged the British propaganda campaign. General Von Hutier warned his troops against the "last resort" of the Allies to a program of "ruses, trickery and other underhand methods" aimed at inducing "in the minds of the German people a doubt in their invincibility."[99] Northcliffe, "the most thorough-going rascal of the Entente," received special attention as master of this campaign of forgery for which he had been given "billions" in funding. A few days after Von Hutier's declaration, Hindenburg released a "Manifesto to the German People," which warned of the Allied war against the "German spirit."[100] Surveying the myriad appeals made by the Allies, which he called a "drum-fire of printed paper" intended to "kill the soul," the German field-marshal warned his people not to allow themselves to be fooled by the propaganda of those who wished to "annihilate us." Haig's secretary, Sir Philip Sassoon, congratulated Northcliffe on his work, writing that "Hindenburg's manifesto was a great tribute to the success of your propaganda."[101]

There had been little contact between the press lord and the commander-in-chief since the dismissal of Robertson and the subsequent changes in staff. Concerned that as the war came to a possible close the British Army was being overshadowed by the French and Americans, Northcliffe resumed his correspondence with Sassoon in September. To advance the position in which Britain would stand when "peace is dictated from Washington," the press lord recommended the trebling of British correspondents.[102] He told Sassoon of his own experience on the golf links in Scotland, where every day the war was discussed, yet he never heard Haig's name, nor the names of any British generals. The cleverness of Foch and Pershing's "coup" at St. Mihiel were the main topics of conversation. The military position had become promising enough for the *Daily Mail* to warn of an expected "armistice dodge" from Germany.[103] Speaking to an audience of foresters in Scotland, Northcliffe called for Prussia to pay "town for town, village for village, ship for ship, jewel for jewel, picture for picture, dollar for dollar... she must pay full compensation for all she has ... stolen, sacked and burnt."[104]

In late September, Bulgaria signed an armistice and left the war. Crewe House moved swiftly to include this victory in the propaganda campaign.[105] In a letter to Colonel House, Josiah Wedgwood called the Bulgarian collapse a glorious occasion, "the second thunderbolt of justice in the West." He also enclosed a cutting from a Northcliffe "rag" to show that, even though it would not last, "at present he has us all off our feet."[106] Based on a letter in *The Times,* Lovat Fraser feared the Bulgarians would be dealt with too lightly. He wrote to his chief, "That narrow, grasping peasant nation was not in the least led astray when it joined the Germans. It went in on the make, exactly as the Sikhs would do.... If we are going to throw all the blame on the Kings and shed tears over the peoples we shall have a rotten peace. If we begin by saying that the Bulgarians are not to blame, but only their King, we shall end by saying the same thing about the Germans."[107] This mirrored Northcliffe's own concern exactly.

While the Allies were taking control on the battlefield, Lloyd George began the 1918 election campaign with a major address at Manchester on

12 September.[108] Negotiations had also started with the Asquithian Liberals for places in the prospective coalition government. At the end of the month, Rothermere and Lord Murray of Elibank approached the prime minister with a proposal for what Riddell called an "old gang" coalition to include Asquith as lord chancellor, as well as Walter Runciman and Herbert Samuel.[109] The following day Rothermere arrived with Northcliffe in tow. Riddell was unsure how much the owner of the *Daily Mail* knew of the plan and felt Rothermere might be using his brother for a "bit of domestic humbug...to dust the eyes of L. G., and others as to Northcliffe's actual knowledge of and participation in the ramp."[110] On 2 October the press lord visited Lloyd George at Danny Park. The next day he warned Riddell that the old gang were "trying to lay hold of the legs of the Prime Minister and drag him down."[111] They would succeed, Northcliffe believed, unless the Welshman realized his position and stopped giving so much credence to the "little people" in the government, such as Walter Long and Austen Chamberlain, who had no real standing in the country. He urged Riddell not to let the prime minister be fooled. The coming election, said the press lord, would turn on the soldier's vote and could be won by a Paris *Daily Mail* appeal to the troops. He offered to go to France for this work, but refused to do so "for the return of the Old Gang."

Northcliffe was disillusioned because he had been assured (or at least believed he had been assured) by the prime minister that a new government of experts would be formed "immediately the new [voting] Register became legal."[112] Under political pressure, Lloyd George now wavered from this earlier position. The press lord therefore wrote to Riddell that he did not propose to use his newspapers and personal influence to "support a new Government elected at the most critical period of the history of the British nations," unless he knew "definitely and in writing" and could approve "the personal constitution of the Government."[113] When Riddell passed along this demand for the names of his prospective ministers to Lloyd George, the prime minister responded that he would "give no undertaking as to the constitution of the Government and would not dream of doing such a thing."[114] Riddell recorded that he "communicated this to N., who said very little." With Northcliffe's support in serious question, Lloyd George moved to shore up the newspapers on which he could count. A group of his political allies completed the purchase of the *Daily Chronicle* in October.[115]

As the end of the worldwide struggle became only a matter of time, Northcliffe convened (at Steed's suggestion) a new policy committee of the British war mission to consider the transition from war to peace. This new committee, with members from all the government departments concerned with propaganda, was designed to assist in furnishing materials for drawing up and revising the various peace proposals.[116] The group undertook, among other things, to study the peace terms, to consider the "utterances by important enemy representatives," to suggest statements to be made by Allied representatives, and to consider the German reaction to efforts at the democratization of that nation. In response to the German peace note to President Wilson and his reply, the committee came together in an emergency session, with Northcliffe in the chair for the first time, to draft a statement of propaganda policy.[117] A 9 October 1918 meeting, again with Northcliffe in the chair, approved a draft of a "Memorandum on Propaganda Peace Policy" to be sent to the Foreign Office, and if approved, to Colonel House.[118] At the same time, the *Daily Mail* labeled the German request for an armistice "not peace but trickery," and printed a warning to the Allies (attributed to a German in Switzerland): "They will cheat you yet, those junkers! Having won half the world by bloody murder, they are going to win the other half with tears in their eyes, crying for mercy."[119] A week later the newspaper wholeheartedly endorsed Wilson's "unconditional surrender" reply to the German entreaties.[120]

On 10 October, Northcliffe addressed a luncheon given for visiting American newspaper editors. He spoke of the role of the United States in the war, of the value of public opinion, and of the good work being done by the ministry of information.[121] Beaverbrook sent a note of thanks for the kind words. He added that, "You made a marked impression on the Americans. One day next week you must allow me to suggest to a friend the putting down of a question on the House of Lords Order paper in relation to Enemy Propaganda."[122] The minister of information, "distressed" by swollen glands in his neck, hoped that if he had to leave office and undergo an operation, his colleague could "be persuaded to take over my Department without taking office." Northcliffe replied,

As to your very kind suggestion that I should take over your ministry, which will of course become a permanent and important government department, I could not do so until the war is over. During the next few weeks I am going to concentrate every moment of my time and of my staff on the Austrians and the Germans.

I shall be glad if you will have a question put in the House of Lords about Enemy Propaganda. If there is anything wrong with it, it ought to be criticised. The more it is talked about the more the Germans get frightened of it, as is obvious from a glance at the German newspapers, practically all of which now assail it.[123]

On 21 October Beaverbrook resigned and had his operation.[124] He was not replaced.

Northcliffe took Steed and Captain Chalmers Mitchell, who had joined Crewe House from Adastral House, to a meeting with Lloyd George to discuss their propaganda peace policy memorandum.[125] The men were disappointed in the prime minister's reaction. He told Steed and Mitchell that "I can't have this.... Here you are laying down principles and conditions which only the Allied Governments are competent to decide." Further, he refused to have his hands bound by "announcing things of this sort." When asked for his specific objections, Lloyd George replied that he could not "be bound by principles and programs such as you lay down. I am a lawyer.... possession is nine tenths of the law," and when the peace conference met the British would have the Germans "in our hands."[126] However, after further discussion, Lloyd George agreed that if the men could persuade Balfour, the memorandum might be used as terms of propaganda.

After changes were made concerning the German colonies, the Foreign Office authorized the revised document to be used "unofficially."[127] The resulting "Propaganda Peace Policy" listed thirteen nonnegotiable and three negotiable conditions for peace with Germany. The nonnegotiable terms included the restoration of Belgium and France (with Alsace-Lorraine as a reparation to France for the "wrong done in 1871"), the readjustment of the disputed frontiers of Italy along lines of nationality, an assurance that the nationalities in Austria-Hungary would be allowed to unite, the evacuation of all Russian territory and the annulment of all treaties since the Russian Revolution, the formation of an independent Polish state with access to the sea, the abrogation of the Treaty of Bucharest, the restoration of Serbia, Rumania, and Montenegro, the removal of Turkish dominion from non-Turkish peoples, a poll of Schleswig to determine its allegiance, reparations for the illegal submarine campaign of Germany, the appointment of a tribunal to consider crimes of war and crimes against humanity, and, finally, the loss of the German colonies as a result of her illegal aggression against Belgium. The negotiable conditions included the adjustment of claims for damages of war and the establishment of a "League of Free Nations" to prevent future wars and improve international relations. The final clause called for the league to be designed "to create a world in which, when the conditions of the Peace have been carried out, there shall be opportunity and security for the legitimate development of all Peoples."[128]

On 22 October Northcliffe spoke at the Washington Inn, an American officer's club in London. He shared a preview of his department's peace policy and discussed the need for a united program against the Germans.[129] He also attacked Milner's 17 October interview in the *Evening Standard*, which supported conditional surrender terms for Germany in order to stave off bolshevism. Northcliffe countered that "the way to create Bolshevism was to let the Hun off."[130] He worried, not of the threat of revolution in Germany, but of the "real danger of social upheaval ... in this country and in other Allied countries, *if an unsatisfactory peace is made*."[131] The *Evening News* of 28 October included the veiled threat to Milner that "his German origin is not forgotten and the man in the street declares that he is acting as a Prussian. Lord Milner should take care. If this impression were to spread the results might surprise him."[132] In the House of Commons, critical note was taken of the statements of both Milner and Northcliffe. The Irish M.P. John Dillon complained that the Members were being treated "like a lot of school children" concerning the peace terms while the press lord was allowed to make public declarations.

The collapse of Austria-Hungary and Turkey in October left Germany alone. Northcliffe's greatest fear was that too lenient a peace would be made with Britain's paramount enemy, and he called for an unconditional surrender in *The Times*.[133] The 14 October *Daily Mail* featured "The Great War of 1938," which occurred only because the Allies had not "seen the thing through" in 1918. At this stage, Crewe House propaganda took on a religious theme that the looming defeat was God's vengeance and that the present government could not be trusted and was the only real obstacle to peace.[134] At what would prove to be the final meeting of the committee for propaganda in enemy countries on 29 October it was announced, at long last, that arrangements had been made with the ministry of information to use aeroplanes for the distribution of propaganda. Five million leaflets had been prepared for this purpose, which emphasized that a clean sweep of the German "old gang" was needed before Germany's suffering would end.[135] Wickham Steed also reported that "the propaganda carried out against Austria-Hungary could claim credit not for the actual breaking-up, but for very materially accelerating the break-up of Austria."[136]

With peace talks looming on the horizon, Colonel House arrived in Britain. Northcliffe sent a note that he was glad to find the colonel "on this side in these critical days" and that he was looking forward very much to seeing him. He gave House a copy of his propaganda peace policy in order to "prepare the ground for full coordination of propaganda policy between the Associated countries."[137] On 28 October the document was distributed to all the members of the Inter-Allied Propaganda Committee.[138] As preliminary peace discussions began in Paris, the *Daily Mail* renewed its "They will cheat you yet, those Junkers" warning to the "Softies" in the government.[139]

In Paris for an Inter-Allied Enemy Propaganda meeting, Northcliffe sought an official peacemaking role for himself and his department after the cessation of hostilities. He met with Lloyd George, who told him to arrange for a house in Paris.[140] The press lord believed he had been given assurances that the British war mission would continue and that he had approval to carry out publicity before and during the Peace Conference.[141] He wrote to Lloyd George for confirmation of his understanding:

> The approach of the Peace conference and the importance of keeping British Public opinion adequately informed in regard to its deliberations and the principles underlying them renders the definition of the sphere of competence hitherto assigned to the Department of Propaganda in Enemy Countries now incorporated in the British War Mission.
>
> ...With the assent of the Foreign Secretary, acting on behalf of the War Cabinet, it has drafted a memorandum to be used as a foundation for peace term propaganda.
>
> The prospective disappearance of enemy countries properly so called naturally brings into greater prominence this aspect of the activities of the British War Mission.
>
> They will henceforth be directed increasingly to the dissemination of knowledge of the essential conditions of peace and of the reasons why these conditions are essential.
>
> It seems therefore indispensable that, pending the convocation of the Peace Conference and during its deliberations, the British War Mission should be definitely entrusted with this work both because it is the logical sequel to the work it has done with considerable success hitherto, and because there is no other organization in existence that possesses in the same degree its special qualifications.
>
> Therefore, in view of the urgency of the matter, I request that I be given, with the least possible delay, authority as Chairman of the British War Mission to undertake this Peace Terms propaganda in the closest collaboration with the various departments of state until the final peace settlement has been concluded.[142]

The prime minister had come to believe that Northcliffe wanted more than the control of publicity. He thought the press lord's ambitions included a seat at the Peace Conference table as a member of the British delegation.[143] When the two men spoke on 3 November Lloyd George bluntly stated that he intended for Northcliffe's position in Paris to be only unofficial and advisory. He later recalled that the press lord was "visibly astonished and upset at my declining to accede to his request."[144] On this occasion the press lord also asked the prime minister for the names of the members of the new government. Howard Corbett, the manager of *The Times,* recorded that Northcliffe told him that Lloyd George had "pursued me vigorously and when I saw him I asked for the names of the new Government. I did not then know that Sir George Younger, the Conservative wire puller, and much the ablest person in English party politics, had frightened the Prime Minister, as he did in December 1916.... to my surprise, the Prime Minister told me that he was unable to give me the names... to which I replied that I would not support a Government with whose *personnel* I was unacquainted."[145] Comparing the prospective government to a business interest, the press lord added that he "would not take shares in a company which declined to make public the names of its Directors. When this proposed company is formed, it will be found that the Directors are not, with two exceptions, experts in anything except politics."

The day after his meeting with Lloyd George, a signed Northcliffe article, "From War to Peace," appeared in the *Daily Mail* and *The Times*. This statement, syndicated internationally, listed and explained, as parts of a three-stage process, the terms of his department's peace policy. The *Daily Mail* also included a further denunciation of the war secretary, "Lord Milner's Blunder: Encouraging the Enemy and Discouraging Our Friends." In the Commons on the same day, John Dillon asked the nature of Northcliffe's trip to Paris and if the views revealed in his "From War to Peace" article were private or official.[146] Bonar Law replied that the press lord had traveled to Paris on private business, though he might have discussed propaganda, and that the article expressed only his private position.

Despite Lloyd George's rejection of him during their 3 November meeting, Northcliffe did not give up hope for a role in Paris. Two days later, Sir Campbell Stuart saw J. T. Davies in an attempt to smooth over the differences. However, any peacemaking effort was complicated by the *Daily Mail* campaign against Milner, which continued with a 6 November editorial, "Milner's Mischief."[147] Along with his public announcement of peace terms, which were soon called "Northcliffe's Thirteen Points," the anti-Milner campaign gave the prime minister an example of the sort of behavior he could expect if he took the press lord to Paris in any capacity. The two men had a final meeting at this time at which Lloyd George, wearied by his conditions of support, claimed he told Northcliffe to "go to Hades."[148] Sir Auckland Geddes, who saw both men after this confrontation, later told Geoffrey Harmsworth that both "described the other as impossible and intolerable," and that he did not believe Northcliffe had asked for a seat at the Peace Conference because, if he had, Lloyd George would have "blurted it out all over the place and there would have been a cloud of witnesses."[149]

The Welshman apparently told at least one person, Sir Edward Carson, who gave L. S. Amery the prime minister's version of the meeting, in which the press lord peremptorily demanded a place in the peace delegation.[150] With Northcliffe's supposed impertinence to Lloyd George and the newspaper offensive against Lord Milner both fresh in his mind, Carson rose during the

7 November Commons debate on funding for the ministry of information to unleash perhaps the most telling attack on Northcliffe of the war:

> I am quite alive to the fact that it is almost high treason to say a word against Lord Northcliffe. I know his power and that he does not hesitate to exercise it to try to drive anybody out of any office or a public position if they incur his royal displeasure. But as at my time of life neither office nor its emoluments, nor anything connected with Governments, or indeed public life, makes the slightest difference... I venture to incur even the possibility of the odium of this great trust owner who monopolises in his own person so great a part of the Press of this country....
>
> Within the last few days there has been an attack made by this noble Lord's papers upon Lord Milner... [who] seems to have given an interview to a rival paper.... having read it and having read the criticism of some of Lord Northcliffe's papers upon it, I believe that it has been purposefully and intentionally misrepresented and misunderstood.... it seems to me to be nothing but indecent that the gentleman engaged in foreign propaganda on behalf of His Majesty's Government should make part of his propaganda an attack on the Secretary of State for War in the Government under which he purports to serve....
>
> I think it is really time to put an end to this kind of thing. The Government may imagine that they gain power and support, but I do not believe it for a moment. I believe that all the best elements in the country resent this kind of thing.... At this present moment, when Lord Milner is in France... dealing with... matters of vital importance to this country... come these attacks from an official of the Government... to drive him out of his office. For What? In order that Lord Northcliffe may get it or get into the War Cabinet, so that he may be present at the Peace Conference.... The whole thing is a disgrace to public life in England and a disgrace to journalism.[151]

After this, Milner informed Carson, he had a "shower of letters from friends simply delighted with the trouncing you gave Northcliffe."[152] Milner thought it was high time that "somebody other than myself" spoke out, and added that the press lord was "only a scarecrow, but still the fact remains that most public men are in terror of him."

The conflicts between Northcliffe and Lloyd George over the Peace Conference, added to the continuing demands for the names of the future government, resulted in a permanent rift between the two men. Though they would afterward communicate sporadically, there were no more personal interviews. The idea of overseeing a "just" peace for the country must have appealed strongly to Northcliffe. He had asserted several times during the war that he would relish this role. Given the brittle state of his health, however, whether he would be up to the rigors of the job was questionable. The predominance of the evidence is that he wished only for his department to run the publicity for the Peace Conference.[153] Perhaps Lloyd George considered this tantamount to a seat at the table. Only in his version of events did the owner of the *Daily Mail* make further demands.

Nevertheless, as the Great War came to its final days, Northcliffe had reason to feel satisfaction at the contribution of his British war mission. Crewe House had helped speed the downfall, first of Austria-Hungary and then of Germany. British propaganda did not create the conditions that led to the enemy's final collapse, but it has rightly been credited with exploiting and accelerating the process.[154] At a 7 November luncheon in Paris, given in appreciation of the efforts of his propaganda colleagues and the staff of the *Continental Daily Mail,* the press lord announced that the signing of the armistice would mean the end of his government service. He remarked to the gathering that "We have to some extent hastened the end.... Ours has been a bloodless campaign and a costless one. I wish that we had embarked upon it at an earlier stage of the War."[155] Though Northcliffe had not gotten the unconditional surrender he wanted from Germany, at the end shortening the war and thereby saving lives had been the press lord's primary aim, and in this his department succeeded.

Elsewhere, however, Northcliffe failed. As late as August there is good evidence that Lloyd George was still considering whether to include him in the war cabinet or a reorganized future government. However, in October, by demanding names in exchange for support, the press lord himself prompted the prime minister to line up alternative newspaper backers. "The Man Who Won the War" gambled he could win the coming election without Northcliffe. The press lord's actions also cost Northcliffe the possibility of an official role at the Peace Conference. Bolstered by Britain's victories in the field, the prime minister could afford to tell the demanding press lord to "go to Hades." In the Byzantine world of high diplomacy, Northcliffe, Steed, and Wells were overmatched by Balfour and his minions. As Wells noted after the war, by allowing the staff at Crewe House to carry out their schemes "unofficially," the Foreign Office used their "quasi-official" peace term assurances as decoys that later could be repudiated.[156]

The day after the armistice was signed, Northcliffe sent his resignation to Lloyd George; it was accepted at once. The prime minister replied that he wished "to assure you how grateful I am for the great services you have rendered to the Allied Cause while holding this important post. I have had many direct evidences of the success of your invaluable work and of the extent to which it has contributed to the dramatic collapse of enemy strength in Austria and Germany."[157] The next day Northcliffe notified his other great wartime antagonist, Arthur Balfour, that he had resigned and thanked him for the "courtesy and promptness" with which the foreign office had dealt with him and his departments.[158] Balfour replied, with the same studied courtesy he had shown throughout, "Though I rejoice in the cause, I am indeed sorry that our cooperation has come to an end. It is a great pleasure to me to feel that our two Departments have worked so smoothly together; and while I am grateful for what you say about the Foreign Office I know that such harmony can only be the result of mutual goodwill."[159] However, it was not with goodwill, but with trepidation that Northcliffe looked toward the election of 1918 and the Peace Conference of 1919.

ELEVEN

"The Huns Must Pay"
Politics & Peacemaking,
November 1918 to June 1919

WHILE OTHERS REJOICED IN BRITAIN'S VICTORY AFTER MORE THAN
four interminably bloody and brutal years of total war, Northcliffe found
little tranquillity. For him the war had not had the "Glorious End" proclaimed by the *Daily Mail*.[1] The armistice fell far short of his demands for a
total surrender and the complete destruction of Prussian militarism. Cut off
from an official role at the Peace Conference that would decide Britain's
place in the postwar world, he feared Germany would be treated lightly, and
had little faith that the politicians could make a truly lasting settlement. "The
Huns Must Pay" *Daily Mail* editorial of 13 November began a drumbeat
that would last well beyond the signing of the Versailles treaty in June 1919.
Northcliffe did not doubt Lloyd George would win the election set for December 1918, but predicted revolution would follow the return of a government dominated by what he saw as Tory remnants of the old regime. Additionally, the press lord's health worsened; a visible lump had appeared on his
throat.[2] Ordered to rest by his doctors, he wrote to the Earl of Selborne from
Elmwood that he was "doing my part of the election from here."[3]

The election season opened in earnest after the armistice was signed.
Despite his calculation that as "The Man Who Won the War" he would triumph, Lloyd George remained unsure of the outcome until the final results
were tabulated. The Welshman promised far-reaching social and economic
reconstruction to a Liberal party meeting on 12 November, but nevertheless
continued his alliance with the Conservatives. Bonar Law explained his decision to carry on with Lloyd George to his party as the only course to head off
Bolshevist radicalism.[4] The Lloyd George–Bonar Law Coalition program
was published on 18 November and supplemented thereafter by regular

manifestos outlining policy. Having led the country to victory, the new coalition mission would be the reconstruction of Britain into a land "fit for heroes." The Asquithian segment of the Liberal party was proscribed from the list of approved candidates given the "Coupon" of approval, partly on the basis of the vote in the Maurice affair of May 1918.[5] One element of the wartime government, Labour, decided not to continue into peacetime. With the exception of George Barnes and a few others, Labour withdrew, and became the official opposition.

Northcliffe was keenly aware of the new political power in the votes of working men and returning soldiers. The *Daily Mail* criticized the Labour party's withdrawal as "the wrong line of cleavage" and recommended to Lloyd George that he not exclude Labour as he separated the "sheep from the goats." The newspaper called for the progressive elements in all the parties, "prepared to go forward fearlessly with a policy of vigorous and unconventional reform," to detach themselves from the reactionaries who cared for nothing but "obstruction and self-interest."[6] The most pressing issues to be addressed, according to the *Daily Mail,* were land for the returning servicemen and reform of "the evils which have caused and are still causing those ravages upon the public health revealed by the National Service."

Other press lords also expressed disillusionment with political developments. Rothermere, a more consistent supporter of Lloyd George than his brother, was also angered by the multitude of Conservatives included in the 1918 coalition slate and felt the prime minister had shown little gratitude for the support the newspapers had given since December 1916. He pointed out to the Welshman that his administration had been "sustained" by a coalition of the press, a section of the Liberal party, and the Conservative party. "Without the aid of the Press," the owner of the *Daily Mirror* and the *Sunday Pictorial* asserted, "it is a fair thing to say that the present Coalition Government could not have survived the storms of the last eighteen months. Some other Government there would have been... quite different from the present one, and many of your associates who now hold high office would have been relegated to the back benches."[7] Despite the support of his newspapers, and those of Northcliffe and Beaverbrook, complained Rothermere, the government had not stopped the "calumnies" aimed at his "press friends" by the Unionist War Committee and other Conservative critics. Rothermere did not understand how he could be expected to endure the return of a majority composed of these reactionaries in the next election and complained that it would be impossible to get "a square deal" from them over land for the soldiers, vital to forestall revolution. Despite this letter, in the end Rothermere trimmed his sails and supported Lloyd George as the man most likely to stave off bolshevism. Beaverbrook's *Daily Express* also supported the coalition.

Unless the needs of the working classes and the soldiers were met, Northcliffe feared a socialist revolution would spread from the Continent. Consequently, he attempted to use his newspapers as a bulwark against the Bolshevists. Hamilton Fyfe wrote to his chief of the general feeling that he held the power "to restrain the forces which threaten to drive Labour into adopting revolutionary methods."[8] Fyfe urged the press lord to give Labour "a fair show" to keep it on "constitutional lines." He was in contact with Arthur Henderson, the Labour leader, and urged Northcliffe to meet with him to dispel the notion among party members that he was an ogre. Since Labour had no daily newspaper of its own, the *Daily Mail* donated free space to the party, under a disclaimer that the paper was not responsible for the opinions offered.

The millions of men in the armed forces, Northcliffe believed, would decide the election. In the months after the armistice, delays in demobilization of the troops became a major problem. The press lord received numerous letters of complaint from the soldiers and their families about the matter, and serious unrest developed in Britain and France. To defuse the situation, he instructed Marlowe to publish an article on demobilization, "carefully explained by someone who understands it."[9] He also feared many soldiers would lose their votes because of the general confusion and instructed the *Daily Mail* staff that "owing to the difficulties that soldiers abroad will have in knowing their real constituencies consequent on the changes made in the Redistribution Act many will lose their votes. Soldiers in France... think they are being tricked. I hope the paper will agitate for the rights of soldiers... to speak at elections. The time has gone for the antiquated regulation on the subject to continue.... That regulation... is totally inapplicable to our new and large citizen and democratic army."[10]

The press lord demanded that the returning soldiers receive a just reward. He explained to his brother Cecil, one of the Coalition candidates, that the men had been "through horrors unspeakable, unwritable, unbelievable, and they must not be fobbed off with mere promises and speeches. I will see to it that they are not so treated."[11] The *Daily Mail* labeled the land-for-soldiers issue a "test question" for the voters and declared that if money could be found to buy land for redistribution in Ireland in the past, surely the country could "do no less for the soldiers of England, Scotland, and Wales."[12] Besides the land issue and social reform another *Daily Mail* "test for candidates" became the settlement with the Hun, which included a trial for the kaiser, the punishment of all those guilty of crimes against innocents, the expulsion and exclusion of enemy aliens, and full reparations and compensation for all losses.[13] Northcliffe told Cecil that his criticism of the government was based on "knowledge of the state of affairs and of the public mind in England" and his fear that "the Government of Tory reactionaries that we are going to get will be a direct incentive to dangerous discontent."[14]

In late November Lloyd George remained uneasy over the electoral prospects. He discussed Northcliffe with Reading and Milner, who was in close contact with Dawson at *The Times*.[15] Robert Sanders, a Conservative party insider, recorded that the prime minister "was anxious to know if anyone could get at Northcliffe."[16] On 30 November, Cecil Harmsworth found the Welshman "low spirited" about the election, pacing "up and down in the Cabinet room more agitated in his manner than I have seen him during the war, save on one or two very critical occasions."[17] The two men discussed Northcliffe's opposition, and later that evening Cecil telephoned his brother to ascertain whether a trip to Broadstairs would be useful. The press lord was adamant that as long as Lloyd George was "tied hand and foot to the Junkers of the Tory 'old party' gang," any further conversation on the subject would not change his position "in the slightest."[18] In the Welshman's version of events, Cecil had come as Northcliffe's envoy and had been told that the prime minister "did not mean to be treated in this way, and if necessary I shall have to say something in public."[19] Lloyd George went on that a public statement would "raise a great accession of support in many quarters," that he really "had little to fear from his opposition," and that he would "rather cease to be Prime Minister than be at the beck and call of Northcliffe, Rothermere, Beaverbrook & Co." At the same time, the prime minister told Riddell that Northcliffe had renewed his demand for a place at the conference and was attempting to "blackmail" him on the issue.[20]

After his resignation from the British war mission, with his official channels of propaganda closed, Northcliffe's publications gained a renewed importance as instruments to reflect his opinions. He also had more time to devote to them, particularly *The Times*. Thus began a struggle between the chief proprietor and the editor over election and peace issues, which culminated in February 1919 with Dawson's resignation.[21] In July the newspaper agreed with the press lord's view of the election, but by late November had become more conciliatory toward the government. Northcliffe had allowed *The Times* a semi-independent course during much of the war, but the disastrous result he foresaw moved the press lord to inform Dawson that he did "not propose to speak anymore with two voices."[22]

In an attempt to have an impact on the formation of the cabinet, the press lord wrote to his editor again on 1 December. He warned that, "unless we speak now," Lloyd George would be influenced by men like Sir George Younger, who ran the "party of wealth," into forming a reactionary government that would not allow the prime minister to carry out the reforms needed to prevent revolution. He instructed Dawson to ask, editorially, who would be in the new government, noting that

> I personally put this question to the Prime Minster...two months ago. I was promised a reply but never got it. I put it to him again in Paris. Turning very red in the face, he "side-slipped," saying that he was in a great hurry to catch his train....
>
> There have been moments in history when *The Times* has rendered great service to the nation. You can render no greater service, in my judgement, than in asking the Prime Minister who are the men that the country is to be asked to vote for. Such a course will strengthen his hands. Surely, it is very simple, if he has the backbone to do it....
>
> If I have not made myself plain, then I am afraid I am incapable of coherence. I feel sure that, had the Prime Minister adopted the plan of The Times, he would have swept the country and returned to power with a great and sufficient majority, and he would be a free man to pick the officers of the ship of State without regard to any questions other than their efficiency.[23]

Another issue over which Northcliffe and Dawson quarreled was reparations, which became a major focus of the election. Despite the prime minister's increasingly anti-German statements during the course of the campaign, the press lord suspected that, after his victory at the polls, Lloyd George would give in to international financial interests and make too-lenient a peace. Thomas Marlowe agreed. He reported that the prime minister was "under suspicion of forgiving the Germans & forgetting the war too quickly. He is acting on the belief that Englishmen like to shake hands after a fight: so they do, but not this time. They don't regard the Hun as a clean fighter and they don't want to shake hands with him. People...resent the impertinence of 'British Sportsmanship' being exploited by international financiers. I am glad you insist on keeping out the Huns & hope you will ram this 'stunt' down the Prime Minister's throat."[24] To answer German protestations of the severity of the Allied terms, Fyfe collected the various statements of the terms of peace the enemy would have imposed and, at Northcliffe's instruction, had them sent to Dawson for publication in *The Times*.[25] The press lord complained to Dawson that he had a great responsibility as chief proprietor of *The Times* and that the paper had "lagged woefully" behind his other journals in pointing out that the prime minister was "evading main issues" and acting in accord with the German financiers in Britain who sought "to prevent Germany from having to pay for the war."[26] He told his editor that he did not believe the Welshman was a "free agent in this matter" and that he was determined to bring "pressure to bear."

In his early speeches the prime minister had pledged that Germany should be forced to pay "up to the limit of her capacity."[27] In the heat of the campaign this had been increased to "the uttermost farthing" and "until the pips squeak" by various coalition figures. When it appeared Lloyd George was wavering on the issue, Northcliffe cabled him in Leeds. He had heard that the French had named a reparations figure for their own country and told the prime minister that "the public are expecting you to say definitely amount of cash we shall get from Germany. They are very dissatisfied with the phrase 'limit of her ability' which…may mean anything or nothing."[28] The prime minister responded, "You are quite wrong about France. No ally has named figure. Allies in complete agreement as to demand for indemnity. Inter-Allied Commission will investigate on behalf of all on identical principles. Don't always be making mischief."[29] However, the prime minister's rhetoric in the following days moved closer to the position of the *Daily Mail* and its proprietor, calling for a trial for the kaiser and the "fullest indemnities." At Bristol the Welshman called for Germany to pay "the whole cost of the war," and the *Daily Mail* crowned it "his best speech of the campaign."[30]

Nevertheless, as the election moved into its last week, the *Daily Mail* warned that the prime minister was still avoiding many of the main issues. It cautioned its readers that it was time to "pin the candidates down to a definite pledge" concerning support for the points it had listed over the preceding weeks: returning soldiers, a trial for the kaiser, "ample provision" for new houses, full indemnity from Germany, expulsion and restrictions on German immigration, and reform of pensions and allowances.[31] By the end of the campaign, the aims of the *Daily Mail* and the coalition had become remarkably similar. The final coalition manifesto, published 11 December, listed five: punish the kaiser, make Germany pay, get the soldier home as quickly as possible, fair treatment for the returned soldier and sailor, and better housing and social conditions.[32]

While electioneering came to an end in Britain, the Peace Conference took shape in Paris. Northcliffe's longtime Liberal adversary, C. P. Scott, editor of the *Manchester Guardian,* cabled him a warning of a reborn censorship. Scott reported to his competitor that British cables from Paris were being suppressed by the French, while the Americans had gotten the censorship lifted for their dispatches.[33] The press lord feared a return to the conditions of earlier in the war, with U. S. publications having a free hand while the British were shackled. He complained to Dawson from Paris that two of his dispatches had already been stopped. "Out of this will come chaos," the press lord declared, "for we shall get our accounts of the Conference via New York and tinged with the American point of view."[34] His correspondence with Scott led Northcliffe to suggest to Dawson that his newspapers should combine with the *Manchester Guardian* and "defy the censor. It is not a very good beginning for a so-called democratic Government that it should gag the newspapers."

After *The Times* received written Press Bureau instructions on news from the conference, Northcliffe complained to Lord Derby, who had replaced Lord Bertie as British ambassador to France, and to Lord Riddell, who had been made British press liaison for the conference. From Paris, the press lord wrote to Riddell, "it is rumoured here that British censors are about to arrive.... President Wilson wants an open conference and our people at home—especially the labour section of them—are entirely in favour of it. I have no desire to embarrass the new Government, but if I had that desire, I could not be presented with a more effective weapon than the censorship."[35] Riddell responded that there would be no censorship and that the notice received by *The Times* had "no legislative sanction" and had only represented the "pious hope" of the government that the press would refrain from "referring to personal incidents and differences of opinion" that might be harmful.[36] Derby also affirmed that there would be no censorship.[37] In the end news was not censored; it was simply withheld.

Northcliffe's fears of a rift with America during the Peace Conference were confirmed by members of the British mission still in the United States. Arthur Willert cabled from Washington of the developing problems concerning the freedom-of-the-seas issue (the second of Wilson's Fourteen Points) and of the general bad feeling toward Britain.[38] Louis Tracy, assigned to the British bureau of information in New York, seconded these opinions and complained to the press lord of the planned closing of his office. "It really does seem to me that some sort of link should be allowed to exist," argued Tracy, "between government policy in Great Britain and the people of the United States, who are simply hungering for the right sort of information."[39] Though he had resigned from Crewe House, Northcliffe opposed the rapid dismantling of the British propaganda establishment that was being carried out at his British mission and at the ministry of information. He thought closing the British bureau in New York would be pure folly, responding to Tracy's importunity that he had "done his best in the matter, and I think something will be done."[40] After negotiation, the Foreign Office, which had resumed control of propaganda, allowed Tracy's bureau to operate another six months. The 9 December "Message From the Chief" suggested to the *Daily Mail* employees that "Anglo-American relations are in a very delicate condition," and insisted in "the utmost care being used in what we print both from and about the United States."[41]

Northcliffe also became involved in the question of whether Woodrow Wilson should take part in the Peace Conference. Some in America doubted whether it was proper for the president to attend and also whether the Europeans would welcome him. The press lord replied to a telegram from E. L. Keen of the United Press, "It would be unthinkable for us that Lloyd George would not be at the Peace Conference.... It is apparent from cables that we are now getting that many citizens of the United States... object to the President's voyage. I can only say that we cannot comprehend that situation.... if these conferences are held without President Wilson, the whole European world would think there was something very wrong indeed with these conferences."[42] Northcliffe cabled Wilson, through his secretary, Joseph Tumulty, that it was "unthinkable that the head of the United States should be absent" and that the "fervour of his reception will exceed that of any foreign visitor on record."[43]

The chief proprietor of *The Times* reported the extraordinary greeting Wilson received on his arrival in France to his editor. He also recorded the dissatisfaction in the president's entourage over the delay in starting the conference and the "infinite harm" that the prime minister's tardiness in coming over, while the president was anxious to get to work, was doing.[44] Northcliffe also suggested that Dawson should travel to France to sample the atmosphere, which the press lord did not like. The freedom-of-the-seas question and Wilson's subsequent statements concerning the building of an American merchant fleet equal to Britain's caused resentment on both sides. The press lord wrote to Derby in Paris about the hostility and suspicion among the arriving Americans, who felt that the "cards have been stacked against them" at the conference.[45]

While waiting for the talks to begin, Colonel House proposed that Wilson should visit England. The press lord sent his strong approval of the idea to Balfour at the Foreign Office, who agreed with the potential importance of a visit by the president.[46] Northcliffe assured Lord Reading that, although some Americans believed Wilson would receive a chilly reception in Britain, he was sure the president would "receive a very hearty welcome" and that a visit to England would "be all to our benefit and... remove from the minds of the entourage any misapprehensions."[47] Before the president traveled to Britain on 26 December, House secured a Paris interview with Wilson for Northcliffe, printed in *The Times* and the *Daily Mail* on 21 December. The published version spent little time on weighty matters, but did report Wilson's view that the main business of the conference was to "create a safeguard against future wars." Concerning the freedom-of-the-seas issue, Wilson reassured Northcliffe that he respected Britain's "peculiar position as an Island Empire."[48]

Reading sent the press lord congratulations for his journalistic coup, stating that he "liked its tone" and found it very "valuable and opportune."[49]

In Northcliffe's talk with the president, the two men discussed the censorship and agreed that the peace sessions should be open. The press lord gave a statement to this effect to the American Associated Press. House congratulated him for his "already famous interview" and added that the Associated Press statement "leaves us all in your debt."[50] Northcliffe sent thanks for House's "very handsome letter." The press lord also explained that his name, and sometimes even photograph and signature, were being used for unauthorized articles "inimical to the United States or its President," published by "mischief makers who invent quotations from my newspapers, or who re-write articles or headlines from them."[51]

Preparations for the Peace Conference were interrupted by the announcement of the British election results at the end of December. The *Daily Mail* remarked on the "Thumping Unionist Majority":

> The forecast made in these columns recently as to the size of the Unionist Majority...were regarded as extravagant by many, but they have proved to be more accurate than the official estimates.
>
> Sir George Younger, Lord Downham (Mr. Hayes Fisher), and Mr. Bonar Law have maneuvered our gallant little Welsh wizard into a position in which he is almost entirely dependent on the votes of those whom he so vigorously denounced at Limehouse a few years ago.
>
> He is now at the mercy of his recent enemies. Will they cajole the Prime Minister, or will he cajole them?[52]

However, the paper discerned at least two bright spots in the result: first, the many seats lost by the Liberal old gang, including Asquith; and second, the gains made by Labour.

Though uneasy over the large number of reactionaries that had been returned, Northcliffe nevertheless felt there was a slim chance something could still be salvaged from the situation. He confided in Rothermere that "the Prime Minister has an immense opportunity, but I doubt he will take it. The country would support him in a clean sweep of the Old Gang people.... The Foreign Office, Diplomatic and... Consular Services could be put right in three months."[53] The *Daily Mail*, however, soon recounted the "ugly rumours about" concerning the formation of an "Old Gang Tory Cabinet... a tied Prime Minister, and the crack of the Tory whip."[54]

At the beginning of 1919, Northcliffe prepared to depart for an extended stay in France. He had been ordered to rest by his doctors and, after a stop in

Paris, his final destination was La Dragonnière, Rothermere's villa at Cap Martin, near Monte Carlo. He instructed his papers to take care in Anglo-American relations, to keep an eye on the demobilization delays, and to watch Ireland. The 7 January "Message from the Chief" warned,

> Before I leave England, I would like to say one word more about Ireland, about which there is cause for great anxiety. I am very certain that something will happen soon … to bring the Irish question before the world. I have reason to believe that Lord French is preparing for martial law there. He had the nerve to ask for the loan of one of my staff to act as military censor. If he starts shooting in Ireland, the noise of his machine-guns will travel to a far greater distance than he imagines.
>
> Hands should be sent to Ireland at once.

While recuperating, Northcliffe kept up his criticism. A signed article the next month in one of his journals, the *New Illustrated*, charged that Lloyd George was under the thumb of the Conservatives and that "he would, if he were a free agent, be in favour of a square deal all around, justice for everybody, and an end to profiteering and privilege."[55] Unfortunately, asserted the press lord, the Tories surrounding the prime minister would never "embrace willingly such social reforms as those which the soldiers now returning to civil life are now contemplating," and Lloyd George "has not that high moral courage which enables a man to stand alone. The most perilous defect in his character is that he is not sure of himself." Turning to Ireland, Northcliffe recommended partitioning North and South as "the only way" for a settlement, adding that he would "make Ulster spend a million pounds in propaganda in the United States to let the American people know why they don't want Home Rule with the South."[56]

When the membership of the new government was announced on 10 January, Northcliffe was appalled at most of Lloyd George's choices, even though they included Cecil Harmsworth, who was elevated from the prime minister's secretariat to a Foreign Office under-secretaryship. Unfortunately, in the press lord's view at least, political considerations had once again over-ridden all other factors. He complained to Andrew Caird at the *Daily Mail* that the "original plan was that the Prime Minister should go to the country on his own, forming a Government of "All the Talents" and Parties.... Then Sir George Younger stampeded the Prime Minister.... even worse than what I foretold has happened. A Government that is a scandal has been formed."[57] Disgusted with a timid article about the new government, Northcliffe cabled Charles Beattie at Carmelite House, "No wonder people say they can tell the difference in the Daily Mail when I have left England."[58]

Prominent among the new ministers who came in for immediate criticism was Winston Churchill, secretary of state for war and air. This recombination of the separate air ministry, for which Northcliffe and his press had fought tirelessly until its creation in late 1917, brought a sharp reaction. The 11 January *Daily Mail* warned that if "we are to return to the chaos from which we were delivered in 1917...this union under such a man as Mr Churchill is asking for trouble, and is a sure cause of future mischief." However, the press lord and his newspapers cooperated with Churchill over another issue, demobilization. Churchill curried favor by sending Northcliffe the details of his plan and the reasoning behind it.[59] The press lord replied from the south of France that he would instruct his editors to give the scheme all their support, and did so.[60]

Because he felt his unheeded calls for stronger criticisms had allowed Lloyd George a free hand in the creation of a reactionary cabinet, the press lord's displeasure descended on Dawson at *The Times*. A letter to his editor reported that the French were "amazed at the new Cabinet" and went on:

I am not given to saying..."I told you so," but I saw the possibilities of the present deplorable Cabinet when I asked you to begin that campaign last summer.

I blame myself greatly for my lack of vigour in regard to "The Times" when I was ill at Elmwood in November and December. The sending of an emissary to me showed that George knew perfectly well that I was the only force that could stop his really timid nature.... It is the timidity of the ...Welsh that hides itself in brave words and gestures. Never again will I allow myself to be overruled in a matter like that. I am very willing to be led in matters I do not understand, but I do understand character....

By the appointment of my brother he has no doubt hopes of deflecting criticism through which I yet trust that I may able to change the Government and avert a semi-Revolution in England. The giving of office, either to brothers or friends, will not move me to the extent of a single column or comma.[61]

Northcliffe was also out of patience with Dawson for his slackness in criticizing the delays in starting the Peace Conference. He gave an ultimatum:

If you do not like my attitude, I beg you to do either one of two things — endeavour to see eye to eye with me, or relinquish your position.

The Times could have accelerated the peace conference....Unless the peace conference can be speeded, I can assure you from my knowledge of what is going on among our troops in France that we may have serious trouble.

My ownership and control of The Times are a great responsibility, and as long as I have health I will act up to that responsibility to the full. In the last three months I have, against my will and owing largely to the inertia of ill-health, fallen far short in my conception of my duty.[62]

To make matters worse, Northcliffe received reports from Rothermere and others concerning "indiscreet" comments by Dawson to his circle of friends, most of whom, like Milner, were decidedly hostile to the press lord. The tenure of the editor of The Times was nearing its end.

Once the Peace Conference opened in mid-January, Lloyd George found himself trapped between the passionate demands of Clemenceau for a peace settlement that would cripple Germany and Wilson's Fourteen Points, capped with a League of Nations to ensure the peace. The prime minister wished Germany again to become a major trading partner of Britain, but he was constantly reminded of his election pledges to make the enemy pay dearly. After Wilson returned from a visit to the United States in February, the important business of the conference took place in the private meetings of the Council of Four, which added Vittorio Orlando of Italy to Clemenceau, Lloyd George, and Wilson.

The Daily Mail coverage of the great event was placed in the overall charge of George Curnock. On 22 January, he passed along to the correspondents their chief's general displeasure with the caliber of their work. At the end of the month Montagu Smith, covering the British delegation, wrote a controversial article for the Paris edition, which asserted that Dominion interests were being sacrificed to the demands of the United States. Smith apparently received most of his information from the colonial premiers, particularly Hughes of Australia.[63] Though Northcliffe was increasingly disillusioned with Wilson's view of the settlement, he was unhappy with his correspondent's disclosures, which had elicited a protest from the president. The press lord warned Smith not to be fooled by the politicians, and added that his actions had placed him in a very difficult position and that another such error would not be tolerated.[64] Riddell recorded that the prime minister was angered by the episode and that Wilson had threatened, "if this sort of thing was repeated," to "break off the Conference and go back to America."[65] Riddell went on that the "PM was very strong about Northcliffe, and was evidently under the impression that N was at the bottom of the newspaper campaign." Harold Nicolson, a junior member of the Peace Conference staff, reflected the Foreign Office view in his assertion that the "ego-maniac" Northcliffe "brooded over the conference as a miasma" and "turned upon Lloyd George a constant stream of boiling water."[66]

Sir Campbell Stuart and Henry Wickham Steed became perhaps the two most important members of the Northcliffe newspaper team in Paris. While the chief proprietor of *The Times* recuperated in the south of France, Stuart joined the *Daily Mail* staff in Paris and became a liaison to all the newspapers. He kept in touch with such figures as House, who, Stuart informed his chief, had become "as you foresaw, the real power of the Conference. Things are not going well, as Steed will have written you."[67] House also suffered from ill health in this period, and Northcliffe sent an invitation for the colonel to rest with him at Rothermere's villa, which he described as being "the California of France."[68] House responded that he was better and would try to come later. He went on that, "Your staff is doing splendid work in helping the cause along. We [are] indeed fortunate in having your powerful co-operation."[69]

The colonel was particularly close to Steed, foreign editor of *The Times,* who became Northcliffe's principal source of information and his advisor on the complicated negotiations. Beginning in mid-January he sent his chief regular memoranda on the work of the conference and also wrote almost daily leaders for the Paris edition of the *Daily Mail.* The press lord told Steed that, for the time being, the Paris *Daily Mail* was "the most important newspaper in the world, because the English-speaking delegates would read it with their morning coffee."[70] Steed had been for some time the press lord's counselor on foreign affairs, which the Peace Conference brought to the forefront. He was also the man the proprietor of *The Times* had in mind to take over its editorship after Dawson. Northcliffe had often been willing to take Dawson's lead on domestic affairs, which cost the editor after the 1918 election disaster. When Dawson resigned in February, Stuart became the agent in the successful negotiations with Steed to assume the position. The new editor of *The Times* was far more philosophically in tune with, and more able to influence, Northcliffe, than his predecessor. Steed was also more compliant, in fact fawning, in his relations with the press lord.[71]

During the conference, Steed was in intimate contact with House and allied himself with the colonel and the French when Wilson and his chief advisor split over compromises in the peace terms.[72] Northcliffe sympathized with the colonel, but still did not wish his newspapers to be overly critical of Wilson. Gordon Auchincloss, House's secretary at the conference, also was in close touch with Steed. Auchincloss met with Northcliffe in late March and recorded that they discussed "the reparations matter, the Russian situation, the German territorial situation and Lloyd George's attitude towards the president's position."[73] Auchincloss found the press lord "very complimentary to the Colonel and the work that he has done." He also suggested that the press lord should take over the ambassadorship in Washington. Steed reported that Auchincloss told him, "Far and away the best man would be Northcliffe. Pilgrims and sinners would run off his back without hurting him & he knows our people."[74] Other Americans present noted Northcliffe's activities. The journalist Ray Stannard Baker wrote that in mid-April House was "still working with Clemenceau and Northcliffe and opposes Lloyd George, while the President works with Lloyd George—and finds Clemenceau his hardest opponent."[75]

Relocated from the south of France to Paris, the press lord became more directly involved in the press coverage of developments in April. He remained anxious over reparations and the terms in general and exhorted his newspapers to keep up the pressure on the prime minister. However, the feud with Lloyd George made it difficult for Northcliffe's correspondents to gain inside information. Consequently, the competition often scooped the *Daily Mail*, much to its owner's displeasure. An interview with a "high authority" (widely believed to be Lloyd George) published in the 28 March *Westminster Gazette* made it appear the prime minister was "going soft" on reparations.[76] Disturbed by this declaration, Northcliffe had his secretary, Humphrey Davy, direct Marlowe to admonish the Welshman to carry out his election promises and not to put the cost of war on the backs of the British people.[77] "They Will Cheat You Yet, Those Junkers," once again became the battle cry of the *Daily Mail*.

The newspaper calls for a statement of the amount of reparations due to Britain infuriated Lloyd George, who told Riddell that he would not "state the terms" and complained of the "disgraceful" attacks of Northcliffe press, which, he said, called him a pro-German. He considered a libel action in the matter, but Riddell counseled against it. "I shall certainly say in public what I think about Northcliffe," continued Lloyd George, "His action is due to vanity and spleen.... His advice has not been asked about a single subject. I ran the election without him and I beat him. He is full of disappointment and bitterness."[78] Lloyd George had come to the view that the treaty should not state a total figure, but that the matter should be left to a reparations commission to decide.[79]

The prime minister's course led the press lord's old newspaper associate, Kennedy Jones, M.P., to contact Northcliffe seeking advice and support. Though often dismissed as a "satellite" of the press lord, Jones followed his own course, which reflected the unrest among many in the Commons who had made rather extravagant election pledges concerning reparations and were concerned at Lloyd George's hedging. After the publication of the *Westminster Gazette* article, Jones sought Northcliffe's opinion, and the press lord recommended that the strongest possible protest should be made from

Parliament.[80] On 8 April, several hundred Members signed a telegram to Lloyd George asking for reassurances on reparations, and a furious Prime Minister saw Northcliffe behind the affair.[81] The next day the press lord wrote to Jones that the Welshman was giving in to the pressure of German financial agents, who claimed the country would go Bolshevik if forced to assume a large debt. "That he is being bluffed is obvious," declared the press lord. "His entourage says that the reasons the Peace terms cannot be published is that the British Government would fall at once, as the people would realize they had been had.... it is a deplorable thing that after all our sufferings and the sacrifices of all the gallant boys that have gone that in the end we should be beaten by financiers."[82] Though it was widely believed that Northcliffe was hostile to President Wilson, he went on to tell Jones that Wilson should not be blamed, that he had tried to help and even snubbed an Irish delegation, which would cost him votes.

Northcliffe's nephew, Esmond Harmsworth, was on Lloyd George's staff at the Peace Conference. The press lord wrote to him that he feared "your chief is giving away the show. He always seems to be led by the nose by those who were at the bottom of the poll at the last election."[83] In the young Harmsworth's view, the prime minister was seeing too many people and had no time for reflection. When Northcliffe heard that Esmond's father, Rothermere, was going to see Lloyd George, he told him that he would be doing a great service if he gave the prime minister the truth about the national "exasperation" caused by the many conflicting statements on the financial settlement.[84] Northcliffe also sent a statement of his views meant for the eyes of Lloyd George. After meeting with the Welshman, Rothermere visited his brother at his hotel in Fontainebleau. The two men played golf, and Rothermere attempted to make peace. His mission was a failure. At this time Riddell considered that Lloyd George had become "more autocratic; more intolerant of criticism, and more insistent upon secrecy. Thus he has given Northcliffe his opportunity, which the latter is not using very skillfully, with the result that LG may give him a nasty shock."[85]

Rebuked in his latest attempt at reconciliation and fed up with Northcliffe's interference and criticism, Lloyd George returned from Paris to defend himself in the Commons, determined to "declare war to the knife" and to follow through with his threats of a public statement.[86] According to Paul Mantoux, the interpreter and the only person taking notes at the Council of Four sessions, before he left, Lloyd George told the Council that he had to return to London to face his critics on the reparations issue. He promised he would be back within a few days "unless the House of Commons refuses me its confidence, in which case it will be with Lord Northcliffe or Horatio Bottomley that you will be resuming these talks."[87]

On 16 April, speaking on the subject of the Peace Conference, the prime minister brutally denounced the press lord in the Commons. Turning aside the *Westminster Gazette* article as the cause of the telegram from Parliament, Lloyd George instead blamed Kennedy Jones's instigation of the affair on the cable of a "reliable source" (undoubtedly Northcliffe) in Paris. Without ever naming his target, the prime minister continued,

> At the beginning of the conference there were appeals to everybody all around to support President Wilson and his great ideals. Where did these come from? From the same "reliable source" that is now hysterically attacking all these great ideals.... Reliable! That is the last adjective I would use. It is here to-day, jumping there to-morrow, and there the next day. I would as soon rely on a grasshopper.
>
> Still I am willing to make some allowance ... when a man is labouring under a keen sense of disappointment, however unjustified and ... ridiculous the expectations may have been.... When a man deludes himself, and all the people whom he ever permits to go near him into the belief that he is the only man who can win the War, and is waiting for the clamour of the multitude that is going to demand his presence there to direct the destinies of the world, and there is not a whisper, not a sound, it is rather disappointing; it is unnerving; it is upsetting.
>
> Then the War is won without him. There must be something wrong. Of course it must be the Government. Then, at any rate, he is the only man to make peace.... So he publishes the Peace Terms, and he waits for the "call." It does not come.... Under these conditions I am prepared to make allowances; but let me say this, that when that kind of diseased vanity is carried to the point of sowing dissension between great Allies, whose unity is essential to the peace and happiness of the world ... then I say that not even that kind of disease is a justification for so black a crime against humanity.[88]

During this denunciation, as he spoke the words "diseased vanity," Lloyd George tapped his forehead to demonstrate the press lord's infirmity. The prime minister ended his indictment with an apology for taking up the time of the House with the matter, which, he explained, was only necessary because he had been many weeks in France, where it was still believed that *The Times* was a "serious organ" and it was not known it was "merely a three-penny edition" of the *Daily Mail*. "On the continent," said Lloyd George, "they really have an idea that it is a semi-official organ of the Government. That shows how long these traditions take to die out.... This is my only apology for taking notice of that kind of trash, with which some of these papers have been filled during the last few weeks."[89]

The prime minister's performance was widely acclaimed, and Riddell reported that the Welshman was in "great spirits" afterward. Lord Robert Cecil remarked to Lloyd George, "I expect N. will burst."[90] Not only had the occasion allowed him to strike at his chief press critic, the theatrics had enabled him to sidestep any detailed discussion of the peace settlement. Frances Stevenson recorded in her diary that the Welshman returned to Paris "in the highest of spirits, & very pleased with himself. He had a wonderful reception and gained complete mastery of the House, while telling them absolutely nothing about the peace conference. But he treated them to an amusing skit on Northcliffe...which will make N. squirm. D. is determined to fight him tooth and nail...Lord Rothermere, who came in tonight, was not quite sure how to take it, but young Harmsworth did not like it at all & has gone to London."[91] Bonar Law commented a few weeks later that the attack had been "very dexterous, but that the speech as a whole was open to serious Parliamentary criticism, had there been anyone to criticise."[92] Besides the fact that the speech cleverly diverted the discussion away from the real subject, Bonar Law would have pointed out the prime minister's previous alliance with the press lord, the fact that he had appointed him to two offices, and that "nothing had occurred warranting LG's change in attitude except the fact that N had the temerity to disagree with him." Expecting an equally stinging response from *The Times* and its chief proprietor, Lord Esher told a confidant on 18 April that he believed the newspaper would survive the battle, but added melodramatically, "No one can say what the result of the conflict will be that now opens between L.G. and Northcliffe."[93]

However, the response of *The Times* under its new editor, Steed, was measured, and Northcliffe chose not to wage a public battle with the prime minister. At the press lord's suggestion, Steed had traveled from Paris to witness Lloyd George's attack. He recalled that the Commons "roared with delight" at the performance; however, in his opinion, the address "showed no critical faculty whatever," and in "view of the gravity of the position in Paris" he found the "spectacle hardly comforting."[94] The editor of *The Times* reported back to his chief that the Welshman's attack was "really beneath contempt. I thought the best way to treat him was to be dignified...and to give him better than he sent. From the number of letters I have received these tactics seem to have been successful."[95] The press lord replied, "Your handling of our Petty P. M. was perfect" and recommended the same course to his other journals.[96] He sent Marlowe a memorandum on the subject: "We must be careful not to involve ourselves in *wrong* quarrels with the Prime Minister....When he is vigorous in fighting Germany I support him; when he sings his "be kind to poor little Germany" song, I oppose him.... I notice a tendency in the staffs of my newspapers to hit back when the Prime Minister makes foolish remarks about me.... Silence is a more effective and dignified weapon."[97]

The day after Lloyd George's speech, an angry Cecil Harmsworth wrote to his older brother that the attack had "gone beyond all reasonable bounds" and that, even though he had not wholly approved of the newspaper methods, he was considering resignation.[98] Northcliffe counseled Cecil not to resign because of the "stupidity of your chief. He is angry because we have found out what is going on in Paris."[99] The whole conference, said the press lord, was dominated by German financiers. He went on that even though he did not believe, as some did, that there was any "sinister financial connection" between them and Lloyd George, there was "no doubt that they are succeeding in shifting the burden of the cost of the war on to the backs of the Allies, and especially the British." The conflict with Lloyd George also elicited comments from America. W. F. Bullock, the New York *Daily Mail* correspondent, informed his owner that the clash with the prime minister had "excited an enormous amount of energy here."[100] Bullock went on that in response to a Paris communiqué that the "situation had resolved itself into a struggle between Wilson and Northcliffe for the Soul of Lloyd George," the American writer Frank Cobb quipped: "That is what I call a damned small stake."

This April 1919 episode proved to be Northcliffe's last major confrontation with Lloyd George. A month after the rather one-sided imbroglio with the prime minister, even his role as critic of the Peace Conference came to an end when his failing health forced him to see a series of doctors about his throat. In their opinion, it was imperative that he have the adenoma that had developed on his thyroid gland removed as soon as possible. The surgery was successfully completed on 18 June. Ten days later, as the press lord recuperated, the Versailles treaty was signed in Paris. Among the many letters wishing him a speedy recovery was the missive from Sir William Robertson Nicoll that opened this study.

Northcliffe's impact on the 1918 Election and 1919 Peace Conference was in stark contrast to his wartime influence. Although the coalition was moved finally to make election pledges that mirrored the demands of the *Daily Mail*, his newspapers failed to derail, or even dent, the candidates anointed by the Lloyd George juggernaut. The most that might be claimed is that by giving a respectable mass newspaper voice to Labour, the *Daily Mail* may have aided the party of the working class in some of its gains. In January 1919, Northcliffe was not able to influence the construction of the cabinet of "Tory nincompoops" that he feared would lead the country to disaster. In Paris, his newspapers can be given some credit for shaping opinion, but in the end it was the politicians who triumphed there as well. Though still feared, as Lloyd

George's April outburst clearly demonstrated, he could only rail from a distance as events passed him by.

The published accounts of the conflict between Northcliffe and Lloyd George after November 1918 have concentrated on the press lord's supposed rage at being left out of the peace process which, it is said, led him to carry out an irrational and megalomaniacal "vendetta" against the prime minister, which was quashed by the Welshman on 16 April.[101] Examining the record, however, reveals that the press lord's course was little different than that of the previous years. The truth of the matter may be closer to Bonar Law's admission in May 1919, that it was Northcliffe's open disagreement that caused the break. The prime minister who had won the war and the election could afford openly to deride his former ally, now no longer needed. For a variety of reasons, including his health, his departure from official office, and the widespread popularity of Lloyd George, in the period from November 1918 to June 1919 Northcliffe completed the fall from indisputable power that had begun in mid-1918. Thereafter, for the few years that remained to him, he returned to the more insubstantial press influence he had achieved well before 1914.

TWELVE

Conclusion
Politicians, the Press, & Propaganda

IN THE FEW YEARS LEFT TO HIM, NORTHCLIFFE NEVER REGAINED HIS
prewar vitality. In 1921 a prolonged world tour failed to improve his health,
and the next year he suffered a complete mental and physical breakdown
from which he never recovered. Consequently, three years after the signing
of the Versailles treaty, the Napoleon of Fleet Street was reduced to a piti-
able invalid confined to a makeshift wooden cabin on the roof of the Duke of
Devonshire's London house.[1] The press lord died 14 August 1922. However,
the tragic finale should not overshadow his earlier accomplishments, which
were unparalleled in the field of journalism and significant to Britain's story
in the Great War. Northcliffe's career from 1914 to 1918 clearly demonstrated
the largely unexamined intimate relationship between British politics and
journalism during the First World War.

By involving himself in a stunning number of the war's problems, the
owner of the *Daily Mail* contributed in substantial ways to the final victory.
Few men outside positions of national leadership made a greater overall impact. The press lord fearlessly challenged his government over almost every
matter of concern, including: censorship, recruiting, munitions, war strategy and policy, conscription, the blockade, finance, food, foreign policy, air
power, propaganda, and the peace. In the process he raised money and recruits, contributed to the fall of governments, speeded the supply of shells, attempted to guard Anglo-American and Anglo-French relations, and lowered
the morale of the enemy. In the war years he developed a degree of power
over political and public opinion that was real, not illusory.

From August 1914 Northcliffe strove to make the government and the
people of Britain realize the seriousness of the conflict in which they were involved. The censorship frustrated this aim and also, he felt, handicapped recruiting for the army he supported against the interference of the politicians.

These two causes were soon overtaken by shortages in munitions that could be traced directly to Liberal mismanagement of the war. Concerning the revelations of the shells, Christopher Addison, Lloyd George's assistant at munitions (and later minister himself), wrote in his memoir that, "in connection ... with the exposure of the munition shortage, the methods adopted by these papers may have been censurable on many grounds ... but Lord Northcliffe did not overstate the case and he rendered a real service in a very vital matter.... It may or may not have been a good newspaper effort, but it was of immense service."[2] Whatever its other effect on the formation of the May 1915 coalition, the "Shells Campaign" helped ensure that Lloyd George would head the new munitions ministry. It also marked a first awakening of the British public to the scale of the war and the sacrifices needed to prevail.

The people had perhaps begun to awaken, but to Northcliffe the prime minister remained in his Liberal repose, even after the press revelations over the shells helped foster the formation of the May 1915 coalition. What the press lord hated most was inaction and vacillation, and this is why he loathed Asquith and his wobbling "old gang." On 12 December 1916, after the fall of Asquith, the Conservative *Globe* declared,

> And Lord Northcliffe has just brought down the Asquith Cabinet.
> I know that the assertion will be jealously contested by those who would be his rivals; indeed, the statement is in some ways a generalization rather than the strict truth. The fact remains that it was after reading the now famous "leader" in Monday's "Times" that Mr. Asquith sent in his resignation. By that alone Lord Northcliffe (we speak now from the solely journalistic point of view) has achieved probably the greatest journalistic feat in history. He has out-lioned all the famous lions of the "Times" itself.

That the imperturbable Prime Minister could be so angered by one article in *The Times* reflected the frustration he felt after eighteen months of unrelenting newspaper criticism by Northcliffe. The cumulative effect of this campaign should be considered, along with the reverses of the war and the political combination of Lloyd George, Bonar Law, and Carson, as a tangible factor in the destruction of Asquith's last government.

The rise of David Lloyd George to the premiership soon brought a change in Northcliffe's role, from external critic to government official. The Welshman first focused the press lord's restless energy on the United States, which Northcliffe had believed since the beginning would play a crucial role in the defeat of Germany. The press lord fought for bolder British propaganda in America from 1914 until June 1917, when he was able to carry out his own personal campaign that smoothed the strained relations that still existed on his arrival. In addition to publicity, Northcliffe appealed directly to American government and business officials for supplies and all-important dollars, cutting, in many cases, through the war's red tape. Working without the wholehearted cooperation of the British embassy (much less the full powers of the ambassadorship that Lord Reading later enjoyed), Northcliffe nevertheless prevailed. Lloyd George, who so skillfully maneuvered the owner of the *Daily Mail* into service across the Atlantic, later noted his "striking success" and remarked that "for a man of his dictatorial temperament and experience he did well."[3]

The press lord returned from America to a homeland deeply troubled by the many Allied reverses of 1917. Speculation that he sought the premiership must have appealed mightily to his vanity; however, Northcliffe did not wish to lead, only that his country do its utmost to defeat the enemy. The press lord's declining health limited his activities; nevertheless, in the six months after he returned, he did all he could to spur his government and its leader to the same level of activity and enthusiasm that he had witnessed abroad. He also lent his prestige and available energy to successful propaganda efforts against Austria-Hungary and Germany, while warning of the domestic Bolshevik menace. Despite complaints and threats to resign from his Crewe House duties in 1918, the press lord continued to work with Lloyd George.

In early 1918, in a reversal of years of complete support, Northcliffe attacked army incompetence and Sir William Robertson, the embodiment of the strategy of attrition. From what he had seen in the United States, Northcliffe believed that, if the army could hold until sufficient reinforcement arrived, it was only a matter of time before the enemy would be defeated. By April 1918, however, with the Prussian wolf at the door, this appeared doubtful. If Britain did hold the line, the question was, where would the country stand in the war's aftermath? Once the German advance had been reversed, Northcliffe redoubled his propaganda efforts and maneuvered to have his British war mission play a role in the peace process. Thwarted in this attempt by the prime minister in the war's final weeks, the press lord found his power greatly reduced after 11 November 1918. Nevertheless, his failures at the end and after the war should not mask his contributions to the British effort between 1914 and 1918, which were considerable.

Winston Churchill, hardly a friend of Northcliffe, writing in *The World Crisis* on the press in the war, said that "no account which excluded its influence would be true."[4] Yet many such accounts have been published in recent years. The present work has been, in part, an attempt to examine the role of the British press in the First World War by chronicling the activities of its most prominent figure. This approach has provided a different perspective, that of a uniquely powerful outsider, on most of the major issues of 1914 through 1918. Until the end of the war, the country's politicians had to take Northcliffe seriously because, like few other men in Britain, when he believed himself right and the official line wrong, he could take substantial action. Although most of Britain's leaders abhorred Northcliffe privately, almost all sought his aid at one time or another. In the face of continuing British military failures, the politicians and the generals both needed publicity to bolster their own positions. Asquith did not deign to deal with him. Lloyd George did not make the same mistake. Perhaps more than any other politician, the Welshman realized the value of publicity.

Lloyd George's relations with Northcliffe during the war revealed a little-examined side of the prime minister. Rather than the towering figure who swept the election of 1918, the Welshman emerged as a fearful and constantly maneuvering politician, clearly aware of his precarious position as a premier without a party, dependent after December 1916 on an unlikely triumvirate made up of the press, the Conservative machine, and whatever Liberal parliamentary support he could muster. These conditions prevailed at least until Austen Chamberlain joined the cabinet in April 1918, and it may well have been Chamberlain's attack on Northcliffe, which underlined just how unpopular he was at Westminster, that emboldened Lloyd George to forego the press lord's support. Still, it was only when the war appeared won and when the premier had secured enough supplemental newspaper and political backing that he could afford to tell the preeminent press lord to "go to Hades." Four months after leading the coalition to victories in the war and at the polls, Lloyd George could proclaim similar sentiments aloud in the Commons, something he never dared to do during the war. This alternative portrait of the "Welsh Wizard" has been one of the valuable results of this study.

Outside the political realm, the generals, as well, struck wartime alliances with Northcliffe to further their own ends or to defend their own shortcomings. The press lord's activities on behalf of the army in the Great War clearly demonstrated both the enhanced power of the press in wartime and his personal influence. Within months of being installed to run the war effort by public and press acclamation, Kitchener's aloof rigidity brought the politicians and Northcliffe to reconsider their support of the war secretary. When the press lord transferred his allegiance to the more cooperative Sir John French, the field-marshal found he could not control his newspaper ally, and his own failures brought his downfall. Once Lloyd George became prime minister, the support of the Northcliffe press for the generals was an important reason the Welshman could neither implement his eastern plans nor rid himself of the troublesome Haig and Robertson. However, by early 1918, after a year and a half of backing the duo against the government, the toll of blood and Robertson's perceived lack of initiative finally led Northcliffe to break with the CIGS. Had the press lord still been supporting Robertson in February 1918, his dismissal would have been that much more difficult for the prime minister. Although he harbored similar doubts about Haig, Northcliffe protected him as the best alternative, believing to the end that to secure a lasting peace, the war must be won on the ground in Germany.

In the face of stalemate on the blood-soaked battlefields, Northcliffe turned his activities more and more to propaganda during the course of the war. From the very beginning he believed that his country overlooked and misused this valuable weapon. After the generals turned down the 1914 plans to attack Germany with airborne leaflets, the press lord gave his attention to efforts aimed at Britain's Allies and at America, where, he believed, Foreign Office amateurs were bungling matters, just as the government mismanaged the rest of the war. Well before the United States joined the war, Northcliffe had his own operatives assessing the situation across the Atlantic. After April 1917 he was able to make an unofficial and long-overlooked publicity contribution in America, which rivaled the much more celebrated Crewe House campaign. Examination of Northcliffe's personal effort from June to November 1917 has revealed a significant gap in the history of British propaganda in the First World War. From February to November 1918 Crewe House also made an important contribution, but the results were due more to the efforts of subordinates such as Henry Wickham Steed, Sir Campbell Stuart, and H. G. Wells, than to the chairman of the British war mission. In failing health for most of this period, Northcliffe was not able to attend most of his propaganda committee meetings, and his value was more in the prestige his name lent to the effort and in his ability to deal directly with the government when problems arose.

Had he the political skills and desires of a Clemenceau, Northcliffe might have been prime minister in a war government. However, in reality, he did not desire to hold the reins of official power, but to advise a ministry sympathetic to his view of the war, which, in many instances the politicians had to admit, proved annoyingly correct. Not even the most grasping politician relishes the responsibilities and dangers that go with leadership, but they accept them as one price of achievement. Northcliffe had no need to pay that price. His position allowed him to escape "official" responsibility. However, that does not mean he took his own self-imposed duty to the nation any less seriously. Because he saw no limits to his endeavors, it was perhaps a heavier burden for him than any political office short of the premiership would have been. He was not limited by a portfolio, and ventured wherever he saw problems—of which, between 1914 and 1918, there were an unlimited number.

Rather than seize the reins of power for himself, like many of his time, Northcliffe looked for "the man" to lead the way. Lord Kitchener was the first incarnation, followed by Sir John French, Sir Douglas Haig, and, finally, David Lloyd George. The name of a politician on this list may seem out of place, but despite all of Northcliffe's criticism, it was apparent to him well before the Welshman assumed the ultimate responsibility that he was ablest among the politicians to do the job. The press lord was well aware that the two other closest candidates in his estimation, Sir Edward Carson and Lord Milner, both had fatal political drawbacks in the British system. The press lord's sizable ego must have cherished fleeting thoughts of anointing himself, but he was too much of a realist to take himself seriously as a candidate, and there is little evidence that he ever did so, except in the imaginations of his press rivals and political targets. More attractive by far was the combination, which Lloyd George wisely tolerated, of criticism and government service without cabinet obligations of loyalty. The Welshman's genius was to turn the press lord's skills to America and against the enemy. However, even Lloyd George's enormous energy was not enough to satisfy the press lord's passion to find a man with "push and go" enough to win the war and to make a suitable settlement afterward. No such man existed, not even Northcliffe himself, and the rigorous pace he set during the conflict almost certainly shortened his life.

Over the years, those who have written about Northcliffe have tended to extreme views. Most have dismissed his activities in the Great War as those of a mere gadfly and dabbler—a dangerously curious boy who never grew up or took his responsibilities seriously; or, similarly, as the uncouth barbarian who somehow gained entrance to the gates of power and influence early in the war and had the run of the palace until late 1918. Alternatively, a few have seen him as a patriot, unafraid to reveal the ineptitude of the bumbling leaders of Britain. Each of these positions contains a kernel of truth. Northcliffe could be rude, overbearing, uncouth, dogmatic, shortsighted, and too sure of himself. He could also be the epitome of charm, but his temper and general behavior did not often conform to the rules of the drawing room or the gentleman's club, for which he had little time and less interest. His duty, as he saw it during the war, was to use whatever influence and power he possessed to preserve Britain and her empire. To this end he relentlessly followed whatever path he believed led to victory. In this pursuit Northcliffe was hardly more irrational or egotistical than numerous other leading figures with whom he vied for power and influence. However, he was different in that he had not attended Oxford or Cambridge and had only made his place by clawing his way to the top with the help of his family. Also, he did not wear the stamp of election or party, and he dared to disagree with those who did. The British ruling class felt the underpinnings of their traditional power slipping away in the war. Northcliffe personified the feared new world to come. The postwar rush to dismantle the British propaganda establishment dominated by press figures was part of the unsuccessful attempt to leave behind the "aberrations" of wartime.

The hatred and distrust of Northcliffe by many of his contemporaries has obscured both his role and that of the press in the war. Few writers have bothered to check the manuscript record for evidence of the charges of megalomania or "diseased vanity" that have clung to him. Most have simply repeated versions of events as recalled by his enemies, such as Churchill, who described him as undoubtedly patriotic, but also "a swaying force, uncertain, capricious, essentially personal, potent alike for good or evil, claiming to make or mar public men, to sustain or displace Commanders, to shape policies or overthrow Governments."[5] At the other extreme, Colonel House, who in the historian Stanley Morison's words came to have a "mystified admiration" and a "superstitious respect" for the press lord, wrote that Northcliffe "has never received the credit due him in the winning of the war. He was tireless in his endeavors to stimulate the courage and energy of the Allies, and he succeeded in bringing them to a realization of the mighty task they had on their hands."[6] It does not require mystery or superstition to have respect for Northcliffe's efforts, for good or bad, during the Great War. It only needs an evenhanded examination of his actions.

Notes

ONE

Introduction: Background and Prelude to War

1. Nicoll to Northcliffe, 28 June 1919, Northcliffe Add. Mss., 62347, f.126, British Library (hereafter BL).

2. The most attention paid to Northcliffe in the war has come in the many biographies published since William Carson's *Northcliffe: Britain's Man of Power* (New York: Dodge Publishing Co., 1918). Reginald Pound and Geoffrey Harmsworth's *Northcliffe* (London: Cassell, 1959) and Henry Hamilton Fyfe's *Northcliffe: An Intimate Biography* (London: Macmillan, 1930) contain the most wartime material.

3. John M. McEwen, "The National Press During the First World War: Ownership and Circulation," *Journal of Contemporary History* 17 (1982): 466–67, 470–71, 474.

4. For an analysis of the different segments of the British press up to 1914, see James D. Startt, *Journalists for Empire: The Imperial Debate in the Edwardian Stately Press, 1903–1913* (New York: Greenwood Press, 1991), 6–7.

5. McEwen, "The National Press During the First World War," 482.

6. Alan J. Lee, *The Origins of the Popular Press in England 1855–1914* (London: Croom Helm, 1976), 18–19; Lucy Brown, *Victorian News and Newspapers* (Oxford: Clarendon Press, 1985), 273.

7. Taxes on advertisements and newspapers were repealed in 1853 and 1855. The duty on paper was removed in 1861. Stephen Koss, *The Rise and Fall of the Political Press in Britain*, vol. 1, *The Nineteenth Century* (Chapel Hill: University of North Carolina Press, 1981), 2.

8. For a view of the debates over the New Journalism, including just how "new" it was, see Joel Wiener, ed., *Papers for the Millions. The New Journalism in Britain 1850–1914* (New York: Greenwood Press, 1985).

9. Mathew Arnold, "Up to Easter," *The Nineteenth Century* 21 (May 1887): 638–39.

10. Asa Briggs, *The Birth of Broadcasting* (London: Oxford University Press, 1961), 42.

11. Koss, *Political Press*, I: 1, 3, 9; Brown, *Victorian News*, 274; David Ayerst, *Garvin of the Observer* (London: Croom Helm, 1985), 1.

12. Tom Clarke, *My Northcliffe Diary* (New York: Cosmopolitan Publishing Co., 1931), 4.

13. Pound and Harmsworth, *Northcliffe*, 12–14.

14. Ibid., 17. Geraldine Harmsworth bore fourteen children, eleven of which survived.

15. Ibid., 26.

16. Tom Clarke, *Northcliffe in History* (London: Hutchinson, 1952), 24; Piers Brendon, *The Life and Death of the Press Barons* (New York: Athenum, 1983), 111.

17. Pound and Harmsworth, *Northcliffe*, 40.

18. Ibid., 35.

19. Northcliffe's nephew, Cecil Harmsworth King, reported in his memoir, *Strictly Personal* (London: Weidenfeld and Nicolson, 1969), 60, that Alfred had been banished from the family premises because "he got the family servant in the family way."

20. Tom Clarke, who worked for Northcliffe at the *Daily Mail*, doubted if Northcliffe "could have tolerated Oxford for six months." *My Northcliff Diary*, 2.

21. Max Pemberton, *Lord Northcliffe: A Memoir* (London: Hodder and Stoughton, 1922), 29.

22. J. A. Hammerton, *With Northcliffe in Fleet Street*, (London: Hutchinson, 1932), 29.

23. Pound and Harmsworth, *Northcliffe*, 92–94.

24. Ibid., 146–60.

25. Brendon, *Press Barons*, 113.

26. Pound and Harmsworth, *Northcliffe*, 116.

27. *Answers*, 23 July 1892.

28. Ibid.

29. Pound and Harmsworth, *Northcliffe*, 170–75. For Kennedy Jones's recollections see *Fleet Street and Downing Street* (London: Hutchinson, 1920).

30. Robert Pierce, "Lord Northcliffe: Trans-Atlantic Influences," *Journalism Monographs* 40 (August 1975): 13. This article gives a balanced view of Northcliffe's journalistic "borrowings" of press innovations, technology, and talent from America and his own influence in return.

31. Pound and Harmsworth, *Northcliffe*, 208.

32. Ibid., 186.

33. Hammerton, *With Northcliffe in Fleet Street*, 162.

34. Pound and Harmsworth, *Northcliffe*, 193.

35. Koss, *Political Press*, 1: 369.

36. Brendon, *Press Barons*, 114.

37. Kennedy Jones, *Fleet Street and Downing Street*, 142.

38. Pound and Harmsworth, *Northcliffe*, 200.

39. *Politics in Wartime* (London: Hamish Hamilton, 1964), 154. Northcliffe gave credit for the paragraph to Edmund Yates of the London *World*. Pound and Harmsworth *Northcliffe*, 65.

40. Brendon, *Press Barons*, 114.

41. Pound and Harmsworth, *Northcliffe*, 260. Northcliffe has been given credit for various other publishing innovations. On the financial side, the Harmsworths began the trend of transforming private publishing empires into public companies. Other features Northcliffe at least helped popularize were the use of comic strips and the serial story.

42. Pound and Harmsworth, *Northcliffe*, 219.

43. The Unionist (in favor of the maintenance of the Union with Ireland) and Conservative political labels were used interchangeably in this period.

44. Pound and Harmsworth, *Northcliffe*, 220.

45. Ibid., 230–31.

46. Ibid., 254.

47. Pierce, "Northcliffe's Trans-Atlantic Influences," 18–23.

48. Ibid., 24.

49. Alfred Gollin, *Proconsul in Politics: A Study of Lord Milner in Opposition and in Power* (New York: Macmillan, 1964), 575.

50. Esher to Maurice Brett, 29 October 1901, in Maurice Brett, ed., *Journals and Letters of Reginald Viscount Esher*, 4 vols. (London: Ivor Nicholson, 1934, 1938), 1: 311. For Esher see Peter Fraser, *Lord Esher: A Political Biography* (London: Hart-Davis, McGibbon, 1973).

51. Koss, *Political Press*, 1: 368–69. This phrase was reputedly a play on the newspaper described in Thackeray's *Pendennis* as "written by gentlemen for gentlemen."

52. Pound and Harmsworth, *Northcliffe*, 151–52.

53. This was published in 1894 as *The Great War in England in 1897*. For a survey of the popular invasion scare literature before the war, see I. F. Clarke, *Voices Prophesying War* (London: Oxford University Press, 1966).

54. Pound and Harmsworth, *Northcliffe*, 152.

55. Twells Brex, *"Scaremongerings" from the Daily Mail 1896–1914* (London, 1915), 9; Pound and Harmsworth, *Northcliffe*, 232. Stevens died of enteric fever while covering the war.

56. Pound and Harmsworth, *Northcliffe*, 250–51.

57. Clarke, *Northcliffe in History*, 23.

58. Richard Bourne, *Lords of Fleet Street: The Harmsworth Dynasty* (London: Unwin, 1990), 30–31.

59. Pound and Harmsworth, *Northcliffe*, 252.

60. A. J. A. Morris, *The Scaremongers: The Advocacy of War and Rearmament, 1896–1914* (London: Routledge, Kegan Paul, 1984), 89.

61. Balfour to Harmsworth, 7 May 1896, Northcliffe Add. Mss., 62153, BL.

62. The name is taken from a part of the coast near his favorite home Elmwood, St. Peters, Kent. In 1922, with the Lloyd George honors scandal brewing, Lord Riddell, the Welshman's press confidant, recorded in his 8 July diary that Sir George Younger told the prime minister that Northcliffe had paid £200,000 for his peerage, £100,000 each to King Edward and his mistress Mrs. Keppel. Though some sort of payment to the party would not have been unusual, funneling the money to the king and his mistress seems rather unlikely. J. M. McEwen, ed., *The Riddell Diaries 1908–1923* (London: Athlong Press, 1986), 371.

63. Northcliffe supported Bonar Law as a compromise candidate for the Conservative leadership in 1911. Bonar Law shared Balfour's appreciation of the political value of press support; however, during the war Northcliffe considered the future prime minister a chronically ineffectual opposition leader. There is little manuscript evidence of the relations between these two men. Robert Blake's *The Unknown Prime Minister* (London: Eyre & Spottiswoode, 1955) remains the standard Bonar Law work.

64. Pound and Harmsworth, *Northcliffe*, 289.

65. For his attempts to keep Northcliffe in the tariff reform camp, see Alfred Gollin, *The Observer and J. L. Garvin 1908–1914: A Study in Great Editorship* (London: Oxford University Press, 1960).

66. An 1891 *Answers* article, "Why the Germans Come to England," had begun the warnings.

67. For views of both the compulsory service issue and the role of Lord Roberts, see R. J. Q. Adams and Philip P. Poirier, *The Conscription Controversy in Great Britain, 1900–1918* (London: Macmillan, 1987).

68. The book was also successfully translated into several languages with corresponding changes in who the invaded and the invader were. For a closer view of the 1906 campaign, see W. Michael Ryan, "The Invasion Controversy of 1906–1908: Lieutenant-Colonel Charles a Court Repington and British Perceptions of the German Menace," *Military Affairs* (February 1980): 8–12.

69. After the outbreak of the war, Northcliffe was merciless in his criticism of what he perceived as Haldane's inadequate prewar efforts and his reported pro-German sympathies. In *The Prerogative of the Harlot: Press Barons and Power* (London: Bodley Head, 1980), Hugh Cudlipp closely considers Northcliffe's anti-Haldane campaign.

70. Pound and Harmsworth, *Northcliffe*, 164.

71. Alfred Gollin, *No Longer an Island: Britain and the Wright Brothers 1902–1909* (London: Heinemann, 1984), 193. Much more on Northcliffe's contribution to the early development of aviation is also to be found in this work.

72. For this see Alfred Gollin, *The Impact of Air Power on the British People and Their Government, 1909–1914* (Stanford: Stanford University Press, 1989).

73. In capturing the new mass audience, Northcliffe was among the earliest to realize that large numbers of women could be courted as customers for his publications. His first weekly paper for women, *Forget-Me-Not*, was published in 1891. Linton Andrews and H. A. Taylor, *Lords and Laborers of the Press: Men Who Fashioned the Modern British Newspaper* (Carbondale: Southern Illinois University Press, 1970), 45; Pound and Harmsworth, *Northcliffe*, 128–29.

74. This bargain gave Rothermere a mass outlet for his own, often conflicting, views during the war, to which he added the *Sunday Pictorial* in 1915.

75. For the official version of the purchase, see *The History of the Times*, vol. 3, *The Twentieth Century Test 1884–1912* (New York, 1947), 555–86.

76. Chief, but far from alone, of Northcliffe's Liberal press antagonists was A. G. Gardiner, editor of the *Daily News*.

77. Brendon, *Press Barons*, 118–19.

78. The journalist Robinson changed his name to Dawson in July 1917 as a condition of an inheritance. He was a protégé of Lord Milner and a graduate of what is called Milner's South African "kindergarten." For Dawson see, John Evelyn Wrench, *Geoffrey Dawson and Our Times* (London: Hutchinson, 1953).

79. Northcliffe owned the *Observer* (one of the most respected London Sunday newspapers) briefly, from 1905 to 1911. Blatchford was a former army sergeant, whose *Clarion* reflected a unique blend of socialism and jingo patriotism.

80. Morris, *Scaremongers*, 169.

81. Pound and Harmsworth, *Northcliffe*, 367. After this trip, persistent rumors spread that Northcliffe was suffering from an incurable disease or, alternatively, that he had suffered a nervous collapse.

82. Fisher, afraid too much was being spent on the army, had been feeding information to Garvin since 1904. After the outbreak of the war in 1914, Blatchford published the 1909 articles he wrote for the *Daily Mail* as *Germany and England: The War that Was Foretold*.

83. Pound and Harmsworth, *Northcliffe*, 369.

84. John Grigg, *Lloyd George: The People's Champion 1902–1911* (Berkeley: University of California Press, 1978), 214–15. The account of this episode by Cecil Harmsworth also appears in Clarke, *Northcliffe in History*, 87–88, and Pound and Harmsworth, *Northcliffe*, 376–77.

85. Bentley Brinkerhoff Gilbert, *David Lloyd George: A Political Life, The Architect of Change 1863–1912* (Columbus: Ohio State University, 1987), 387.

86. Ibid., 388; Morris, *Scaremongers*, 205.

87. Northcliffe to Balfour, 13 December 1910, Northcliffe Add. Mss., 62153, f. 4, BL.

88. Balfour to Northcliffe, 17 December 1910, Northcliffe Add. Mss., 62153, f. 42, BL.

89. Pound and Harmsworth, *Northcliffe*, 400.

90. Morris, *Scaremongers*, 207.

91. Ibid., 158. This also can be seen as a continuation of the earlier fears of German spies generated during the 1906 invasion scare.

92. The British government had let a contract to the British Marconi Company to build a series of transmitting stations to link the empire. Reports soon surfaced that the attorney-general, Sir Rufus Isaacs (later Lord Reading), Lloyd George, and others had traded in the shares of the American Marconi company, which was not, at least directly, involved in the contract.

93. Lloyd George to Northcliffe, 21 March 1913, Lloyd George Papers, C16/8112, House of Lords Record Office.

94. Northcliffe to Lloyd George, 24 March 1913, Lloyd George Papers, C16/8/1a, House of Lords Record Office. The "lucid explanation" apparently came from Winston Churchill.

95. For this see Geoff Elley, "Some Thoughts on the Nationalist Pressure Groups in Imperial Germany," in Paul Kennedy and Anthony Nichols, eds., *Nationalist and Racialist Movements In Britain and Germany Before 1914* (London: Oxford University Press, 1981).

96. For an overview of developments in Germany in the years leading up to the war, see Immanuel Geiss, *German Foreign Policy 1871–1914* (London: Routledge & Kegan Paul, 1976) and Fritz Fischer, *World Power or Decline: The Controversy over Germany's Aims in the First World War* (New York: W. W. Norton, 1974).

97. General Freidrich Von Bernhardi, *Germany and the Next War* (New York: Edward J. Clode, 1914). The original German edition was published in 1912.

98. Pound and Harmsworth, *Northcliffe*, 442–43.

99. Clarke, *Northcliffe in History*, 23.

100. For a vivid account of these years, see George Dangerfield's *The Strange Death of Liberal England*. Ever since the 1801 Act of Union failed to include Catholic Emancipation for Ireland, the mostly Catholic southern portion of the country had carried on a running battle with England which culminated in the late nineteenth century with several failed attempts to carry Home Rule for Ireland. In the spring of 1914 yet another Home Rule bill finally was about to be passed, to the extreme displeasure of the Protestant Ulster counties of Northern Ireland who wished the Union to continue. In the summer of 1914 both sides were armed and, in the view of some accounts of the period, perhaps at the brink of civil war. Though from the south, Sir Edward Carson was the leader of the Irish Unionist party.

101. For the Irish question in this period see George Dangerfield, *The Damnable Question* (Boston: Lippincott, 1976).

102. In the usual *Daily Mail* layout, page one was devoted to advertising. The editorial was on page four, with the news leader on page five of ten to twelve total pages. The paper also featured a city page with financial and legal news, a sports page, and a women's page. Almost every page carried advertising. Though the *Daily Mail* did not use as many photographs as, for example, the pictorial *Daily Mirror,* during the war the final page was devoted to a full-page photo essay at least vaguely associated with the paper's lead editorial or articles.

103. *Daily Mail,* 22 May 1914.

104. L. C. F. Turner, *Origins of the First World War* (New York: W. W. Norton, 1970), 78.

105. *Daily Mail,* 26 June 1914. Since 1886 the earl had published *Brassey's Naval Annual,* an authoritative survey of world naval affairs.

106. "The Hapsburg Tragedy," *Daily Mail,* 29 June 1914.

107. J. M. N. Jeffries, *Front Everywhere* (London: Hutchinson, 1935), 63.

108. Jeffries described Prioleau as a man of "pretty style," the epitome of the English Cricket tradition. When told he might be sent to the Balkans, Prioleau reportedly exclaimed "But I don't speak Balkan." *Front Everywhere,* 44.

109. Pound and Harmsworth, *Northcliffe*, 456.

110. *Daily Mail,* 11 July 1914.

111. Jeffries, *Front Everywhere*, 64. Jeffries was sent instead to Spithead on July 20 to report on the great review of the fleet by the king.

112. The Curragh incident involved a threatened mutiny of British army officers who preferred to resign rather than follow orders to take action against Ulster.

113. "The Home Rule Crisis," *Quarterly Review* 440 (July 1914): 276.

114. Two years before he had remarked that the "Liberal press was written by boobies for boobies." Stephen Koss, *The Rise and Fall of the Political Press in Britain,* vol. 2, *The Twentieth Century* (Chapel Hill: University of North Carolina Press, 1984), 191.

115. Michael and Eleanor Brock, eds., *H. H. Asquith Letters to Venetia Stanley* (Oxford: Oxford University Press, 1982), 99–100. Asquith's biographer, Roy Jenkins, considers these letters to Miss Stanley to be the most truly representative record of Asquith's innermost thoughts.

116. Ibid., 100–101. The Covenanters were the supporters of Sir Edward Carson who had signed the Ulster Covenant on 28 September 1912 and pledged to use any methods necessary to maintain the union of Ulster and Britain against attempts to force Home Rule.

117. Ibid., 104.

118. He wrote to Venetia Stanley that "it is annoying on every ground, & puts the whole Liberal press in the worst of tempers: they are as jealous as cats & naturally resent the notion that *The Times* has been preferred to them." Brock, *H. H. Asquith Letters,* 107.

119. Turner, *Origins of the First World War,* 88.

120. *Daily Mail,* 23 July 1914. The spellings "Serbia" and "Servia" were both used in 1914.

121. Cameron Hazlehurst, *Politicians at War July 1914 to May 1915: A Prologue to the Triumph of Lloyd George* (London: Jonathan Cape, 1971), 14.

122. Ibid., 25–31.

123. *Daily Mail,* 29 July 1914.

124. "A United Front," *Daily Mail,* 31 July 1914.

TWO

"A Boomerang Policy": Censorship and Recruiting Battles, August to December 1914

1. Reginald Pound and Geoffrey Harmsworth, *Northcliffe,* 457.

2. For Conservative fears about Liberal mismanagement of defense before the war, see Rhodri Williams, *Defending the Empire: The Conservative Party and British Defense Policy 1899–1915* (New Haven: Yale University Press, 1991).

3. John Evelyn Wrench, *Struggle 1914–1920* (London: Ivor Nicholson & Watson, 1935), 41–42.

4. The *Daily Mail* assigned Lindsay Bashford to Vienna, Harold Pemberton to Switzerland, and Atkinson to Holland, the latter departing in the morning coat and silk hat he had been wearing to a London function. For a general history of war correspondents, see Phillip Knightley, *The First Casualty* (New York: Harper & Row, 1975).

5. Valentine Williams, *World of Action* (Boston: Houghton, Mifflin, 1938), 137.

6. Pound and Harmsworth, *Northcliffe,* 461.

7. Jeffries, *Front Everywhere,* 66–67. Jeffries had been recalled to London from Dublin after spending only two days there covering the Irish crisis. He arrived back on 30 July. On Saturday, 1 August he was called to the *Daily Mail* office at 11:00 A.M. and informed by the foreign editor, Fenton Macpherson, that he was to take the 2:30 P.M. train out of London—his destination being Brussels.

8. Ibid., 67.

9. The *Daily Mail* office on Carmelite Street just off Fleet Street was dubbed Carmelite House. *The Times* office was called Printing House Square.

10. Pound and Harmsworth, *Northcliffe,* 462.

11. Henry Wickham Steed, *Through Thirty Years 1892–1922,* 2 vols. (New York: Doubleday Page & Co., 1924), 2: 10. Stephen Koss, in *The Rise and Fall of the Political Press in Britain,* 2: 253, traces this information back to General Sir Henry Wilson, the director of military operations (DMO) and consummate British political intriguer.

12. Steed, *Through Thirty Years,* 2: 11.

13. Pound and Harmsworth, *Northcliffe,* 463.

14. 1914 Diary, Milner Papers, dep F85, Bodleian Library.

15. Turner, *Origins of the First World War,* 108–9.

16. Keith Wilson, "The Foreign Office and the 'Education' of Public Opinion Before the First World War," *The Historical Journal* 26, 2 (1983): 410.

17. Hazlehurst, *Politicians at War,* 67–70, 100.

18. Turner, *Origins of the First World War,* 114.

19. Lord Beaverbrook, *Politicians and the War 1914–1916* (London: Collins, 1960), 36–37. Beaverbrook reported that Churchill "stood out strongly for the despatch…all the more strongly perhaps because of Northcliffe's intervention."

20. Clarke, *My Northcliffe Diary,* 53.

21. Ibid., 54–55.

22. Steed, *Through Thirty Years,* 2: 34.

23. Ibid., 33.

24. Sir George Arthur, *Lord Kitchener,* 3 vols. (New York: Doran, 1920), 3: 3.

25. W. Michael Ryan, *Lieutenant-Colonel Charles a Court Repington: A Study in the Interaction of Personality, the Press, and Power* (New York: Greenwood Press, 1987), 147.

26. For one example of the press idolization, see G. W. Steevens, *With Kitchener to Khartum* (London, 1898).

27. Earl of Oxford and Asquith, *Memories and Reflections. 1852–1927,* 2 vols. (Boston: Little Brown, 1928), 2: 30; Roy Jenkins, *Asquith* (London: Collins, 1964), 342.

28. Hazlehurst, *Politicians at War,* 153.

29. Viscount Grey of Fallodon, *Twenty-Five Years,* 2 vols. (New York: Frederick Stokes, 1925), 2: 20.

30. Philip Magnus, *Kitchener: Portrait of an Imperialist* (New York: Dutton, 1959), 278–79.

31. David French, *British Strategy and War Aims 1914–1916* (London: Allen & Unwin, 1986), 25.

32. Steed recorded in *Through Thirty Years,* 2: 33, that Northcliffe told him on 6 August 1914, "this is going to be a long, long war." Magnus states that Kitchener foresaw a war of three or four years. *Kitchener,* 282.

33. David French, *British Economic and Strategic Planning 1905–1915* (London: Allen & Unwin, 1982), 51–70.

34. Ibid., 124–35.

35. Magnus, *Kitchener,* 288.

36. Ibid., 279–81. French had made his reputation as a cavalry officer in the Boer War. For more on his career see Richard Holmes, *The Little Field-Marshal: Sir John French* (London: Jonathan Cape, 1981).

37. Wrench, *Struggle,* 62.

38. Jeffries, *Front Everywhere,* 152; Hamilton Fyfe, *My Seven Selves* (London: George Allen & Unwin, 1935), 178.

39. For Wile's own account of his departure from Germany and other recollections of Northcliffe, see his memoir, *News Is Where You Find It* (Indianapolis, 1939), particularly 278–310. Northcliffe soon sent Wile on a reconnaissance mission to America. Wile also wrote a continuing series on conditions inside Germany for the *Daily Mail* called "Germany Day by Day."

40. Price to Northcliffe, 10 August 1914, Northcliffe Add. Mss., 62210B, ff. 16–17, British Library (hereafter BL).

41. Northcliffe to Price, 18 August 1914, Northcliffe Add. Mss., 62210B, f. 18., BL.

42. Philip Towle, "The Debate on Wartime Censorship in Britain 1902–1914," in Brian Bond and Ian Roy, eds., *War and Society: A Yearbook of Military History* (New York, 1975), 110.

43. Ibid., 104–7.

44. Pound and Harmsworth, *Northcliffe,* 363.

45. Colin Lovelace, "British Press Censorship During the First World War," in George Boyce, James Curran, and Pauline Wingate, eds., *Newspaper History from the Seventeenth Century to the Present Day* (London, 1978), 309.

46. George Cassar, *Kitchener: Architect of Victory* (London: William Kimber, 1977), 350–51; J. M. McEwen, "'Brass Hats' and the British Press During the First World War," *Journal of Canadian History* 18 (April 1983): 45–46.

47. Lovelace, "British Press Censorship During the First World War," 310.

48. Lord Riddell, *Lord Riddell's War Diary 1914–1918* (London, 1933), 9. The Press Bureau, staffed mainly with over-aged military men brought out of retirement, opened in a decrepit Admiralty building in Charing Cross on August 10.

49. Towle, "The Debate on Wartime Censorship in Britain," 112.

50. Smith to Northcliffe, 12 August 1914, Northcliffe Papers, Harmsworth Archive.

51. Towle, "The Debate on Wartime Censorship in Britain," 113.

52. Deian Hopkins, "Domestic Censorship in the First World War," *Journal of Contemporary History* 5 (1970): 154.

53. Lovelace, "British Press Censorship During the First World War," 310; Koss, *The Rise and Fall of the Political Press*, 2: 244.

54. Riddell Diary, 25 August 1914, Add. Mss. 62974, ff. 155–57, BL.

55. Ibid.

56. Regulation 18 forbade the collection and publication of information useful to the enemy. Regulation 27 forbade the spread of false reports that would cause either disaffection among the armed forces or prejudice Britain's relations with its Allies. Regulation 51 gave powers to the military both to search and to seize machinery at any place suspected of breaching these regulations. Violations were punishable by court-martial with possible life sentences.

57. *The History of The Times*, 4, pt. 1: 220. Soon, however, *The Times* and *Daily Mail* did report "official" German news, as better than no news.

58. Towle, "The Debate on Wartime Censorship in Britain," 113.

59. Robert Blatchford, "Do You Understand?" *Daily Mail*, 25 August 1914.

60. *Daily Mail*, 27 August 1914.

61. On the 14th, Sir John French arrived at Boulogne, and by the 17th he was at his headquarters at Le Cateau. Magnus, *Kitchener*, 292.

62. Fyfe to Northcliffe, 18 August 1914, Northcliffe Add. Mss., 62206, ff. 89–90, BL.

63. J. M. Bourne, *Britain and the Great War 1914–1918* (London: Edward Arnold, 1989), 18–19.

64. Holmes, *The Little Field-Marshal*, 219–20.

65. Hazlehurst, *Politicians at War*, 140–41.

66. Denis Gwynn, *The Life of John Redmond* (1932 reprint, London: Books for Libraries Press, 1971), 355–57.

67. For the home fronts during the war, see John Williams, *The Other Battleground: The Home Fronts Britain, France and Germany 1914–1918* (Chicago: ?? 1972).

68. *The History of the Times*, 4, pt. 1, 232–33.

69. During the war the *Daily Mail* correspondents placed important Sunday news in the *Weekly Dispatch*. These two papers and the *Evening News* made up Northcliffe's Associated Newspapers. They all supported and advertised for each other, and to a certain extent, shared staff.

70. Since the British army would not officially allow correspondents, the two men had been forced to glean their stories from reports given them by retreating soldiers they came upon on the road to Amiens. Fyfe, *My Seven Selves*, 177–80. Fyfe's first reports based on the accounts of the wounded from Mons appeared in the Friday, 28 August 1914, *Daily Mail*.

71. The original Amiens dispatch, with F. E. Smith's changes, is at the Archive of *The Times*. See Amiens Dispatch File, World War I Box.

72. *Daily Mail*, 1 September 1914. Smith was called to account for the affair in the Commons and tried unsuccessfully to defend himself on the grounds that his action was meant to bolster recruiting. John Campbell, *F. E. Smith, First Earl of Birkenhead* (London: Jonathan Cape, 1983),

375–77; R. F. V. Heuston, *Lives of the Lord Chancellors 1885–1940* (Oxford: Oxford University Press, 1964), 370.

73. Riddell Diary, entry beginning August 25, 1914, Add. Mss. 62974, ff. 155–57, BL. In Riddell's opinion, Smith had no doubt been "endeavouring to curry favour" with Northcliffe, so he had "only himself to blame."

74. Buckmaster was replaced in May 1915 by the colonial administrator Sir Frank Swettenham, who shared duties with the Liberal editor Sir Edward Cook. Cook served to the end of the war.

75. Martin Gilbert, *Winston S. Churchill*, vol. 3, *The Challenge of War 1914–1916* (Boston: Houghton Mifflin, 1971), pt. 1: 127.

76. Churchill to Northcliffe, 5 September 1914, Northcliffe Add. Mss., 62156, BL, in ibid., 126.

77. Northcliffe to Churchill, 7 September 1914, Northcliffe Add. Mss., 62156, BL.

78. For naval censorship during the war, see Sir Douglas Brownrigg, *Indiscretions of the Naval Censor* (London, 1920).

79. Neville Lytton, *The Press and the General Staff* (London: W. Collins Sons & Co., 1920), viii.

80. Swinton's name was not announced, but soon became common knowledge. He was recommended to Kitchener by Churchill and was later better known as one of the fathers of the tank. For his account of the assignment see Major General Sir Ernest Swinton, *Eyewitness: Being Personal Reminiscences of Certain Phases of the Great War, Including the Genesis of the Tank* (1933; reprint, New York, 1972).

81. Lord Riddell, *War Diary*, 17.

82. Northcliffe to Murray, 1 December 1914, Northcliffe Add. Mss., 62158, f. 55, BL.

83. R. Macnair Wilson, *Lord Northcliffe: A Study* (Philadelphia: J. B. Lippincott, 1927), 206.

84. Ibid.

85. Maps were a staple of the *Daily Mail*. A 4 September 1914 advertisement claimed 500,000 *Daily Mail* war maps had already sold separately. The commercial possibilities seemed endless. By 1 September the *Daily Mail* was already advertising the second volume of *The Times History of the War*. The *Daily Mail War Album* with pictures of the heroes of the war also sold well. Advertisers lost no opportunity to make patriotic the purchase of their products for the men in the trenches, from Wrigley's gum to Zig Zag cigarette papers.

86. *Daily Mail*, 3 September 1914; Jeffries, *Front Everywhere*, 137.

87. *Daily Mail*, 4 September 1914.

88. Price to Marlowe, 6 September 1914, Northcliffe Add. Mss., 62199, f. 15, BL.

89. Wilson, *Lord Northcliffe*, 205; Wrench, *Struggle*, 117.

90. Repington to Roberts, 22 October 1914, Roberts Papers, quoted in Towle, "The Debate on Wartime Censorship in Britain," 113.

91. This feature began in September 1914 as "Soldier's Letters." In the following years it would be called, among other things, "Letters from the Front," "Letters from the Firing Line," and "Letters from the Trenches."

92. Swinton, *Eyewitness*, 38–39.

93. In Swinton's view, though Northcliffe's patriotism was obvious, to favor one newspaper proprietor over another with a personal visit was not wise. Ibid., 39.

94. Northcliffe to General Charteris, 6 August 1916, Northcliffe Add. Mss., 62159, ff. 112–15, BL. Sir Campbell Stuart wrote that Northcliffe and Swinton actually worked together on a scheme in October 1914 and that pamphlets were printed and distributed by airplane, but that their project was not supported by the Army and did not go any further. *Secrets of Crewe House* (London: Hudder and Stoughton, 1920), 51.

95. Fyfe, *Northcliffe*, 179.

96. Northcliffe to Maxse, 13 October 1914, Northcliffe Add. Mss., 62175, f. 60, BL.

97. *Daily Mail,* 13 November 1914.

98. Riddell Diary, 5 November 1914, Add. Mss. 62974, ff. 231–32, BL.

99. Captain B. H. Liddell Hart, *The Real War 1914–1918* (1930; reprint, Boston 1964), 68–70. The press was not allowed to report fully about this episode for several months.

100. The first *Daily Mail* map showing the spreading line appears on 5 October 1914.

101. The attacks began on 13 October 1914 in the *Morning Post* and were soon picked up by other papers. Gilbert, *Winston Churchill,* vol. 3, pt. 1, 193–94.

102. He led a volunteer force across the channel which suffered heavy casualties. Further, the foray was blamed (because it gave false hope) for delaying and therefore making more costly the retreat of the Belgian army.

103. *Daily Mail,* 14 October 1914.

104. Northcliffe to Fisher, 24 November 1914, Fisher Papers, Churchill College Archive, Cambridge.

105. Northcliffe complained to Lord Murray of Elibank that, "so far as the naval censors are concerned; a message I sent to a string of American newspapers, in response to a request from them, was altered so as to be meaningless, and the name of Lord Fisher, on which the whole message turned, was struck out." 1 December 1914, Northcliffe Add. Mss., 62158, f. 55, BL.

106. Riddell Diary, 7 November 1914, Add. Mss. 62974, ff. 233–34, BL.

107. Northcliffe to Brisbane, 22 December 1914, Northcliffe Add. Mss., 62180, ff. 116–21, BL.

108. Bullock to Northcliffe, 16 November 1914, Northcliffe Add. Mss., 62208, f. 80, BL.

109. Northcliffe to Murray, 1 December 1914, Northcliffe Add. Mss., 62158, f. 55, BL. The Admiralty never officially admitted the sinking during the war.

110. Riddell Diary, 10 November 1914, Add. Mss. 62974, ff. 239–40, BL. At a dinner party, the wife of Reginald McKenna, the home secretary, told Riddell that her husband "would have had Northcliffe court-martialed if he had his way."

111. Riddell Diary, 7 November 1914, Add. Mss. 62974, ff. 233–34, BL.

112. At first, British voluntary enlistment had been enthusiastic, so much so that the 750,000 who joined by the end of September completely overwhelmed the system in place to train and equip them. In the following months, partly because Lord Kitchener raised the standards, the numbers fell off drastically. The raising of standards apparently was taken by many to mean that the crisis must not have been as severe as first thought. Adams and Poirier, *The Conscription Controversy,* 60.

113. Northcliffe to Sir Henry Wilson, 17 November 1914, Northcliffe Add. Mss., 62327, ff. 73–76, BL.

114. Northcliffe to Campbell, 1 November 1914, Northcliffe Add. Mss., 62327, f. 52, BL.

115. Northcliffe to Asquith, 3 November 1914, Northcliffe Add. Mss., 62327, ff. 59–60, BL.

116. Northcliffe to Robinson, 4 November 1914, Northcliffe Add. Mss., 62244, ff. 233–34, BL.

117. *Daily Mail,* 1 December 1914.

118. *Daily Mail,* 3 December 1914.

119. Koss, *The Rise and Fall of the Political Press,* II: 256.

120. See the *Daily Mail,* 2 October 1914, p. 2, for a notice that Schweppes was Swiss, not German.

121. However, the *Daily Mail* treated these two cases very differently. The 27 October *Daily Mail* account of Prince Louis's German connections was actually sympathetic. The 30 October editorial called his decision to resign as First Sea Lord "wise and chivalrous." There was no call for his head as with Haldane. The press campaign against Haldane continued throughout the war.

122. On 5 August 1914 an Alien Restriction Act had given aliens not of military age until 10 August to leave the country. Others were restricted and had to register with the police. By mid-October 10,000 enemy alien men of military age were in custody. For internment, see J. C. Bird,

Control of Enemy Aliens in Great Britain 1914–1918 (New York, 1986), and A. W. Brian Simpson, *In the Highest Degree Odious: Detention without Trial in Wartime Britain* (Oxford: Clarendon Press, 1992).

123. This order was soon suspended because of overcrowding in available facilities.

124. *Daily Mail*, 28 August 1914.

125. James Read, *Atrocity Propaganda 1914–1919* (New Haven: Yale University Press, 1941), 56.

126. The Bryce Committee findings were published in the United States in 1915 as the *Report of the Committee on Alleged German Outrages.*

127. See for example, "The Glad Eye That Failed," *Daily Mail*, 12 August 1914, 2, article by F. W. Wile on the Kaiser's twelve-year campaign for American sympathy.

128. *Daily Mail*, 7 September 1914, 6.

129. Willert to Northcliffe, 22 September 1914, Northcliffe Add. Mss., 62255, ff. 43–45, BL.

130. Enclosure, Northcliffe to Maxse, 13 October 1914, Northcliffe Add. Mss., 62175, f. 60, BL.

131. Northcliffe to Willert, 9 August 1917, Willert Papers, Box 6, Sterling Library, Yale University.

132. Northcliffe to Riddell, 30 December 1914, Northcliffe Add. Mss., 62173, f. 36, BL.

133. *Daily Mail*, 21 September 1914.

134. Northcliffe to Lloyd George, 27 October 1914, Northcliffe Add. Mss., 62157, BL.

135. Lloyd George to Northcliffe, 3 November 1914, Northcliffe Add. Mss., 62157, BL.

136. Quoted in Wilson, *Lord Northcliffe*, 213.

137. Northcliffe to Brisbane, 26 October 1914, Northcliffe Add. Mss., 62180, ff. 112–15, BL.

138. Clarke, *My Northcliffe Diary*, 59.

139. Stephen Koss, *Fleet Street Radical: A. G. Gardiner and the Daily News* (London: Archon Books, 1973), 81.

140. *Daily News*, 5 December 1914. The "Pekin falsehood" refers to the report published in the *Daily Mail* during the 1900 Boxer rebellion in China that the German minister had been murdered and the foreign legations in Peking destroyed. The *Daily Mail* delayed publishing the story for several days and it reflected the best information available at the time. Only the death of the German minister turned out to be accurate.

141. *Daily Mail*, 12 December 1914.

142. Northcliffe to Fraser, 15 December 1914, Northcliffe Add. Mss., 62251, f. 114, BL.

143. Riddell diary, 14 January 1915, in McEwen, ed., *The Riddell Diaries*, 98.

144. *Daily Mail*, 18 December 1914.

145. Ibid., 15 October 1914.

146. Ibid., 30 December 1914.

THREE
"A Very Big and Difficult Thing": Munitions and Coalition, January to June 1915

1. Gollin, *Proconsul in Politics* (New York, 1964), 249. Winston Churchill, *The World Crisis*, 2 vols. (New York: Scribners, 1927) 1: 248–51.

2. Gollin, *Proconsul in Politics*, 249–50.

3. Trevor Wilson, *The Myriad Faces of War: Britain and the Great War, 1914–1918* (Cambridge: Polity Press, 1986), 165, 182.

4. For a still useful study of the Dardanelles, see Alan Moorehead, *Gallipoli* (New York, 1956).

5. For the easterner/westerner split and Lloyd George's Balkans strategy, see David Woodward, *Lloyd George and the Generals* (London: Associated University Presses, 1983). Some historians, notably David French in *British Strategy and War Aims 1914–1916* and *The Strategy of the Lloyd George*

Coalition 1916–1918 (Oxford: Oxford University Press, 1995), have seriously questioned the accuracy of this division in the debate carried on within the British government. Nevertheless, this model remains useful for Northcliffe's role as an ally of the generals.

6. Churchill proposed a joint action with Greece even before Turkey entered the war. For Churchill and the Dardanelles see Martin Gilbert, *Winston S. Churchill, The Challenge of War 1914–1916.*

7. French, *British Strategy and War Aims 1914–1916,* 25.

8. Barrow to Northcliffe, 1 January 1915, Northcliffe Add. Mss., 62328, f. 3, British Library (hereafter BL). The same offending paragraph had been cut from the London *Daily Mail* edition of 29 December 1914 by the British authorities. The article revealed troop massings near the Swiss frontier.

9. Three lines were cut, concerning French pilots flying low to see German positions, but the French censorship claimed to have banned the whole article.

10. Northcliffe to A. M. Story, 2 January 1915, Northcliffe Add. Mss., 62328, f. 15, BL.

11. Northcliffe to Macpherson, 2 January 1915, Northcliffe Add. Mss., 62328, f. 19, BL.

12. Northcliffe to Cook, 5 January 1915, Northcliffe Add. Mss., 62328, f. 29, BL.

13. Northcliffe to Storey, 14 January 1915, Northcliffe Add. Mss., 62328, f. 50, BL.

14. This conscription theme was followed up in the 11 January editorial, "Drifting to Compulsion."

15. Fyfe to Northcliffe, 18 February, 12 April 1915, Northcliffe Add. Mss., 62206, f. 105. Northcliffe to Fyfe, 12 March, 24 April, 11 May 1915, Northcliffe Add. Mss., 62206, ff. 106, 110, 114–16, BL.

16. Wilton to Northcliffe, 24 April 1915, Northcliffe Add. Mss., 62253, ff. 143–45, BL.

17. Rodd to Northcliffe, 26 May 1915, Northcliffe Add. Mss., 62329, BL.

18. Northcliffe to Asquith, 1 January 1915, Asquith Mss. 14, f. 1, Bodleian Library; Northcliffe to Grey, 1 January 1915, Northcliffe Add. Mss., 62328, f. 8, BL.

19. Asquith to Northcliffe, 3 January 1915, Northcliffe Add. Mss., 62328, f. 24; Grey to Northcliffe, 4 January 1915, Northcliffe Add. Mss., 62328, f. 25, BL.

20. Brade to Drummond, 4 January 1915, Asquith Mss. 14, ff. 3–5, Bodleian Library.

21. Northcliffe to Asquith, 6 January 1915, Northcliffe Add. Mss., 62328, f. 32, BL.

22. Northcliffe to Grey, 8 January 1915, Northcliffe Add. Mss., 62328, f. 37, BL.

23. Northcliffe to Bonar Law, 4 February 1915, Northcliffe Add. Mss., 62158, BL.

24. Northcliffe to Fitzgerald, 4 March 1915, Fitzgerald Papers, Imperial War Museum.

25. Jan Cohn, *Improbable Fiction: The Life of Mary Roberts Rinehart* (Pittsburgh, 1980), 81.

26. Mary Roberts Rinehart, *My Story* (New York: Farrar and Rinehart, 1931), 152; Cohn, *Improbable Fiction,* 81–82.

27. *The History of The Times,* vol. 4, pt. 1: 273.

28. Northcliffe to F. Henriksson, 24 March 1915, Northcliffe Add. Mss., 62328, f. 227, BL.

29. Ingram to Northcliffe, 29 March 1915, Northcliffe Add. Mss., 62328, f. 238; Northcliffe to Ingram, 31 March 1915, Northcliffe Add. Mss., 62328, f. 239, BL.

30. Charles Grey to Northcliffe, n.d., Northcliffe Add. Mss., 62328, ff. 163–67; Brisbane to Northcliffe, 11 March, 12 April 1915, Northcliffe Add. Mss., 62180, f. 154, BL.

31. Marion Siney, *The Allied Blockade of Germany 1914–1916* (Ann Arbor: The University of Michigan Press, 1957), 12.

32. A set of wartime blockade rules had been drawn up and agreed to by most of the international community in the 1909 Declaration of London. At the time Northcliffe campaigned against it, and Britain never ratified the agreement. Ibid., 22–23.

33. Armin Rappaport, *The British Press and Wilsonian Neutrality* (Stanford: Stanford University Press, 1951), 27. The German submarines were expected to follow rules of engagement designed

for surface ships. Their size made it impossible for them to remove passengers and made them vulnerable to armed merchantmen, whose guns were often concealed.

34. Rappaport, *The British Press and Wilsonian Neutrality*, 14.

35. Willert to Northcliffe, 8 January 1915, Northcliffe Add. Mss., 62255, ff. 48–49, BL.

36. Northcliffe to Grey, n.d., Northcliffe Add. Mss., 62328, f. 101, BL.

37. *Daily Mail*, 22 January 1915, 5.

38. Wile to Northcliffe, 9 February 1915, Northcliffe Add. Mss., 62207, ff. 145–48, BL.

39. Northcliffe to Fisher, 24 February 1915, Fisher Papers, 3/7 2336, Churchill College Archive, Cambridge.

40. Ibid.

41. *Daily Mail*, 6, 8 February 1915.

42. Northcliffe to Robinson, 21 February 1915, Northcliffe Add. Mss., 62245, f. 3, BL. The Northcliffe papers were eventually all cut in page count and size.

43. Siney, *The Allied Blockade of Germany*, 66–67. The new measures were announced 1 March.

44. O'Laughlin to Northcliffe, 3 March 1915, Northcliffe Add. Mss., 62328, ff. 175–78, BL.

45. Rappaport, *The British Press and Wilsonian Neutrality*, 34–36.

46. Willert to Northcliffe, 1 June 1915, Northcliffe Add. Mss., 62255, f. 51, BL. Woodrow Wilson stayed true to his unwavering desire to keep the United States out of the war. Though numerous diplomatic notes were issued in response to the tightening of the British blockade, American sentiment, political philosophy, and economic self-interest kept the United States from extreme measures. Any economic losses were more than made up for by the increased Allied orders that inundated American factories and farms. In the end the lives lost to German submarine activity counted more seriously. This economic link, which by late 1915 also included loans, continued to expand until America officially became an associate of the Allied cause in April 1917.

47. John Evelyn Wrench, *Alfred Lord Milner: The Man of No Illusions* (London: Eyre & Spottiswode, 1958), 301.

48. R. J. Q. Adams, *Arms and the Wizard: Lloyd George and the Ministry of Munitions, 1915–1916* (London: Macmillan, 1978), 19. The shortage of heavy artillery was also examined.

49. John Grigg, *Lloyd George: From Peace to War 1912–1916* (London: HarperCollins, 1985), 183.

50. Reginald Viscount Esher, *The Tragedy of Lord Kitchener* (New York: E. P. Dutton, 1921), 8; Lord Hankey, *The Supreme Command 1914–1918* (London: Allen & Unwin, 1961), 1: 186.

51. Magnus, *Kitchener*, 285.

52. Ibid., 283–88.

53. Holmes, *The Little Field-Marshal*, 275; Williams, *World of Action*, 242. It had been arranged that Kitchener was a cabinet minister and also a serving field-marshal with seniority over French.

54. For the larger strategic considerations of the first two years of the war, see French, *British Strategy and War Aims 1914–1916*.

55. Magnus, *Kitchener*, 310. For Kitchener's strategic considerations of Russia and the Dardanelles operation, see Keith Neilson, *Strategy and Supply: The Anglo-Russian Alliance, 1914–17* (London: George Allen & Unwin, 1984), 61–77.

56. There were severe shortages as well of machine guns (which British headquarters tended to think overrated) and artillery.

57. Magnus, *Kitchener*, 332.

58. Adams, *Arms and the Wizard*, 12–14, 23. Some attempts have been made to rehabilitate Kitchener's reputation against what has been seen as a bias toward Lloyd George's version of events. For example, see Cassar, *Kitchener: Architect of Victory*, and Peter Fraser, "The British 'Shell's Scandal' of 1915," *Journal of Canadian History* 18 (April 1983), 69–86.

59. Cassar, *Kitchener*, 352.

60. Magnus, *Kitchener*, 333.

61. Northcliffe to French, 3 March 1915, Northcliffe Add. Mss., 62159, ff. 47–49, BL.

62. French to Northcliffe, 6 March 1915, Northcliffe Add. Mss., 62159, f. 50, BL.

63. Northcliffe to French, 20 March 1915, French Papers, Imperial War Museum.

64. Repington and Williams visited French as "private guests" to circumvent the restrictions against correspondents. Williams's Neuve Chappelle article was published 19 April. See Williams, *World of Action*, 243.

65. French to Northcliffe, 25 March 1915, Northcliffe Add. Mss., 62159, f. 56, BL.

66. Pound and Harmsworth, *Northcliffe*, 473.

67. Magnus, *Kitchener*, 334.

68. Some would say he originated them. Lloyd George accused McKenna of inspiring articles against him. Roy Jenkins, *Asquith*, 356.

69. Michael and Eleanor Brock, eds., *H. H. Asquith Letters to Venetia Stanley*, 517. Unfortunately, Asquith told Miss Stanley he could not write down the nature of McKenna's evidence, and it remains unknown; however, Margot Asquith recorded in her diary that McKenna had mistakenly opened a letter to the Treasury, meant for Lloyd George, which outlined the plot. Robert Skidelsky, *John Maynard Keynes: Hopes Betrayed 1883–1929* (London: Macmillan, 1983), 306.

70. Williams, *World of Action*, 259.

71. Northcliffe to Geraldine Harmsworth, 5 April 1915, Northcliffe Papers, Harmsworth Archive.

72. Northcliffe to Kenealy, n.d., Northcliffe Add. Mss., 62234, ff. 95–96, BL.

73. Williams, *World of Action*, pp. 242–43. Northcliffe had also been in contact with the French foreign minister, Theophile Delcassé, concerning the correspondent problem, which, he argued, hindered British and French understanding of the other's sacrifices. Northcliffe Add. Mss., 62328, ff. 110–12, BL.

74. 6 April 1915, Fitzgerald Papers, Imperial War Museum; Memorandum, 6 April 1915, Northcliffe Add. Mss., 62329, ff. 3–9, BL.

75. Northcliffe was allowed to choose F. Douglas Williams, the brother of Valentine, for this Reuters post.

76. Northcliffe to Riddell, 20 April 1915, Northcliffe Add. Mss., 62173, ff. 44–46, BL.

77. Lord Riddell, *War Diary*, 20–23.

78. Williams, *World of Action*, 247.

79. Northcliffe to Fraser, 11 April 1915, Northcliffe Add. Mss., 62251, ff. 115–17, BL.

80. Fraser to Northcliffe, 13 April 1915, Northcliffe Add. Mss., 62251, ff. 118–23, BL.

81. For this controversy, see Grigg, *Lloyd George: From Peace to War: 1912–1916*, 230–38.

82. *Daily Mail*, 30 March 1915.

83. Northcliffe to Beattie, 2 April 1915, Northcliffe Add. Mss., 62203, f. 11, BL.

84. Lloyd George to Northcliffe, 15 April 1915, Lloyd George Papers, C/6/8/2, House of Lords Record Office.

85. The same edition quoted a recruiting speech by Lord Durham that repeated Sir John French's call for more shells, "I want to pound the enemy and go on pounding them regardless of the expense, regardless of the number of shells I use because by doing so I am saving the lives of our gallant men. The more ammunition the less the danger are our men incurring in making these advances." *Daily Mail*, 13 April 1915, 5.

86. *Daily Mail*, 15 April 1915.

87. *Daily Mail*, 19 April 1915.

88. *Daily Mail*, 21 April 1915; George Cassar, *Asquith as War Leader* (London: The Hambledon Press, 1994), 88.

89. The 22 April *Daily Mail* quoted Kitchener's 15 March House of Lords statement, "I can only say that the supply of war materials at the present moment and for the next two or three months is causing me very serious anxiety."

90. Brock and Brock, *H. H. Asquith Letters to Venetia Stanley*, 562.

91. Northcliffe to French, 1 May 1915, Northcliffe Add. Mss., 62159, ff. 67–69, BL. The private correspondent mentioned almost certainly refers to Repington, whose army connections allowed him to visit French at general headquarters as a private citizen, not a war correspondent.

92. *The History of the Times*, vol. 4, part 1, 272.

93. *Daily News*, 1 May 1915.

94. "The War, the Government and the Critics," *Daily News*, 8 May 1915.

95. Edward David, ed., *Inside Asquith's Cabinet: From the Diaries of Charles Hobhouse* (London: John Murray, 1977), 242–43.

96. Magnus, *Kitchener*, 335.

97. Holmes, *The Little Field-Marshal*, 287–88; Magnus, *Kitchener*, 336.

98. *The Times*, 14 May 1915. Repington had previously pointed out the artillery ammunition problem on 27 April. After the 14 May disclosure, he claimed not to have known about Northcliffe's correspondence with French. Repington's biographer, W. Michael Ryan, thinks this "possible." See *Lieutenant-Colonel Charles à Court Repington*, 155.

99. For the munitions details in brief see Fraser, "The British 'Shells Scandal' of 1915," 69–86.

100. The historian John Grigg found "credible" Repington's claim to this in *The First World War 1914–1918*, 1: 39. *Lloyd George: From Peace to War, 1912–1916*, 248.

101. Pound and Harmsworth, *Northcliffe*, 476. Lucas was the son of Northcliffe's elder sister Geraldine. Having no children of his own, Northcliffe became very attached to several of his nieces and nephews, particularly the sons of his brother Lord Rothermere.

102. Lord Riddell, *War Diary*, 87, entry for 17 May 1915.

103. For a detailed view of the political developments surrounding the formation of the new government, see Cameron Hazlehurst, *Politicians at War July 1914 to May 1915*.

104. Pound and Harmsworth, *Northcliffe*, 477–78.

105. *Daily Mail*, 21 May 1915.

106. *Daily News*, 22 May 1915.

107. MacDonagh, *In London During the Great War*, 67.

108. Wilson, *The Myriad Faces of War*, 210.

109. Haig to Fitzgerald, 24 May 1915, Kitchener Papers, PRO 30/57/53, Public Record Office, Cassar, *Kitchener*, 357.

110. Rawlinson to Fitzgerald, 24 May 1915, Kitchener Papers, PRO 30/57/51, Public Record Office, Cassar, *Kitchener*, 357.

111. Ian B. M. Hamilton, *The Happy Warrior: A Life of General Sir Ian Hamilton* (London: Cassell, 1966), 322.

112. *Daily News*, 22 May 1915.

113. *Daily News*, 24 May 1915.

114. Wrench, *Geoffrey Dawson and Our Times*, 116.

115. *Daily Mail*, 24 May 1915.

116. *Manchester Guardian*, 20 May 1915, quoted in 21 May 1915 *Daily Mail*.

117. *Daily Mail*, 24 May 1915.

118. *Daily Mail*, 2 June 1915.

119. Bentley Brinkerhoff Gilbert, *David Lloyd George: Organizer of Victory 1912–1916* (Columbus: Ohio State University Press, 1992), 206.

120. 26 May 1915 entry, Riddell diaries, Add. Mss., 62975, BL, quoted in Gilbert, *David Lloyd George: Organizer of Victory 1912–1916*, 206.

121. *Daily Mail*, 4 June 1915.

122. *Daily Mail*, 8 June 1915.

123. *Daily Mail*, 10 June 1915.

124. Williams to Northcliffe, 6 June 1915, Northcliffe Add. Mss., 62210A, ff. 57–58, BL.

125. Northcliffe to Hornby, 15 June 1915, Northcliffe Add. Mss., 62172, f. 206, BL.

126. Lincoln to Northcliffe, 8 June 1915, Northcliffe Papers, WDM/3/1(3), Archive of *The Times*.

127. Bullock to Northcliffe, 17 June 1915, Northcliffe Add. Mss., 62208, f. 95, BL.

128. Lord Riddell, *War Diary*, 87, entry for 16 May 1915.

129. Gwynne to Fitzgerald, 27 May 1915, Gwynne Papers, Box 23, quoted in J. M. McEwen, " 'Brass Hats' and the British Press During the First World War," 50.

130. Magnus, *Kitchener*, 334.

131. Holmes, *The Little Field-Marshal*, 275.

132. Northcliffe to Lloyd George, undated, but postmarked 29 May 1915, Lloyd George Papers, D/18/1/4, House of Lords Record Office.

133. R. F. V. Heuston, *The Lives of the Lord Chancellors*, 221–22.

134. Nicoll to Northcliffe, 18 June 1915, Northcliffe Add. Mss., 62329, ff. 184–85, BL. Buller was a British Boer War general widely blamed for several defeats, but championed by some.

135. Esher, *The Tragedy of Lord Kitchener*, 120. Esher reported (p. ix) that he came to France at Kitchener's request in September 1914 as a sub-commissioner of the British Red Cross. He was an intimate of the king and a behind-the-scenes power whose job "brought him into contact with many phases of the war."

136. Beaverbrook's position has been questioned in some quarters. In *The Downfall of the Liberal Party 1914–1935* (Ithaca, New York, 1966), 54, Trevor Wilson has pointed out that the shells scandal was indeed a "live issue" before May 15, but that it was not the shells scandal or Fisher's resignation that drove Asquith to coalition, but the use Conservatives would make of these matters. The Beaverbrook thesis is also questioned by John Stubbs in "Beaverbrook as Historian: 'Politicians and the War, 1914–1916' Reconsidered," *Albion* 14 (1982): 241–44. Stubbs finds Beaverbrook too much a Bonar Law partisan and thus misleading in his analysis of Unionist actions.

137. Wilson, *The Downfall of the Liberal Party 1914–1935*, 54.

138. *Field-Marshal Viscount French of Ypres, 1914* (London: Constable and Co., 1919), 360.

139. Churchill, *The World Crisis*, 1: 251–52.

140. Grigg, *Lloyd George: From Peace to War, 1912–1916*, 244–45. Hazlehurst, *Politicians at War*, 261.

141. Adams, *Arms and the Wizard*, 35; Pound and Harmsworth, *Northcliffe*, 480; *The History of the Times*, vol. 4, pt. 1, 275.

142. Gilbert, *David Lloyd George: Organizer of Victory 1912–1916*, 192.

143. Adams, *Arms and the Wizard*, 188–89; Alfred Gollin, "Freedom and Control in the First World War," *Historical Reflections* 2 (1975): 147.

144. Esher, *The Tragedy of Lord Kitchener*, 130–31.

FOUR

"A Very Hard Nut to Crack": The Conscription Question, July to December 1915

1. Winston Churchill, *The World Crisis*, 1: 250–51. Other Conservative voices also found a new credence. In a letter to Northcliffe, Leo Maxse, editor of the *National Review* and an ally in the call for compulsory service, commented that, "after having been regarded as a hopeless lunatic for half a generation it is a curious sensation to be treated as a comparatively sane being, though I do not suppose it will last." Maxse to Northcliffe, 8 July 1915, Northcliffe Add. Mss., 62175 ff. 64–66, British Library (hereafter BL).

2. General Sir Ian Hamilton, *Gallipoli Diary*, 2 vols. (New York, 1920), 1: 340.

3. Robert Blake, ed., *The Private Papers of Douglas Haig 1914–1919* (London: Eyre & Spottiswoode, 1952), 102.

4. For the conscription issue, see Adams and Poirier, *The Conscription Controversy in Great Britain, 1900–1918.*

5. Oliver to Amery, 23 July 1915; quoted in John Barnes and David Nicholson, eds., *The Leo Amery Diaries, Volume 1: 1896–1929* (London: Hutchinson, 1980), 123. Oliver had first crossed swords with Northcliffe over tariff reform, and he felt the press lord hurt Milner's conscription campaign.

6. Ibid.

7. David Dutton, *Simon: A Political Biography of Sir John Simon* (London: Aurum Press, 1992), 36.

8. Northcliffe wrote to Thomas Marlowe at the *Daily Mail* that he was "delighted to accept an invitation to a very simple function on my fiftieth birthday. I am much touched by the fact that my friends have thought of me at this busy time in our history." 13 July 1915, Northcliffe Add. Mss., 62199, f. 39, BL.

9. Wrench, *Struggle,* 142.

10. The considerable profits from this book were donated to the British Red Cross.

11. *Daily Mail,* 3 July 1915.

12. *Daily Mail,* 5 July 1915.

13. *Daily Mail,* 6, 8, 9 July 1915.

14. Harrison to Northcliffe, 11 July 1915, Northcliffe Add. Mss., 62174, f. 111, BL. Lloyd George was officially made minister for munitions by a 16 June Order in Council. For his career at the ministry, see Adams, *Arms and the Wizard: Lloyd George and the Ministry of Munitions, 1915–1916.*

15. Northcliffe to Harrison, 14 July 1915, Northcliffe Add. Mss., 62174, f. 112, BL.

16. J. M. McEwen, "Northcliffe and Lloyd George at War, 1914–1918," *The Historical Journal* 24, 3 (1981): 654.

17. Northcliffe to Lloyd George, 19 August 1915, Lloyd George Papers, D/18/1/27, House of Lords Record Office (hereafter HLRO).

18. For one example, see extract of a letter of an English officer at the front censored by Press Bureau dated 15 June 1915, Lloyd George Papers, D/18/1/13, HLRO.

19. Wrench, *Struggle,* 143.

20. Carson to Northcliffe, n.d., Northcliffe Add. Mss., 62158, f. 131, BL.

21. Carson to Northcliffe, 29 May 1915, Northcliffe Add. Mss., 62158, f. 126, BL.

22. Northcliffe to Carson, 15 June 1915, Northcliffe Add. Mss., 62158, f. 129, BL.

23. Ian Colvin, *The Life Lord Carson,* 4 vols. (London: Victor Gollancz, 1936), 3: 77.

24. McKenna to Northcliffe, 29 May 1915, Northcliffe Add. Mss., 62157, f. 188, BL.

25. McKenna to Northcliffe, 25 June 1915, Northcliffe Add. Mss., 62157, f. 191, BL. For the varied publicity activities of Le Bas in the war, see Nicholas Hiley, "Sir Hedley Le Bas and the Origins of Domestic Propaganda in Britain 1914–1917," *Journal of Advertising History* 10, 2 (1987): 31–45.

26. Northcliffe to McKenna, 4 July 1915, McKenna Papers, 5/10, f. 1, Churchill College Archive, Cambridge.

27. Northcliffe to McKenna, 6 July 1915, Northcliffe Add. Mss., 62157, f. 194, BL.

28. For the most recent view, see David Gilmour, *Curzon* (London: John Murray, 1994).

29. Northcliffe to Curzon, 11 June 1915, Northcliffe Add. Mss., 62153, BL.

30. Adams and Poirier, *Conscription Controversy,* 94–95.

31. Ibid., 98.

32. Northcliffe to Balfour, 1 August 1915, Northcliffe Add. Mss., 62153, f. 53, BL.

33. Northcliffe to Grey, 1 September 1915, Northcliffe Add. Mss., 62330, f. 196, BL.

34. Northcliffe to Murray, 7 October 1915, Murray to Northcliffe, 12, 18 October 1915, Northcliffe Add. Mss., 62158, ff. 72, 74, 82, BL.

35. Northcliffe to Fyfe, 20 August 1915, Northcliffe Add. Mss., 62206, ff. 129–30, BL.

36. Wilton to Northcliffe, 5 July 1915, Northcliffe Add. Mss., 62253, ff. 149–50, BL.

37. Northcliffe to Wilton, 19 July 1915, Northcliffe Add. Mss., 62253, ff. 151–52, BL.

38. Fyfe to Northcliffe, 16 September, 12 October 1915, Northcliffe Add. Mss., 62206, ff. 131–62, BL. Wilton to Northcliffe, 1 November 1915, Northcliffe Add. Mss., 62253, ff. 161–64, BL.

39. Wilton to Northcliffe, 4 November 1915, Northcliffe Add. Mss., 62253, ff. 165–66, BL.

40. Reick to Northcliffe, 9 August 1915, Northcliffe Add. Mss., 62180, f. 83, BL. Northcliffe to Reick, 14 September 1915, Northcliffe Add. Mss., 62180, f. 86, BL.

41. Curtin to Northcliffe, 26 October 1915, Northcliffe Add. Mss., 62331, ff. 89–90, BL.

42. Northcliffe to Melis, 29 July 1915, Northcliffe Add. Mss., 62330, f. 100, BL.

43. Northcliffe to Willert, 14 September 1915, Northcliffe Add. Mss., 62255, f. 53, BL.

44. Adams and Poirier, *Conscription Controversy*, 88. In May 1915, conscription, not munitions, had been the issue over which the Conservatives were prepared to challenge Asquith before other matters, as we have seen, intervened. In the reorganization that followed, the prime minister placed the Conservative conscriptionists where they could be supervised. The opposition leader, Bonar Law, did not make compulsion a condition of the new political arrangement. Despite pressure from within his party, he was not convinced that the need for conscription outweighed the perils.

45. Gollin, *Proconsul in Politics*, 279.

46. Northcliffe to Milner, 19 August 1915, Northcliffe Add. Mss., 62330, f. 147, BL.

47. Milner to Strachey, 21 August 1915, Strachey Papers, S/10/11/7, HLRO.

48. Milner Memorandum, 29 August 1915, Milner Papers, quoted in Koss, *The Rise and Fall of the Political Press in Britain*, vol. 2, 283–84, and Gollin, *Proconsul in Politics*, 283–84.

49. Adams and Poirier, *Conscription Controversy*, 69.

50. Ibid., 73–74.

51. Frank Owen, *Tempestuous Journey: Lloyd George, His Life and Times* (New York: McGraw-Hill, 1955), 300.

52. Wedgwood to Northcliffe, 20 August 1915, Northcliffe Add. Mss., 62330, f. 158, BL. Northcliffe to Wedgwood, 20 August 1915, Northcliffe Add. Mss., 62330, f. 160, BL.

53. *Daily Mail*, 24 June 1915. A sharper appeal is reported in the 29 July 1915 *Daily Mail*.

54. Adams and Poirier, *Conscription Controversy*, 99.

55. Statement dated 25 August 1915, Burnham Papers, PP/MCR/196, Imperial War Museum. Lawson was at this point already overseeing the day-to-day operations of the *Daily Telegraph* for his father.

56. Adams and Poirier, *Conscription Controversy*, 67.

57. Statement dated 2 September 1915, Burnham Papers, PP/MCR/196, Imperial War Museum.

58. Asquith to the Sovereign, 28 May 1915, Cab. 37/128/25, fols. 110–11, quoted in Koss, *Rise and Fall of the Political Press*, 2: 281.

59. Colvin, *The Life of Carson*, 3: 74.

60. Smith to Carson, 11 September 1915, quoted in Colvin, *The Life of Carson*, 3: 74. When Carson resigned in October 1915, Smith took his place.

61. Repington to Northcliffe, 2 September 1915, Northcliffe Add. Mss., 62253, f. 40, BL.

62. Northcliffe to Repington, 4 September 1915, Northcliffe Add. Mss., 62253, f. 42, BL.

63. Repington to Northcliffe, 16 September 1915, Northcliffe Add. Mss., 62253, ff. 43–54, BL.

64. Northcliffe to Milner, 6 October 1915, Milner Papers, Dep. 351, f. 36, Bodleian Library, Oxford.

65. *The History of The Times 1912–1948*, vol. 4, pt. 1: 282.

66. For the roles of Hamilton and Murdoch in the Gallipoli affair, see Alan Moorehead, *Gallipoli*; Ian B. M. Hamilton, *The Happy Warrior: A Life of General Sir Ian Hamilton* (London: Cassell, 1966); and Desmond Zwar, *In Search of Keith Murdoch* (Melbourne: Macmillan, 1980).

67. He also came under the influence of the discontented and hostile press representative on the spot, Ellis Ashmead-Bartlett, a *Daily Telegraph* correspondent whose reports were shared by the

London newspapers. Ashmead-Bartlett believed disaster was imminent unless immediate action was taken. Moorehead, *Gallipoli,* 308.

68. An original report, addressed to Asquith and written by Ashmead-Bartlett, had been seized at Marseilles by British representatives warned by Hamilton. Murdoch then simply wrote another, and equally hostile, 8,000-word report on his own. This was the document he gave to Northcliffe and others. Moorehead, *Gallipoli,* 308–9. A copy is in the Northcliffe Add. Mss. at the British Library and is largely reproduced in Zwar, *In Search of Keith Murdoch.*

69. Zwar, *In Search of Keith Murdoch,* 27.

70. Northcliffe to Murdoch, 30 September 1915, Northcliffe Add. Mss., 62179, ff. 58–59, BL.

71. Moorehead, *Gallipoli,* 311.

72. Murdoch to Northcliffe, 19 October 1915, Northcliffe Add. Mss., 62179, f. 63, BL.

73. Northcliffe to Carson, 16 October 1915, Northcliffe Papers, WDM/2/15, Archive of *The Times* (hereafter TA).

74. Riddell, *Lord Riddell's War Diary,* 127–28.

75. Ibid.

76. Ibid.

77. Colvin, *The Life of Lord Carson,* 3: 106–10.

78. *Daily Mail,* 29 October 1915.

79. Northcliffe to Carson, 1 and 9 November 1915, Carson to Northcliffe, 5 November 1915, Northcliffe Add. Mss., 62158, ff. 134–36, BL.

80. Northcliffe to Marlowe, 6 January 1916, Northcliffe Add. Mss., 62199, f. 45, BL. Northcliffe to Robinson, 30 December 1915, Northcliffe Add. Mss., 62245, f. 17, BL. This same tactic was employed against Churchill in this period.

81. Northcliffe to Murray, 8 November 1915, Northcliffe Add. Mss., 62158, ff. 87–88, BL.

82. For example, the salutation "Dear Sir John" had become "Dear Sir John French."

83. McEwen, ed., *The Riddell Diaries,* 127.

84. *Daily Mail,* 21 December 1915.

85. Randolph S. Churchill, *Lord Derby: King of Lancashire* (New York: Putnam's Sons, 1959), 195–96.

86. Adams and Poirier, *Conscription Controversy,* 112–15.

87. E. Sylvia Pankhurst, *The Home Front* (1932; reprint, London, 1987), 256.

88. Adams and Poirier, *Conscription Controversy,* 119.

89. Ibid., 120; Churchill, *Lord Derby: King of Lancashire,* 187.

90. Churchill, *Lord Derby: King of Lancashire,* 194.

91. Jameson to Northcliffe, 29 June 1915, Northcliffe Add. Mss., 62329, ff. 200–201, BL.

92. Le Bas to Northcliffe, 5 July 1915, Northcliffe Add. Mss., 62170, ff. 144–45, BL.

93. Margot Asquith to Strachey, 10 October 1915, Strachey Papers, S/11/7/52, HLRO.

94. Strachey to Margot Asquith, 12 October 1915, Strachey Papers, S/11/7/52, HLRO.

95. Adams and Poirier, *Conscription Controversy,* 121.

96. The same letter listed several suggestions: stop emigration to the colonies and the escape of men to Ireland and Jersey; shame men into the ranks by requiring an armlet to be worn (under penalty of law) that would identify their status; advertise the scheme, especially in the provinces; have a definite statement made by the cabinet that if the scheme fails, compulsion is inevitable; and finally, tell "more truth," so that young men cannot say, "What is the use of all this boresome drilling only to find the war is over." Northcliffe to Derby, 20 October 1915, Northcliffe Papers, WDM/2/98, TA.

97. Derby to Northcliffe, 23 October 1915, Northcliffe Papers, WDM/2/99, TA.

98. Northcliffe to Derby, 25 October 1915, Northcliffe Papers, WDM/2/100, TA.

99. Northcliffe to Derby, 29 October 1915, Northcliffe Papers, WDM/2/102, TA. Northcliffe to Derby, 1 November 1915, Derby Papers, Liverpool City Library.

100. Derby to Northcliffe, 27 October 1915, Northcliffe Papers, WDM/2/101, TA. Selborne was president of the Board of Agriculture and Fisheries and more concerned with home food production.

101. Derby to Northcliffe, 31 October 1915, Northcliffe Papers, WDM/2/103, TA.

102. Ibid.

103. Northcliffe to Derby, 1 November 1915, Northcliffe Papers, WDM/2/104, TA.

104. Derby to Northcliffe, 2 November 1915, Northcliffe Papers, WDM/2/106, TA.

105. Derby to Northcliffe, 11 November 1915, Northcliffe Papers, WDM/2/112, TA.

106. Northcliffe to Derby, 12 November 1915, Northcliffe Papers, WDM/2/113, TA.

107. *Daily Mail*, 11 December 1915.

108. Churchill, *Lord Derby: King of Lancashire*, 201–2.

109. Trevor Wilson, ed., *The Political Diaries of C. P. Scott 1911–1928* (Ithaca: Cornell University Press, New York, 1970), 160.

110. Wrench, *Struggle*, 147.

111. A. J. P. Taylor, ed., *Lloyd George: A Diary by Frances Stevenson* (New York, 1971), 90.

112. Adams and Poirier, *Conscription Controversy*, 135–38. See also the 27–30 December *Daily Mail*.

113. *Daily Mail*, 6 January 1916.

114. Robert Rhodes James, *Memoirs of a Conservative: J. C. C. Davidson's Memoirs and Papers 1910–1937* (London: Constable, 1969), 37.

115. *The Northcliffe Press and Foreign Opinion*, marked "secret" and "printed for the use of the Cabinet," dated 1 November 1915, Ministry of Information Records, INF4/1B, Public Record Office, London.

116. The newspapers cited included the *Kolnische Zietung*, the *Berliner Tagblatt*, and the *Frankfurter Zietung*.

117. Pound and Harmsworth recorded that Carson defeated Simon's cabinet proposal to have the *Daily Mail* suppressed over this map. *Northcliffe*, 489.

118. Ibid.

119. *The History of The Times*, vol. 4, pt. 1: 283; pt. 2: 1069–70.

120. *Parliamentary Debates*, Commons, 5th Series, vol. 76, cols. 547–670.

121. Gilbert, *Churchill: The Challenge of War 1914–1916*, vol. 3, pt. 2, 751.

122. Quoted in Dudley Sommer, *Haldane of Cloan: His Life and Times 1856–1928* (London: George Allen & Unwin, 1960), 333, n. 1.

123. 15 December 1915, Strachey Papers, S/11/7/54, HLRO.

124. Margot Asquith to Strachey, n.d., Strachey Papers, S/11/5/54, HLRO.

125. Rinehart to Northcliffe, 26 November 1915, Northcliffe Add. Mss., 62331, ff. 164–65, BL.

126. Williams to Northcliffe, 1 December 1915, Northcliffe Add. Mss., 62210A, f. 63, BL.

127. Dutton, *Simon*, 36.

128. MacDonagh, *In London During the Great War*, 86. The *Globe* falsely reported that Kitchener had resigned from the cabinet because of conflicts with his colleagues. It was soon back in business after delivering an abject apology to the government. Lovelace, "British press censorship during the First World War," 313. This press incident also may once again have saved Kitchener from dismissal by showing his continued popularity in the country. Blake, *The Unknown Prime Minister*, 276.

129. MacDonagh, *In London During the Great War*, 87.

FIVE

"*No More Shilly-Shallying*": Air Power and Conscription, *January to June 1916*

1. Walter to Northcliffe, 1 January 1916, Northcliffe Add. Mss., 62239, f. 1, British Library (hereafter BL). The Walters had retained an interest in the paper when Northcliffe gained control in 1908.

2. Brisbane to Northcliffe, 7 February 1916, Northcliffe Add. Mss., 62180, f. 171, BL.

3. Repington to Northcliffe, 12 January 1916, Northcliffe Add. Mss., 62253, f. 53, BL.

4. Northcliffe to Repington, 20 January 1916, Northcliffe Add. Mss., 62253, f. 54, BL.

5. Riddell diary, 23 January 1916, in McEwen, ed., *The Riddell Diaries,* 144.

6. Northcliffe to Massingham, 13 January 1916, Northcliffe Add. Mss., 62176B, f. 116, BL. McKenna was chancellor of the exchequer.

7. *Daily Mail,* 4 January 1916.

8. During the newspaper campaign Northcliffe issued periodic "Messages from the Chief," which alternately lauded, criticized, or advised his employees. For example, the 16 February 1916 declaration suggested that the newspaper placards be used to issue air raid warnings and called the scheme for warnings by "hooters" a "ridiculous one." Subsequent missives stressed points to be emphasized about the German zeppelin attacks, including that asphyxiating bombs were used. He also decried accounts that minimized the serious damage done by reporting "havoc among chickens." "Message from the Chief," 2, 14 April 1916, Ms. Eng. Hist d. 303, Bodleian Library.

9. Northcliffe to Bonar Law, 13 January 1916, Northcliffe Add. Mss., 62158, f. 25, BL.

10. Bonar Law to Northcliffe, 20 January 1916, Northcliffe Add. Mss., 62158, f. 26, BL.

11. In February 1916 the navy was responsible for enemy aircraft to the British coast, where the army took charge. Arthur Marwick, *The Deluge, British Society and the First World War* (Boston: Houghton-Mifflin, 1965), 232.

12. Northcliffe to Bonar Law, 20 January 1916, Northcliffe Add. Mss., 62158, f. 29, BL.

13. Bonar Law to Northcliffe, 21 January 1916, Northcliffe Add. Mss., 62158, f. 30, BL. Sir David Henderson was director of Military Aeronautics. His counterpart, the director of the Naval Air Service, was Rear Admiral Vaughan-Lee. Neither of them, the *Daily Mail* charged on 16 February, had "practical air experience."

14. Northcliffe to Bonar Law, 2 February 1916, Northcliffe Add. Mss., 62158, f. 33, BL.

15. *Daily Mail,* 3, 4, 5, 7, 8, 10 February 1916.

16. Bonar Law to Northcliffe, 18 February 1916, Northcliffe Add. Mss., 62158, f. 35, BL.

17. *Daily Mail,* 16 February 1916.

18. McEwen, "Northcliffe and Lloyd George at War 1914–1918," 655.

19. Lord Riddell, *Lord Riddell's War Diary,* 153. Frances Stevenson, Lloyd George's secretary, feared and distrusted Northcliffe. In her 12 February diary entry, she worried that "Sir G. says that if Lord N. once gets a footing inside the Government, he will not rest until he is made Dictator. I think there is something in it. Lord N. is unscrupulous, & a dangerous man I do feel that D. [Lloyd George] should not have too much to do with him. N. will use him for his own ends, & throw him over when he has no further use for him." Taylor, ed., *Lloyd George, A Diary by Frances Stevenson,* 98.

20. *Daily Mail,* 14 February 1916.

21. Northcliffe to Nicoll, 17 February 1916, Northcliffe Add. Mss., 62333, f. 150, BL.

22. Nicoll to Northcliffe, 18 February 1916, Northcliffe Add. Mss., 62333, ff. 158–60, BL.

23. Northcliffe to Nicoll, 24 February 1916, Northcliffe Add. Mss., 62333, ff. 167–68, BL.

24. Gilmour, *Curzon,* 450.

25. Derby to Northcliffe, 23 February 1916, Northcliffe Papers, WDM/2/119, Archive of *The Times* (hereafter TA).

26. Northcliffe to Derby, 24 February 1915, Northcliffe Papers, WDM/2/120, TA. Farnborough was the headquarters of the air corps.

27. Derby to Northcliffe, 25 February 1916, Northcliffe Papers, WDM/2/121, TA.

28. Gilmour, *Curzon,* 450.

29. Ibid., 451.

30. Ibid., 451–52.

31. *Parliamentary Debates,* Lords, 5th Series. vol. 22, 23 May 1916, cols. 124–26.

32. Northcliffe to McKenna, n.d., Northcliffe Add. Mss., 62157, ff. 213–14, BL.

33. Northcliffe to Carson, 5 January 1916, Northcliffe Add. Mss., 62158, f. 137, BL.

34. Steed, *Through Thirty Years,* 2: 82.

35. Since February the Germans had been launching massive assaults on the French fortresses surrounding the French city of Verdun. Both sides suffered immense casualties, but after early German successes, the French rallied behind General Petain and held the line.

36. Steed, *Through Thirty Years,* 2: 91.

37. The first dispatch appeared in the 6 March 1916 *Daily Mail.*

38. Pound and Harmsworth, *Northcliffe,* 496.

39. Northcliffe to Clemenceau, 10 February 1916, Northcliffe Add. Mss., 62333, f. 99, BL.

40. Lady Algernon Gordon Lennox, ed., *The Diary of Lord Bertie of Thame 1914–1918,* 2 vols. (London: Hodder and Staughton, 1924), 1: 305.

41. Northcliffe to Le Roux, 22 April 1916, Northcliffe Add. Mss., 62334, f. 57, BL.

42. Wilton to Northcliffe, 3 June 1916, Northcliffe Add. Mss., 62253, f. 170, BL.

43. Northcliffe to Wilton, 5 June 1916, Northcliffe Add. Mss., 62253, f. 171, BL.

44. David French, *British Strategy & War Aims 1914–1916,* 168.

45. Ibid., 174.

46. Amery, *My Political Life,* 2: 72.

47. Northcliffe to Derby, 24 February 1916, Northcliffe Papers, WDM/2/120, TA.

48. Derby to Northcliffe, 23 February 1916, Northcliffe Papers, WDM/2/119, TA.

49. Derby to Northcliffe, 25 February 1916, Northcliffe Papers, WDM/2/121, TA.

50. *Daily Mail,* 1, 3, 15, 16, 27 March 1916.

51. Northcliffe to Derby, 23 March 1916, Northcliffe Papers, WDM/2/124, TA.

52. Derby to Northcliffe, 26 March 1916, Northcliffe Papers, WDM/2/125, TA.

53. Northcliffe to Derby, 28 March 1916, Northcliffe Papers, WDM/2/126, TA.

54. Strachey to Margot Asquith, 21 March 1916, Strachey Papers, S/11/7/56, House of Lords Record Office (hereafter HLRO).

55. Robertson was in close contact with Geoffrey Robinson at *The Times.* For the spring campaign to extend compulsion, Adams and Poirier, *The Conscription Controversy in Great Britain, 1900–1918.*

56. *Daily Mail,* 6 April 1916.

57. Northcliffe to Massingham, 16 April 1916, Northcliffe Add. Mss., 62176B, ff. 129–30, BL. The last line translates into English as "It is the work that makes the life sweet."

58. A. M. Gollin, *Proconsul in Politics,* 340.

59. Harrison to Northcliffe, 20 April 1916, Northcliffe Add. Mss., 62174, f. 120, BL.

60. Northcliffe to Harrison, 24 April 1916, Northcliffe Add. Mss., 62174, f. 121, BL.

61. Northcliffe to Willison, 22 April 1916, Northcliffe Add. Mss., 62334, f. 54, BL.

62. Riddell diary, 24 April 1916, in McEwen, ed., *Riddell Diaries,* 153.

63. Norman and Jeanne MacKenzie, *The Life of H. G. Wells* (London, 1987), 308.

64. Northcliffe to Wells, 22 April 1916, Northcliffe Add. Mss., 62161, ff. 97–98, BL.

65. For this issue, see L. Margaret Barnett, *British Food Policy During the First World War* (London: George Allen & Unwin, 1985).

66. C. Paul Vincent, *The Politics of Hunger, The Allied Blockade of Germany, 1915–1919* (Athens: Ohio University Press, 1985), 10.

67. Northcliffe to Wells, 8 May 1916, Northcliffe Add. Mss., 62161, ff. 100–101, BL.

68. For the Irish Easter Rising, see Dangerfield, *The Damnable Question: A Study in Anglo-Irish Relations.*

69. Harmsworth to Northcliffe, 23 May 1916, Lloyd George Papers, D/14/1/8, HLRO.

70. *Daily Mail,* 26 May 1916.

71. Lord Riddell, *Lord Riddell's War Diary,* 185.

72. Pound and Harmsworth, *Northcliffe,* 500.

73. Ibid., 500–501.

74. "Message from the Chief," 8 June 1916, Ms. Eng. Hist d. 303, Bodleian Library.

75. Strachey to Margot Asquith, 24 June 1916, Strachey Papers, S/11/7/1916, HLRO.

76. A. J. P. Taylor, *English History 1914–1945* (London: Oxford University Press, 1965), 58.

77. Riddell diary, 15 June 1916, in McEwen, ed., *Riddell Diaries*, 160. Riddell had recorded on 21 May that he believed Northcliffe and Lloyd George were working to "dethrone" Asquith, 156.

78. David R. Woodward, *The Military Correspondence of Field-Marshal Sir William Robertson, Chief of the Imperial General Staff, December 1915–February 1918* (London: Bodles Head, 1989), 20.

79. *Daily Mail*, 7 July 1916. In "Northcliffe and Lloyd George at War 1914–1918," J. M. McEwen has suggested that the muted response came because the two men had "mysteriously" drifted apart in June. The combination of their disagreement over the Irish question and Lloyd George's taking the War Office against Northcliff's advice would seem to make this understandable.

80. Hankey Diary, 8 July 1916, quoted in Stephen Roskill, *Hankey, Man of Secrets,* vol. 1, *1877–1918* (London: Collins, 1970), 283.

81. Northcliffe to Lloyd George, 8 June 1916, Lloyd George Papers, D/18/1/32, HLRO.

82. Ibid. Northcliffe sent Churchill's letter to Lloyd George, and it remains in his papers.

83. Gilbert, *Churchill,* vol. 3, pt. 2: 977.

84. Northcliffe to Churchill, 8 June 1916, Lloyd George Papers, D/118/1/33, HLRO.

85. McEwen, "'Brass-Hats' and the British Press During the First World War," 51–52. Robertson was also often in contact with Geoffrey Robinson.

86. Gerard De Groot, *Douglas Haig, 1861–1928* (London: John Murray, 1988), 193.

87. Robertson to Haig, 2 June 1916, quoted in Woodward, *The Military Correspondence of Field-Marshal Sir William Robertson,* 55.

SIX

"Asquith's Head on a Plate": The Fall of Asquith and the Rise of Lloyd George, July to December 1916

1. He had been invited, as well, to visit the Australian troops by William Hughes, the Australian prime minister, and planned to inspect the Red Cross installations at the front that were supported by a fund drive in *The Times*. Duff Cooper, *Haig* (New York: Doubleday, Doran, 1935), 109.

2. Although Northcliffe later stated that he did not know Haig before this visit and Pound and Harmsworth state this was their first meeting, General John Charteris wrote that the two men first met in 1915 while Haig was commander of the First Army in France. See John Charteris, *Field-Marshal Earl Haig* (London: Cassell, 1929), 155.

3. Haig diary, 21 July 1916, Haig Papers, ACCS. 3155/97, National Library of Scotland.

4. 21 July 1916, "Lord Northcliffe's Visit to the War," Northcliffe Papers, Harmsworth Archive.

5. Haig diary, 23 July 1916, Haig Papers, ACCS. 3155/97; Blake, *The Private Papers of Douglas Haig,* 155.

6. 26 July 1916, "Lord Northcliffe's Visit to the War," Northcliffe Papers, Harmsworth Archive.

7. Pound and Harmsworth *Northcliffe*, 502.

8. Blake, *Private Papers of Douglas Haig,* 157.

9. 2 August 1916, "Lord Northcliffe's Visit to the War," Northcliffe Papers, Harmsworth Archive.

10. Northcliffe to Lloyd George, 6 August 1916, Lloyd George Papers, E/2/21/1, House of Lords Record Office (hereafter HLRO).

11. Northcliffe to Derby, 4 August 1916, Northcliffe Papers, WDM/2/129, Archive of *The Times* (hereafter TA).

12. For Lloyd George's strained relations with the military, see Woodward, *Lloyd George and the Generals*.

13. Strachey to Margot Asquith, 16 August 1916, Strachey Papers, S/11/7/61, HLRO.

14. Pound and Harmsworth, *Northcliffe*, 503.

15. McEwen, " 'Brass-Hats' and the British Press During the First World War," 54.

16. McEwen, ed., *The Riddell Diaries*, 168.

17. Ibid.; *Lord Riddell, Lord Riddell's War Diary,* 208.

18. Northcliffe to Lee, n.d., Northcliffe Papers, Harmsworth Archive; McEwen, "Northcliffe and Lloyd George at War," 659.

19. Northcliffe to Lee, 27 August 1916, Northcliffe Add. Mss., 62334, ff. 138–41, British Library (hereafter BL).

20. Northcliffe to Robinson, 6 August 1916, quoted in Pound and Harmsworth, *Northcliffe*, 503.

21. For a recent view of Italy in the Great War, see James Burgwyn, *The Legend of the Mutilated Victory: Italy, the Great War, and the Paris Peace Conference, 1915–1919* (London: Greenwood Press, 1993).

22. Lady Lennox, ed., *The Diary of Lord Bertie of Thame,* 2: 10.

23. Haig diary, Haig Papers, ACCS. 3155/97, National Library of Scotland; Blake, *The Private Papers of Douglas Haig,* 164–65.

24. Ibid.

25. Haig Papers, ACCS. 3155/144, National Library of Scotland.

26. Northcliffe to Charteris, 6 August 1916, Northcliffe Add. Mss., 62159, ff. 112–15, BL.

27. Charteris to Northcliffe, 19 August 1916, Northcliffe Add. Mss., 62159, f. 116, BL.

28. Northcliffe to Robinson, 8 August 1916, Northcliffe Add. Mss., 62245, ff. 29–31, BL.

29. Steed, *Through Thirty Years,* 2: 122.

30. Ibid.; Northcliffe had long since lost the trim figure of his youth. He kept a diary of his continuing battles with his waistline, "A Fat Man's Gallant Fight Against Fate." Northcliffe Papers, TA.

31. Sassoon to Northcliffe, 19 September 1916, Northcliffe Add. Mss., 62160, f. 18, BL.

32. Northcliffe to Charteris, 25 October 1916, Northcliffe Add. Mss., 62159, f. 126, BL.

33. Northcliffe to Murdoch, 20 September 1916, Northcliffe Add. Mss., 62179, f. 71, BL.

34. Wrench, *Alfred Lord Milner,* 312.

35. "Message from the Chief," 20, 21 September 1916, Ms., Eng. Hist d. 303, Bodleian Library.

36. Grigg, *Lloyd George: From Peace to War 1912–1916,* 384.

37. Sassoon to Northcliffe, 14 September 1916, Northcliffe Add. Mss., 62160, ff. 9–12, BL.

38. Sassoon reported further that Haig's last words to Lloyd George were, "when you have finished your joy riding come and stay two days with me" and that overall, Lloyd George's visit left Haig "terribly disappointed in him." Lloyd George further infuriated the army by discussing British generalship with the French general Foch. Woodward, *Lloyd George and the Generals,* 106.

39. Ibid., 108.

40. Repington to Northcliffe, 21 October 1916, Northcliffe Add. Mss., 62253, ff. 98–99, BL.

41. Northcliffe to Lloyd George, 25 September 1916, Lloyd George Papers, E/2/21/2, HLRO.

42. *The Times* and *Daily Mail,* 29 September 1916. See Grigg, *Lloyd George,* 415–34 for an insightful appraisal of the importance of this interview.

43. Woodward, *Lloyd George and the Generals,* 108–9.

44. Derby to Northcliffe, 2 October 1916, Northcliffe Papers, WDM/2/131, TA.

45. Northcliffe to Sassoon, 2 October 1916, Northcliffe Add. Mss., 62160, f. 35, BL.

46. Sassoon to Northcliffe, 6 October 1916, Northcliffe Add. Mss., 62160, f. 36, BL.

47. Northcliffe to Sassoon, n.d., Northcliffe Add. Mss., 62160, f. 38, BL.

48. McEwen, "Northcliffe and Lloyd George at War," 660.

49. Sommer, *Haldane of Cloan*, 341.

50. Pound and Harmsworth, *Northcliffe*, 507.

51. Sassoon to Northcliffe, 15 October 1916, Northcliffe Add. Mss., 62160, ff. 42–44, BL.

52. Woodward, *Lloyd George and the Generals*, 110.

53. Robertson to Lloyd George, 11 October 1916, Robertson Papers, Liddell Hart Centre for Military Archives.

54. Robertson to Northcliffe, 11 October 1916, quoted in Woodward, *Military Correspondence of Field-Marshal Sir William Robertson*, 91.

55. Northcliffe to Sassoon, 18 October 1916, Northcliffe Add. Mss., 62160, ff. 45–48, BL. Lord Beaverbrook's more melodramatic version of this story has Northcliffe telling Davies, "You can tell him that I hear he has been interfering with strategy and that if he goes on I will break him." *Politicians and the War* (London, 1960), 323. Frances Stevenson's diary entry for October 12 recorded a version much closer to Northcliffe's. Taylor, *Lloyd George: A Diary by Frances Stevenson*, 115.

56. Repington, *The First World War 1914–1918*, 2: 359–61; McEwen, "'Brass-Hats' and the British Press During the First World War," 56.

57. Taylor, *Lloyd George: A Dairy by Frances Stevenson*, 117.

58. Lloyd George to Robertson, 11 October 1916, quoted in Woodward, *The Military Correspondence of Field-Marshal Sir William Robertson*, 93–96.

59. Repington to Northcliffe, 13 October 1916, Northcliffe Add. Mss., 62253, f. 95, BL.

60. Northcliffe to Repington, 18 October 1916, Northcliffe Add. Mss., 62253, f. 83, BL.

61. Repington to Northcliffe, 19 October 1916, Northcliffe Add. Mss., 62253, f. 97, BL.

62. McEwen, *Riddell Diaries*, 171.

63. Taylor, *Lloyd George, A Diary by Frances Stevenson*, 117.

64. Repington, *The First World War*, 1: 374.

65. Lord Riddell, *Lord Riddell's War Diary*, 217.

66. Notes of a conversation between Lord Burnham and Mr. Lloyd George, Wednesday, 1 November 1916. First World War Papers of Viscount Burnham, Imperial War Museum, 8. On 13 November Frances Stevenson recorded in her diary that "Northcliffe has been bragging that the War Office has broken everyone who went there, & that D. [Lloyd George] will be no exception to the rule. If it were only for the sake of defeating that man, I hope that D. will remain & make a fight of it. N. certainly has a swelled head, & I wonder the public stand him as they do." Taylor, *Lloyd George: A Diary by Frances Stevenson*, 122–23.

67. For example, Lloyd George defended Northcliffe in a November Commons debate on Northcliffe's October Aldwych Club speech against demands that he should be prosecuted under DORA. Northcliffe was accused of revealing troop strengths, slighting Russia's contribution, and stating that compulsion should be forced on Ireland. *Parliamentary Debates*, Commons, 5th Series, vol. 87, 23 November 1916, cols. 1710–11; *The Times*, 24 November 1916.

68. Northcliffe to Sassoon, n.d., Northcliffe Add. Mss., 62160, ff. 50–51, BL.

69. Le Bas to Northcliffe, 30 October 1916, Northcliffe Add. Mss., 62170, f. 189, BL.

70. Northcliffe to Sassoon, 30 October 1916, Northcliffe Add. Mss., 62160, f. 57, BL.

71. Pound and Harmsworth, *Northcliffe*, 512.

72. Although Bonar Law won the vote in this debate over the disposition of captured enemy businesses in Nigeria, many Unionists followed Sir Edward Carson (who since he left the government in October 1915 had been the effective leader of the political opposition) and voted to allow only British interests to bid. See Robert Blake, *The Unknown Prime Minister*, 298–99.

73. Robinson's account of the crisis began with a Monday, 27 November dinner that included himself, Milner, Carson, Waldorf Astor, F. S. Oliver, and Derby. The group discussed whether

"Lloyd George should come out of the government, which he was convinced was going the best way to lose the war? And was it, or was it not, desirable that Bonar Law should come with him?" They were unanimous that Lloyd George should "make a definite effort to set things right or to come out at once" and Bonar Law "should, if possible, support him." "The Political Upheaval of December 1916," Dawson Ms. 66, f. 178, Bodleian Library.

74. Ibid., ff. 179–80.

75. Alan Clark, ed., "*A Good Innings*": *The Private Papers of Viscount Lee of Fareham* (London: John Murray, 1974), 158. In *Politicians and the War*, 360, Beaverbrook claimed that he also tried to bring Northcliffe and Lloyd George together around this time, but with no success.

76. Ruth Lee's diary of 1 December 1916, quoted in Clark, "*A Good Innings*," 160.

77. Ibid.

78. Lord Riddell, *Lord Riddell's War Diary*, 225.

79. Lloyd George's recollection of events was that when Northcliffe saw "something was going on, he made an effort to resume friendly relations. But he was not only left out of the negotiations, but as far as I know he was not informed as to what was actually taking place." *War Memoirs*, 3: 388. Frances Stevenson, his mistress and secretary, feared and hated Northclffle. She recorded on 1 December 1916 that "Northcliffe has turned up again, groveling, and trying to be friends with D. again. He sees that the other game will not work and if there is anything big happening Northcliffe would hate to be out of the know. But D. has beaten him once again. He (N.) acknowledges that D. is the only man who can save the country, and N. will back him." Taylor, *Lloyd George, A Diary by Frances Stevenson*, 130.

80. In *My Northcliffe Diary*, 94, Tom Clarke reported that Marlowe changed Northcliffe's original advertising placards, which read, "Asquith: A National Danger."

81. Balfour was actually only sixty-eight in December 1916, Lansdowne was seventy-one. Grey had been ill for some time, and his eyesight was failing.

82. Grigg, *Lloyd George: From Peace to War 1912–1916*, 452.

83. Northcliffe to Derby, 2 December 1916, Northcliffe Papers, WDM/2/134, TA.

84. Derby to Northcliffe, 2 December 1916, Northcliffe Papers, WDM/2/135, TA.

85. Pound and Harmsworth, *Northcliffe*, 513. Apparently on 3 December, other matters, including a possible lucrative writing contract for Lloyd George, were discussed as well, although both men later denied this. See McEwen, "Northcliffe and Lloyd George at War," 664.

86. Wrench, *Geoffrey Dawson and Our Times*, 140. Robinson flatly stated that, without Northcliffe's knowledge or advice, he wrote the editorial after talking to Carson, although Lloyd George may well have been Carson's source. Tom Clarke reported in *My Northcliffe Diary*, 95, that Northcliffe wrote a two column article on the political crisis, giving some the impression he had written *The Times* piece. A 4 December *Daily Mail* article called for "A War Council That Will Act." This may have been the piece referred to.

87. McEwen, "The Press and the Fall of Asquith," 881.

88. Asquith to Lloyd George, 4 December 1916, Asquith MS. 31, f. 20, Bodleian Library.

89. Lloyd George to Asquith, 4 December 1916, Asquith MS. 31, f. 21, Bodleian Library.

90. Montagu Memo, quoted in Jenkins, *Asquith*, 448.

91. McEwen, "The Struggle for Mastery in Britain," 150.

92. Montagu Memo, quoted in Jenkins, *Asquith*, 448.

93. Montagu to Asquith, 5 December 1916, Asquith MS. 27, f. 186, Bodleian Library.

94. Montagu to Bongy [Carter], 6 December 1916, Asquith MS. 17, f. 193, Bodleian Library.

95. Asquith's biographer, Roy Jenkins, did not see his resignation as a tactical move, but as forced, simply because he "did not have sufficient support to carry on." Asquith also feared that if he served in another government, he would be the butt of newspaper attacks on any failures. Jenkins viewed Arthur Balfour's "switch of allegiance" as "the most decisive single event of the crisis." *Asquith*, 454, 456–59, 461.

96. *The Times,* 6 December 1916.

97. Dawson diary, 5 December 1916, Dawson Ms. 66, ff. 181–84, Bodleian Library.

98. Pound and Harmsworth, *Northcliffe,* 514.

99. Arthur Lee reported that on 6 December Northcliffe told him that Lee should be made blockade minister (rather than Robert Cecil) because of his understanding of America, "the only country that counts." Ruth Lee's diary, 7 December 1916, quoted in Clark *"A Good Innings,"* 162.

100. Dawson diary, 8 December 1916, Dawson Ms. 66, f. 190, Bodleian Library.

101. Beaverbrook had expected this position but instead accepted a peerage. Stanley later credited Northcliffe's influence for his gaining the office. Stanley to Northcliffe, 9 May 1919, Northcliffe Add. Mss., 62158, f. 229, BL.

102. Isaac Marcosson, *Adventures in Interviewing* (London: John Lane, 1919), 129.

103. Gollin, *Proconsul in Politics,* 373–74. Pleased that Milner had been included in the war cabinet, Northcliffe sent a congratulatory note to Milner, who replied, "Many thanks. It's an appalling job, as you know better than anyone, still it won't be our fault if we can't pull it off." Milner to Northcliffe, 12 December 1916, Northcliffe Add. Mss., 62335, f. 103, BL.

104. Lord Beaverbrook, *Politicians and the War,* 526.

105. Ibid., 512. Lloyd George had already declared this sentiment in the 23 November Commons debate on DORA.

106. Samuel, *Memoirs,* 123–24.

107. Lord Beaverbrook, *Politicians and the War,* 544. Beaverbrook's biographer, A. J. P. Taylor, casts doubt on this story by questioning whether Beaverbrook was actually with Lloyd George in the first few days of his administration. See Taylor, *Beaverbrook,* 120–27.

108. Hankey's diary, 10 December 1916, quoted in Koss, *The Rise and Fall of The Political Press in Britain,* II: 310.

109. MacDonagh, *In London During the Great War,* 156. MacDonagh covered the event for *The Times.* In *The Downfall of the Liberal Party 1914–1935* (Ithaca: Cornell University Press, 1966), 101, Trevor Wilson marks this meeting as the final gathering of the old Liberal party. Roy Jenkins (*Asquith,* 461) places this speech at the National Liberal Club.

110. Strachey to Margot Asquith, 13 December 1916, Strachey Papers S/11/7/64, HLRO.

111. Clarke, *My Northcliffe Diary,* 98.

112. *The History of The Times,* vol. 4, pt. 1: 307.

113. Northcliffe to Stanley, 15 December 1916, Northcliffe Add. Mss., 62158, f. 176, BL.

114. Northcliffe to Carson, 10 December 1916, Northcliffe Papers, WDM/2/16, TA.

115. Northcliffe told Carson that he had heard of these problems from both Philadelphia and New York and advised Carson to speak to Admiral De Chair, who "could tell you something."

116. Northcliffe to Lloyd George, 18 December 1916, Lloyd George Papers, F/4/7/1, HLRO.

117. Strachey to Margot Asquith, 29 December 1916, Strachey Papers, S/11/7/64, HLRO.

118. This article was reproduced in the next morning's *Daily Mail* and *The Times.*

119. Particularly after the recent "Knock-Out Blow" article.

120. House to Wilson, 3 December 1916, in Arthur Link, ed., *The Papers of Woodrow Wilson* (Princeton: Princeton University Press, 1982), 40: 133.

121. "Message from the Chief," Ms. Eng. Hist d. 303, Bodleian Library.

122. Page to Lansing, 22 December 1916, in Link, *Papers of Woodrow Wilson,* 40: 319.

123. Northcliffe to Lloyd George, 27 December 1916, Lloyd George Papers, F/41/7/2, HLRO.

124. These include, among the biographers of the principals: Jenkins, *Asquith;* Gilbert, *David Lloyd George: Organizer of Victory 1912–1916;* Grigg, *Lloyd George: From Peace to War 1912–1916;* Blake, *The Unknown Prime Minister;* Taylor, *Beaverbrook;* and Anne Chisholm and Michael Davie, *Lord Beaverbrook* (New York, 1993). The most recent political work to address the crisis is John Turner's *British Politics and the Great War: Coalition and Conflict 1915–1918* (London: Oxford University Press, 1992). A number of journal articles have also considered the problem, including John Fair, "Politicians,

Historians and the War: A Reassessment of the Political Crisis of December 1916," *Journal of Modern History* 49 (September 1977), On Demand Supplement, D1329–43; and J. M. McEwen, "The Struggle for Mastery in Britain: Lloyd George Versus Asquith, December 1916," *The Journal of British Studies* 18 (Fall 1978): 131–56. Stephen Koss's *The Rise and Fall of the Political Press in Britain*, vol. 2, considers the question from the press perspective, as does J. M. McEwen, "The Press and the Fall of Asquith," *The Historical Journal* 21, 4 (1978): 863–83.

125. Beaverbrook, *Politicians and the War*, 400–403.

126. Buckmaster was replaced by Lord Finlay as lord chancellor in December 1916.

127. Heuston, *Lives of the Lord Chancellors*, 263.

128. McEwen, "The Press and the Fall of Asquith," 863–83.

129. Ibid., 883.

130. Williams to Northcliffe, 22 December 1916, Northcliffe Add. Mss., 62210A, ff. 74–76, BL.

SEVEN
"To Tell the People of America the Truth": The United States Enters the War, January to May 1917

1. V. H. Rothwell, *British War Aims and Peace Diplomacy 1914–1918* (Oxford: Oxford University Press, 1971), 66. The Germans gambled that the already weakened British and French could be brought to their knees before the United States could make a significant contribution.

2. Northcliffe to Devonport, 18 January 1917, Northcliffe Add. Mss., 62335, f. 146, British Library (hereafter BL).

3. Northcliffe to Devonport, 20 January 1917, Northcliffe Add. Mss., 62335, f. 149, BL.

4. Ms. Eng. Hist d. 303, Bodleian Library.

5. 1 February 1917 entry, Lord Riddell, *Lord Riddell's War Diary*, 238.

6. Northcliffe to Bonar Law, 12 February 1917, Northcliffe Add. Mss., 62158, f. 36, BL.

7. Northcliffe to Bonar Law, 19 February 1917, Northcliffe Add. Mss., 62158, f. 38, BL.

8. Bonar Law to Northcliffe, 20 February 1917, Northcliffe Add. Mss., 62158, f. 39, BL.

9. Le Bas to Northcliffe, 3 January 1917, Northcliffe Add. Mss., 62170, f. 191, BL.

10. Northcliffe to Le Bas, 7 January 1917, Northcliffe Add. Mss., 62170, f. 192, BL.

11. British propaganda in World War I, particularly in America, has received recent attention from several scholars. For an overview of this topic see, M. L. Sanders and Philip M. Taylor, *British Propaganda During the First World War* (London: Macmillan, 1982). For a work that considers many of the personalities involved, including Northcliffe, see Gary S. Messinger, *British Propaganda and the State in the First World War* (Manchester: Manchester University Press, 1992). Other, less recent works, still of value include H. C. Peterson, *Propaganda for War: The Campaign Against American Neutrality* (Norman: University of Oklahoma Press, 1939) and James Duane Squires, *British Propaganda at Home and in the United States* (Cambridge: Harvard University Press, 1935).

12. No recent overview has been published on the German propaganda campaign headed by Ambassador Count Bernstorff. Perhaps this is because the German effort has been traditionally viewed as overdone and ineffective in comparison to the British. However, some information can be gleaned from Bernstorff's *My Three Years in America* (New York: Scribners, 1920) as well as from the recent Bernstorff biography by Reinhard Doerries, *Imperial Challenge: Ambassador Count Bernstorff and German-American Relations, 1908–1917* (Chapel Hill: University of North Carolina Press, 1989). The *Memoirs* (New York: Doran, 1953) of Franz Von Papen, the future German chancellor, who carried on propaganda activities in the United States, also contain some useful information.

13. For Masterman and Parker, see, Messinger, *British Propaganda and the State in the First World War*, 24–84. Masterman's own memoirs make few comments on his career as a propagandist. Also see the biography by his wife, Lucy Masterman, *C. F. G. Masterman* (London: Cassell, 1939), par-

ticularly 272–308. The most recent work on Parker is John C. Adams, *Seated with the Mighty: A Biography of Sir Gilbert Parker* (Ottawa: Borealis Press, 1979).

14. Arthur Willert, *The Road to Safety: A Study in Anglo-American Relations* (London: Derek Verschoyle, 1952), 97.

15. David Burton, *Cecil Spring Rice: A Diplomat's Life* (London: Associated University Presses, 1990), 197. Burton believed it unlikely that Northcliffe was behind *The Times* attack.

16. 2 January 1917 entry, House diary, vol. 10, House Papers, Series II, Sterling Library, Yale University.

17. Ibid.

18. Insull to Northcliffe, n.d., Northcliffe Papers, WDM/2/63, Archive of *The Times* (hereafter TA).

19. Cecil to Northcliffe, 16 January 1917, Northcliffe Papers, WDM/2/64, TA.

20. Link, *The Papers of Woodrow Wilson*, 41: 196.

21. Northcliffe to Philpotts, 30 January 1917, Northcliffe Add. Mss., 62335, f. 159, BL.

22. Northcliffe to Lloyd George, 23 January 1917, Lloyd George Papers, F/41/7/4, House of Lords Record Office (hereafter HLRO).

23. Northcliffe to Charteris, 25 January 1917, Northcliffe Add. Mss., 62159, f. 134, BL.

24. Burton was an American whom Northcliffe had lured away from Joseph Pulitzer and who had widespread press and business connections in the United States. Burton suggested that he should return to the United States to make the situation clear to his American publishing contacts and to enlist their aid. Burton to Northcliffe, 30 January 1917, Northcliffe Add. Mss., 62193, f. 102, BL.

25. This new organization would combat the preponderance of German war news in the American papers and widespread editor's complaints of how impossible it was to obtain authentic Allied news. It would have branches in all important neutral countries, with trained newspaper executives, if possible, in charge.

26. Memo, Burton to Northcliffe, n.d., Northcliffe Add. Mss., 63193, ff. 103–9, BL.

27. The January 1917 reorganization partly followed recommendations made by the journalist Robert Donald in a report prepared at Lloyd George's request. See *Report on Propaganda Arrangements,* INF4/4B, Public Record Office. The ongoing propaganda changes culminated in spring 1918 with a ministry of information, under Lord Beaverbrook, which coordinated the often-competing efforts of the Foreign Office, War Office, Admiralty, and Department of Information.

28. There is no record of Northcliffe's exact conversations with Lloyd George and Milner. For the most recent appraisal of Buchan, see Andrew Lownie, *John Buchan: The Presbyterian Cavalier* (London: Constable, 1995), particularly, 127–36, concerning his propaganda duties. For a brief view, see the chapter on Buchan in Messinger, *British Propaganda and the State in the First World War,* 85–97. Buchan's memoir, *Memory Hold the Door* (London: Hodder and Stoughton, 1941), says little about propaganda.

29. Northcliffe to Davies, 31 January 1917, Northcliffe Add. Mss., 62157, BL.

30. The other members included Lord Burnham, Robert Donald, and C. P. Scott. When Northcliffe went to America in June, Beaverbrook replaced him on the committee. Squires, *British Propaganda at Home and in the United States From 1914 to 1917,* 36.

31. Masterman's Wellington House operation became one of the branches of Buchan's organization. Buchan was supposed to report to the prime minister, but he and Lloyd George soon disagreed over policy, and Buchan found it more and more difficult to gain access to the Welshman.

32. Northcliffe to Charteris, 1 February 1917, Northcliffe Add. Mss., 62159, f. 136, BL.

33. Northcliffe to Buchan, 20 February 1917, Northcliffe Add. Mss., 62161, f. 177, BL.

34. Messinger, *British Propaganda and the State in the First World War,* 90–91.

35. Blake, ed., *The Private Papers of Douglas Haig,* 189; McEwen, "Northcliffe and Lloyd George at War, 1914–1918," 665.

36. Blake, *The Private Papers of Douglas Haig*, 189; McEwen, " 'Brass-Hats' and the British Press During the First World War," 57–58.

37. Haig diary, ACCS. 3155/97, National Library of Scotland.

38. Haig diary, 6 January 1917, ACCS. 3155/97, National Library of Scotland.

39. Blake, *The Private Papers of Douglas Haig*, 189–90.

40. Repington, *The First World War*, 1: 428–30.

41. Northcliffe to Charteris, 25 January 1917, Northcliffe Add. Mss., 62159, f. 134, BL.

42. Neilson, *Strategy and Supply: The Anglo-Russian Alliance*, 226–29.

43. Ibid., 251–53.

44. Ibid., 262.

45. French, *The Strategy of the Lloyd George Coalition*, 53–55.

46. Northcliffe to Charteris, 8 February 1917, Northcliffe Add. Mss., 62159, f. 135, BL.

47. For Marcosson's recollections of this episode, see his *Adventures in Interviewing*, 103–4.

48. Northcliffe to Sassoon, 1 February 1917, Northcliffe Add. Mss., 62160, ff. 69–70, BL. Impressed by the French general Nivelle's optimism, Lloyd George had agreed to put British troops under his operational control for an April offensive that ultimately failed.

49. Sassoon to Northcliffe, 6 February 1917, Northcliffe Add. Mss., 62160, ff. 78–79, BL.

50. Northcliffe to Repington, 12 February 1917, Northcliffe Add. Mss., 62253, ff. 104–5, BL.

51. Ibid.

52. Ibid. Repington later called the complaints about wasted civilian brains "all gammon." Repington, *The First World War*, 1: 459.

53. Northcliffe to Maxse, 20 February 1917, Northcliffe Add. Mss., 62175, ff. 91–92, BL.

54. Northcliffe to Haig, 21 February 1917, Northcliffe Papers, Harmsworth Archive; Northcliffe to Sassoon, 21 February 1917, Northcliffe Add. Mss., 62160, ff. 87–89, BL. The press lord wrote to Sir William Robertson on the subject as well. Robertson replied to his letter on civilian brains that "it is a very difficult business getting people into their proper places. The only sure time to do this is before war comes and not after, and as you know our country would not look at war at all until it was forced upon us. I quite agree that the thing can only be done by rough and ready measures, and so far as I am concerned I am not afraid to apply them." Northcliffe to Robertson, 15 February 1917, Robertson Papers, I/36/77, Liddell Hart Centre for Military Archives; Robertson to Northcliffe, 20 February 1917, Northcliffe Add. Mss., 62335, f. 208, BL.

55. Haig to Northcliffe, 23 February 1917, Northcliffe Add. Mss., 62335, ff. 213–15, BL.

56. Ibid.

57. "Message from the Chief," 26 February 1917, Ms. Eng. Hist d. 303, Bodleian Library. The gardener's cottage still stands, the plainly visible shell hole filled in by a window.

58. Wilson to Northcliffe, 26 February 1917, Northcliffe Add. Mss., 62201, ff. 81–82, BL.

59. Northcliffe to Brade, 22 March 1917, Northcliffe Add. Mss., 62336, f. 105, BL.

60. Chamberlain gave up the position of lord mayor of Birmingham to answer Lloyd George's call. For Chamberlain's short career as director-general of National Service, see David Dilks, *Neville Chamberlain 1869–1929* (Cambridge: Cambridge University Press, 1984), 1: 199–250.

61. Northcliffe to Stanley, 22 February 1917, Northcliffe Add. Mss., 62158, f. 187, BL.

62. Northcliffe to Higginbottom, 10 March 1917, Northcliffe Add. Mss., 63336, f. 9, BL.

63. Higginbottom to Northcliffe, 13 March 1917, Northcliffe Add. Mss., 63336, f. 30, BL.

64. Keith Grieves, *The Politics of Manpower, 1914–1918* (Manchester: Manchester University Press, 1988), 122.

65. For the civilian compulsion issue, see Adams and Poirier, *The Conscription Controversy in Great Britain*, particularly 192–216.

66. Dilks, *Neville Chamberlain 1869–1929*, 1: 223.

67. Ibid., 1: 203.

68. Ibid., 1: 218.

69. Northcliffe to Davies, 18 February 1917, Northcliffe Add. Mss., 62157, BL.

70. Northcliffe to Riddell, 18 February 1917, Northcliffe Add. Mss., 62173, f. 70, BL.

71. Northcliffe to Davies, 25 February 1917, Northcliffe Add. Mss., 62157, BL.

72. Northcliffe to Davies, 31 March 1917, Northcliffe Add. Mss., 62157, BL.

73. Cowdray to Northcliffe, 8 April 1917, Northcliffe Add. Mss., 62336, f. 159, BL. The only Cowdray biography is J. A. Spender's *Weetman Pearson, First Viscount Cowdray 1856–1927* (London, 1930).

74. Northcliffe to Cowdray, 10 April 1917, Northcliffe Add. Mss., 62336, f. 165, BL.

75. Speaking to a Birmingham audience in 1918 about his National Service experience, Chamberlain quipped, "here was a problem big enough to satisfy the most super-eminent of supermen. Why it might even have taxed the energies of Lord Northcliffe himself." Dilks, *Neville Chamberlain 1869–1929,* 1: 203.

76. Northcliffe to Stanley, 19 February 1917, Northcliffe Add. Mss., 62158, f. 186, BL.

77. Northcliffe to Riddell, 5 March 1918, Northcliffe Add. Mss., 62173, f. 97, BL.

78. "Message from Lord Northcliffe to *The Times,*" 3 March 1917, Northcliffe Papers, NOR2/1/7, TA. Cadbury, owner of the *Daily News,* was often attacked by the *Daily Mail.*

79. Ibid.

80. Northcliffe to Stanley, 23 March 1917, Northcliffe Add. Mss., 62158, f. 194, BL. Previously the *Daily Mail* had allowed newsdealers to return unsold copies. Also, on 5 March the paper announced that it had been forced to reduce from 1,200,000 to 850,000 copies printed.

81. Pound and Harmsworth, *Northcliffe,* 524–25. By the end of the war, the *Daily Mail* was down to four pages from its 1914 twelve or fourteen.

82. Northcliffe to Thorpe, 11 March 1917, Northcliffe Add. Mss., 63336, f. 24, BL.

83. Northcliffe to Devonport, 13 March 1917, Northcliffe Add. Mss., 62336, ff. 31–32, BL.

84. *Daily Mail,* 24 March 1917.

85. Marcosson, *Adventures in Interviewing,* 129.

86. Ibid.

87. Northcliffe to Sassoon, 21 February 1917, Northcliffe Add. Mss., 62160, f. 89, BL.

88. Northcliffe to Carson, 5 March 1917, Northcliffe Add. Mss., 62158, f. 147, BL.

89. Carson to Northcliffe, 7 March 1917, Northcliffe Add. Mss., 62158, f. 148, BL. These so-called "Q-ships," disguised as defenseless merchantmen were one of Britain's most effective weapons against the submarines, which they lured to surface under their camouflaged guns.

90. Repington, *The First World War,* 1: 479.

91. Fisher to Lambert, 10 March 1917, in Arthur J. Marder, *Fear God and Dread Nought: The Correspondence of Admiral of the Fleet Lord Fisher of Kilverstone,* 3 vols. (London: Jonathan Cape, 1959), 3: 437.

92. Northcliffe to Carson, 11 March 1917, Northcliffe Papers, WDM/2/17, TA.

93. Carson to Northcliffe, 14 March 1917, Northcliffe Papers, WDM/2/18, TA.

94. Colvin, *The Life of Lord Carson,* 3: 251.

95. Ibid., 3: 251–52. After the war, Jellicoe claimed that Northcliffe confused him with Paine, which resulted in subsequent attacks by the *Daily Mail* and Northcliffe's other newspapers. A. Temple Patterson, ed., *The Jellicoe Papers,* 2 vols. (London: Navy Records Society, 1966, 1968) 2: 412.

96. Northcliffe to Carson, 29 March 1917, Northcliffe Papers, WDM/2/22, TA.

97. Carson to Northcliffe, 29 March 1917, Northcliffe Papers, WDM/2/23, TA.

98. Northcliffe to Carson, 30 March 1917, Northcliffe Papers, WDM/2/24, TA.

99. Northcliffe to Cowdray, 13 January 1917, Northcliffe Add. Mss., 62335, f. 143, BL. The 3 January *Daily Mail* greeted the choice with a full-page headline proclaiming "Business Man to 'Run' the Air Board."

100. Cowdray to Northcliffe, 28 January 1917, Northcliffe Add. Mss., 62335, f. 155, BL.

101. Northcliffe to Cowdray, 30 January 1917, Northcliffe Add. Mss., 62335, f. 158, BL.

102. Cowdray to Northcliffe, 1 February 1917, Northcliffe Add. Mss., 62335, ff. 166–67, BL.

103. Cowdray to Northcliffe, 31 March 1917, Northcliffe Add. Mss., 62336, BL. "Civil" was added at Northcliffe's suggestion to keep it distinct from aerial military transportation.

104. Pearson to Northcliffe, 27 April 1917, Northcliffe Add. Mss., 62172, f. 61, BL.

105. Northcliffe to Robinson, 18 March 1917, Northcliffe Add. Mss., 62245, f. 38, BL.

106. "The Remaking of Ireland," speech made by Northcliffe to the Irish Club, 17 March 1917, as reported in *The Times,* 19 March 1917, privately printed by Clement Shorter, London, March 1917, after being revised by Northcliffe, BL Reading Room.

107. Ibid.

108. For his recollection, see his *In London During the Great War: The Diary of a Journalist,* 182–84.

109. Northcliffe to Robinson, 18 March 1917, Northcliffe Add. Mss., 62245, f. 38, BL.

110. Northcliffe to Marlowe, 18 March 1917, Northcliffe Add. Mss., 62199, f. 53, BL.

111. Northcliffe to O'Connor, 18 March 1917, Northcliffe Add. Mss., 62336, ff. 60–61, BL.

112. Burton to Northcliffe, 16 March 1917, Northcliffe Add. Mss., 62193, ff. 113–14, BL.

113. Ibid.

114. *Daily Mail,* 4 April 1917.

115. Northcliffe to Lloyd George, 4 April 1917, Lloyd George Papers, F/41/76, HLRO.

116. Lloyd George to Northcliffe, 4 April 1917, Lloyd George Papers, F/41/7, HLRO.

117. For Balfour's mission, see Kathleen Burk, *Britain, America and the Sinews of War 1914–1918* (Boston: Houghton Mifflin, 1985). The mission arrived in America on 21 April and stayed until late May.

118. Northcliffe to Balfour, 5 April 1917, Northcliffe Add. Mss., 62153, BL; Northcliffe to Balfour, 11 April 1917, quoted in Pound and Harmsworth, *Northcliffe,* 527. He also urged Balfour to make use of the experience of Arthur Willert in Washington and W. F. Bullock in New York.

119. Northcliffe to Lady Northcliffe, 9 June 1917, Northcliffe Papers, Harmsworth Archive. Lord Bertie also noted in his diary of 11 June that "Lloyd George wanted to substitute Northcliffe for Spring-Rice but that was stopped." Lady Lennox, ed., *The Diary of Lord Bertie of Thame 1914–1918* 2: 136.

120. Burton to Northcliffe, 11 April 1917, Northcliffe Add. Mss., 62193, ff. 146–47, BL.

121. Northcliffe to Howard, 12 April 1917, Northcliffe Add. Mss., 62336, f. 166, BL.

122. Howard to Northcliffe, 18 April 1917, Northcliffe Add. Mss., 62336, f. 178, BL. Northcliffe had already forwarded the FTC request to Sir Albert Stanley, who replied he would take the matter up with the shipping controller. Stanley to Northcliffe, 1 April 1917, Northcliffe Add. Mss., 62158, f. 198, BL.

123. Burton to Northcliffe, 11 April 1917, Northcliffe Add. Mss., 62193, f. 151, BL.

124. Northcliffe to Burton, 11, 16 April 1917, Northcliffe Add. Mss., 62193, f. 150, f. 152, BL.

125. Burton to Northcliffe, 17 April 1917, Northcliffe Add. Mss., 62193, f. 145, BL.

126. Northcliffe to Burton, n.d., Northcliffe Add. Mss., 62193, f. 155, BL.

127. A copy of this report can be found in the Arthur Willert Papers, Series II, Box 13, Sterling Library, Yale University Archive.

128. According to the report, these included Bruce Barton, Irving Cobb, Douglas Fairbanks, Booth Tarkington, William Allen White, and Mary Roberts Rinehart.

129. Burton to Northcliffe, 17, 24 May 1917, Northcliffe Add. Mss., 62193, ff. 169–76, BL.

130. At one point during this crisis, the British had only a six-week supply of food in the country.

131. *Daily Mail,* 23 April, 4 May 1917.

132. "55 Ships Sunk. Growing Peril of the Submarine Campaign," *Daily Mail,* 26 April 1917.

133. French, *Strategy of the Lloyd George Coalition*, 60–61.

134. Northcliffe to Charteris, 24 April 1917, Northcliffe Add. Mss., 62159, ff. 178–79, BL.

135. In Repington's view, the only way to make the government move was to have a secret parliamentary session to "give the Government the figures if they will not produce them." He felt he had support for this in the House of Commons, and was convinced that, were he in Parliament, he "could make the Government move. One cannot give the figures in the press." Repington to Northcliffe, 5 April 1917, Repington Papers, TA. Geddes replaced Neville Chamberlain in August as head of National Service.

136. Repington to Northcliffe, 27 April 1917, Repington Papers, TA.

137. *Daily Mail*, 10 May 1917.

138. *Daily Mail*, 18, 21 May 1917.

139. Willert to Northcliffe, 16 May 1917, Northcliffe Add. Mss., 62255, f. 57, BL.

140. Garrett to Northcliffe, 15 May 1917, Northcliffe Add. Mss., 62158, ff. 167–69, BL.

141. Ibid.

142. Northcliffe to Balfour, n.d., Northcliffe Add. Mss., 62153, BL.

143. Cecil to Drummond, 17 May 1917, Balfour Add. Mss., 49738, f. 77, BL. Grey demurred, saying that he was not well enough to accept the post. See ff. 80–81.

144. Cecil to Drummond, 17 May 1917, Balfour Add. Mss., 49738, f. 84, BL.

145. Balfour to Cecil, 20 May 1917, Balfour Add. Mss., 49738, ff. 90–91, BL.

146. Northcliffe to Repington, 27 May 1917, Northcliffe Add. Mss., 62253, f. 117, BL.

147. *Daily Mail*, 28 May 1917.

148. Northcliffe to Lady Ripon, 28 May 1917, Northcliffe Add. Mss., 62336, ff. 123–28, BL.

149. A copy of this report can be found in the Northcliffe Papers, NOR13/4/4, TA.

150. Lord Beaverbrook's account in *Men and Power 1917–1918* (London: Collins, 1956), 63–64, emphasizes that Lloyd George was considering bringing Winston Churchill back into the government, a move Beaverbrook and Lloyd George believed Northcliffe would bitterly oppose.

151. Lord Beaverbrook, *Men and Power 1917–1918*, 64. Unfortunately, no record appears to exist of how Lloyd George convinced his colleagues to cooperate.

152. House shared the hostile telegram with the president. The Balfour message claimed that the Americans thought of Northcliffe as a "vigorous hustler and loud voiced propagandist," and continued, "whether this is the best way to treat our new Allies is a matter for argument." Balfour to Cecil, May 27, 1917, FO 115/2295, 165–66, in Link, *Papers of Woodrow Wilson*, vol. 42, 428. Lloyd George recorded in his *War Memoirs*, 3: 551 that "a satisfactory response was cabled by Mr. Balfour on 28th May."

153. Stephen Roskill, *Hankey, Man of Secrets*, 3 vols. (London, 1970–74) 1: 390–91.

154. Northcliffe to Lady Northcliffe, 9 June 1917, Northcliffe Papers, Harmsworth Archive. In this letter, Northcliffe claimed he accepted only reluctantly after he first tried to convince Lloyd George to send Churchill (because of his American mother) or the more businesslike Rothermere. Northcliffe also feared he would be vulnerable in America without his "newspapers to defend him against his many enemies." On the other hand, Lloyd George, in his *War Memoirs*, 3: 552, recorded that Northcliffe accepted "without a fuss."

155. Roskill, *Hankey, Man of Secrets*, 3: 393.

156. Lord Beaverbrook, *Men and Power 1917–1918*, 71–72. Northcliffe's brothers Lord Rothermere and Cecil Harmsworth were already involved in government, with Rothermere in charge of the Royal Clothing Supply Department at the War Office and Cecil in Lloyd George's "garden suburb" secretariat at Downing Street. This outburst by Davies, coupled with other disagreements with Lloyd George, caused the Welshman and Davies to become estranged soon after this.

157. 27–28 June 1917 entry, Wilson, ed., *The Political Diaries of C. P. Scott, 1911–1928*, 296.

158. Repington, *The First World War*, 1: 590–91.

1. Burk, *Britain, America and the Sinews of War 1914–1918,* 7. Burk gives a detailed account of the financial and supply sides of all the British missions to the United States, but does not consider Northcliffe's more personal and unofficial activities, which represent the focus of this chapter.

2. Colonel W. G. Lyddon, *British War Missions to the United States 1914–1918* (London: Oxford University Press, 1938), 18. Lyddon was an officer with the British War Mission.

3. Willert, *The Road to Safety,* 73, 80.

4. For this see Alan J. Ward, *Ireland and Anglo-American Relations 1899–1921* (London, 1969).

5. Northcliffe's biographers suggested that his Irish background was one of the reasons he was chosen for this mission. Pound and Harmsworth, *Northcliffe,* 546. For Balfour's role, see Catharine B. Shannon, *Arthur J. Balfour and Ireland 1874–1922* (Washington: Catholic University Press, 1988).

6. Willert, *Road to Safety,* 99. At Northcliffe's insistence, Willert became a mission secretary.

7. Carson, *Northcliffe, England's Man of Power,* 381.

8. Lloyd George, *War Memoirs,* 3: 547. Balfour met with the president and congressional leaders, smoothing the way for Northcliffe. He also became the first Englishman to address a joint session of Congress. The occasion was called a "triumphant success." Sydney Zebel, *Balfour: A Political Biography* (Cambridge: Cambridge University Press, 1973), 235–36; Willert, *The Road to Safety,* 276.

9. Wilson to House, 1 June 1917, Series I, Box 121, House Papers, Sterling Library, Yale University.

10. Stanley Morison, "Personality and Diplomacy in Anglo-American Relations, 1917," in Richard Pares and A. J. P. Taylor, eds., *Essays Presented to Sir Lewis Namier* (London: Macmillan, 1956), 432.

11. Alfred G. Gardiner, "The Times," *Atlantic Monthly* 119 (January 1917): 111–22. Gardiner may also have penned an anonymous and hostile article in the March issue.

12. Pound and Harmsworth, *Northcliffe,* 530.

13. Wilson to Daniels, 4 June 1917, Reel 65, Daniels Papers, Library of Congress.

14. Robinson to Willert, 4 June 1917, Series I, Box 1, Arthur Willert Papers, Sterling Library, Yale University. In this letter Geoffrey Robinson also told Willert that their chief had "started for America in a great hurry—too much of a hurry perhaps to give him a chance of grasping the business at this end."

15. Balfour sailed for England on 31 May, arriving 9 June, whereupon he resumed his Foreign Office duties.

16. The terms are listed in a confidential cabinet document dated 31 May 1917 and signed by Lloyd George. See the copy in the Northcliffe Add. Mss., 62157, ff. 76–77, British Library (hereafter BL).

17. Lloyd George, *War Memoirs,* 3: 553; Pound and Harmsworth, *Northcliffe,* 529.

18. Lord Beaverbrook, *Men and Power 1917–1918,* 71.

19. L. J. Maxse, *National Review,* July 1917, quoted in Pound and Harmsworth, *Northcliffe,* 543.

20. Robinson to Northcliffe, 22 June 1917, Northcliffe Add. Mss., 62245, ff. 41–42, BL. Robinson added that Buckmaster's diatribe reminded him of Simon's attack on *The Times.* He called Curzon's defense "characteristically lame, but not so bad as the early reports suggested." See *Parliamentary Debates:* Commons, Fifth Series, vol. 94, cols. 606–7, 956–57; Lords, Fifth Series, vol. 25, cols. 522–37.

21. Buckmaster to Gardiner, 21 June 1917, 1/4, Gardiner Papers, London School of Economics.

22. Charles Graves, *Mr. Punch's History of the Great War* (London: Cassell, 1919), 162.

23. Steed, *Through Thirty Years 1892–1922,* 2: 140–41.

24. In June the *Daily Mail* also kept up its attacks on the government's food policy and called for punishment for the "Mesopotamia Culprits" after the publication of the Mesopotamia Report.

25. That morning's *Daily Mail* carried a small page-5 notice that at the invitation of the war cabinet, Northcliffe had accepted the mission to America as "Successor to Mr. Balfour" and that he had already sailed for the United States. Northcliffe left his business affairs in the hands of George Sutton, Manager of the Amalgamated Press. He notified Lloyd George that if Sutton were forced into the military, he would have to return.

26. Northcliffe to Davies, 1 June 1917, Northcliffe Add. Mss., 62157, f. 79, BL. Lloyd George read and approved this, and it was released 7 June.

27. House to Wilson, 7 June 1917, in Link, ed., *The Papers of Woodrow Wilson*, 42: 461.

28. Howard to Northcliffe, 9 June 1917, Howard Papers, Library of Congress.

29. House Diaries, 9, 11 June 1917, Series II, vol. 11, House Papers, Sterling Library, Yale University. Wiseman monitored Northcliffe's communications, often showing them to House, and the many cables retained in his papers constitute a valuable resource for the mission period. He played a key role in Anglo-American relations during the war. Wounded in Flanders in 1915 and sent home to London where he joined the intelligence service, by 1916 Wiseman had become the British liaison with Wilson and House. Arthur Willert recorded that Wilson "opened his mind to him as no other foreigner" and to House "he was practically a private secretary." *Road to Safety*, 15. On 31 May 1917, Wiseman gave House a "Memorandum on Proposed War Mission" detailing Northcliffe's task. For Wiseman, see W. B. Fowler's *British American Relations 1917–1918, The Role of Sir William Wiseman* (Princeton: Princeton University Press, 1969).

30. House to Northcliffe, 12 June 1917, Series I, Box 83a, House Papers.

31. Northcliffe to House, 12 June 1917, Series I, Box 83a, House Papers.

32. House to Wilson, 12 June 1917, in Link, *Papers of Woodrow Wilson*, 42: 487–88. House also told the president that Northcliffe had refused to see a representative of Wilson's critic, Hearst, telling him that if his employer wished to see him he should come himself. If Hearst did, House continued, Northcliffe planned to tell "him some home truths which may be good for his soul." Rumors at the time that Northcliffe supported Hearst were false.

33. Willert, *Road to Safety*, 109.

34. Frederic Boyd Stevenson, *Brooklyn Daily Eagle*, 17 June 1917.

35. George Harvey, "The Man of the War," *North American Review* 206 (July 1917): 15–23.

36. *The New Republic* 11, 137 (16 June 1917): 168. Despite the journal's criticism, Pound and Harmsworth recorded that Northcliffe dined with the *New Republic* editorial staff and told them, among other things, that he believed Labour would come to power after the war, naming G. D. H. Cole as a possible prime minister. *Northcliffe*, 557.

37. *The New Republic* 11, 139 (30 June 1917): 230.

38. Lord Hardinge, *Old Diplomacy* (London: John Murray, 1947), 213.

39. Northcliffe to Lloyd George, 2 June 1917, Northcliffe Papers, Harmsworth Archive. The reports apparently came from the department heads who had briefed Northcliffe in London.

40. Spring Rice claimed he did not know on which ship Northcliffe was arriving, but he obviously did not make much of an attempt to discover the information, as a crowd of journalists was present. For his explanation to the Foreign Office, see his 14 June letter to Cecil in the Balfour Add. Mss., 49738, ff. 121–22, BL.

41. Northcliffe to Geraldine Harmsworth, 14 June 1917, Northcliffe Papers, Harmsworth Archive.

42. Daniels diary, 15 June 1917, in E. David Cronon, ed., *The Cabinet Diaries of Josephus Daniels 1913–1921* (Lincoln: University of Nebraska Press, 1963), 164.

43. For the CPI, see Stephen Vaughn, *Holding Fast the Inner Lines: Democracy, Nationalism and the Committee on Public Information* (Chapel Hill: University of North Carolina Press, 1980). Relations between the CPI and Northcliffe remain unclear. His many conversations with Daniels suggest there

may have been some cooperation. Creel makes no mention of Northcliffe's American activities in his memoir *Rebel at Large*. Professor Vaughn has been kind enough to report to the author that a majority of the CPI's records have been lost or destroyed and that he could recall no mention of Northcliffe in the large amount of surviving material surveyed for his study.

44. House Diaries, 15 June 1917, Series II, vol. 11. In his 19 June entry, House recorded that Polk told him that "Spring Rice is brilliant but at times abnormal. The British Government should never have allowed him to return to the US when the war broke out which found him an invalid in London."

45. Northcliffe to Davies, 20 June 1917, Lloyd George Papers, F/41/7/8, House of Lords Record Office (hereafter HLRO).

46. Sir Arthur Willert, *Washington and Other Memories* (Boston: Houghton Mifflin, 1972), 101; W. B. Fowler, *British-American Relations 1917–1918,* 33. However, realizing his own precarious position, Spring Rice soon began sending rosy reports of his relations with Northcliffe that were belied by his comments to House.

47. Spring Rice to Robert Cecil, 14 June 1917, Balfour Add. Mss., 48738, f. 133, BL; Pound and Harmsworth, *Northcliffe,* 539.

48. Northcliffe to Lady Northcliffe, 1 July 1917, Northcliffe Papers, Harmsworth Archive.

49. Link, *Papers of Woodrow Wilson,* 42: 542.

50. Willert, *Road to Safety,* 104–5.

51. Northcliffe to Davies, 20 June 1917, Lloyd George Papers, F/41/7/8, HLRO. The other Americans Northcliffe included as voicing his argument were Lane, at the interior department; Houston, at the agriculture department; and Hoover, the food administrator.

52. Ibid.

53. Gordon was a Canadian financial expert whose brusque manner caused some problems. At the time, Wiseman and others criticised Northcliffe's decision to locate his office in New York, but later agreed with it.

54. Louis Tracy, "The British War Mission in the United States: Its Objects and Personnel," in *Who's Who in the British War Mission to the United States 1917* (New York: William J. Clode, 1917), x.

55. Ibid., xi.

56. Balfour to House, 28 June 1917, Series I, Box 10, House Papers. House responded the next day that the matter was receiving his "undivided attention."

57. Northcliffe cabled Balfour concerning his breach of diplomatic etiquette, Northcliffe to Balfour, 29 June 1917, FO 800/209, Public Record Office.

58. Ray Stannard Baker, *Woodrow Wilson, Life and Letter, War Leader,* 8 vols. (1939, reprint; New York, 1968) 7: 138.

59. William G. McAdoo, *Crowded Years* (Boston, 1931) 400. McAdoo vividly described Northcliffe. "I have met few men who had such a quick comprehension as Northcliffe. It was never necessary to explain anything to him twice. He was dynamic, his phrases were vivid, his ideas crisp and clear, he had a way of getting down at once to the vital thought in any question under discussion.... His strong point was in determining how to do things—the shortest and surest road to accomplishment. He had a fine political and public sense; he always thought of the effect of actions on public opinion."

60. Northcliffe to Lady Northcliffe, 1 July 1917, Northcliffe Papers, Harmsworth Archive. To handle the technical details of the financial arrangements, Northcliffe was assisted by R. H. Brand of Lazard Freres and Sir Hardman Lever, financial secretary of the Treasury.

61. Northcliffe to House, 20 July 1917, Series I, Box 83a, House Papers.

62. House to Wilson, 17 July 1917, in Link, *The Papers of Woodrow Wilson,* 43: 194. House also told the president of a conversation he had with Wiseman over Spring Rice's attitude. Both felt he should return to England, but the Foreign Office feared this would be considered a triumph for Northcliffe and cause criticism at home.

63. Northcliffe to Prime Minister, 17 July 1917, F/41/7/10, Lloyd George Papers, HLRO.

64. Northcliffe to Prime Minister, 10 July 1917, F/41/7/9, Lloyd George Papers, HLRO.

65. On 3 July 1917, as a condition of an inheritance, Robinson was granted (by Royal License) the right to use Dawson. From this point Dawson will be used in this work.

66. Dawson to Northcliffe, 26 July 1917, Series I, Box 36, House Papers.

67. Charles Seymour, ed., *The Intimate Papers of Colonel House,* 4 vols. (Boston: Houghton Mifflin, 1928) 3: 112, n. 1.

68. Northcliffe Circular Letter, 12 August 1917, Northcliffe Papers, Harmsworth Archive.

69. Seymour, *Intimate Papers of Colonel House,* 3: 105.

70. McAdoo to House, 14 July 1917, Series I, Box 73, House Papers. By this time McAdoo also found it impossible to work with Hardman Lever, one of the reasons Northcliffe was so involved. McAdoo, himself not a technical expert, seemed to prefer dealing with Northcliffe. Burk, *Sinews of Power,* 163.

71. André Tardieu, *France and America: Some Experiences in Cooperation* (Boston: Houghton Mifflin, 1927), 227. Kathleen Burk has argued further that, "supercession of Britain by the United States as the leading financial power can be seen occurring, step-by-step, in the negotiations between the British Treasury mission and the American government during 1917–18; in the daily dealings of the Treasury mission can be seen the passing of hegemony from Britain to the United States." *Britain, America and the Sinews of War 1914–1918,* 5.

72. Denis Judd's *Lord Reading* (London: Weidenfeld and Nicholson, 1982) is the most recent biography.

73. Judd, *Lord Reading,* 135–36.

74. For a detailed organizational chart, see *Who's Who in the British War Mission to the United States.*

75. Northcliffe to Sutton, 7 August 1917, Northcliffe Papers, Harmsworth Archive.

76. Lyddon, *War Missions,* 33.

77. During the period of neutrality, Morgan & Company played a key intermediary role, both in negotiating American loans for the Allies and coordinating the actual purchase. The hostility of the Wilson administration to such a bastion of Wall Street continuing to profit from the Allied loans and purchases played a part in their giving up control to the British, although the firm continued to give advice. For more on this subject, see Burk, *Britain, America and the Sinews of War.*

78. Burk, *Britain, America and the Sinews of War,* 156. During Northcliffe's tenure the U.S. government moved to control the purchasing activities of the Allied missions. This was accomplished administratively by the American War Trade Board and the creation of the Allied Purchasing Commission, which had the same membership and duties as the American War Industries Board.

79. *Public Ledger* (Philadelphia), 11 November 1917.

80. Northcliffe to Prime Minister, 2 July 1917, FO 800/209, Public Record Office.

81. Lyddon, *War Missions,* 29–30. Before it was taken over by the American government, railroad transport was a major problem.

82. Northcliffe to Prime Minister, 25 August 1917, F/41/7/14, Lloyd George Papers, HLRO.

83. Daniels Diary, 2 July 1917, in Cronon, *Cabinet Diaries of Josephus Daniels 1913–1921,* 171.

84. Ibid., 173, 185.

85. Northcliffe to Davies, 3 July 1917, Series I, Box 3, Sir William Wiseman Papers.

86. Northcliffe to Page, 13 August 1917, Northcliffe Papers, Harmsworth Archive.

87. Northcliffe to Lloyd George, 5 July 1917, Series I, Box 3, Wiseman Papers.

88. Northcliffe to J. T. Davies, 20 June 1917, Lloyd George Papers, F/41/7/8, HLRO.

89. Ibid.

90. Northcliffe to Prime Minister, 18 July 1917, FO 371/3072, Public Record Office.

91. Northcliffe to Page, 20 July 1917, Northcliffe Add. Mss., 62337, ff. 109–110, BL.

92. Northcliffe to Prime Minister, 15 August 1917, Series I, Box 3, Wiseman Papers.

93. Northcliffe to Prime Minister, 17 August 1917, Series I, Box 3, Wiseman Papers. To buoy up domestic morale, Lloyd George told the House of Commons on 16 August that with "reasonable economy" there was "no chance of starving out the population of these islands" and that losses were diminishing, antisubmarine measures were working, and the construction of new tonnage was "quickening." *Parliamentary Debates;* Commons, Fifth Series, vol. 97, cols. 1471–84.

94. Daniels Diary, 22 August 1917, in Cronon, *Cabinet Diaries of Josephus Daniels,* 194.

95. House to Wiseman, 11 August 1917, Series I, Box 123, House Papers.

96. House Diaries, 12 August 1917, Series II, vol. 11.

97. Wiseman to House, 12 August 1917, Series I, Box 123, House Papers. Wiseman opposed this idea and suggested that the ambassador be called home for consultations.

98. Northcliffe to Wiseman, 17 August 1917, FO 800/209, Public Record Office. Alternatively, he suggested that the matter should be left until Reading arrived. Some were dismissive of both the British ambassador and Northcliffe. Eustace Percy, at the British embassy in this period, later wrote that during the press lord's time in America, "I hardly think it would be unfair to say that the result was to leave the representation of British power and policy in the hands of two political nonentities … one prematurely aged and one a boy who had never grown up." *Some Memories* (London, 1958), 55.

99. Northcliffe to Prime Minister, Balfour, War Cabinet, and Shipping Controller, 21 August 1917, F/41/7/13, Lloyd George Papers, HLRO.

100. Northcliffe to House, 25 August 1917, in Seymour, *Intimate Papers of Colonel House,* 3: 90.

101. Northcliffe to Prime Minister, 23 August 1917, F/41/7/13, Lloyd George Papers, HLRO.

102. Lloyd George, *War Memoirs,* 3: 564–69; Lyddon, *War Missions,* 31; Pound and Harmsworth, *Northcliffe,* 574. For an overview, see William Williams, *The Wilson Administration and the Shipping Crisis of 1917* (New York, 1992).

103. See Burk, *Britain, America and the Sinews of Power,* 164. Northcliffe's repeated requests finally got results. At the end of August, he cabled Reading directly, urging him to accept the mission. Reading replied on 31 August that he was "impressed" with the message and would leave the next week, on the same ship with Wiseman. Seymour, *Intimate Diaries of Colonel House,* 3: 121.

104. Northcliffe to Prime Minister, Balfour, and Chancellor of the Exchequer, 7 September 1917, F/41/7/20, Lloyd George Papers, HLRO.

105. House to Lloyd George, 24 September 1917, Series I, Box 70a, House Papers.

106. Northcliffe to Steed, 10 October 1917, Series I, Box 3, Wiseman Papers.

107. Northcliffe Circular Letter, 5 August 1917, Northcliffe Papers, Harmsworth Archive.

108. Northcliffe Circular Letter, 12 August 1917, Northcliffe Papers, Harmsworth Archive.

109. Lyddon, *British War Mission to the United States 1914–1918,* 35.

110. Northcliffe Circular Letter, 12 August 1917, Northcliffe Papers, Harmsworth Archive.

111. Pound and Harmsworth, *Northcliffe,* 551.

112. Butler to Buchan, 22 August 1917, FO395/80 News America File, Public Record Office. Concerning propaganda, Northcliffe wrote to Lloyd George that he "did not know how much House spoke for the President on this matter," but that House had referred to it "again and again," particularly propaganda aimed at Germany. House also said that the war was being fought "without imagination." Northcliffe to Prime Minister, 15 August 1917, Series I, Box 3, Wiseman Papers.

113. Northcliffe later complained that his name was falsely attached to more than one controversial article.

114. Howard to Northcliffe, 13 June 1917, Reel 3, Howard Papers, Library of Congress.

115. The United Press articles appeared in the 17–18 September and 4 October 1917 *Philadelphia Ledger* (as well as other American papers) and were reprinted in the *Daily Mail.*

116. Lord Northcliffe, "What America Is Fighting For," *Current Opinion* 63 (October 1917): 236.

117. House Diaries, 1 October 1917, Series II, vol. 12.

118. Wiseman to Drummond, 4 October 1917, FO 800/209, Public Record Office.

119. Willert, *Washington and Other Memories*, 105.

120. House Diaries, 18 October 1917, Series II, vol. 12.

121. For example, Amos Pinchot had informed him that Northcliffe was "making a vigorous campaign to get the American newspapers to stand behind the British program. Doubtless you know all about this." Pinchot to Wilson, 25 July 1917, in Link, *Papers of Woodrow Wilson*, 43: 276–78.

122. Morison, "Personality and Diplomacy," 449.

123. *New York Times*, 29 June 1917. Marcosson had traveled on the *St. Paul* with Northcliffe. For his view of the trip, Northcliffe's speech and his mission, see *Adventures in Interviewing*, 131–34.

124. Geoffrey Butler to Eric Drummond (FO), 9 July 1917, Lloyd George Papers, F/60/2/25, HLRO. In a 27 June 1917 letter to John Buchan at the Foreign Office Department of Information, Butler complimented Northcliffe on his "masterly restraint" and the good impression he had made generally. FO 395/79 News America File, Public Record Office.

125. Pound and Harmsworth, *Northcliffe*, 558.

126. *New York Times*, 22 July 1917.

127. Northcliffe to Geraldine Harmsworth, 13 July 1917, Northcliffe Papers, Harmsworth Archive.

128. Clarke, *Northcliffe in History*, 123.

129. *Public Ledger* (Philadelphia), 20 September 1917. Max Pemberton reprints an unidentified American speech with similar themes in *Lord Northcliffe, A Memoir*, 181–82.

130. Northcliffe Speech to ABA, 27 September 1917, British War Mission Box, Northcliffe Papers, Harmsworth Archive. A Northcliffe article with these same themes, "Win the War with Thrift," promoted saving and the Liberty Loans while it defended extending credit to England. It appealed to the American public to "Pull together! That is our motto: Every man, every woman putting their very souls into the war. The Hun must be crushed. The evil thing he has reared must be driven out of our lives, and the way to do it is with steel in the battlefield, and with silver bullets in the world's marts." *The Forum* 58 (November 1917): 509–16.

131. One of Geoffrey Butler's duties was to organize a traveling British exhibit which toured the country in 1917, including a stop at the Texas State Fair, where 7,000 people visited it in one day.

132. Northcliffe to Geddes, 12 September 1917, Series I, Box 3, Wiseman Papers.

133. Northcliffe to Cowdray, 29 September 1917, Series I, Box 3, Wiseman Papers.

134. Butler to Buchan, 14 September 1917, FO 395/80 New America File, Public Record Office.

135. Northcliffe to Prime Minister, Balfour, Bonar Law, and Churchill, 30 September 1917, F/41/7/26, Lloyd George Papers, HLRO.

136. F. M. Carroll, *American Opinion and the Irish Question 1910–1923* (New York, 1978), 99–101.

137. The FO 395 Department of Information 1917 American News Files in the Public Record Office are full of examples pulled from U.S. newspapers in the Midwest as evidence for this assertion. The Foreign Office also tracked American public opinion in a regularly published "American Press Resume" in 1916 and 1917.

138. Butler to Buchan, 27 June 1917, FO 395/79 New America File, Public Record Office.

139. Northcliffe to Page, 20 July 1917, Northcliffe Add. Mss., 62337, ff. 109–10, BL.

140. Dawson to Northcliffe, 27 August 1917, Northcliffe Add. Mss., 62245, ff. 82–83, BL. When Dawson approached Sir Edward Carson with the idea of Lloyd George taking a three-week American tour, Carson replied that he was agreeable, and said his colleagues would be as well, "except for the fact that Bonar Law would be temporarily left in charge…and this would be disastrous." Ibid. f. 87.

141. Dawson to Northcliffe, 1 September 1917, Northcliffe Add. Mss., 62245, ff. 93–97, BL. When Dawson reported this to Lord Milner, he replied, "What colleagues?"

142. This committee was one more attempt by Lloyd George to blunt the plans of Haig. See Adams and Poiner, *The Conscription Controversy in Great Britain, 1900–1918*, 203–4.

143. Northcliffe to Smuts, 21 August 1917, Series I, Box 3, Wiseman Papers.

144. Northcliffe to Prime Minister and War Cabinet, 21 August 1917, F/41/7/13, Lloyd George Papers, HLRO.

145. Report of Smuts to Buchan letter, 29 August 1917, FO 395/83, Public Record Office.

146. Northcliffe to Smuts, 30 August 1917, Series I, Box 3, Wiseman Papers.

147. Willert, *Washington and Other Memories*, 105.

148. Dawson to Northcliffe, 23 August 1917, Northcliffe Add. Mss., 62245, ff. 79–81, BL.

149. Northcliffe to Churchill, 6 October 1917, Series I, Box 3, Wiseman Papers. In an additional complication, Northcliffe had ridiculed Ford earlier in the war, when Ford backed a "Peace Ship" voyage to Europe.

150. For this episode, see Alan Nevins and Frank Ernest Hill, *Ford: Expansion and Challenge 1915–1933* (New York, 1957), 61–63.

151. *Detroit Free Press,* 17 October 1917.

152. *Cleveland Press,* 23 October 1917; *Daily Mail,* 24 October 1917.

153. *Daily Mail,* 24 October 1917.

154. Northcliffe Circular Letter, 21 October 1917, Northcliffe Papers, Harmsworth Archive. In Cleveland Northcliffe also met with Thomas Edison, who he reported was "doing very good anti-submarine work and hates the Germans like poison … they stole all his patents."

155. "Lord Northcliffe Scorns Sugar in His Tea," *Cleveland Press,* 22 October 1917.

156. Northcliffe Circular Letter, 21 October 1917, Northcliffe Papers, Harmsworth Archive.

157. *Daily Mail,* 25 October 1917.

158. *Chicago Tribune,* 25 October 1917.

159. *Chicago Herald,* 25 October 1917, quoted in 26 October *Daily Mail.*

160. The 25 October *Kansas City Star* noted that Northcliffe had outdrawn Helen Keller and America's former German ambassador, Gerard.

161. *Kansas City Times,* 26 October 1917.

162. *St. Louis Post-Dispatch,* 26 October 1917.

163. *St. Louis Post-Dispatch,* 27 October 1917.

164. *St. Louis Post-Dispatch,* 26 October 1917.

165. Katherine Wright to Colonel Campbell Stuart, n.d., Northcliffe Add. Mss., 62337, ff. 121–23, BL. Since before the war, Northcliffe had maintained a correspondence with Katherine Wright, the sister of the aviators. She thanked him on 2 October 1917 for his help in obtaining for Orville the Albert Medal from the Royal Society of Arts. Also see Fyfe, *Northcliffe,* 218–19; Seymour, *Intimate Papers of Colonel House,* 3: 93–94.

166. Daniels diary, 29 October 1917, in Cronon, *Cabinet Diary of Josephus Daniels,* 228.

167. Pound and Harmsworth, *Northcliffe,* 591.

168. Rinehart, *My Story,* 235.

169. Extract of letter, Borden to Northcliffe, 31 October 1917, Northcliffe Papers, WDM/3/1(20), Archive of *The Times.*

170. Butler to Buchan, 17 November 1917, FO 395/89 1917 News America File, Public Record Office.

171. *Some Memories,* 57.

172. Brendon, *The Life and Death of the Press Barons,* 122.

173. Willert, *Washington and Other Memories,* 101.

174. Northcliffe cabled Rothermere on 7 September requesting him to come in early November. He told his brother that he planned to return to England to give his views to the government and then return with some "urgently needed people." After initial enthusiasm for the idea, Rothermere replied in October that labor problems in Britain would keep him there. Sir Frederick Black became the temporary head of the mission in Northcliffe's absence. Series I, Box 3, Wiseman Papers.

175. *Washington and Other memories*, 106.

176. C. J. Philips to Northcliffe, 1 November 1917, Northcliffe Add. Mss., 62157, f. 90, BL.

"Pegasus in Harness": Politics and Propaganda, November 1917 to April 1918

1. Several correspondents had pointed out this flatness to Northcliffe, but he feared they were simply appealing to his vanity. *The Times* continued on its semi-independent course. With Geoffrey Dawson under Lord Milner's influence, it generally supported the government. Dawson enjoyed the tranquillity Northcliffe's absence had given him. Hankey noted in his diary that at a dinner on November 19 he was amused at the "intense desire of Geoffrey Dawson that Lord Northcliffe... should return to America," quoted in Roskill, *Hankey: Man of Secrets*, 1: 460.

2. Lloyd George, *War Memoirs*, 4: 416.

3. Even when the rain stopped, the low water table devastated by millions of shells, kept the terrain saturated.

4. For example, in October *The Times* reported, "The particular task which Sir Douglas Haig set his armies has been very nearly accomplished.... The German defence system has been broken." Quoted in Owen, *Tempestuous Journey*, 398.

5. Ibid., 430–32. Robertson and Haig were opposed to any such "interference."

6. Ibid., 433–34.

7. *Daily Mail*, 12 November 1917. The most active campaign carried out by the *Daily Mail*, in Northcliffe's absence was the fall 1917 crusade against air service incompetence.

8. Maxse to Northcliffe, 12 November 1917, Northcliffe Add. Mss., 62175, f. 95, British Library (hereafter BL).

9. Repington to Northcliffe, 12 November 1917, Northcliffe Add. Mss., 62253, ff. 118–19, BL.

10. Northcliffe Circular Letter, 5 November 1917, Northcliffe Papers, Harmsworth Archive.

11. 29 October 1917, Daniels diary, in Cronon, ed., *The Cabinet Diaries of Josephus Daniels 1913–1921*, 228.

12. House diary, 13 November 1917, Series II, Diary 12, House Papers, Sterling Library, Yale University. House received a parade of British notables and journalists, including the Asquiths. The day after his return, Northcliffe met with House at the Colonel's suite at Claridge's. When Northcliffe arrived, House spirited out C. P. Scott, of the Liberal *Manchester Guardian*, so that the two proprietors would not have a "fatal" meeting.

13. House diary, 14 November 1917, Series II, Diary 12.

14. Ibid.

15. House diary, 15 November 1917, Series II, Diary 12.

16. Fowler, *British-American Relations 1917–1918*, 98–99; House diary, 15 November 1917. Wiseman later told House that Northcliffe could be "used to club LG into any plan we consider wise," and House wrote President Wilson in a similar vein.

17. Wiseman told House that he had heard Northcliffe tell Lloyd George that he did not propose to give up the right to criticize when necessary. House to President Wilson, 16 November 1917, in Link, ed., *The Papers of Woodrow Wilson*, 45: 70–71.

18. Lord Beaverbrook, *Men and Power 1917–1918*, 85; Owen, *Tempestuous Journey*, 421.

19. Reading had first called on House to explain Lloyd George's position.

20. House diary, 15 November 1917.

21. Beaverbrook had called the prime minister on the evening of 15 November to inform him that the Press Association had just issued a statement that Northcliffe had declined the air ministry. Owen, *Tempestuous Journey*, 421. Fowler suggested that Wiseman "planted the seed" that led

to Northcliffe's letter, although he would not have wanted it published. *British American Relations 1917–1918*, 105.

22. *The Times*, 16 November 1917. This was also published in the same day's *Daily Mail*. The almost identical 15 November letter to Lloyd George is in the Northcliffe Add. Mss., 62157, ff. 93–96, BL.

23. *The Times*, 16 November 1917.

24. Ibid.

25. J. A. Spender, *Weetman Pearson: First Lord Cowdray 1856–1927* (London: Cassell, 1930), 234–35.

26. For Lloyd George's explanation of this affair, see *War Memoirs*, 4: 124–28. Cowdray apparently did not hold Northcliffe responsible, although it must be admitted that Northcliffe did not treat Cowdray, with whom he had been friendly, very well in this affair.

27. Beaverbrook, *Men and Power*, 86–87.

28. Ibid.; Pound and Harmsworth, *Northcliffe*, 593–94.

29. Riddell Diary, 17 November 1917, Riddell Add. Mss., 62980, f. 162, BL. Lloyd George also mentioned that Rothermere was supporting him, not his brother, in this affair because Rothermere was angling for the War Office, for which Lloyd George said he was unsuited.

30. Riddell diary, 24 November 1917, Riddell Add. Mss., 62980, ff. 174–75, BL.

31. Brisbane to Northcliffe, 19 November 1917, FO 395/86, Public Record Office.

32. Willert to Northcliffe, 16 November 1917, Lloyd George Papers F/41/7/32, House of Lords Record Office (hereafter HLRO).

33. Butler to Buchan, 17 November 1917, FO 395/86, Public Record Office. This was copied to Robert Cecil, the War Office, and the prime minister.

34. Butler to Buchan, 18 November 1917, FO 395/86, Public Record Office.

35. Strachey to Asquith, 16 November 1917, Strachey Papers, S/11/6/18, HLRO.

36. Owen, *Tempestuous Journey*, 436.

37. House diary, 16 November 1917, Series II, Diary 12.

38. Ibid.

39. Daniels diary, 29 October 1917, in Cronon, *Cabinet Diaries of Josephus Daniels*, 228.

40. F. E. Smith to Geddes, 31 October 1917, in Patterson, ed., *The Jellicoe Papers*, 2: 222–34.

41. Jellicoe Papers, Add. Mss., 49039, ff. 1–9, BL.

42. Milford Haven to Jellicoe, 27 December 1917, Jellicoe Papers, Add. Mss., 49039, ff. 139–40, BL, in Patterson, ed., *The Jellicoe Papers*, 2: 258.

43. House diary, 20 November 1917, Series II, Diary 12.

44. Ibid.

45. Riddell diary, 24 November 1917, Riddell Add. Mss., 62980, ff. 174–75, BL.

46. House diary, 20 November 1917, Series II, Diary 12.

47. House diary, 27 November 1917, Series II, Diary 12. Honors were distributed to many members of the American Mission. Willert and Campbell Stuart both received knighthoods.

48. Ibid. Northcliffe had suggested Rothermere to the prime minister in an undated note in the Northcliffe Add. Mss., 62157, f. 91, BL. He served until April 1918.

49. Amery, *My Political Life*, 2: 129. Amery had been on Hankey's war cabinet staff and became political secretary of the British section and liaison officer with the war cabinet.

50. House diary, 1 December 1917, Series II, Diary 12.

51. House diary, 5 December 1917, Series II, Diary 12.

52. Ibid. Northcliffe speculated to House that "George's incredible timidity at certain times, is due to his humble origin and the fear of criticism by the aristocracy. He says that LG has a brother who is a carpenter and quite without education." House added that "N himself thinks of the aristocracy as we do in the US, praising them when they deserve it, condemning them when they do not, but never allowing the fact of their high birth to make a difference in estimating them."

53. House diary, 11 December 1917, Series II, Diary 12. He recorded in his diary that "I cannot help dwelling upon the thought that my particular work might have been very much more effective if I had had a different man to deal with than LG. He makes an appealing speech, states his case well, has a charming personality, and there, as far as I can see, his usefulness ends...."

54. House to Northcliffe, 6 December 1917, Northcliffe Papers, Harmsworth Archive.

55. Lansdowne, who had held numerous posts, including foreign minister, had put a similar proposal before the cabinet a year earlier.

56. For Dawson's account, see Wrench, *Geoffrey Dawson and Our Times*, 156–57.

57. *The History of the Times*, vol. 4, pt. 1: 336–42.

58. Riddell Diary, 3 December 1917, Riddell Add. Mss., 62980, f. 193, BL.

59. Some thought the continuing attacks of *The Times* on Lansdowne went too far. Lord Burnham reported to Riddell that the king was annoyed at the "bad taste" of the attack. Burnham also complained to Riddell that Northcliffe was running the country. Curzon had told him that he had "gone into the Cabinet room and found the press lord stalking up and down and laying down the law to L.G. in a loud voice and arrogant manner." Riddell diary, 3 December 1917, Riddell Add. Mss., 62980, f. 198, BL.

60. Owen, *Tempestuous Journey*, 441–42.

61. "Message from the Chief," 15 December 1917, Ms. Eng. Hist. d. 303.

62. Tracy to Northcliffe, 5 December 1917, Northcliffe Add. Mss., 62164, f. 1, BL.

63. John J. Pershing, *My Experience in the War*, 2 vols. (New York: Frederick A. Stokes, 1931), 1: 252.

64. Northcliffe to Curtis, 17 December 1917, Northcliffe Add. Mss., 62337, f. 182, BL.

65. Pershing, *My Experiences in the War*, 1: 254. For the controversy about the use of American troops and American cooperation in general, see David R. Woodward, *Trial by Friendship: Anglo-American Relations 1917–1918* (Lexington: University of Kentucky Press, 1993).

66. Pershing, *My Experiences in the War*, 1: 255. Pershing believed that he had persuaded Northcliffe to his view, writing that, "at the conclusion of the conversation, he very frankly said we were perfectly right. After that, so far as I am aware, he became a consistent advocate of an American army."

67. 7 December 1917 diary entry, in Brigadier-General John Charteris, *At G.H.Q.* (London: Casell, 1931), 273.

68. In his biography of Haig, Charteris attempted to shift the blame for the national depression after Cambrai to Northcliffe and his reporters for exaggerating the initial successes and then turning against Haig after the reversals. He also speculated that Northcliffe's wounded vanity after his 7 December visit to GHQ was a contributing factor. *Field-Marshal Earl Haig*, 292–93. Duff Cooper also follows this line in *Haig*, 199–200. Both these works also consider Northcliffe hostile to Haig in his newspapers from December 1917.

69. Northcliffe to Sassoon, 13 December 1917, in Grieves, *The Politics of Manpower*, 165.

70. Northcliffe to Charteris, 11 December 1917, Northcliffe Add. Mss., 62159, f. 184, BL.

71. Northcliffe to Sassoon, 13 December 1917, Northcliffe Add. Mss., 62160, f. 101, BL.

72. Northcliffe to Reading, 27 December 1917, Northcliffe Add. Mss., 62156, BL.

73. Northcliffe to Caird, 3 January 1918, in Pound and Harmsworth, *Northcliffe*, 607.

74. Wiseman to House, 19 December 1917, Series I, Box 123, Wiseman Papers.

75. Tracy to Northcliffe, 4 January 1918, Northcliffe Add. Mss., 62164, ff. 11–14, BL.

76. Reading soon after became ambassador as well as head of the War Mission.

77. "Message from the Chief," 21 December 1917, Ms. Eng. Hist d. 303, Bodleian Library.

78. Healy to Northcliffe, 21 December 1917, Northcliffe Add. Mss., 62337, BL.

79. Northcliffe to Healy, 30 December 1917, Northcliffe Add. Mss., 62337, BL.

80. For this, see Colvin, *The Life of Lord Carson*, 3: 301–11.

81. Pound and Harmsworth, *Northcliffe*, 614.

82. Northcliffe to Prime Minister, 14 February 1918, Northcliffe Add. Mss., 62157, f. 102, BL.

83. Decies to Northcliffe, 21 February 1918, Northcliffe Add. Mss., 62338, f. 226, BL.

84. Healy to Northcliffe, 25 February 1918, Northcliffe Add. Mss., 62338, f. 226, BL.

85. Northcliffe to Healy, Northcliffe to Decies, 27 February 1918, Northcliffe Add. Mss., 62338, ff. 231–32, BL.

86. Wilton to Northcliffe, 27 December 1917, Northcliffe Add. Mss., 62253, f. 174, BL.

87. Wilton to Northcliffe, 7 January 1918, Northcliffe Add. Mss., 62253, ff. 186–87, BL.

88. Neilson, *Strategy and Supply: The Anglo-Russian Alliance*, 296.

89. Repington, *The First World War*, 2: 149.

90. Repington to Howard Corbett, 16 January 1918, Northcliffe Add. Mss., 62253, ff. 122–23, BL. The major disagreement was with his editor, Geoffrey Dawson, over revisions of Repington's articles.

91. Repington to Northcliffe, 16 January 1918, Northcliffe Add. Mss., 62253, f. 121, BL.

92. Strachey to Repington, 26 January 1918, Strachey Papers, S/12/1/2, HLRO.

93. Repington to Strachey, 29 January 1918, Strachey Papers, S/12/1/2, HLRO.

94. Fraser, *Private Notes for Lord Northcliffe*, n.d., Northcliffe Add. Mss., 62251, f. 143, BL.

95. *Daily Mail*, 21 January 1918.

96. *Daily Mail*, 24, 28 January 1918.

97. Robertson to Gwynne, 22 January 1918, in Woodward, ed., *The Military Correspondence of Field-Marshal Sir William Robertson*, 273–74.

98. *Daily Mail*, 31 January 1918.

99. Strachey to Bonham Carter, 23 January 1918, Strachey Papers, quoted in McEwen, "'Brass-Hats' and the British Press During the First World War," 61. As usual, he suspected that Northcliffe was using this as an opportunity to "support L.G. against Robertson in Order to bring him down ... he will lead L.G. into the soup and leave him there."

100. "Message from the Chief," 22 January 1918, Ms. Eng. Hist. d. 303, Bodleian Library.

101. Woodward, *Lloyd George and the Generals*, 246.

102. Ibid.

103. Amery, *My Political Life*, 2: 138.

104. Buchan to Northcliffe, 23 January 1918, Northcliffe Papers, Harmsworth Archive.

105. Hedging his bets, Buchan at the same time expressed anxiety to Beaverbrook that Northcliffe might take over; Riddell Diary, 28 January 1918, Riddell Add. Mss., 62981, f. 29, BL.

106. Northcliffe to Ribblesdale, 24 January 1918, Northcliffe Add. Mss., 62338, f. 96, BL.

107. This scheme grew out of the results of a propaganda investigation done at Lloyd George's request by Robert Donald, editor of the *Daily Chronicle*.

108. Riddel Diary, 28 January 1918, Riddell Add. Mss., 62981, ff. 29–30, BL.

109. Northcliffe told Steed that during the propaganda discussions it was hinted that he might be asked to go to the War Office instead. Wickham Steed, *The Fifth Arm*, (London, 1940), 15.

110. Riddell Diary, 28 January 1918, Riddell Add. Mss., 62981, ff. 29–30, BL.

111. 26 January 1918 Statement, Beaverbrook Papers, C261, HLRO. A further unsigned undated document in the Beaverbrook Papers, which appears to be in Lloyd George's hand, states that the "Prime Minister, at the request of the Chancellor of the Duchy of Lancaster, has appointed Lord Northcliffe to undertake the direction of all propaganda in foreign countries." It was not unreasonable for Northcliffe to report to Lloyd George, with whom he had been in direct contact since June 1917 on mission affairs. Those who point to this arrangement as unorthodox, such as Taylor in *Beaverbrook*, 138, apparently were unaware that Northcliffe continued his duties as head of the British War Mission in London (though admittedly nominal after he tackled Enemy Propaganda). See p. 138, n. 2.

112. Northcliffe to Beaverbrook, 7 February 1918, Beaverbrook Papers, C261, HLRO; A. J. P. Taylor, *Beaverbrook*, 139.

113. Northcliffe to Beaverbrook, 13 February 1918, Northcliffe Add. Mss., 62161, f. 24, BL. For an overview of British propaganda in enemy countries, see Sanders and Taylor, *British Propaganda During the First World War, 1914–1918*, 208–45.

114. "Message from the Chief," 19 February 1918, Ms. Eng. Hist. d. 303, Bodleian Library.

115. Fraser, *Lord Esher*, 382.

116. Northcliffe to Prime Minister, 14 February 1918, Northcliffe Add. Mss., 62157, f. 102, BL.

117. Hankey diary, 13 February 1918, in Lord Hankey, *The Supreme Command 1914–1918*, 2 vols. (London: George Allen & Unwin, 1965), 2: 777.

118. Owen, *Tempestuous Journey*, 461. The final disagreement came over the command of the Allied reserve.

119. Haig diary, 17 February 1918, quoted in Churchill, *Lord Derby: King of Lancashire*, 332.

120. Northcliffe to Rosebery, 17 February 1918, Northcliffe Add. Mss., 62154, BL.

121. *Field-Marshal Earl Haig*, 293.

122. Northcliffe to Beattie, 5 February 1917, Northcliffe Add. Mss., 62203, f. 17, BL.

123. Northcliffe to Marlowe, 14 February 1918, Northcliffe Add. Mss., 62199, f. 81, BL.

124. Esher to Haig, 14 February 1918, Esher Papers, quoted in Fraser, *Lord Esher*, 382.

125. Sir Charles Petrie, *The Life and Letters of the Right Honourable Sir Austen Chamberlain*, 2 vols. (London: Cassell, 1940), 2: 105. The Conservative Austen (older brother of Neville) had been secretary for India from May 1915 until he resigned over the Mesopotamia Report in July 1917.

126. *Parliamentary Debates*, Commons, 5th Series, vol. 103, cols. 633–45.

127. Ibid.

128. Petrie, *Austen Chamberlain*, 2: 107.

129. David Dutton, *Austen Chamberlain Gentleman in Politics* (London: Russ Anderson, 1985), 140. His associate Leo Amery told Chamberlain that bringing press lords into the government was no different from bringing in great landlords for their influence. Amery thought Chamberlain acted as though Britain was still in the genteel political world of the 1880s.

130. Beaverbrook, *Men and Power*, 279.

131. Ibid., 282–83.

132. Guest to the Prime Minister, 26 February 1917, quoted in *The History of The Times*, vol. 4, part I, 351.

133. Milner to the Prime Minister, 27 February 1918, quoted in ibid., 353.

134. "Message from the Chief," 20 February 1918, Ms. Eng. Hist. d. 303, Bodleian Library. Potatoes and pigs were highly recommended because they grew quickly and were economical.

135. Northcliffe to Reading, 8 March 1917, Reading Papers, F118.61, ff. 65–68, India Office Library.

136. Ibid.

137. *Parliamentary Debates*, Commons, 5th Series, vol. 104, cols. 40–42.

138. Ibid., cols. 73–79.

139. *Daily Mail*, 12 March 1918.

140. On his return from the United States, Northcliffe's mission operations had been set up in cramped quarters in Abingdon Street, across from the House of Lords. This site appears now to be part of a small park from which interviews with government figures (with the House of Parliament in the background) are regularly televised—a fitting use for the first location of Northcliffe's headquarters.

141. Steed was perhaps the greatest enemy of the Dual Monarchy in Britain, where many were still sympathetic. He had served as *The Times* correspondent in Vienna from 1902 to 1913 and wrote a book on the subject, *The Hapsburg Monarchy* (London, 1913).

142. Steed's role in the propaganda effort, particularly against Austria-Hungary cannot be overestimated. Sir Peter Chalmers Mitchell, who later joined him at Crewe House, described Steed as the "heart and soul" of Crewe House. *My Fill of Days* (London: Faber and Faber, 1937), 296.

143. For this, see Rothwell, *British War Aims and Peace Diplomacy 1914–1918,* and Kenneth J. Calder, *Britain and the Origins of the New Europe 1914–1918* (London: Cambridge University Press, 1978).

144. Rothwell, *British War Aims and Peace Diplomacy,* 147. The Bolsheviks had released and repudiated the so-called "Secret Treaties," which revealed the promises made to Russia concerning Constantinople in the peace settlement.

145. The British National War Aims Committee, founded in August 1917 to strengthen home morale, had been urging the government for some time to declare war aims that would appeal to the working classes.

146. Rothwell, *British War Aims and Peace Diplomacy,* 153.

147. French, *The Strategy of the Lloyd George Coalition 1916–1918.*

148. Lloyd George, *War Memoirs,* 5: 63–73.

149. *The History of The Times,* vol. 4, pt. 1, 347.

150. Unofficial talks had been ongoing, the latest in December between General Smuts and the Austrian Count Mensdorff in Switzerland. For this and other peace moves, see David Stevenson, *The First World War and International Politics* (Oxford: Oxford University Press, 1988).

151. Northcliffe to Balfour, 24 February 1918, FO 899/764, Public Record Office.

152. The letter broke down the Dual Monarchy as follows: "Austria contains some 31,000,000 inhabitants. Of these, less than one-third, i.e., the 9,000,000 or 10,000,000 Germans of Austria are pro-German. The other two-thirds (including the Poles, Czecho-Slovaks, Rumanes, Italians, and Southern Slavs) are actively or passively anti-German. The Kingdom of Hungary... has a population of... 21,000,000 of which one-half (Magyars, Jews, Saxons and Swabians) may be considered pro-German, and the rest (Slovaks, Rumanes, and Southern Slavs) actively or passively anti-German."

153. He added that expressions such as "self-government" or "autonomous-development" should be avoided, because they have a "sinister" meaning in Austria-Hungary and tend to discourage the friends of the Allies. Also, statements that the Allies do not wish to "dismember Austria" should be avoided.

154. According to this plan, the Germans of Austria would be free to join the Confederated States of Germany. They would, in any case, tend to secede from a transformed Austria in which they would no longer be able to rule over non-German peoples.

155. Balfour to Northcliffe, 26 February 1918, FO 899/764, Public Record Office. Sir Eric Drummond drafted most of Balfour's response.

156. Ibid.

157. Northcliffe to Balfour, 27 February 1918, FO 899/764, Public Record Office; Steed, *The Fifth Arm,* 17.

158. War Cabinet 359, 5 March 1918, Cab. 23–5, quoted in Calder, *Britain and the Origins of the New Europe 1914–1918,* 179. Northcliffe also agreed to submit the leaflets produced to Balfour for approval. Also see Harry Hanak, *Great Britain and Austria-Hungary During the First World War: A Study in the Formation of Public Opinion* (London, 1962), 276; and Dr. Eduard Benes, *My War Memoirs* (London, 1928), 329.

159. Steed to Northcliffe, 7 March 1918; Northcliffe to Steed, 19 March 1918, Northcliffe Add. Mss., 62246B, ff. 13–14, 17, BL.

160. For the propaganda activities of Steed and Seton-Watson in the war, see Messinger, *British Propaganda and the State in the First World War,* 163–83.

161. For Italy's continuing territorial aspirations, see Burgwyn, *The Legend of the Mutilated Victory,* 109–63.

162. Fyfe to Northcliffe, 21 March 1918, Northcliffe Add. Mss., 62206, f. 185, BL.

163. *Daily Mail,* 23 March 1918.

164. Pershing, *My Experience in the War,* 1: 356.

165. Northcliffe to Bullock, 24 March 1918, Northcliffe Add. Mss., 62209, ff. 24, BL.

166. The details of the campaign, including samples of the leaflet messages, can be found in Steed's 30 April 1918, "Report on the British Mission for Propaganda in Austria-Hungary," Northcliffe Add. Mss., 62163, ff. 24–37, BL.

167. Ibid.; Steed, *The Fifth Arm*, 29–30.

168. Stuart, *Secrets of Crewe House*, 38–39.

169. Ibid., 40; Steed, *The Fifth Arm*, 30–31.

170. Lloyd George sent Northcliffe these reports on 22 April 1918.

171. Maxse to Northcliffe, 4 April 1918, Northcliffe Add. Mss., 62175, f. 97, BL.

172. Northcliffe to Maxse, 10 April 1918, Northcliffe Add. Mss., 62175, f. 98, BL.

173. Maxse to Northcliffe, 13 April 1918, Maxse Papers, quoted in Fraser, *Lord Esher*, 391–92.

174. Northcliffe to Maxse, 16 April 1918, answering Maxse of the 15th, Maxse Papers, quoted in Fraser, *Lord Esher*, 392.

175. Edwards to Northcliffe, 27 April 1918, Northcliffe Add. Mss., 62339, f. 186, BL.

176. Lord Beaverbrook, "Death of Lord Northcliffe," *Daily Express*, 15 August 1922.

177. Captain B. H. Liddell Hart, *The Real War 1914–1918* (Boston: Houghton Mifflin, 1964), 403.

178. Northcliffe to Lloyd Goerge, 14 April 1918, Lloyd George Papers, F/41/8/6, HLRO. Burton had recently been added to the mission staff in Paris after months in limbo because of unwise remarks he had made in a speech about Wilson in late 1917.

179. 10 April 1917 Memo, Lloyd George Papers, F/41/8/6, HLRO. To halt delays, Burton also recommended that an American of cabinet rank be installed in France.

180. Lloyd George to Reading, 18 April 1918, quoted in Owen, *Tempestuous Journey*, 476.

181. Pound and Harmsworth, *Northcliffe*, 630.

182. This shift has also been viewed as a maneuver by Lloyd George to remove Milner, with whom he disagreed, from the war cabinet. Derby replaced Lord Bertie at the British embassy in Paris.

183. Dutton, *Austen Chamberlain*, 140–41. As usual, Lloyd George was eager to harness the energies of his critics. Chamberlain's main assignment was Ireland.

184. Petrie, *Austen Chamberlain*, 2: 118.

185. *The History of The Times*, vol. 4, pt. 1, 357–58.

186. *Daily Mail*, 19 April 1918. It added that, in protesting the choice, it voiced the "feeling of every father, mother or relative of the boys whose names appear in the sad lists printed in the last page of the journal every morning. They had expected better things of Mr. Lloyd George than indulgence in the old game of political juggling in such a tremendous hour."

187. Petrie, *Austen Chamberlain*, 2: 118.

188. Northcliffe to Milner, 22 April 1918, Northcliffe Add. Mss., 62339, ff. 169–71, BL. Lloyd George had assured Northcliffe's brother that he would support *The Times* in its campaign for Home Rule "to the finish" or resign. Cecil Harmsworth diary, 15 April 1918, in Pound and Harmsworth, *Northcliffe*, 615.

189. Milner to Northcliffe, 22 April 1918, Northcliffe Add. Mss., 62339, ff. 172–74, BL.

190. Pound and Harmsworth, *Northcliffe*, 631.

191. Northcliffe to Cecil Harmsworth, 20 April 1918, Northcliffe Papers, Harmsworth Archive.

192. Northcliffe to Beaverbrook, 19 April 1918, Northcliffe Add. Mss., 62161, f. 29, BL. He considered him an ideal man, as well, to look after British propaganda in the United States.

193. Northcliffe to Beaverbrook, 19 April 1918, Northcliffe Add. Mss., 62161, f. 29, BL.

194. Beaverbrook to Northcliffe, 22 April 1918, Northcliffe Add. Mss., 62161, f. 30, BL.

195. Northcliffe to Beaverbrook, 23 April 1918, Beaverbrook Papers, C/261, HLRO.

196. Lloyd George to Northcliffe, 22 April 1918, Lloyd George Papers, F/41/8/7, HLRO.

197. Northcliffe to Lloyd George, 28 April 1918, Lloyd George Papers, F/41/8/8, HLRO. The 27 April 1918 *Daily Mail* announced that Northcliffe was recuperating from a nine-week bout of the flu and had agreed to stay in his job until the government could find someone to replace him.

198. Beaverbrook, *Men and Power*, 87.

199. Ibid., 88. Stanley Morison in "Personality and Diplomacy in Anglo-American Relations," 465, also marks the November 16 publication of Northcliffe's letter as "the end of Northcliffe, though not immediately."

200. E. T. Raymond, *Uncensored Celebrities* (New York: Henry Holt and Co., 1919), 165.

201. Wrench, *Geoffrey Dawson and Our Times*, 162.

202. Northcliffe to R. B. Marston, 25 March 1918, in Pound and Harmsworth, *Northcliffe*, 629. Marston was editor of the *Fishing Gazette*.

203. Wells to Northcliffe, n.d., Northcliffe Add. Mss., 62161, ff. 130–32, BL.

TEN

"Great Propaganda": From War to Peace, May to November 1918

1. For this affair, see Turner, *British Politics and the Great War*, 288–307; Owen, *Tempestuous Journey*, 480–82; Blake, *The Unknown Prime Minister*, 368–75.

2. The prime minister was able to refute Maurice's accusations point by point, including the fact that the figures he had used came from Maurice's department. This episode further exposed the fracture lines of the Liberal party, and this vote was one of the factors used to mark those who would be supported by the Coalition in the "coupon" election of December 1918.

3. Northcliffe to Reading, 26 May 1918, F118, ff. 70–72, Reading Papers, British Library, Oriental and India Collections. His letter continued that, in the "opinion of a good many people, your absence has weakened the Government here. The Prime Minister is dragged hither and thither about Great Britain and needs those evening visits which you used to pay to Downing Street. Never having any time to think and having no steady brain near him, now that Lord Milner is at the War Office, the Prime Minister often sees things out of perspective in regard to our internal politics."

4. Lloyd George to Northcliffe, 16 May 1918, in the 27 May 1918, "Minutes of the Second Meeting of the Committee for Propaganda in Enemy Countries." Beaverbrook Papers, E/3/9, House of Lords Record Office (hereafter HLRO).

5. Northcliffe to Prime Minister, 22 May 1918, Lloyd George Papers, F/41/8/13, HLRO; Northcliffe Add. Mss., 62157, f. 107, British Library (hereafter BL).

6. Northcliffe to Beaverbrook, 30 April 1918, Beaverbrook Papers, E/3/9, HLRO.

7. *The History of The Times*, vol 4, pt. 1: 354, n. 1.

8. Northcliffe to Dawson, 14 May 1918, Northcliffe Add. Mss., 62245, ff. 116–17, BL.

9. Ibid.

10. Northcliffe and others, including Colonel Swinton, had suggested propaganda by airplane in the fall of 1914. The Germans tried it first at Nancy in September 1914, but were soon outclassed by British efforts. Sanders and Taylor, *British Propaganda During the First World War, 1914–1918*, 211.

11. Northcliffe to Beaverbrook, 30 April 1918, Beaverbrook Papers, E/3/9, HLRO.

12. Ibid. Though airplanes were forbidden, many other means of dissemination were available including balloons, the Belgian Air Service, interviewing German sentries, evasion of postal censorship, wrapping pamphlets and leaflets in neutral newspapers, smuggling, and bribery. Crewe House had secret organizations in neutral countries for this work and carried out an important part of their propaganda through the neutral press. 14 May Report of the Committee for Propaganda in Enemy Countries, Beaverbrook Papers, E/3/9, HLRO.

13. Milner to Northcliffe, 14 May 1918, in the 27 May 1918, "Minutes of Second Meeting of the Committee for Propaganda in Enemy Countries," Beaverbrook Papers, E/3/9, HLRO.

14. Northcliffe to Balfour, 11 June 1918, Northcliffe Add. Mss., 62153, f. 63, BL.

15. Northcliffe to the Committee for Propaganda in Enemy Countries, 14 May 1918. This letter makes up the entire 14 May 1918 Committee Report, Beaverbrook Papers, E/3/9, HLRO.

16. For operations against Germany, see Sir Campbell Stuart, *Secrets of Crewe House: The Story of a Famous Campaign* (London: Collins, 1920). Besides Germany and Austria-Hungary, the 14 May 1918 report also listed Turkey, and propaganda among enemy prisoners, as Crewe House responsibilities. Lord Denbigh was asked to assume the Turkish duties; however, he declined. Turkey was later transferred to the Ministry of Information. Sir Charles Nicholson was given responsibility for enemy prisoners. He gained permission from the War Office to visit the camps where the German prisoners were interned. For this, see the "Minutes of the Second Meeting of the Committee for Propaganda in Enemy Countries."

17. Wells, *Experiment in Autobiography*, 2: 697. Wells also thought that Northcliffe "knew something of what I had in mind and sympathized with it and wanted to forward it. But his undoubtedly big and undoubtedly unco-ordinated brain was like a weather-chart in stormy times; phases of high and low pressure and moral gradients and depressions chased themselves across his mental map. His skull held together, in a delusive unity, a score of flying fragments of purpose." Ibid., 700.

18. Wells's undated draft plan for a "Directorate of Propaganda (German)" can be found in the Northcliffe Add. Mss., 62163, ff. 10–22, BL.

19. An undated synopsis of the "Great Propaganda" plan is in the Northcliffe Add. Mss., 62162, f. 10, BL.

20. "Minutes of the Third Meeting of the Committee for Propaganda in Enemy Countries," 31 May 1918, Beaverbrook Papers, E/3/9, HLRO. To Wells, beside its propaganda value, an international organization was critical to rebuilding the postwar world and its economy. It would act as a damper to control problems such as the calls for disastrous economic revenge on Germany, and inflation, which, without international cooperation, might mean a collapse of world credit.

21. Ibid. Before the Wells plan was presented to Balfour, Wickham Steed added a preface that pointed out that the "real" Allied aim was not only to beat the enemy, but to establish a lasting peace. To do this, Crewe House propaganda would need to bring home to the Germans that the war would continue until Germany accepted the Allied terms. Steed repeated the call for a League of Nations and a "Changing of Germany" in the interest of both sides. Germany now had to choose between "her own permanent ruin by adhering to her present system of government and policy and the prospect of economic and political redemption by overthrowing her present militarist system."

22. Northcliffe to Balfour, 10 June 1918, FO 899/780, Public Record Office.

23. Ibid. Northcliffe went on that this would, in effect, amount to the constitution of a League of Free Nations which, presumably, Germany would eventually be invited to join. Germany's admission would be its guarantee against the establishment of, for example, a hostile monopoly on raw materials. The terms of peace, therefore, could be represented as the conditions on which Germany should be invited to take part. In order to secure the economic benefits, it would have to accept the political conditions. This would greatly lighten the task of propaganda, as it would put British aims in a form more acceptable to moderate elements in Germany, than if they were put forward "merely as terms to be imposed on a defeated enemy."

24. Ibid.

25. Balfour to Northcliffe, 11 June 1918, recorded in the 25 June 1918, "Minutes of the Fifth Meeting of the Committee for Propaganda in Enemy Countries," Beaverbrook Papers, E/3/9, HLRO.

26. Northcliffe to Balfour, 13 June 1918, in the "Minutes of the Fifth Meeting of the Committee for Propaganda in Enemy Countries," Beaverbrook Papers, E/3/9, HLRO.

27. "Minutes of the Fifth Meeting of the Committee for Propaganda in Enemy Countries," Beaverbrook Papers, E/3/9, HLRO.

28. For this, see Stuart, *Secrets of Crewe House,* 134–42.

29. Northcliffe to Balfour, n.d., in the 27 May 1918, "Minutes of the Second Meeting of the Committee for Propaganda in Enemy Countries."

30. Balfour to Northcliffe, 6 June 1918, in the 11 June 1918, "Minutes of the Fourth Meeting of the Committee for Propaganda in Enemy Countries," Beaverbrook Papers, E/3/9, HLRO.

31. Northcliffe to Steed, 2 June 1918, Northcliffe Add. Mss., 62246B, BL.

32. Balfour to Northcliffe, 8 June 1918, Northcliffe Add. Mss., 62153, f. 61, BL.

33. Curnock to Northcliffe, 14 June 1918, Northcliffe Add. Mss., 62205, BL.

34. *The History of the Times,* vol. 4, pt. 1, 359–61. Sharp also gathered intelligence for the government in Stockholm.

35. Sharp to Steed, 13 June 1918, in *The History of The Times,* vol. 4, pt. 1, 360–61.

36. For Milner's "appeasement" of Germany, see Gollin, *Proconsul in Politics,* 522–77.

37. Pound and Harmsworth, *Northcliffe,* 645.

38. Northcliffe to Dawson, 5 July 1918, Northcliffe Add. Mss., 62245, ff. 127–28, BL.

39. Northcliffe to Milner, 17 June 1918, in the 25 June 1918, "Minutes of the Fifth Meeting of the Committee for Propaganda in Enemy Countries," Beaverbrook Papers, E/3/9, HLRO.

40. Hankey to Northcliffe, 29 June 1918, in the 9 July 1918, "Minutes of the Sixth Meeting of the Committee for Enemy Propaganda," Northcliffe Add. Mss., 62162, ff. 138–40, BL.

41. Wells to Northcliffe, 27 June 1918, Northcliffe Add. Mss., 62161, ff. 138–40, BL.

42. Ibid. Wells had asked Beaverbrook about his policy and so far as any general idea went, Wells found he hadn't one.

43. Sanders and Taylor, *British Propaganda During the First World War,* 219.

44. Wells to Northcliffe, 27 June 1918, Northcliffe Add. Mss., 62161, ff. 138–40 BL.

45. Ibid.

46. Northcliffe to Wells, 29 June 1918, Northcliffe Add. Mss., 62161, ff. 141–43, BL.

47. Ibid.

48. Wells to Northcliffe, 2 July 1918, Northcliffe Add. Mss., 62161, ff. 146–48, BL.

49. Ibid.

50. Turner, *British Politics and the Great War,* 308. The new law had extended the franchise to almost all men of legal age and women over thirty, as a response to their sacrifice in the war.

51. "Message from the Chief," 5 June 1918, Ms. Eng. Hist. d. 303, Bodleian Library.

52. For Beaverbrook's struggle with the official mind of the Foreign Office, see Taylor, *Beaverbrook,* 148–53; and Chisholm and Davie, *Lord Breaverbrook,* 160–62.

53. Northcliffe to Beaverbrook, 6 July 1918, Beaverbrook Papers, C261, HLRO.

54. Northcliffe to Philips, 7 July 1918, Northcliffe Add. Mss., 62341, f. 36, BL.

55. Northcliffe to Balfour, 7 July 1918, Northcliffe Add. Mss., 62153, f. 66, BL.

56. Balfour to Northcliffe, 9 July 1918, Northcliffe Add. Mss., 62153, f. 69, BL. He asked only that his "Department should be consulted and my advice followed on matters where questions of foreign policy are concerned, that officers who undertake propaganda in foreign countries should be under the ultimate control of the Ambassador or Minister, sending him ... copies of their reports, when they concern political conditions, and that when the Ministry of Information desire that important British presonage [*sic*] should visit foreign countries I should have an opportunity of consulting our Diplomatic representative on the subject." Balfour did not think this "impossible or unreasonable."

57. Northcliffe to Prime Minister, 12 July 1918, Northcliffe Add. Mss., 62157, ff. 115–16, BL.

58. Beaverbrook to Northcliffe, 11 July 1918, Northcliffe Add. Mss., 62161, f. 49, BL.

59. Northcliffe to Beaverbrook, 10 July 1918, Beaverbrook Papers, E/3/9, HLRO.

60. *The Dropping of Leaflets Behind Enemy Lines,* Beaverbrook to Cabinet, 12 July 1918, Beaverbrook Papers, E/3/33, HLRO.

61. Northcliffe to Beaverbrook, 19 July 1918, Beaverbrook Papers, E/3/9, HLRO.

62. Northcliffe to Beaverbrook, 23 July 1918, Beaverbrook Papers, E/3/9, HLRO.

63. Beaverbrook to Northcliffe, 24 July 1918, Beaverbrook Papers, E/3/9, HLRO.

64. As the son of an enemy alien, the man could not continue in his employment under new government regulations. Sir Campbell Stuart brought the "young German" to Wells's attention and dismissed him. Sir Campbell Stuart, *Opportunity Knocks Once* (London, 1952), 71.

65. Wells to Northcliffe, n.d., Northcliffe Add. Mss., 62161, ff. 149–50, BL. He added that the former St. Paul's boy was "no doubt full of sinister designs against this country." Wells could imagine "nothing more utterly mischievous then this campaign to make every human being of German origin hate us as bitterly as possible & I can see no possibility of conducting a propaganda against the German Government while it goes on."

66. Ibid.

67. Northcliffe to Wells, 16 July 1918, Northcliffe Add. Mss., 62161, f. 151, BL.

68. Wells to Northcliffe, 17 July 1918, Northcliffe Add. Mss., 62161, f. 152, BL.

69. Northcliffe to Wells, 25 July 1918, Northcliffe Add. Mss., 62161, f. 153, BL. Wells remained on the committee and made occasional comments at its meetings.

70. Northcliffe to Dawson, 5 July 1918, Northcliffe Add. Mss., 62245, ff. 127–28, BL.

71. Ibid. Sir William Sutherland was one of Lloyd George's secretaries. Part of his responsibility included dealing with the press.

72. "Message from the Chief," 13 July 1918, Ms. Eng. Hist. d. 303, Bodleian Library.

73. "Business as Usual Never Again!" *Daily Mail,* 1 July 1918.

74. *Daily Mail,* 2 August 1918.

75. *Parliamentary Debates,* Commons, Fifth Series, vol. 109, cols, 947–1035, 5 August 1918. For the businessmen in the Ministry of Information, see Chisholm and Davie, *Lord Beaverbrook,* 159.

76. Baldwin to Northcliffe, 5 August 1918, Northcliffe Add. Mss., 62341, f. 1612, BL.

77. Northcliffe to Beaverbrook, 6 August 1918, Northcliffe Add. Mss., 62161, ff. 55–56, BL. One of the "Old Gang" to which Northcliffe referred was Charles Masterman. Northcliffe wrote to Beaverbrook that he hoped it was "not true that Masterman had been reappointed to the Ministry of Information. He is overripe for ejection." Northcliffe to Beaverbrook, 8 August 1918, Northcliffe Add. Mss., 62161, f. 57, BL.

78. Beaverbrook to Northcliffe, n.d., Beaverbrook Papers, E/3/42, HLRO.

79. General Ludendorff, *My War Memories 1914–1918,* 2 vols. (London: Hutchinson, 1919), 2: 679.

80. 6 August 1918, in Pound and Harmsworth, *Northcliffe,* 650.

81. For this see Stuart, *Secrets of Crewe House,* 146–200.

82. Northcliffe to Prime Minister, 7 August 1918, Lloyd George Papers, F/41/8/20, HLRO. He also asked the chief of the naval intelligence department to attend, as well as the regular liaison officers with the department of state, including the Foreign Office, so that "our Government will be in the closest touch with our deliberations."

83. "Minutes of the Tenth Meeting of the Committee for Propaganda in Enemy Countries," 3 September 1918, Northcliffe Add. Mss., 62162, f. 44, BL. Steed, *Through Thirty Years,* 2: 241.

84. In addition to being director of propaganda in enemy countries, Northcliffe was also chairman of the London headquarters of the British War Mission to the United States and chairman of the committee responsible for British propaganda to Italy.

85. Northcliffe to Prime Minister, 16 August 1918, Lloyd George Papers, F/41/8/21, HLRO. The new organization would be directly responsible to the war cabinet and have direct relations with the treasury, which Propaganda in Enemy Countries did not have.

86. 12 August 1918, Riddell diary, Add. Mss., 62982, f. 28, BL.

87. Northcliffe to Caird, 12 January 1919, in Pound and Harmsworth, *Northcliffe*, 693.

88. August 1918, Riddell diary, Add. Mss., 62982, ff. 44–45, BL.

89. Ibid.

90. Lord Beaverbrook, *Men and Power 1917–1918*, 88.

91. No evidence of this episode has been found in the Northcliffe, Reading, Beaverbrook, Lloyd George, or other papers consulted for this work. Northcliffe was in Scotland in September; however, Pound and Harmsworth reported that Campbell Stuart did not accompany him and had no recollection of this affair. *Northcliffe*, 661–62.

92. "Summary of Speeches by and about Lord Northcliffe 1908–1922," Northcliffe Papers, Harmsworth Archive.

93. Pound and Harmsworth, *Northcliffe*, 661.

94. "To Berlin," *Daily Mail*, 19 August 1918.

95. House to Northcliffe, 18 July 1918, Northcliffe Add. Mss., 62180, f. 2, BL. House Papers, Series I, Box 83a, Sterling Library, Yale University.

96. "Minutes of the Tenth Meeting of the Committee for Propaganda in Enemy Countries," 3 September 1918, Northcliffe Add. Mss., 62162, f. 47, BL.

97. "Minutes of the Eleventh Meeting of the Committee for Propaganda in Enemy Countries," 17 September 1918, Northcliffe Add. Mss., 62162, f. 54, BL. Activity had expanded so much that additional quarters at the adjacent No. 16 Curzon Street were needed.

98. "Minutes of the Twelfth Meeting of the Committee for Propaganda in Enemy Countries," 1 October 1918, Northcliffe Add. Mss., 62162, f. 63, BL. For this see Stuart, *Secrets of Crewe House*, 105–33.

99. 29 August 1918 General Order, in Lutz, *Fall of the German Empire*, 1: 162. A captured copy of this order was reproduced in the 21 September 1918 *Daily Mail*.

100. "A Hindenburg Manifesto to the German People," 2 September 1918, in Lutz, *Fall of the German Empire*, 1: 163.

101. Sassoon to Northcliffe, 2 October 1918, Northcliffe Add. Mss., 62160, f. 116, BL.

102. Northcliffe to Sassoon, n.d., Northcliffe Add. Mss., 62160, ff. 113–15, BL.

103. *Daily Mail*, 7 September 1918.

104. *Daily Mail*, 20 September 1918.

105. "Minutes of the Twelfth Meeting of the Committee for Enemy Propaganda," 1 October 1918, in the Northcliffe Add. Mss., 62162, f. 64, BL. This meeting included a final report on Bulgaria by Dr. Seton-Watson.

106. Wedgwood to House, 28 September 1918, House Papers, Series I, Box 117, Sterling Library, Yale University.

107. Fraser to Northcliffe, 30 September 1918, Northcliffe Add. Mss., 62251, f. 144, BL.

108. Turner, *British Politics and the Great War*, 312.

109. 27 September 1918, Riddell diary, Add. Mss., 62982, f. 93, BL.

110. Ibid.

111. Northcliffe to Riddell, 3 October 1918, in the Riddell diaries, Add. Mss., 62982, f. 119, BL.

112. Howard Corbett, "Why Northcliffe Quarreled with Lloyd George," *World's Press News*, 5 May 1952.

113. Northcliffe to Riddell, 3 October 1918, in the Riddell diaries, Add. Mss., 62982, f. 119, BL.

114. Lord Riddell, *Lord Riddell's War Diary*, 366.

115. Koss, *The Rise and Fall of the Political Press in Britain*, 2: 334–38. This purchase, which had been discussed for some time, converted a formerly critical paper and also allowed Lloyd George

to repay two enemies by dismissing the editor, his former supporter Robert Donald, and also General Maurice, who had joined the paper at Donald's invitation.

116. "Report on the 4 October 1918 First Meeting of the Policy Committee of the British War Mission," Beaverbrook Papers, E/3/9, HLRO.

117. The German peace feelers began on 4 October and a formal Note was presented through the Swiss to Wilson on 7 October 1918. At the same time, Lloyd George and the French and Italian prime ministers were meeting in Paris. The negotiations went on for a month before the armistice was signed, in part because on 10 October a German submarine sank the Irish Mail packet *Leinster,* killing 451 passengers and crew.

118. Reports on 8, 9 October Emergency Meetings of the British War Mission Policy Committee, Beaverbrook Papers, E/3/9, HLRO.

119. "The German Offer, What it Means," *Daily Mail,* 7 October 1918.

120. *Daily Mail,* 16 October 1918.

121. "Summary of Speeches by and about Lord Northcliffe 1908–1922," Northcliffe Papers, Harmsworth Archive.

122. Beaverbrook to Northcliffe, 11 October 1918, Northcliffe Add. Mss., 62161, f. 60, BL.

123. Northcliffe to Beaverbrook, 13 October 1918, Beaverbrook Papers, E/3/9, HLRO.

124. Taylor, *Beaverbrook,* 156.

125. Steed, *Through Thirty Years,* 2: 244; Mitchell, *My Fill of Days,* 297. Steed dated this meeting 9 October and Mitchell 15 October 1918.

126. Steed, *Through Thirty Years,* 2: 244–45. Mitchell gave much the same account in *My Fill of Days,* 297.

127. "Report on British War Mission Policy Committee Meeting," 19 October 1918, Beaverbrook Papers E/3/9, HLRO.

128. *Propaganda Peace Policy,* Beaverbrook Papers, E/3/9, HLRO.

129. "Summary of Speeches by and about Lord Northcliffe 1908–1922," Northcliffe Papers, Harmsworth Archive.

130. *The History of The Times,* vol. 4, pt. 1, 383.

131. *Daily Mail,* 23, 25 October 1918.

132. Gollin, *Proconsul in Politics,* 573.

133. "Towards a United Policy," 23 October 1918.

134. "Minutes of the Thirteenth Meeting of the Committee for Propaganda in Enemy Countries," 15 October 1918, Northcliffe Add. Mss., 62162, f. 78, BL.

135. "Minutes of the Fourteenth Meeting of the Committee for Propaganda in Enemy Countries," Northcliffe Add. Mss., 62162, ff. 87–88, BL.

136. Ibid., f. 85. He continued that unless "the Home Congress had been organized and the propaganda accentuated, it was probable that we should not have had the capitulation of Austria so soon, or have had Germany isolated so quickly."

137. Northcliffe to House, 27 October 1918, House Papers, Series I, Box 83a, Sterling Library, Yale University.

138. *The History of The Times,* vol. 4, pt. 1, 383.

139. *Daily Mail,* 30 October 1918.

140. Steed, *Through Thirty Years,* 2: 249; Beaverbrook, *Men and Power,* 88–89.

141. *The History of The Times,* vol. 4, pt. 1, 385–86.

142. Northcliffe to Prime Minister, 3 November 1918, Lloyd George Papers, F/41/8/26, HLRO.

143. Almost a year after Northcliffe's death, Leo Amery reported in his diary that the king confided to him at a dinner that he had seen letters from the press lord to Lloyd George that confirmed that Northcliffe suggested he be included in the war cabinet and demanded to be made

a part of the peace commission at Paris and that Lloyd George had civilly turned down the first request and had not responded at all to the second. 17 July 1923, Amery Diary, in Barnes and Nicolson, eds., *The Leo Amery Diaries,* 1: 334.

144. David Lloyd George, *Memoirs of the Peace Conference,* 2 vols. (New Haven: Yale University Press, 1939) 1: 176.

145. Corbett, "Why Northcliffe Quarreled with Lloyd George."

146. *Parliamentary Debates,* Commons, Fifth Series, vol. 110, cols. 1780–99.

147. *The History of The Times,* vol. 4, pt. 1: 393–96, argues that someone other than Northcliffe was behind the attack.

148. Lloyd George, *Memoirs of the Peace Conference,* 1: 176. After receiving these instructions, Bonar Law dryly noted, Northcliffe "promptly came to see me at the Treasury." Robert Blake, *The Unknown Prime Minister,* 391.

149. Geddes to Harmsworth, 9 December 1953, in Pound and Harmsworth, *Northcliffe,* 682–83.

150. L. S. Amery, *My Political Life,* 2 vols. (London, 1953) 2: 180. Perhaps the wiley Lloyd George (who knew Carson already to be incensed at the attacks on Milner) incited Carson to attack Northcliffe by conveying his version of the demands.

151. *Parliamentary Debates,* Commons, Fifth Series, vol. 110, cols. 2350–52.

152. Colvin, *The Life of Lord Carson,* 3: 367.

153. Steed, *Through Thirty Years,* 2: 249. Steed took this position and added that Northcliffe never told him he wished a seat at the peace conference. Northcliffe was soon after ordered to the south of France by his doctors and had a throat operation in June 1919.

154. Sanders and Taylor, *British Propaganda During the First World War,* 238.

155. *Daily Mail,* 11 November 1918.

156. Wells, *Experiment in Autobiography,* 2: 705.

157. Northcliffe to Prime Minister, 12 November 1918, Lloyd George Papers, F/41/8/27; Lloyd George to Northcliffe, 12 November 1918, F/41/8/28, HLRO. The Welshman asked for Sir Campbell Stuart to remain at Crewe House until the end of the year to close down the operation. John Buchan served the same end at the Ministry of Information.

158. Northcliffe to Balfour, 13 November 1918, Northcliffe Add. Mss., 62153, BL.

159. Balfour to Northcliffe, 13 November 1918, Northcliffe Add. Mss., 62153, BL.

ELEVEN

"The Huns Must Pay": Politics and Peacemaking, November 1918 to June 1919

1. *Daily Mail,* 12 November 1918.

2. Pound and Harmsworth, *Northcliffe,* 675.

3. Northcliffe to Selborne, 22 November 1918, Northcliffe Add. Mss., 62344, f. 65, British Library (hereafter BL).

4. John Turner, *British Politics and the Great War,* 318. For Bonar Law's role in the continuance of the coalition, see Blake, *The Unknown Prime Minister.*

5. For a recent view of the "coupon" election, see Turner, *British Politics and the Great War.* For Lloyd George's swift reversal in his relations with the Liberal party, see Wilson, *The Downfall of the Liberal Party,* 135–83.

6. *Daily Mail,* 15 November 1918.

7. Rothermere to Lloyd George, 14 November 1918, Churchill Papers, Chartwell 2/103, Churchill College Archive, Cambridge. Lloyd George apparently gave the letter to Winston Churchill.

8. Fyfe to Northcliffe, 27 November 1918, Northcliffe Add. Mss., 62206, f. 195, BL.

9. "Message from the Chief," 28 November 1918, Ms. Eng. Hist d. 303, Bodleian Library.

10. "Message from the Chief," 18 November 1918, Ms. Eng. Hist d. 303, Bodleian Library.

11. Northcliffe to Cecil Harmsworth, 18 December 1918, Northcliffe Papers, Harmsworth Archive.

12. *Daily Mail,* 21 November 1918.

13. *Daily Mail,* 27 November 1918.

14. Northcliffe to Cecil Harmsworth, 18 December 1918, Northcliffe Papers, Harmsworth Archive.

15. *The History of The Times 1912–1948,* vol. 4, pt. 1: 448.

16. 27 November 1918 diary entry, in John Ramsden, ed., *The Political Diaries of Sir Robert Sanders, Lord Bayford 1910–1935* (London, 1984), 117.

17. Pound and Harmsworth, *Northcliffe,* 676.

18. Ibid., 676–77.

19. Riddell diary, 30 November 1918, in McEwen, ed., *The Riddell Diaries,* 250.

20. Ibid. The prime minister did not reveal any specifics of the "blackmail" attempt; however, a month later the political gossip, Moreton Frewen, informed St. Loe Strachey that Northcliffe held two compromising letters concerning the Marconi affair that he was attempting to use to secure a seat at the conference. This seems unlikely given Northcliffe's previous statements on the Marconi affair. Frewen to Strachey, 1 January 1919, Strachey Papers, S/6/4/17, House of Lords Record Office (hereafter HLRO).

21. For the struggle between the two men, see Wrench, *Geoffrey Dawson and Our Times,* 170–91 and *The History of The Times,* vol. 4, pt. 1: 446–86.

22. Northcliffe to Dawson, 30 November 1918, Northcliffe Add. Mss., 62245, f. 149, BL.

23. Northcliffe to Dawson, 1 December 1918, Northcliffe Add. Mss., 62245, f. 142, BL.

24. Marlowe to Northcliffe, 27 November 1918, Northcliffe Add. Mss., 62199, ff. 142–43, BL.

25. Fyfe to Northcliffe, 21 November 1918, Northcliffe to Fyfe, 23 November 1918, Northcliffe Add. Mss., ff. 191–92, BL.

26. Northcliffe to Dawson, 30 November 1918, Northcliffe Add. Mss., 62245, f. 149, BL.

27. Owen, *Tempestuous Journey,* 501.

28. Northcliffe to Lloyd George, 6 December 1918, Lloyd George Papers, F/41/8/30, HLRO.

29. Lloyd George to Northcliffe, 7 December 1918, Lloyd George Papers, F/41/8/31, HLRO.

30. *Daily Mail,* 12 December 1918.

31. *Daily Mail,* 9 December 1918.

32. Bunselmeyer, *The Cost of the War 1914–1919,* 133.

33. Scott to Northcliffe, 6 December 1918, Northcliffe Add. Mss., 62344, ff. 164–66, BL.

34. Northcliffe to Dawson, 17 December 1918, Northcliffe Add. Mss., 62245, f. 153, BL.

35. Northcliffe to Riddell, 17 December 1918, Northcliffe Add. Mss., 62173, f. 127, BL.

36. Riddell to Northcliffe, 31 December 1918, Northcliffe Add. Mss., 62173, f. 130, BL.

37. Derby to Northcliffe, 18 December 1918, Northcliffe Papers, Archive of *The Times* (hereafter TA).

38. Willert to Northcliffe, 15, 22 November 1918, Northcliffe Add. Mss., 62255, ff. 97–98, BL.

39. Tracy to Northcliffe, 22 November 1918, Northcliffe Add. Mss., 62164, ff. 102–3, BL.

40. Northcliffe to Tracy, 4 December 1918, Northcliffe Add. Mss., 62164, f. 104, BL.

41. "Message from the Chief," Ms. Eng. Hist d. 303, Bodleian Library.

42. Northcliffe to Keen, 29 November 1918, Northcliffe Add. Mss., 62344, ff. 103–4, BL.

43. Northcliffe to Tumulty, 24 November 1918, Northcliffe Add. Mss., 62344, f. 75, BL.

44. Northcliffe to Dawson, 18 December 1918, Northcliffe Add. Mss., 62245, f. 155, BL.

45. Northcliffe to Derby, 17 December 1918, Northcliffe Papers, TA.

46. Northcliffe to Balfour, 17 December 1918, Balfour Add. Mss., 49748, ff. 296–98, BL. Balfour to Northcliffe, 18 December 1918, Balfour Add. Mss., 49748, f. 299, BL.

47. Northcliffe to Reading, 20 December 1918, Northcliffe Add. Mss., 62156, BL.

48. *The Times,* 21 December 1918.

49. Reading to Northcliffe, 25 December 1918, Northcliffe Add. Mss., 62156, BL. On the other hand, Dawson, in whose absence the interview had been published, called it "appalling."

50. House to Northcliffe, 21 December 1918, House Papers, Series I, Box 83a.

51. Northcliffe to House, 3 January 1919, House Papers, Series I, Box 83a.

52. *Daily Mail,* 30 December 1918. Fisher, a Conservative M.P. and president of Local Government Board since June 1917, had been in charge of organizing the new electoral register after the passing of the Reform Act of 1918. Lloyd George felt Fisher had mismanaged this duty. Fisher was elevated to the peerage as Lord Downham to remove him. Robert Blake, *The Unknown Prime Minister,* 381–83.

53. Northcliffe to Rothermere, 31 December 1918, Northcliffe Papers, Harmsworth Archive.

54. *Daily Mail,* 3 January 1919.

55. Fyfe, *Northcliffe: An Intimate Biography,* 259–60.

56. Ibid.

57. Northcliffe to Caird, 12 January 1918, in Pound and Harmsworth, *Northcliffe,* 693.

58. Northcliffe to Beattie, 19 January 1919, Northcliffe Add. Mss., 62203, f. 26, BL.

59. Martin Gilbert, *Winston S. Churchill,* vol. 4, 191.

60. Northcliffe to Dawson, 30 January 1919, Northcliffe Add. Mss., 62245, f. 169, BL.

61. Northcliffe to Dawson, 12 January 1919, Northcliffe Add. Mss., 62245, f. 161, BL.

62. Northcliffe to Dawson, 25 January 1919, Northcliffe Add. Mss., 62245, ff. 165–66, BL.

63. Hughes had been unhappy since November that the armistice had been arranged on the basis of Wilson's Fourteen Points. Bunselmeyer, *Cost of the War,* 88.

64. Northcliffe to Smith, 5 February 1919, Northcliffe Add. Mss., 62345, ff. 51–52, BL.

65. 30 January 1919, in McEwen, *Riddell Diaries,* 256.

66. Harold Nicolson, *Peacemaking 1919* (London, 1933), 19–20, 60.

67. Stuart to Northcliffe, 28 January 1919, Northcliffe Add. Mss., 62240, ff. 34–35, BL.

68. Northcliffe to House, 26 January 1919, House Papers, Series I, Box 83a.

69. House to Northcliffe, 29 January 1919, House Papers, Series I, Box 83a.

70. Steed, *Through Thirty Years,* 2: 259–60.

71. For an example of this, see Steed to Northcliffe, 12 March 1919, Northcliffe Add. Mss., 62246B, ff. 77–78, BL.

72. For House in 1919, see Inga Floto, *Colonel House in Paris: A Study of American Policy at the Paris Peace Conference 1919* (Copenhagen, 1972).

73. Auchincloss diary, 28 March 1919, in Floto, *Colonel House in Paris,* 197, n. 249.

74. Steed to Northcliffe, 15 March 1919, Northcliffe Add. Mss., 62246B, ff. 79–80, BL.

75. Baker diary, 17 April 1919, in Floto, *Colonel House in Paris,* 198.

76. Pound and Harmsworth, *Northcliffe,* 710.

77. Humphrey Davy to Marlowe, 8 April 1919, Northcliffe Add. Mss., 62199, f. 161, BL.

78. Riddell diary, 5 April 1919, in McEwen, *Riddell Diaries,* 265.

79. Blake, *The Unknown Prime Minister,* 407.

80. Pound and Harmsworth, *Northcliffe,* 710.

81. For Lloyd George's version of the "Parliamentary Revolt," see his *Memoirs of the Peace Conference.*

82. Northcliffe to Jones, 13 April 1919, Northcliffe Add. Mss., 62196, ff. 110–11, BL.

83. Pound and Harmsworth, *Northcliffe,* 710–11.

84. Northcliffe to Rothermere, 10 April 1919, in Pound and Harmsworth, *Northcliffe,* 712.

85. 9 April 1919, in McEwen, *Riddell Diaries,* 266–67.

86. A. J. P. Taylor, ed., *Lloyd George: A Diary by Frances Stevenson,* 180. Miss Stevenson recorded that the prime minister told her that "N is intent on trying to oust him so he … is going to attack

him now in order that people may know that N's motives are purely personal, & that he may be descredited from the outset. He told me part of his speech before he left, & I must say it is very clever and amusing & will make N very sorry for himself."

87. Quoted in Howard Alcock, *Portrait of a Decision: The Council of Four and the Treaty of Versailles* (London, 1972), 206. Bottomley, the owner of *John Bull*, had also been elected in December to a seat in the Commons.

88. *Parliamentary Debates*, Commons, 5th Series, vol. 114, cols. 2951–53.

89. Ibid.

90. Alcock, *Portrait of a Decision*, 208.

91. Taylor, *Lloyd George: A Diary by Frances Stevenson*, 180.

92. Riddell Diary, 4 May 1919, in McEwen, *Riddell Diaries*, 272.

93. Oliver, Viscount Esher, ed., *Journals and Letters of Reginald Viscount Esher*, 4: 231.

94. Steed, *Through Thirty Years*, 2: 321–22.

95. Steed to Northcliffe, 18 April 1919, Northcliffe Add. Mss., 62246B, ff. 92–94, BL.

96. Northcliffe to Steed, 19 April 1919, Steed Papers, TA.

97. "Lord Northcliffe and the Prime Minister," 22 April 1919, Northcliffe Add. Mss., 62199, ff. 181, BL.

98. Cecil Harmsworth to Northcliffe, 17 April 1919, Northcliffe Papers, Harmsworth Archive.

99. Northcliffe to Cecil Harmsworth, 19 April 1919, Northcliffe Papers, Harmsworth Archive.

100. Bullock to Northcliffe, 6 May 1919, Northcliffe Add. Mss., 62209, ff. 21–23, BL.

101. For a recent work in this vein, see A. Lentin, *Guilt at Versailles: Lloyd George and the Pre-History of Appeasement* (London, 1984).

TWELVE:
Conclusion: Politicians, the Press, and Propaganda

1. When Northcliffe's own roof proved unsuitable to building a shelter from the summer heat, the duke, his Carlton Gardens neighbor, agreed to allow this.

2. Christopher Addison, *Politics from Within*, vol. 1, *1911–1918* (London: Herbert Jenkins, 1925), 62.

3. Lloyd George, *War Memoirs*, 3: 558–62.

4. Winston Churchill, *The World Crisis*, 1: 246.

5. Ibid., 1: 251.

6. Stanley Morison, "Personality and Diplomacy in Anglo-American Relations, 1917," 453–55; Seymour, *The Intimate Papers of Colonel House*, 3: 87.

Selected Bibliography

Primary Sources

PRIVATE PAPERS

Asquith Manuscripts. Bodleian Library, Oxford University.

Balfour Manuscripts. British Library, London.

Beaverbrook Manuscripts. House of Lords Record Office, London.

Bonar Law Manuscripts. House of Lords Record Office, London.

Burnham Manuscripts. Imperial War Museum, London.

Robert Cecil Manuscripts. British Library, London.

Churchill Manuscripts. Churchill College Archive, Cambridge University.

Dawson Manuscripts. Bodleian Library, Oxford Univeristy; Archive of *The Times*, London.

French Manuscripts. Imperial War Museum, London.

Gardiner Manuscripts. British Library of Economic and Political Science, London.

Garvin Manuscripts. Ransom Humanities Research Center, The University of Texas at Austin.

Haig Manuscripts. National Library of Scotland, Edinburgh.

Hardinge of Penshurst Manuscripts. Cambridge University Library.

House Manuscripts. Sterling Library, Yale University.

Kitchener Manuscripts. Public Record Office, London.

Lloyd George Manuscripts. House of Lords Record Office, London.

Milner Manuscripts. Bodleian Library, Oxford University.

Northcliffe Manuscripts. British Library, Archive of *The Times*, Harmsworth Archive, London.

Reading Manuscripts. British Library Oriental and Indian Collections, London.

Rennell of Rodd Manuscripts. Bodleian Library, Oxford University.

Repington Manuscripts. Archive of *The Times,* London.
Riddell Diaries. British Library, London.
Robertson Manuscripts. Liddell Hart Center, King's College, London.
Spring Rice Manuscripts. Churchill College Archive, Cambridge University.
Steed Manuscripts. Archive of *The Times,* London.
Strachey Manuscripts. House of Lords Record Office, London.
Wedgwood Manuscripts. Imperial War Museum, London.
Willert Manuscripts. Sterling Library, Yale University.
Wiseman Manuscripts. Sterling Library, Yale University.

NEWSPAPERS

Brooklyn Daily Eagle
Chicago Tribune
Cleveland Press
Daily Mail (London)
Daily News (London)
Detroit Free Press
Evening News (London)
London Globe
Kansas City Star
Kansas City Times
Manchester Guardian
New York Sun
New York Times
Philadelphia Journal Ledger
St. Louis Post-Dispatch
The Times (London)
Weekly Dispatch (London)

PERIODICALS

Atlantic Monthly
The Century
Current Opinion
The Forum
The Nation
New Republic
North American Review

COLLECTIONS OF PRINTED PRIMARY DOCUMENTS

Barnes, John and Nicholson, David, eds. *The Leo Amery Diaries,* vol. 1, *1896–1929.* London: Hutchinson, 1980.

Blake, Robert. *The Private Papers of Douglas Haig 1914–1919.* London: Eyre & Spottiswoode, 1952.

Boyce, George, ed. *The Crisis of British Unionism: Lord Selborne's Domestic Political Papers, 1885–1922.* London: The Historian Press, 1987.

Brett, Maurice, ed. *Journals and Letters of Reginald Viscount Esher.* London: Ivor Nicholson & Watson Limited, 1934, 1938.

Brex, Twells. *"Scaremongerings" from the Daily Mail 1896–1914.* London: Daily Mail, 1915.

Brock, Michael and Eleanor, eds. *H. H. Asquith: Letters to Venetia Stanley.* Oxford: Oxford University Press, 1982.

Clark, Alan, ed. *"A Good Innings": The Private Papers of Viscount Lee of Fareham.* London: John Murray, 1974.

Cronon, E. David, ed. *The Cabinet Diaries of Josephus Daniels 1913–1921.* Lincoln: University of Nebraska Press, 1963.

David, Edward, ed. *Inside Asquith's Cabinet: From the Diaries of Charles Hobhouse.* London: John Murray, 1977.

Graves, Charles. *Mr. Punch's History of the War.* London: Cassell and Company, Ltd., 1919.

Gwynn, Stephen, ed. *The Anvil of War: Letters Between F. S. Oliver and His Brother 1914–1918.* London: Macmillan and Co., Limited, 1936.

———, ed. *The Letters and Friendships of Sir Cecil Spring Rice.* Boston: Houghton Mifflin Co., 1929.

Hamilton, General Sir Ian. *Gallipoli Diary.* New York: George Doran, 1920.

Hendrick, Burton, ed. *The Life and Letters of Walter H. Page.* New York: Doubleday, Page & Co., 1925.

Lennox, Lady Algernon Gordon, ed. *The Diary of Lord Bertie of Thame 1914–1918.* London: Hodder and Stoughton, 1924.

Link Arthur. *The Papers of Woodrow Wilson,* vols. 40–44. Princeton: Princeton University Press, 1982–83.

Lord Riddell. *Lord Riddell's Intimate Diary of the Peace Conference and After 1918–1923.* New York: Reynal & Hitchcock, 1934.

———. *Lord Riddell's War Diary 1914–1918.* London: Ivor Nicholson & Watson Limited, 1933.

Marder, Arthur, ed. *Fear God and Dread Nought: The Correspondence of Admiral of the Fleet Lord Fisher of Kilverstone,* vol. 3, London: Jonathan Cape, 1959.

McEwen, J. M., ed. *The Riddell Diaries 1908–1922.* London: The Athlone Press, 1986.

Seymour, Charles, ed. *The Intimate Papers of Colonel House.* Boston: Houghton Mifflin Co., 1928.

Taylor, A. J. P., ed. *Lloyd George: A Diary by Frances Stevenson.* New York: Harper and Row, 1971.

Wilson, Trevor, ed. *The Political Diaries of C. P. Scott 1911–1928.* Ithaca, New York: Cornell University Press, 1970.

Woodward, David, ed. *The Military Correspondence of Field-Marshal Sir William Robertson, Chief of the Imperial General Staff, December 1915–February 1918.* London: The Bodley Head, 1989.

Addison, Christopher. *Politics from Within*. London: Herbert Jenkins Limited, 1925.

Amery, L. S. *My Political Life*. London: Hutchinson, 1953.

Asquith, Herbert Henry. *Memories and Reflections, 1852–1927*. Boston: Little Brown, 1928.

Buchan, John. *Memory Hold the Door*. London: Hodder & Stoughton Ltd., 1941.

Count Bernstorff. *My Three Years in America*. New York: Scribner's, 1920.

Carson, William. *Northcliffe, Britain's Man of Power*. New York: Dodge Publishing Co., 1918.

Viscount Cecil of Chelwood. *All the Way*. London: Hodder and Stoughton, 1949.

Charteris, John. *At G. H. Q*. London: Cassell and Company, Ltd., 1931.

Clarke, Tom. *My Northcliffe Diary*. New York: Cosmopolitan Book Corp., 1931.

Cook, Sir Edward. *The Press in War-Time*. London: Macmillan, 1920.

French of Ypres, Field-Marshal Viscount. *1914*. London: Constable and Company, 1919.

Fyfe, Henry Hamilton. *Northcliffe, An Intimate Diary*. New York: Macmillan, 1930.

Hammerton, J. A. *With Northcliffe in Fleet Street*. London: Hutchinson & Co., 1925.

Jeffries, J. M. N. *Front Everywhere*. London: Hutchinson & Co., 1935.

King, Cecil. *Strictly Personal*. London: Weidenfeld and Nicolson, 1969.

Lloyd George, David. *Memoirs of the Peace Conference*. 1939; reprint, Howard Fertig: New York, 1972.

————. *War Memoirs of David Lloyd George*. Boston: Little, Brown and Co., 1934.

Lord Beaverbrook. *Men and Power 1917–1918*. London: Collins, 1956.

————. *Politicians and the War 1914–1916*. London: Collins, 1960.

Lord Esher. *The Tragedy of Lord Kitchener*. New York: E. P. Dutton and Company, 1921.

Lord Hankey. *The Supreme Command 1914–1918*. London: George Allen and Unwin Ltd., 1961.

Lord Hardinge of Penhurst. *Old Diplomacy*. London: John Murray, 1947.

Lord Northcliffe. *Lord Northcliffe's War Book*. New York: George H. Doran Co., 1917.

General Ludendorff. *My War Memories*. London: Hutchinson & Co., 1919.

Lytton, Neville. *The Press and the General Staff*. London: W. Collins Sons & Co. LTD., 1920.

MacDonagh, Michael. *In London During the Great War: The Diary of a Journalist*. London: Eyre and Spottiswoode, 1935.

McAdoo, William G. *Crowded Years*. Boston: Houghton Mifflin Co., 1931.

Mitchell, Sir Peter Chalmers. *My Fill of Days*. London: Faber and Faber, 1937.

Pankhurst, E. Sylvia. *The Home Front*. 1932; reprint, London; The Cresset Library, 1987.

Pemberton, Max. *Lord Northcliffe, A Memoir*. London: Hodder and Stoughton, 1922.

Repington, Charles à Court. *The First World War 1914–1918*. Boston: Houghton Mifflin Co., 1920.

Rhodes James, Robert. *Memoirs of a Conservative: J. C. C. Davidson's Memoirs and Papers*. London: Macmillan, 1969.

Rinehart, Mary Roberts. *My Story*. New York: Farrar and Rinehart, 1931.

Samuel, The Rt. Hon. Viscount. *Memoirs*. London: The Cresset Press, 1945.

Steed, Henry Wickham. *Through Thirty Years 1892–1922*. New York: Doubleday, Page and Co., 1924.

Stuart, Sir Campbell. *Opportunity Knocks Once*. London: Collins, 1952.

———. *Secrets of Crewe House: The Story of a Famous Campaign*. London: Hodder and Stoughton, 1920.

Swinton, Sir Ernest. *Eyewitness*. 1932; reprint, New York: Arno Press, 1972.

———. *Over My Shoulder: The Autobiography of Major-General Sir Ernest Swinton*. Oxford: George Ronald, 1951.

Wells, H. G. *Experiment in Autobiography*. London: Victor Gollancz Ltd., 1934.

Who's Who in the British War Mission to the United States of America 1917. New York: Edward J. Clode, 1917.

Wile, Frederic William. *News Is Where You Find It*. New York: Bobbs-Merrill, 1939.

Willert, Sir Arthur. *Washington and Other Memories*. Boston: Houghton Mifflin Co., 1972.

Williams, Valentine. *World of Action*. Boston: Houghton Mifflin, 1938.

Wrench, John Evelyn. *Struggle 1914–1920*. London: Ivor Nicholson & Watson, 1935.

Secondary Works

Adams, John Coldwell. *Seated with the Mighty: A Biography of Sir Gilbert Parker*. Ottawa: Borealis Press, 1979.

Adams, R. J. Q. *Arms and the Wizard, Lloyd George and the Ministry of Munitions, 1915–1916*. College Station: Texas A&M Press, 1978.

Adams, R. J. Q. and Philip Poirier. *The Conscription Controversy in Great Britain, 1900–1918*. London: Macmillan, 1987.

Ayerst, David. *Garvin of the Observer*. London: Croom Helm, 1985.

Blake, Robert. *The Unknown Prime Minister: The Life and Times of Andrew Bonar Law 1858–1923*. London: Eyre & Spottiswoode, 1955.

Bourne, Richard. *Lords of Fleet Street: The Harmsworth Dynasty*. London: Unwin, 1990.

Brendon, Piers. *The Life and Death of the Press Barons*. New York: Atheneum, 1983.

Briggs, Asa. *The Birth of Broadcasting*. London: Oxford University Press, 1961.

Brown, Lucy. *Victorian News and Newspapers*. Oxford: Clarendon Press, 1985.

Bruntz, George. *Allied Propaganda and the Collapse of the German Empire in 1918*. Stanford: Stanford University Press, 1938.

Burgwyn, H. James. *The Legend of the Mutilated Victory: Italy, the Great War, and the Paris Peace Conference, 1915–1919*. London: Greenwood Press, 1993.

Burk, Kathleen. *Britain, America and the Sinews of War 1914–1918*. Boston: Houghton Mifflin Co., 1985.

Burton, David. *Cecil Spring Rice, A Diplomat's Life*. London: Associated University Presses, 1990.

Calder, Kenneth. *Britain and the Origins of the New Europe 1914–1918*. London: Cambridge University Press, 1978.

Campbell, John. *F. E. Smith, First Earl of Birkenhead*. London: Jonathan Cape, 1983.

Cassar, George. *Kitchener: Architect of Victory*. London: William Kimber, 1977.

Churchill, Randolph S. *Lord Derby: King of Lancashire*. New York: G. P. Putnam's Sons, 1959.

Churchill, Winston. *The World Crisis 1916–1918*. New York: Scribners, 1927.

Clarke, Tom. *Northcliffe in History*. London: Hutchison, 1952.

Colvin, Ian. *The Life of Lord Carson*. London: Victor Gollancz Ltd, 1936.

Cooper, Duff. *Haig*. New York: Doubleday, Doran, 1936.

Cudlipp, Hugh. *The Prerogative of the Harlot: Press Barons & Power*. London: Bodley Head, 1980.

Curran, James and Jean Seaton. *Power without Responsibility—The Press and Broadcasting in Britain*. London: Macmillan, 1981.

Dilks, David. *Neville Chamberlain*, vol. 1, *1869–1929*. Cambridge: Cambridge University Press, 1984.

Doerries, Reinhard. *Imperial Challenge: Ambassador Count Bernstorff and German-American Relations, 1908–1917*. Chapel Hill: University of North Carolina Press, 1989.

Dutton, David. *Austen Chamberlain: Gentleman in Politics*. London: Ross Anderson Publications, 1985.

———. *Simon: A Political Biography of Sir John Simon*. London: Aurum Press, 1992.

Ferris, Paul. *The House of Northcliffe, The Harmsworths of Fleet Street*. London: Weidenfeld and Nicholson, 1971.

Fowler, W. B. *British-American Relations 1917–1918, The Role of Sir William Wiseman*. Princeton: Princeton University Press, 1969.

Fraser, Peter. *Lord Esher: A Political Biography*. London: Hart-Davis, MacGibbon, 1973.

Gilbert, Bentley. *David Lloyd George: A Political Life, Organizer of Victory 1912–1916*. Columbus: Ohio State University Press, 1992.

Gilbert, Martin. *Winston S. Churchill*, vol. 4, *1916–1922 The Stricken World*. Boston: Houghton Mifflin, 1975.

Gilmour, David. *Curzon*. London: John Murray, 1994.

Gollin, A.M. *Proconsul in Politics: A Study of Lord Milner in Opposition and in Power*. New York: Macmillan, 1964.

Grieves, Keith. *The Politics of Manpower, 1914–1918*. Manchester: Manchester University Press, 1988.

———. *Sir Eric Geddes: Business and Government in War and Peace*. Manchester: Manchester University Press, 1989.

Grigg, John. *Lloyd George: From Peace to War 1912–1916*. London: Methuen, 1985.

Hamilton, Ian B. M. *The Happy Warrior: A Life of General Sir Ian Hamilton*. London: Cassell, 1966.

Hanak, Harry. *Great Britain and Austria-Hungary During the First World War: A Study in the Formation of Public Opinion*. London: Oxford University Press, 1962.

Hazlehurst, Cameron. *Politicians at War July 1914 to May 1915: A Prologue to the Triumph of Lloyd George*. London: Jonathan Cape, 1971.

Holmes, Richard. *The Little Field-Marshal: Sir John French*. London: Jonathan Cape, 1981.

Jenkins, Roy. *Asquith*. London: Collins, 1964.

Judd, Denis. *Lord Reading*. London: Weidenfeld and Nicholson, 1982.

Koss, Stephen. *Fleet Street Radical: A. G. Gardiner and the Daily News*. London: Archon Books, 1973.

———. *The Rise and Fall of the Political Press in Britain*. Chapel Hill: University of North Carolina Press, 1981.

Lee, Alan J. *The Origins of the Popular Press in England 1855–1914*. London: Croom Helm, 1976.

Link, Arthur. *Wilson the Diplomatist*. Baltimore: Johns Hopkins Press, 1957.

Lownie, Andrew. *John Buchan: The Presbyterian Cavalier*. London: Constable, 1995.

Lutz, Ralph, ed. *Fall of the German Empire 1914–1918*. Stanford: Stanford University Press, 1932.

Lyddon, W. G. *British War Missions to the United States 1914–1918*. London: Oxford University Press, 1938.

Martin, Lawrence. *Peace without Victory: Woodrow Wilson and the British Liberals*. New York: Kennikat Press, 1973.

Messinger, Gary. *British Propaganda and the State in the First World War*. Manchester: Manchester University Press, 1992.

Morris, A. J. A. *The Scaremongers. The Advocacy of War and Rearmament 1896–1914*. London: Routledge and Kegan Paul, 1984.

Peterson, H. C. *Propaganda for War: The Campaign Against American Neutrality, 1914–1917*. Norman: University of Oklahoma Press, 1939.

Petrie, Sir Charles. *The Life and Letters of the Right Hon. Sir Austen Chamberlain*. London: Cassell and Company Ltd., 1940.

Pound, Reginald and Geoffrey Harmsworth. *Northcliffe*. London: Cassell, 1959.

Rappaport, Armin. *The British Press and Wilsonian Neutrality*. London: Oxford University Press, 1951.

Raymond, E. T. *Uncensored Celebrities*. New York: Henry Holt and Co., 1919.

Read, James. *Atrocity Propaganda 1914–1919*. New Haven: Yale University Press, 1941.

Roskill, Stephen. *Hankey: Man of Secrets 1877–1918*. London: Collins, 1970.

Rothwell, V. H. *British War Aims and Peace Diplomacy 1914–1918*. Oxford: Clarendon Press, 1971.

Sanders, M. L. and Philip M. Taylor. *British Propaganda During the First World War 1914–1918*. London: Macmillan, 1982.

Simpson, A. W. *In the Highest Degree Odious: Detention without Trial in Wartime Britain*. Oxford: Clarendon Press, 1992.

Siney, Marion. *The Allied Blockade of Germany 1914–1916*. Ann Arbor: University of Michigan Press, 1957.

Sommer, Dudley. *Haldane of Cloan: His Life and Times, 1856–1928*. London: George Allen & Unwin, 1960.

Spender, J. A. *Weetman Pearson First Viscount Cowdray 1856–1927*. London: Cassell and Company Ltd., 1930.

Squires, J. D. *British Propaganda at Home and in the United States from 1914–1917*. Cambridge: Harvard University Press, 1935.

Stephenson, David. *The First World War and International Politics*. Oxford: Oxford University Press, 1988.

Taylor, A. J. P. *Beaverbrook*. New York: Simon and Schuster, 1972.

———. *Politics in Wartime*. London: Hamish Hamilton, 1964.

Taylor, S. J. *The Great Outsiders: Northcliffe, Rothermere and the Daily Mail*. London: Weidenfeld & Nicholson, 1996.

The Times. The History of the Times. New York: Macmillan, 1947, 1952.

Turner, John. *British Politics and the Great War*. New Haven: Yale University Press, 1992.

Turner, L. C. F. *Origins of the First World War*. New York: W. W. Norton & Company, 1970.

Vaughan, Stephen. *Holding Fast the Inner Lines: Democracy, Nationalism and the Committee on Public Information*. Chapel Hill: University of North Carolina Press, 1980.

Vincent, C. Paul. *The Politics of Hunger: The Allied Blockade of Germany, 1915–1919*. Athens: Ohio University Press, 1985.

Wiener, Joel, ed. *Papers for the Millions, The New Journalism in Britain 1850–1914*. New York: Greenwood Press, 1988.

Willert, Sir Arthur. *The Road to Safety, A Study in Anglo-American Relations*. London: Derek Verschoyle, 1952.

Wilson, R. Macnair. *Lord Northcliffe: A Study*. Philadelphia: J. B. Lippincott Company, 1927.

Wilson, Trevor. *The Downfall of the Liberal Party 1914–1935*. Ithaca, New York: Cornell University Press, 1966.

———. *The Myriad Faces of War: Britain and the Great War, 1914–1918*. Cambridge: Polity Press, 1986.

Woodward, David. *Lloyd George and the Generals*. London: Associated University Presses, 1983.

———. *Trial by Friendship: Anglo-American Relations 1917–1918*. Lexington: University of Kentucky Press, 1993.

Wrench, John Evelyn. *Alfred Lord Milner: The Man of No Illusions 1854–1925*. London: Eyre and Spottiswoode Ltd., 1958.

———. *Geoffrey Dawson and Our Times*. London: Hutchinson, 1953.

Zebel, Sydney. *Balfour, A Political Biography*. Cambridge: Cambridge University Press, 1973.

ARTICLES

Fair, John, "Politicians, Historians and the War: A Reassessment of the Political Crisis of December 1916," *Journal of Modern History* 49, 3 (September 1977 On Demand Supplement): D1329–43.

Fraser, Peter, "The British 'Shells Scandal' of 1915," *The Journal of Canadian History* 18, 1 (1983): 69–86.

Gollin, Alfred, "Freedom or Control in the First World War," *Historical Reflections* 2, 2 (1975): 135–55.

Hopkins, Deian, "Domestic Censorship in the First World War," *Journal of Contemporary History* 5, 4 (1970): 151–69.

Lovelace, Colin, "British Press Censorship During the First World War," in George Boyce, James Curran, and Pauline Wingate, eds., *Newspaper History from the Seventeenth Century to the Present Day*. London: Constable, 1978.

McEwen, J. M., "'Brass-Hats' and the British Press During the First World War," *Journal of Canadian History* 18, 1 (1983): 43–67.

———, "The National Press During the First World War: Ownership and Circulation," *Journal of Contemporary History* 17 (1982): 459–86.

———, "Northcliffe and Lloyd George at War, 1914–1918," *Historical Journal* 24, 3 (1981): 651–72.

———, "The Press and the Fall of Asquith," *Historical Journal* 21, 4 (1978): 863–83.

———, "The Struggle for Mastery in Britain: Lloyd George Versus Asquith, December 1916," *Journal of British Studies* 1, 18 (Fall 1978): 131–56.

Morison, Stanley, "Personality and Diplomacy in Anglo-American Relations 1917," in Richard Pares and A. J. P. Taylor, eds., *Essays Presented to Sir Lewis Namier*. London: Macmillan, 1956.

Pierce, Robert N., "Lord Northcliffe: Trans-Atlantic Influences," *Journalism Monographs* 40 (August, 1975): 1–41.

Towle, Philip, "The Debate on Wartime Censorship in Britain," in Brian Bond and Ian Roy, eds., *War and Society*. New York: Holmes and Meier Publishers Inc., 1975.

Index

Addison, Christopher, 239
Air Board, 93, 137, 163–64
Air Coordination Committee, 92–93
Air defenses, 90–91, 135–37
Air power, development of, 14
Air services: division of, 90–93; Northcliffe's
    advice to, 92, 93, 137
Aitken, William Maxwell. *See* Beaverbrook,
    Lord Amery, L. S., 19, 67, 176
Answers, 6, 7, 11–12
Arnold, Matthew, 4
Asquith, Herbert Henry, viii, 2, 10, 21, 29, 35,
    42, 174, 195, 210, 227; and Amiens dis-
    patches incident, 30–31; and conscription,
    73, 74–75, 80, 97; and Derby recruitment
    scheme, 82; fall of coalition government,
    113–15, 117–18, 121–22, 239; fall of Liberal
    government, 64–65; formation of coalition
    government, 62; and Irish Question, 19;
    and Kitchener's appointment, 25–26; on
    munitions shortages, 56; Northcliffe's
    criticism of war policies, 44–45, 49, 51,
    64–65, 66, 78, 87, 89, 97–99; on press
    freedom, 86–87; resignation of, 115, 117
Asquith, Margot, 81, 85, 96, 101, 104, 117, 119,
    258n.69
Astor, Waldorf, 112, 133
Atlantic Monthly, 149
At the War (Northcliffe), 68
Auchincloss, Gordon, 231–32
Audacious, 18, 34
Austria-Hungary: British propaganda in,
    186–88; collapse of, 213

Baker, Ray Stannard, 232
Baldwin, Stanley, 205
Balfour, Arthur, 57, 62, 70, 122, 135, 176;
    American mission of, 141, 144, 146, 149;
    and enemy propaganda, 187, 198, 199,
    202–3; as foreign secretary, 116, 226; on
    naval preparedness, 15–16; as prime
    minister, 12–13
Barnes, George, 220
Battenberg, Louis (Milford Haven), 37, 175,
    254n.121
Battles and campaigns: Arras, 142; Aubers
    Ridge, 57, 59; Cambrai, 177–78, 180–81;
    Caporetto, 170; Festubert, 57; Flanders,
    170; Jutland, 100; Marne, 32; Mons, 29;
    Neuve Chappelle, 50, 51, 55; for Paris, 199;
    Somme, 103, 104, 106, 111, 112; Verdun, 94,
    112; Ypres (First), 34, 46. *See also*
    Dardanelles campaign
Beattie, Charles, 54, 183, 228
Beaverbrook, Lord, vii, 1, 64, 117, 121, 190,
    193, 200, 201; dispute with Foreign Office,
    202–3; in information ministry, 182, 192,
    196, 202, 204, 205–6, 211; in Northcliffe
    appointment to propaganda post, 181–82;
    on Northcliffe's plan to replace Lloyd
    George, 207–8
Bernhardi, Friedrich von, 17
Bernstorff, Count, 272n.12
Bertie, Lord, 95, 105
Bicycling News, 6
Birdwood, General, 104
Birkenhead, Lord. *See* Smith, F. E.

Birmingham Post, 60
Blatchford, Robert, 15, 40
Boer War, 12
Bonar Law, Andrew: 13, 22, 29, 46, 57, 91, 112, 115, 145, 150, 195, 200, 247n.63; in Asquith coalition, 63, 90; in coalition of 1918, 219; and conscription, 262n.44; on Lloyd George–Northcliffe conflict, 235, 237; on Northcliffe, 98; rejection of negotiated peace, 176–77; in War Cabinet, 117; and war loans, 124, 156
Bonham Carter, Maurice, 115, 181
Borden, Robert, 137, 167–68
Bourne, J. M., x
Bourne, Richard, viii–ix
Boy's Home Journal, 6
Brade, Reginald, 27, 45, 131
Brest-Litovsk, treaty of, 179, 186
Brex, Twells, 39
Briand, Aristide, 94, 107, 128
Brisbane, Arthur, 34, 39, 88, 173
British Expeditionary Force (BEF): ban on correspondents with, 27–28; decision to dispatch to France, 25; embarkation of, 26, 27, 29; and munitions shortage, 49, 50, 51, 56–65, 239; retreat from Mons, 29, 30. *See also* Battles and campaigns
British War Mission to United States, x, 125; appointment of Northcliffe, 144–47, 150–51; under Balfour, 141, 149, 160; British ambassador's interference with, 125–26, 152–53, 159; closing of, 225; contributions of Northcliffe, 168–69, 240; in cooperation with allies, 148, 156; departure of Northcliffe for U.S., 150; financial assistance negotiations of, 155–57, 160, 281n.77; and food procurement, 157–58; and Irish-American relations, 148–49, 158–59; London headquarters, 178–79, 192, 193, 289n.140; and munitions procurement, 157; in New York, 154; and oil, steel, and metal procurement, 158; publicity efforts of, 151–52, 160–68; and ship confiscation issue, 159–60; tasks of, 150; and Wilson, 149, 151, 154, 155, 161, 162
British Weekly, 1, 91
Brooklyn Daily Eagle, 152
Buchan, John, 127–28, 160, 174, 181
Buckmaster, Stanley, 31, 33–34, 35, 121, 181
Bulgaria: armistice with, 209; British propaganda in, 199
Buller, General, 12
Bullock, W. F., 34, 47, 62, 236
Burbidge, Richard, 119

Burton, Pomeroy, 126–27, 139, 140–42, 190, 273n.24
Butler, Geoffrey, 160, 164, 168, 174
Butt, Alfred, 119, 124
Byng, Julian, 104, 106

Caird, Andrew, 178, 207, 228
Carson, Edward: 22, 75, 76, 78, 94, 112, 114, 173, 185, 243, 269n.72; at Admiralty, 119, 124, 134, 135, 136–37; attack on Northcliffe, 215–16; and Irish question, 17, 18, 249n.100; and Northcliffe, 68–69; resignation from Asquith government, 77; resignation from Lloyd George government, 179
Carson, William, viii
Carter, Kate, 165
Cecil, Robert, 116, 122, 126, 144
Censorship: and Amiens dispatches incident, 30–32; circumventing by quoting foreign press accounts, 35; under Defense of the Realm Act (DORA), 28, 86, 121; French, 26, 28, 43–44; House of Commons debate on, 33–34; naval, 31, 34, 135; Northcliffe's conflicts over, 29, 32, 34–36, 43–44, 50; under Official Secrets Act, 27, 28; at Peace Conference, 224–25, 227; and Press Bureau clearances, 28; recruitment problems linked to, 35–36; of Russian correspondents, 71; and Simon's attack on patriotism of Northcliffe press, 83–86; voluntary system of, 27
Chamberlain, Austen, 3, 132, 173; appointment to war cabinet, 190–91, 193; attack on press power, 184–86, 241
Chamberlain, Joseph, 8, 13
Chamberlain, Neville, 119, 131–33
Charteris, John, 103, 105, 126, 128, 177, 178, 183, 287n.68
Chicago Herald, 166, 173–74
Chicago Tribune, 139–40, 166, 175
Churchill, Clementine, 85
Churchill, Randolph, 7
Churchill, Winston, ix, 1, 10, 25, 35, 51, 62, 117, 118, 165; and Dardanelles campaign, 43, 49; on fall of Liberal government, 64, 66; and naval censorship, 31; and Northcliffe, 10, 101–2, 229; on Northcliffe's influence, 66, 240, 244; press attacks on, 34; on Somme offensive, 104
Civil Aerial Transport Committee, 137, 144, 145
Clemenceau, Georges, 94–95, 128, 176, 230, 232
Coffin, Howard, 141

Comedy Cuts, 6

Committee on Public Information (CPI), 153, 161

Conscription: extension of, 99, 102, 111; Liberal supporters of, 73–74; for married men, 95–97; Northcliffe's campaign for, 36, 67, 72–73, 75; opponents of, 74, 75; for single men, 83, 87

Continental Daily Mail, 14, 17, 23, 32, 46

Cook, Edward, 44

Corbett, Howard, 214

Cowdray, Lord, 133, 137, 163, 173

Creel, George, 153

Crewe, Lord, 80

Cudlipp, Hugh, ix

Curnock, George, 36, 199, 230

Current Opinion, 161

Curtin, Thomas, 71

Curtis, Cyrus, 177

Curzon, Lord, 10, 68, 70, 93, 117, 150, 184, 200

Daily Chronicle, 210

Daily Express, 220

Daily Mail, vii–viii; air flight prizes of, 14; on air services, 90–91, 92–93; on alcohol prohibition plan, 54; on armistice request, 211; and Asquith government, campaign against, 44–45, 55–56, 58, 78, 113, 118; and Asquith government, fall of, 115–16, 121–22; battlefront coverage of, 30, 32, 34, 35, 188, 199; and Berlin edition proposal, 17; Boer War coverage of, 12; on bombardment of civilians, 40; on Carson's resignation, 77; conscription campaign of, 67, 72, 75, 96–97, 99; on Dardanelles evacuation, 80; on election of 1918, 220, 224, 227; European crisis coverage of, 18, 20–22; on food shortages, 123, 124, 142, 143; German "atrocity" reports in, 37; on German propaganda in U.S., 37–38, 47–48; layout of, 249n.102; and Lloyd George government, 118, 119; on *Lusitania* sinking, 48; mass audience of, 2–3, 9; on munitions shortage, 58–60, 64; as national newspaper, 9; on National Service Department, 132, 133; naval criticism in, 34, 143, 174–75; and New Journalism, 4; on paper shortage, 134; Paris edition of, 43–44; patriotism of, 12; Peace Conference coverage of, 219, 230–31, 232; prewar political coverage of, 17–20; Simon's attack on patriotism of, 85–86; and single-men-first recruitment, 81, 82, 83; soldiers' letters in, 32–33; soldiers' news in, 183; on U.S. entry, 140–41; war correspon-

dents of, 23–24, 27, 36; war scare stories in, 11, 15, 16, 39; on war's outbreak, 24–25; on Wilson's appointment, 183

Daily News, 39–40, 57, 59–60, 116, 118, 150

Daily Telegraph, 6, 74, 112, 176

Dalrymple, W. L., 61

Dangerfield, George, 249n.100

Daniels, Josephus, 149, 153, 159, 166, 171, 174

Dardanelles campaign: condition of Anzac forces, 76–77; evacuation from, 80; and munitions shortage, 50, 51, 57; Northcliffe's criticism of, 78; "Westerners" opposition to, 43, 67, 78–79

Davidson, J. C. C., 84

Davies, David, 146

Davies, J. T., 109–10, 127, 132, 133, 151

Davy, Humphrey, 232

Dawson, Geoffrey. *See* Robinson, Geoffrey

Decies, Lord, 179

Defense of the Realm Act (DORA) of 1914, 28, 35, 121

Derby, Lord, 104, 128, 181, 183, 190, 225; and air service, 92–93; and conscription, 95–96; in fall of Asquith government, 113, 114; recruitment plan of, 80, 81–83

Devonport, Lord, 116, 123, 124, 134–35

Dilke, Charles, 8

Dillon, John, 64

Drummond, Eric, 45

Edge, S. F., 165

Edison, Thomas, 165

Education Act of 1870, 4

Edwards, J. Hugh, 189–90

Esher, Lord, 11, 63, 65, 235

Evening News, 3, 7, 70, 116, 201, 213, 252n.69

Evening Post, 174

Evening Standard, 212

Everybody's Magazine, 126

Federal Trade Commission (FTC), 141

Ferris, Tom, viii

Fish, W. G., 23

Fisher, Andrew, 76

Fisher, John, 15, 34, 57–58, 64, 91–92

Fitzgerald, Brinsley, 46, 50, 52, 62

Fitzgerald, Oswald, 59

Foch, Marshal, 206

Food supply: rationing, 142, 143; shortages in, 99, 123–24, 134–35, 142, 143, 185; and U.S. procurement, 157–58

Ford, Henry, 165

Forget-Me-Not, 248n.73

Fortescue, John, 46

France: American mission of, 148, 156;
British correspondents in, 23, 27, 32, 36;
censorship policy of, 26, 28, 43–44;
Northcliffe's contacts in, 45–46, 51–52,
94–95. *See also* Battles and campaigns
Franz Ferdinandz, Archduke, 18, 20
Fraser, Lovat, 34, 40, 44–45, 53, 70, 180,
209
French, John, 26, 29, 33, 43, 46, 108, 243; and
Kitchener, 49, 50, 62, 102; on munitions
shortages, 50, 51, 54, 55, 57, 62, 64; and
Northcliffe, 50–51, 52, 56–57, 79, 241
Frewen, Moreton, 299n.20
Fyfe, Henry Hamilton, 23, 32, 33, 167, 223;
Amien dispatches of, 30; banned from
Front, 29; defense of war coverage, 188;
German "atrocity" stories of, 37; and
Labour party, 221; in Russia, 45, 71

Gallipoli campaign. *See* Dardanelles
campaign
Gardiner, A. G., 39–40, 57, 59–60, 64, 116,
118, 149, 150
Garrett, Garet, 143–44
Garvin, J. L., 4, 13, 15, 60, 83
Geddes, Auckland, 142
Geddes, Eric, 163, 175, 176
German propaganda: expansionist, 17; *Times*
articles used by, 83–84; in U.S., 16, 37–38,
47–48, 272n.12
Germany: air defenses of, 136; allied defeat
of, 206; armistice request of, 211; bombardment of Northcliffe's home, 131;
British blockade of, 43, 47, 48, 119; British
propaganda in, 105–6, 196–99, 203–4,
208–9; business interests in Britain, 93–94,
105; internment of nationals, 201, 204–5;
reparations of, 223–24, 232–33; sanctions
against, 205, 209; Schlieffen plan of, 24;
spy mania in Britain, 16, 36–37; submarine
campaign of, 47, 48, 123–24, 135; war
correspondents of, 28–29. *See also* Battles
and campaigns; German propaganda;
Peace Conference
Gilbert, Bentley, 65
Gilbert, Martin, x
Gladstone, William Ewart, 7, 9
Globe, 86–87, 174
Gollin, Alfred, 11, 73, 116
Gordon, Charles, 154, 157
Grey, Edward, 21, 24–25, 26, 45, 47, 95, 118,
120, 144
Guest, Frederick, 57, 74, 184, 201
Gwynne, H. A., 62, 181

Haig, Douglas, 59, 66, 80, 243; and
Northcliffe, 103, 104–5, 106–7, 112, 128,
129–30, 151, 180, 183, 209, 268n.38; at
Cambrai, 177–78; and German advance,
178, 190; Parliamentary support for, 181;
press relations of, 102; response to critics,
130–31
Haldane, R. B., 13–14, 25, 27, 39, 63, 68, 109,
118, 200
Hamilton, Ian, 66, 76
Hampstead & Highgate Express, 5
Hankey, Maurice, 101, 117, 145–46, 183,
200, 203
Hardinge, Lord, 202
Harmsworth, Alfred Charles William.
See Northcliffe, Lord
Harmsworth, Alfred (father), 5
Harmsworth, Cecil (brother), 6, 10, 15, 16,
109, 110, 114, 116, 190, 191, 208; in Ireland,
100; in Lloyd George coalition, 221, 222,
228, 236, 277n.156
Harmsworth, Esmond (nephew), 206–7, 233,
235
Harmsworth, Gerald, viii
Harmsworth, Geraldine Maffett (mother),
4–5
Harmsworth, Harold Sidney (brother).
See Rothermere, Lord
Harmsworth, Hildebrand (brother), 6, 10
Harmsworth, Leicester (brother), 6, 10, 16
Harmsworth, Mary Elizabeth Milner (wife).
See Northcliffe, Lady
Harmsworth Archive, viii
Harrison, Austin, 68, 97–98
Harvey, George, 71, 152
Hazlehurst, Cameron, ix–x, 26
Healy, John, 179
Hearst, William Randolph, 149
Henderson, Arthur, 29, 80, 117
Henderson, David, 90, 91
Henley House School Magazine, 5
Herrick, Myron, 165
Higginbottom, Frederick, 131–32
Hindenburg, Paul von, 209
Hoover, Herbert, 157, 160, 163
House, Colonel: on fall of Asquith gov-
ernment, 120; and Lloyd George, 172,
174, 175; and Northcliffe, 125–26, 149, 151,
154, 156, 159, 161–62, 213, 244; at Paris
Inter-Allied Conference, 176; at Peace
Conference, 231–32; and peace mediation,
108
Howard, Roy, 108, 151, 161
Humphries, Alexander, 163

Hurley, Edward, 159, 160, 167
Hutton-Wilson, Colonel, 130

Imperialism, 8, 9–10
Imperial Press Conference of 1909, 15
Information, Ministry of, 182, 192, 196, 202, 204, 205–6
Ingram, Edward, 47
Insull, Samuel, 126
Inter-Allied Propaganda Committee, 207, 213
Invasion of 1910, The (Le Queux), 13
Ireland: and Home Rule, 17, 18–19, 249n.100, 137–38, 179; military recruitment in, 80–81; partition of, 228; reaction to Easter Rising, 100, 148–49
Italy: British propaganda in, 199; in Pact of Rome, 188

Jameson, Eustace, 80
Jameson, Leander Starr, 8
Jealous, George Samuel, 5
Jeffries, J. M. N., 18, 23, 32
Jellicoe, John, 136–37, 174–75
Joffre, Joseph, 51, 52
Johnson, Claude, 119
Jones, Kennedy, 9, 232, 234
Jones, William Kennedy, 7

Kansas City Star, 166
Kansas City Times, 166
Keen, E. L., 226
Kenealy, Alexander, 52
Kiggell, Lancelot, 103
King, Lucas, 57, 259n.101
Kitchener, Lord, 241, 243; appointment of, 25–26, 35; ban on correspondents, 27–28, 36; conflicts with colleagues, 49, 50; and conscription question, 74, 80, 83; and Dardanelles campaign, 49–50, 57; Dardanelles inspection tour of, 79, 80; death of, 101; on munitions shortages, 49, 50, 51, 56; Northcliffe's attacks on, 57–62, 63, 64, 79; press relations of, 27, 28, 45, 50; removal of ban on correspondents, 52

Labor unrest, 17, 30, 202
Labour party: in election of 1918, 227; and Northcliffe, 221, 236; withdrawal from coalition, 220
Lansdowne, Lord, 176–77
Lansing, Robert, 120
Lawson, Harry, 74
Le Bas, Hedley, 70, 80, 81, 112, 124–25
Le Matin, 95

Le Queux, William, 11, 13
Le Temps, 32
Lee, Arthur, 105, 112–13
Liberal party, 13, 19, 21; and coalition government, 62–63; and conscription, 73–74; and imperialism, 8, 9–10. *See also* Asquith, Herbert Henry
Liberal War Committee, 74
Lincoln, Charles M., 62
Liverpool Courier, 60
Lloyd George, David, viii, ix, x, 1, 18, 38, 40, 49, 51, 57; alcohol prohibition program of, 53–55; Chamberlain appointment to war cabinet, 190–91, 193; and conscription, 73, 75, 83; and fall of Asquith government, 113–16, 121, 122; formation of government, 116–17; and German reparations, 224, 232–33; and Irish Home Rule, 149, 179; and Kitchener, 49, 61; "Knock-Out Blow" interview of, 108; Maurice letter accusations against, 195; and military, 101, 102, 104–5, 107–8, 109, 110, 128, 181, 183–84; as munitions minister, 62, 63; at Paris Inter-Allied Conference, 176; and parliamentary rebellion against press power, 184–86; at Peace Conference, 230, 232–33; and peace policy memorandum, 21; press relations of, 2; on press's role, 89–90; and propaganda in U.S., 127, 164; replacement of Robertson, 183–84; and Supreme War Council, 170–71, 174; war aims of, 186–87; war cabinet of, 116, 117, 190–91
Lloyd George, David, and Northcliffe, 68, 91, 100, 119–20, 241, 243, 270n.79; and anti-Robertson campaign, 181, 183; appointment to American mission, 144, 145–47, 169; appointment to propaganda post, 182; and coalition of 1918, 210, 219–20, 222–23; in conscription campaign, 83; criticism of government, 118–19, 144–45, 172–73, 174–76, 190–91, 196, 228–29, 232; decline of Cabinet posts, 173, 182, 193; distrust between, 111, 191–92, 200; in election of 1918, 210, 221–22; and fall of Asquith government, 113, 114, 121; first meeting of, 15; loyalty to government, 182, 189–90; and Marconi scandal, 16, 299n.20; plan to replace Lloyd George government, 207–8; resignation from propaganda post, 217–18; and resignation threat, 191–93; rift over military strategy, 104, 108, 111, 112–13; rift over Peace Conference, 213–15, 216–17, 232–37

London Inter-Allied Enemy Propaganda
Council, 207
London Opinion, 147
Long, Walter, 49, 70, 184
Ludendorff, Erich von, 206
Lusitania, sinking of, 48

McAdoo, William Gibbs, 155
MacDonagh, Michael, 139
McEwen, J. M., 121
McKenna, Reginald, 51, 69–70, 90, 94, 114,
118, 122, 258n.69
Magnus, Philip, 62
Manchester Courier, 8
Manchester Guardian, 4, 8, 60–61, 90, 224,
225
Mantoux, Paul, 233
Marconi scandal, 16, 157, 247n.92, 299n.20
Marcosson, Isaac, 126, 129–30, 134, 162
Marlowe, Thomas, 2, 23–24, 25, 139, 183, 221,
223, 232, 235
Massingham, H. W., 90, 97
Masterman, C. F. G., 70, 125, 128
Maurice, Frederick, 195
Maxse, Leo, 33, 109, 130, 150, 171, 189,
260n.1
Men and Power (Beaverbrook), 193, 207
Milne, A. A., 7
Milne, John Vine, 5
Milner, Alfred, 8, 24, 75, 127, 176, 181, 184,
207, 243; and conscription question, 67,
72–73, 74, 97; and enemy propaganda, 197,
204; on Lloyd George, 191; Northcliffe's
campaign against, 212–13, 215–16; peace
initiative of, 199–200, 212, 213; Russian
mission of, 128–29; in War Cabinet, 116,
117, 190
Mitchell, Chalmers, 202, 212
Mond, Alfred, 26
Monro, Charles, 78–79
Montagu, Edwin, 114, 115
Moore, Arthur, 30
Morgan & Company, 281n.77
Morison, Stanley, 244
Munitions: procurement in U.S., 157;
shortage of, 49, 50, 51, 56–65, 239
Murdoch, Keith, 76
Murphy, William, 100
Murray of Elibank, Lord, 32, 70–71, 79, 210

Nation, The, 60, 162
National Registration Act, 70
National Service Department, campaign
against, 131–33
National War Aims Committee, 201, 202

Navy: and air defenses, 136–37; Battle of
Jutland, 100; blockade of Germany, 43, 47,
48, 119; censorship policy of, 31, 34, 135; in
Dardanelles campaign, 43, 49; Kiel canal
visit by, 18; Northcliffe's criticism of, 34,
143, 174–75; preparedness of, 11–12, 15–16
New Illustrated, 228
New Journalism, ix, 4
New Liberal Review, 10
Newnes, George, 6
New Republic, The, 152
Newspaper Proprietor's Association (NPA),
27, 28
Newspapers. *See* Press
Newsprint supply, 12, 48, 133–34, 141
New Witness, 60
New York Evening Journal, 34
New York Sun, 38, 152
New York Times, 117, 163
New York Tribune, 144, 152
Nicholson, Charles, 293n.16
Nicoll, William Robertson, 1, 63, 91, 236
Nicolson, Harold, 230
1914 (French), 64
Nivelle, Robert, 129, 130, 142
Northcliffe, Lady (Mary Elizabeth Milner
Harmsworth), 6, 9, 51
Northcliffe, Lord (Alfred Charles William
Harmsworth): on air defenses, 90–91,
135–37; and airplane development, 14; as
air services advisor, 92, 93, 137; ambition
of, vii, 99, 117, 124–25, 193–94, 242–43; and
Asquith government attacks, 44, 52–53,
64–65, 66, 78, 87, 89, 97–99, 118, 122;
Asquith government contacts of, 67–71,
101; and Asquith government fall, 113–16,
117–18, 239; and Balfour, 12–13; battlefront
visits of, 33, 44, 51–52, 68, 94, 103–4, 177;
and Beaverbrook, 181–82, 201, 203, 205–6,
211; on blockade of Germany, 43, 47, 119;
Carson's attack on, 215–16; and censorship,
conflicts over, 29, 31, 32, 34–36, 43–44, 50,
135, 175, 224–25; on Chamberlain appointment, 190–91; and Churchill, 10, 101–2,
229; on Civil Aerial Transport Committee,
137, 144, 145; commitment to war effort, 25,
32, 44; in conscription campaign, 36, 67,
72–73, 75, 95–97; on Dardanelles policy,
76–77, 78; death of, 238; and Derby recruitment scheme, 80, 81–83; education of, 5;
electoral defeat of, 8; entry into journalism,
5–6; establishment hostility to, 10–11,
243–44; family background of, 4–5; on
food shortages, 99, 123–24, 134–35, 185;
French contacts of, 45–46, 51–52, 94–95,

128; German bombardment of home, 131; on German interests in Britain, 93–94, 105; on German internment, 201, 204–5; on German propaganda in U.S., 16, 37–38, 47; on German reparations, 223–24, 232–33; on German sanctions, 205, 209; health of, 7, 181, 192, 193, 197, 217, 219, 227–28, 236, 238; historical neglect of, ix–xi, 1; historical studies of, viii–ix; intelligence network of, 46–47, 70–71, 143–44; and Irish Question, 17, 19–20, 100, 137–39, 179, 228; and Irish recruitment, 80–81; and Kitchener, 25, 57–62, 63, 64, 79; and Labour party, 221, 236; Liberal press attacks on, 39–40, 57, 59–60, 116; marriage to Mary Elizabeth Milner, 6; megalomania of, viii; as military critic, 56–62, 63, 64, 79, 178, 180–81, 240, 241–42; military preparedness warnings of, 11–12, 13, 15–16, 23; military support of, 50–51, 103–5, 106–7, 128, 129–30, 151, 170, 209; military support against government interference, 108–13; on munitions shortage, 57–62, 64, 65, 239; and National Service Department, campaign against, 131–33; newsprint supply of, 12, 48, 133–34, 141; as Peace Conference critic, 230–37; peace negotiation opposed by, 108, 120–21, 176–77, 191, 199–200, 208, 211, 212–13; peace policy memorandum of, 210–11, 212, 213; peerage of, 13, 247n.62, 175, 193; political influence of, ix, viii, 3, 66, 122, 236–37, 238, 240–41; political views of, 8, 9–10, 140; press empire of, 2–3, 6–7, 14–15; and tariff reform, 13; in U.S., 7, 10, 16; and war loans, 124; and war scare, 13, 15, 16, 17. *See also* British War Mission to United States; *Daily Mail;* Lloyd George, David; Northcliffe; *Times, The;* Propaganda

Observer, 4, 14, 60, 112, 247n.79, 133
O'Connor, T. P. O., 139
Official Secrets Act of 1912, 27, 28
O'Laughlin, J. C., 48
Oliver, F. S., 67
Orlando, Vittorio, 230
Outlook, 4
Overseas Daily Mail, 14

Page, Walter Hines, 120, 145
Pall Mall Gazette, 4
Pankhurst, Emmeline, 17
Paris Inter-Allied Conference, 172, 176
Paris Peace Conference. *See* Peace Conference
Parker, Gilbert, 125

Peace Conference: censorship of, 224–25, 227; *Daily Mail* coverage of, 230–31; Northcliffe–Lloyd George clash over reparations, 232–36; Northcliffe's exclusion from, 213–15, 216–17, 237, 240; Wilson's presence at, 226
Peace initiatives, Northcliffe's opposition to, 108, 120–21, 176–77, 191, 199–200, 208, 211, 212–13
Peace policy memorandum, of British War Mission, 210–11, 212, 213
Pearson, Arthur, 137
Pemberton, Max, 5, 6
Percy, Eustace, 168
Pershing, John, 177, 190
Phillips, C. J., 155, 202
Philpotts, Eden, 126
Pluck Library, 6
Poincaré, Raymond, 23
Politicians and the War (Beaverbrook), 64
Polk, Frank, 153
Pound, Reginald, viii
Press: atrocity propaganda in, 37, 42; New Journalism, ix, 4; Northcliffe's holdings, 2–3, 6–7, 14–15; parliamentary attack on domination of, 184–86; political influence of, 2, 3–4, 42; spy paranoia fed by, 16, 36–37; wartime function of, 89–90; wartime prestige of, 42. *See also* Censorship; War correspondents; *names of newspapers*
Press Bureau, 28, 30, 83–86
Price, George Ward, 18, 23, 27, 36
Prioleau, John, 18
Propaganda: against aliens, 205; in allied countries, 95, 199; under Buchan, 127–28; in U.S., 38–39, 125–26, 128, 143–44, 160–68, 239–40, 242; reorganization of, 181–82. *See also* German propaganda
Propaganda, enemy: appointment of Northcliffe, 182–83; in Austria-Hungary, 186–88; in Bulgaria, 199; contribution of, 217; and Foreign office, 202–3; in Germany, 105–6, 195–99, 203–4, 208–9; Inter-Allied Conference on, 207; and peace policy memorandum, 210–11, 212, 213; among prisoners, 293n.16; resignation of Northcliffe, 217–18
Pulitzer, Joseph, 10
Pulitzer, Ralph, 71
Punch, 150

Rapallo Agreement, 171–72
Rawlinson, General, 104
Raymond, E. T., ix, 193

Reading, Lord, 156–57, 160, 161, 175, 176, 178, 185, 226, 240
Recruitment: censorship linked to failure of, 35–36; decline in, 254n.112; Derby Scheme, 80, 81–83; in Ireland, 80–81; Kitchener's first appeal, 26; Parliamentary committee for, 29; and registration law, 70. *See also* Conscription
Redmond, John, 29
Reick, William Charles, 71
Repington, Charles à Court, 27, 50, 89, 102, 108, 110, 128, 130, 171; in conscription campaign, 74, 75; and Kitchener's appointment, 25; on manpower shortage, 142–43; on munitions shortage, 57, 59, 64; support for Robertson, 180, 191
Review of Reviews, 4
Rhodes, Cecil, 8
Ribblesdale, Lord, 181
Riddell, George, 28, 38, 52, 61, 78, 79, 90, 91, 98, 100, 105, 124, 132, 133, 173, 182, 207, 210; at Peace Conference, 225, 230, 232, 233
Rinehart, Mary Roberts, 46, 86, 167
Roberts of Kandahar, Lord, 11–12
Robertson, William: 90, 95, 96, 101, 128, 176, 191, 274n.54; appointment of, 79; and government interference, 108, 109–10; Northcliffe's campaign against, 178, 180–81, 183, 240, 241–42; on press relations, 102; replaced as CIGS, 183
Robinson, Geoffrey (Dawson), 2, 34, 76, 105, 194; communications with Northcliffe, 36, 48, 106, 110, 137, 139, 154, 156, 165, 204–5; and fall of Asquith government, 114, 115, 116; intermediary between Northcliffe and Lloyd George, 112–13; resignation of, 231; rift with Northcliffe, 196, 222–24, 229–30
Rodd, Rennell, 45, 199
Roosevelt, Theodore, 159
Rosebery, Lord, 8, 9–10, 13
Rothermere, Lord (Harold Sidney Harmsworth): 2, 5, 14, 19, 112, 133, 184, 207, 230, 235, 277n.156; as air minister, 176; in British War Mission, 168; and coalition of 1918, 210, 220; in Northcliffe's publishing business, 6, 7; at Peace Conference, 233; political views of, 7, 16
Runciman, Walter, 210
Russia: Bolsheviks in, 179–80; in Brest-Litovsk treaty, 179, 186; March revolution in, 129; Milner mission to, 128–29; war correspondents in, 45, 71, 95

Sala, George Augustus, 6
Salisbury, Lord, 8, 11, 12
Samuel, Herbert, 117, 210
Sanders, Robert, 222
Sassoon, Philip, 107, 108, 109, 112, 129–30, 178, 209
Saturday Evening Post, 35, 46
Schlieffen plan, 24
Scott, C. P., 4, 83, 146, 224
Selborne, Lord, 81, 84
Seton-Watson, R. W., 188
Sharp, Clifford, 199–200
Shaw, George Bernard, 9
Simon, John, 118; attack on Northcliffe press, 83–86
Smith, F. E., 28, 30, 31, 75, 104, 175
Smith, Montagu, 230
Smuts, J. C., 164–65, 181
Southern Daily Mail, 8
Spectator, 60, 119
Spring-Rice, Cecil, 125–26, 152–53, 159, 178–79
Stamfordham, Lord, 85, 181
Stanhope, Earl, 61
Stanley, Albert, 116, 119
Stanley, Venetia, 19, 51, 56, 250n.115
Steed, Henry Wickham, 4, 24, 25, 151, 160, 199, 200, 212; enemy propaganda role of, 186, 188, 197, 213, 242, 289n.142; at front, 94, 105, 106–7; on Lloyd George's attack on Northcliffe, 235; at Peace Conference, 231
Steevens, G. W., 8, 12, 79
Stevenson, Frances, 83, 265n.19, 269n.66, 270n.79
Storey, Samuel, 44
Strachey, John St. Loe, 72, 81, 96, 101, 104, 117–18, 119–20, 174, 180, 181, 194
Stuart, Campbell, x, 157, 192, 197, 208, 231, 253n.94
Submarine campaign, 48, 123–24, 135, 154
Suffrage movement, 17, 29–30, 140
Sunday Pictorial, 133
Sunday *Weekly Dispatch,* 3
Supreme War Council, 170–71, 174
Sutton, George, 6, 134, 157
Swettenham, Frank, 66
Swinton, Ernest, 31–32, 33, 253n.80

Tardieu, André, 51, 148, 156
Taylor, A. J. P., ix, 9
Taylor, S. J., ix
Thomas, Albert, 111
Thorpe, Winton, 134

Times, The: Amiens dispatches in, 30; appointment of Steed, 231; Archive of, viii; on Carson's resignation, 77; criticism of Lloyd George government, 172–73, 196; editorial independence of, 2, 14–15, 196, 204–5, 222–24, 229–30; and fall of Asquith government, 114, 117–18, 121, 122, 239; Northcliffe's acquisition of, 14; Peace Conference coverage of, 231; and Shells Scandal, 57; Simon's attack on patriotism of, 84, 85–86; war correspondents of, 25, 27, 30, 45

Tit-Bits, 6

Tracy, Louis, 7, 178–79, 225

Trenchard, General, 104

Tumulty, Joseph, 226

Turner, John, x

United States: and British blockade, impact of, 43, 47, 48, 78; British propaganda in, 38–39, 125–26, 128, 160–68, 239–40; committment of troops, 177, 190; entry into war, 140–41; German propaganda in, 16, 37–38, 47–48; and mobilization aid, 141, 143–44; Northcliffe's prewar visits to, 7, 10; in peace mediation attempts, 108, 120–21, 124; uncensored military reports from, 34, 35. *See also* British War Mission to United States; Wilson, Woodrow

Versailles treaty (1919), 1, 219, 236

Viviani, René, 148

Von Donop, Stanley, 50, 68

Von Hutier, General, 208–9

Walter, John, 88

War Cabinet, 116, 117, 190–91

War correspondents: banned from BEF, 27–28, 36; in Belgium, 23–24; in France, 23, 27, 32, 36; German, 28–29; removal of ban, 52; in Russia, 45, 71, 95; women, 46. *See also* Censorship

War Policy Committee, 164

Waterbury, John, 155

Wedgwood, Josiah, 73–74, 209

Weekly Dispatch, 14, 30, 120, 252n.69

Wells, H. G., 98, 99; enemy propaganda role of, 194, 197–99, 201–2, 242; on German internment issue, 201, 204

Westminster Gazette, 232, 234

Wile, Frederic William, 27, 47

Wilhelm, Kaiser, 10

Willert, Arthur, 38, 71, 143, 149, 152, 154, 162

Williams, Valentine, 18, 23, 50, 52; on European crisis, 21; on fall of Asquith government, 122; on Shells Scandal, 61; on Simon's attack on Northcliffe press, 86

Wilson, Henry, 35, 128, 171, 176, 183, 191

Wilson, Herbert, 15, 131

Wilson, John, 98

Wilson, R. Macnair, 32

Wilson, Sarah, 12

Wilson, Trevor, 260n.136

Wilson, W. G., 58

Wilson, Woodrow, 48, 140, 200, 211; in Britain, 226–27; and British War Mission, 149, 151, 154, 155, 161, 162, 225; at Peace Conference, 225, 226, 230, 232, 233; peace mediation efforts of, 108, 120–21, 124

Wilton, Robert, 45

Wiseman, William, 126, 151, 159, 161–62, 172, 175, 279n.29

World War I: and British entry, 24–25; events leading to, 18, 20–23; forecasts of brief war, 26; and U.S. entry, 140–41. *See also* Battles and campaigns; Peace settlement

Wrench, John Evelyn, 14, 23, 60, 107

Yorkshire Post, 191

Younger, George, 214–15, 222, 228, 247n.62

Youth, 6

Politicians, the Press, & Propaganda
was designed by Will Underwood.
It was composed in 10.2/13.5 Monotype Baskerville
Old Style with titles set in Monotype Bulmer Display
on an Apple Quadra System using QuarkXPress
by The Book Page, Inc.
It was printed by sheet-fed offset lithography on 50-pound
Turin Book stock (an acid-free, totally chlorine-free paper),
Smyth sewn and bound over binder's boards
in Roxite B cloth with Multicolor endpapers,
and wrapped with dust jackets printed in three colors
finished with polypropylene matte film lamination
by Thomson-Shore, Inc.;
and published by
The Kent State University Press
KENT, OHIO 44242 USA